AFRICAN AMERICAN WOMEN
AND HIV/AIDS

The Research and Reference books
in Political and Justice Studies,
Addiction Studies and Social Work
are made possible by a 2003 grant
from the Library Services and
Technology Assistance act (LSTA)
and the Illinois State Library.

AFRICAN AMERICAN WOMEN AND HIV/AIDS
CRITICAL RESPONSES

Edited by Dorie J. Gilbert and Ednita M. Wright

Foreword by Mindy Thompson Fullilove, M.D.

Library of Congress Cataloging-in-Publication Data

African American women and HIV/AIDS : critical responses / edited by Dorie J. Gilbert
and Ednita M. Wright ; foreword by Mindy Thompson Fullilove, M.D.
　　p.　cm.
　　Includes bibliographical references and index.
　　ISBN 0-275-97127-9 (alk. paper) — ISBN 0-275-97128-7 (pbk. : alk. paper)
　　1. AIDS (Disease)—United States. 2. African American women—Diseases. I.
Gilbert, Dorie J. II. Wright, Ednita M.
RA643.83.A35 2003
362.1′969792′00820973—dc21　　　　2001058040

British Library Cataloguing in Publication Data is available.

Library of Congress Catalog Card Number: 2001058040
ISBN: 0-275-97127-9
　　　0-275-97128-7 (pbk.)

First published in 2003

Praeger Publishers, 88 Post Road West, Westport, CT 06881
An imprint of Greenwood Publishing Group, Inc.
www.praeger.com

Printed in the United States of America

The paper used in this book complies with the
Permanent Paper Standard issued by the National
Information Standards Organization (Z39.48-1984).

10 9 8 7 6 5 4 3 2 1

*To my sisters, Sandra, Joyce, Sarah, Marilyn, Dee Dee, and
Barbara and to my mother, Jewel Daniels Arceneaux*

Dorie J. Gilbert

*To my son, Joshua, and my best friend, Jinny, and to
Karen Kirkhart, my mentor*

Ednita M. Wright

Contents

Foreword

June Osborne, who was then chair of the President's Commission on AIDS, gave a speech in 1991 at the 7th International AIDS Conference in Florence on the topic of "feeling like Cassandra." Cassandra was the Greek heroine who heard the warriors inside the Trojan Horse, but, because no one would listen to her, failed in her efforts to warn her city about the hidden invaders. Dr. Osborne was feeling a great deal like Cassandra, and I had nothing but empathy for her. When I started to do AIDS research in 1986, I used to say in speeches, "African Americans account for 12 percent of the U.S. population but 25 percent of the people with AIDS." Each year I have watched the difference grow: Dorie Gilbert, writing in 2002, opens this book by pointing out that African Americans make up 13 percent of the U.S. population but over 50 percent of newly diagnosed cases of AIDS. The numbers each year get worse. Like Dr. Osborne, we all feel like Cassandra.

It is not comforting to know that there are structural factors or mistaken ideas that underlie this growing disparity. It is certainly not comforting to know that the numbers are not so much *up* for African Americans, as they are *down* for other groups. It is not comforting to know that we have built treatment centers and prevention organizations. It is not comforting to know that, by now, AIDS 101 has been inculcated into the minds of every American, including every African American. It is not comforting to know those things, because we are failing in our major goal: to control the epidemic among African Americans.

We must somehow stop being Cassandra—who was not heard—and become Harriet Tubman, who was heard. Or Sojourner Truth, who was heard. Or Ida B. Wells, who was heard. Or Pernessa Seele, who is being heard all over the country—only her one voice must be multiplied until the insistence upon life has driven out the sorriest, saddest excuses for death that linger in the minds of our people, especially our women.

We cannot tolerate the denial, the self-deceit, the paranoia that rebound on us as death. We must confront head-on the wallowing in misery that has become so much a theme in Black culture that it seems as if it is our culture. Certainly there is, as there has been since we were stolen from Africa, more sorrow, more betrayal, more pain, more injury than a body ought to be asked to bear. But what did that grandmother tell us, through the lilting voice of Langston Hughes? Keep on climbin'.

Our poets, leaders, writers, and singers have given us the signs and symbols of the struggle for life. These are our banners. We must carry them everywhere before us. Yes, there is too much pain, but we embrace life. Yes, there is too much injury, but we embrace life. Yes, there is too much deceit, but we embrace life. Never have a people had such a need to say that the mostly used-up glass was half-full.

And we know, that if we can be fervent enough—and that is the key here— our people will not resist us. The Spirit is too strong. The Spirit will jump up and shout, "Hallelujah! The glass is half-full! Hallelujah, we are about life!" The Spirit knows truth when it hears it.

It may not seem that in a book filled with numbers and citations you will find food to make you fervent. But it is here—here in the words of women thinking about AIDS, in the words of women living with AIDS. It is here. It will fill your heart, and you will be transformed. Go forth from reading—and do read every page in preparation for your new life—and fervently share with everyone you meet, "We must be about life."

After we turn that corner, we might go on to reinvent life in our community without sexism, homophobia, and patriarchy. When the Spirit is strong, we are, indeed, open to cherishing life in its most glorious diversity. That is what took Frederick Douglass to the first Seneca Falls conference for women's rights. That is what took Paul Robeson behind the Iron Curtain, singing in the joy of life though the establishment had forbidden his doing that. Let us remember that heritage, too, the heritage of universalism which is a great strain in our history, one that takes us even more into life: life shared, life cherished, life open as we dream it might be.

Read, and then preach. Preach so that the seductive moan of death is drowned out and the pulsing, deliriously delicious beat of life is everywhere. AIDS cannot stand—it will not stand—in the face of that.

—*Mindy Thompson Fullilove, M.D.*
Professor of Clinical Psychiatry
Columbia University, School of Public Health

Introduction

Dorie J. Gilbert and Ednita M. Wright

In speaking about the health issues facing African American women, R. B. Daniel stated several years ago that "AIDS is killing us. . . . our community, our women, our men, our children, our families, our futures" (1996, 13). We cannot say this any simpler. However, what we would like to add is that, sadly, the problem is not going away anytime soon. AIDS is now the leading cause of death for African American men from thirty-five to forty-four years of age and is the second leading cause of death among African American women between the ages of twenty-five and thirty-four, according to the 2001 National Vital Statistics Report (Anderson 2001). African American women now constitute 63 percent of all cases of AIDS among women in the United States. In states reporting data on HIV and AIDS diagnoses from January 1996 through June 1999, African Americans represented 50 percent of all AIDS diagnoses and an even greater number—57 percent—of all HIV diagnoses. Among young people (ages thirteen to twenty-four), 65 percent of the HIV diagnoses were among African Americans (Centers for Disease Control and Prevention [CDC], 2001), and even though AIDS cases among Whites are declining, by the year 2005, African Americans are estimated to represent over 60 percent of all AIDS cases in the United States (Harvard AIDS Institute, Figure i.1). These facts alone provide the impetus for this book.

Both of us have devoted a substantial amount of time interviewing, counseling, and studying the life circumstances of women, and specifically African American women, living with HIV/AIDS. The number of books addressing women and HIV/AIDS has increased substantially over the past decade; many volumes include chapters that focus on African American women and other subgroups, related to both prevention and intervention efforts. However, there is no single volume that has focused on African American women alone, although they continue to shoulder a disproportionate burden of the HIV/AIDS impact on individuals, families, and communities.

Figure i.1
Proportion of AIDS Cases in the U.S. by Race (actual and projected)

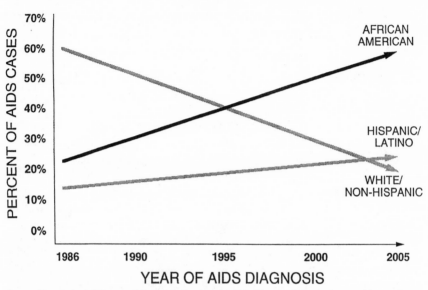

Source: Foster, A. and Pagano, M. (1996). *Leading for Life: The AIDS Crisis Among African Americans.* Harvard AIDS Institute, 1997.

In this book we highlight the life stories, relationship dynamics, challenges, and perseverance of African American women, the primary population of women impacted by AIDS. Authored by African American women from across the country who are directly involved in research, scholarship, and/or prevention and intervention programming related to HIV/AIDS and/or substance abuse, the book is an interdisciplinary approach to examining the critical responses necessary to attack HIV/AIDS head-on in the African American community. The book is grounded in Black feminist and social construction theory; we are guided by our desire to privilege the voice of African American women, arguably, the most disenfranchised and least understood population in AIDS-related research and literature on women. The societal construction of women living with HIV infection has a profound impact on the ideological representation and institutional response to this population. We recognize that African American women were without a voice long before AIDS came along, and there has been a growing need to comprehensively examine their unique situations that place them at heightened risk for HIV infection.

This book uniquely combines the intellectual with the practical, and represents academicians joining practitioners in an effort to reach multiple audiences through scholarly analyses of the problem and down-to-earth discussions of working solutions. Integrated into the book are what we have termed *Focus on*

Solutions sections, accounts of interventions and programs that are currently in place and can effectively address the AIDS crisis within the African American community. Another unique aim of the book is to target the population addressed in the book. In our own work with women living with HIV/AIDS, we have found that women are eager to read meaningful writings on their situation. Women have a need and right to know that the literature is accurately portraying their lives to the public. We hope this book reaches a wide audience—from academics to practitioners to the average individual who wants to have a better understanding of what critical responses are needed to reverse the disturbing trends.

This book is divided into four sections. In Part I, we begin acknowledging that AIDS has been constructed in sociopolitical ways, and those constructions have not always accurately nor kindly reflected the true experiences of the groups primarily affected by HIV infection and AIDS. In this first section, the aim is to reconstruct the meaning of individual and group risks for HIV-infection, as this pertains to African American women. This is addressed first by a comprehensive discussion that answers the question, Why are African Americans, and specifically African American women, so overrepresented among U.S. AIDS cases? The discussion outlines the sociocultural factors underlying the alarming statistics and directly challenges the deficit-based notion of a "Black culture" that casts African Americans as inherently dysfunctional and "in denial" regarding risky behavior leading to HIV infection. A crucial element in reconstructing the disease in the lives of African American women is the need to hear from the women themselves, to understand through their voices how they have conceptualized their lives before and after learning of their HIV-positive status. Brief accounts of the experiences of eight women interviewed by Wright are highlighted in this section. Each woman gives us a glimpse into the life circumstances that put them at risk initially. The intersecting roles of substance abuse, poverty, and survival outside the mainstream, Eurocentric culture in the United States is now extremely apparent as underlying the AIDS epidemic among African Americans. Substance abuse, especially intravenous drug use and crack cocaine, has been appropriately labeled as "the twin epidemic" to AIDS. Accordingly, this section's *Focus on Solutions* highlights the need for and effectiveness of an Afrocentric-based substance abuse treatment program.

In Part II, we examine the individual and collective (family and community) concerns about and responses to the AIDS crisis among African Americans. There has been meager representation, within clinical trials, for example, that inform us of the reality of living with HIV/AIDS for African American women. The fact that many of these women have continued their historic role of caring for their families and their communities with little or no recognition is clear. Yet, we need to look closer at the challenges and ways of coping for African American women. First, quality-of-life issues for women living with the disease are discussed in relation to their primary relationships with spouses and intimate partners, children and extended families. There is a growing number of

HIV-affected children, the vast majority of whom are African American. These children face multiple developmental obstacles due to being orphaned by AIDS or living with a chronically ill parent with HIV-infection or AIDS. In response to this crisis, child and family services agencies are challenged to provide culturally sensitive, family-based interventions for HIV-positive women and their families. The *Focus on Solutions* discussion highlights a component of one community-based agency in Harlem that has effectively demonstrated how comprehensive, family-centered services for HIV-infected women, their HIV-affected children, and extended families can be offered in a culturally competent manner. With effective interventions, many women can and do experience remarkable resilience, and even overcome life circumstances such as drug addiction and traumatic experiences that placed them in the path of HIV-infection in the first place. The "transformations" that women experience has led some women to give back to their community through becoming peer educators and prevention advocates to curb the HIV-infection rates, and the factors that support and hinder that transformative process for women are discussed. A common theme of the women's transforming experiences has centered around spirituality and reliance on God to "make a way out of no way," and, in the later part of this section, we revisit the lives of the eight women introduced in Chapter 2 to examine the role of spirituality in their coping styles. Historically, Black churches have been a pillar of hope for the African American community, but churches are now being challenged to rethink moral codes (specifically the teaching that homosexuality is a sin) that keep them, as an organized body, from leading the fight against AIDS. Although the struggle to involve Black churches is far from over, The Balm In Gilead, a nationally organized response to AIDS from Black churches, is making a difference for many, and this organization is highlighted as a *Focus on Solutions*.

Part III is devoted to our young women who face incredible challenges to a healthy coming of age in the midst of the AIDS crisis, which is already ravishing African American adolescents, especially those in poor, urban environments. The emergent literature supports that family-based interventions are critical in addressing HIV prevention among African Americans, and this has special importance for reaching young girls through working simultaneously with their mothers. One of the *Focus on Solutions* highlights a mother/daughter, community-based intervention. Young African American women on college campuses, particularly historically Black college campuses, also must be included in prevention programs targeting African American adolescents. This group of women is in need of sensitive prevention approaches that are congruent with their college environment, such as computer-based, culturally centered programs which reflect their unique challenges of negotiating safe sex practices, and such a program is highlighted in a second *Focus on Solutions* discussion for this section.

Finally, in Part IV we turn to the broader issues of HIV prevention and intervention efforts for African Americans, as well as an analysis of AIDS-related public policy and how more action is needed in this area. This section addresses the need for change efforts from both within the minds and communities of African Americans and from the larger policy-making bodies. As a critical response, this section presents a description of one Black-initiated agency that responds holistically to HIV prevention and intervention needs of Blacks.

We hope this book will serve to further the dialogue about what critical responses are needed to alleviate the devastating impact of AIDS on the African American community. Some programs are already making great differences, and we have only highlighted a few of these in this volume. We encourage more widespread reporting of prevention and intervention programs that are working. We have taken the discussion thus far; we welcome others to join in this discourse, and continue to react with the level of urgency this crisis warrants.

A NOTE ABOUT TERMINOLOGY

African Americans make up 13 percent of the U.S. population, and although the term African American may accurately reflect those individuals who descended from slaves in this country, many prefer the term Black, which more accurately reflects the various ethnic subgroups (Haitian Americans, for example). Throughout this book, the term Black is used interchangeably with African American. We have chosen to capitalize all ethnic/racial terms, such as Black and White; although this may not conform to certain publication and writing standards, we have done so to recognize that these are political terms as well as group names. Yet, we also recognize and honor that the terms do not describe monolithic group experiences.

The more than 33 million individuals comprising this group include people with roots in the West Indies, South America, Africa, and the Caribbean and many have Native American, White, or Latino ancestors. Although the discussions in this book are addressing the situation of African Americans or Blacks, we acknowledge and stress the great diversity among those described by these terms. There is diversity regarding age, class, educational background, mixed ethnicity, assimilation, geographic locations, personality factors, family dynamics, and so on. There is no single description of the "African American woman," yet, we do not ignore that larger societal structures are designed in such a way as to impact the lives of diverse African American women collectively. It is from this collective impact that we speak of African American or Black women's experiences. Similarly, we use the terms, African American community or Black community to express the collective experiences of people who are bound, not geographically, but in relation to their common experience of societal discrimination and historical oppression of Blacks in the country.

ACKNOWLEDGMENTS

This book has been and is a labor of love. Love for the African American women who have shared their stories about living with HIV/AIDS. They shared their stories out of love for other women facing, living, and suffering in the same situation. This book is a dedication—a monument—to those African American women who have died and for those women who remain cloaked in silence. We want to thank those women who have shared their personal life stories for the benefit of others. We are also grateful to our many colleagues who provided enthusiastic support and constructive criticism throughout the course of this project.

REFERENCES

Anderson, R. N. (2001). Deaths: Leading Causes for 1999. *National Vital Statistics Reports*, 49 (11), 1–88.

Centers for Disease Control and Prevention (2001). HIV/AIDS Among African American Fact Sheet.

Daniel, R. B. (1996). Allowing illness in order to heal: Sojourning African-American women and the AIDS pandemic. In C.F. Collins (Ed.), *African-American Women's Health and Social Issues* (pp. 13–24). Westport, CT: Greenwood Publishing Group.

I

Reconstructing the Reality of African American Women and HIV/AIDS

AIDS is a socially constructed disease, and much of the response to and attitudes toward HIV-infected individuals center around the preexisting concepts, paradigms, and societal constructions of those affected. Social construction theory is concerned with the ways in which societies interpret, judge, and ascribe meaning to groups, conditions, and events (Berger and Luckman 1966), interpretations that may or may not reflect the reality.

From the beginning of the AIDS epidemic, the concept of "culture" has been used to interpret, define, and further distance the "other," or members of groups deemed socially deviant. As has been aptly stated, "In the construction of AIDS risk groups, 'culture' has been used as a distinguishing criterion defining membership in 'high risk groups' and as an explanation of why members of these groups continue to practice 'risky behavior'" (Schiller, Crystal, and Lewellen 1994, 1337). The CDC's unique and problematic initial approach of identifying entire subgroups as "at risk" provided the foundation for the public's view that people with AIDS were part of a differentiated group at risk because of their shared culture, be it a gay culture or in the case of Haitians, a unique Haitian ethnic or biological culture.

As we enter the third decade of AIDS, African Americans now constitute the subgroup of HIV-infected persons most disproportionately impacted, and also a group with relatively little powerful but a heavily burdened segment of U.S. society (Quinn 1993). There is a need to look closer at the lives of women living with or at increased risk for HIV-infection. In the first chapter, we begin with an overview of the many factors that place African American women at risk and examine the context of "risky behavior," much of which can be traced to the historical and ongoing oppression experienced by Blacks in this country. Rather than cultural descriptions meant to be generalized to all African American women, this analysis considers the many layers that, when mounted, place some African American women at an especially high risk. Research has helped to differentiate these factors by investigating the connections between, for example, poverty and sexually transmitted diseases, drug use and incarceration, and past sexual abuse and HIV-infection. Individual research (both large survey studies and smaller ethnographic interviews) has added to our increased understanding of the actual experiences of African American women who are already HIV-positive or who live in social contexts that increase their risk for HIV-infection. Chapter 1 simply adds it all up. What it amounts to is a clear picture that helps explain the complexity of risks among African American women, particularly poor African American women.

African American women have long suffered from being defined by mainstream dominant society's cultural characteristics or popular images of them, examining their behavior and creating policies that have affected their well-being. Reconstructing realities for HIV-positive African American women also requires that we hear from them, directly, and that we understand the meanings they attach to the disease. In Chapter 2, Wright introduces us to eight women who talk about their experiences of being diagnosed as HIV-positive. The women represent a range of ages, backgrounds, and life experiences. What becomes clear from their stories is the large role that untreated substance abuse played in increasing their risk for HIV-infection.

It has been said that next to racism, substance abuse is the primary health and social problem of the African American community (Watts and Wright 1983). This statement was made before the onslaught of the crack epidemic, and obviously before the full impact AIDS hit home in the African American community. By many accounts, racism is not so much situated next to substance abuse but is one of the underlying causes of it and other negative social and psychological outcomes experienced disproportionately by African Americans. Traditional substance abuse treatment programs have not been significantly successful in curbing substance abuse problems among African Americans for a number of reasons, including a lack of clear understanding of issues of motivation for treatment, cultural needs, and underlying reasons for the initiation of substance abuse. To fully understand the individual behavior and psychological processes of African Americans within the context of their historical oppression, we must first ask the right questions in our research. Rowe and Grills (1993) explain that, with substance abuse, "systemic, cultural-political or institutional factors (e.g., easy entrance of drugs into the African American communities, complicit or neglectful law enforcement, Euro-American cultural hegemony) are denied validity in explaining the development or maintenance of addictive behaviors" (25). However, when these issues are considered, certain requirements for effective treatment become clear. Within an Afrocentric paradigm (Asante 1980), treatment would include elements to help individuals counter oppressive external conditions, develop and maintain a core set of values that are congruent with healthy cultural identity, and participate in specific culturally congruent rituals.

Grills, in Chapter 3, provides a comprehensive overview of African-centered psychology. The discussion is followed by a *Focus on Solutions* highlighting the Culturally Congruent Treatment Engagement Project and reports findings from this project which examined the effectiveness of an Afrocentric-based substance abuse treatment program compared with a traditional treatment approach.

REFERENCES

Asante, M.K. (1980). *Afrocentricity: The theory of change*. Buffalo, NY: Amulefi.

Berger, P.L., and Luckman, T.L. (1966). *The social construction of reality*. Garden City, NY: Doubleday.

Quinn, S.C. (1993). "AIDS and the African-American woman: The triple burden of race, class, and gender." *Health Education Quarterly*, 20 (3), 304–320.

Rowe, D., and Grills, C. (1993). African-centered drug treatment: An alternative conceptual paradigm for drug counseling with African-American clients. *Journal of Psychoactive Drugs*, 25 (1), 21–33.

Schiller, N.G., Crystal, S., and Lewellen, D. (1994). Risky business: The cultural construction of AIDS risk groups. *Social Science Medicine*, 38 (10), 1337–1346.

Watts, T.D., and Wright, R. (1983). *Black alcoholism: Toward a comprehensive understanding*. Springfield IL: C.C. Thomas.

1

The Sociocultural Construction of AIDS among African American Women

Dorie J. Gilbert

African Americans constitute only 13 percent of the U.S. population but account for over 50 percent of newly reported cases of HIV-infection (CDC 2001a). African American women represent 63 percent of AIDS cases among women, and researchers estimate that about one in fifty African American men and one in 160 African American women are infected with HIV (CDC 2000). Among HIV-infected African American women, injection drug use has accounted for 42 percent of all AIDS case reports since the epidemic began, with 38 percent due to heterosexual contact with infected male partners, primarily male injection drug users (CDC 2001b). Among African American men with AIDS, the two greatest exposure categories are sex with men (37 percent) and injection drug use (34 percent); heterosexual exposure accounts for 8 percent (CDC 2001b). The devastating impact of this disease on African American men and women is clear. However, much of what we know about these trends has focused either on specific behavioral subgroups of "high-risk" populations (e.g., men who have sex with men, drug users), which, without the social context, puts emphasis on individual behavior. In other cases entire ethnic/racial groups, such as African Americans or Hispanics, are said to be in "high-risk" groups, which emphasizes race/ethnicity and obscures the pervasive forms of disempowerment of the group. Both ignore sociopolitical constructions of HIV/AIDS.

Perceptions and interpretations of a disease are sociopolitically constructed but rarely by those who are primarily affected by the disease. Epidemics evoke human reactions of exclusion, fear, denial, and naming and blaming some "other." Since its beginning, HIV/AIDS has been a disease of some differentiated populations characterized with deficits of individual behavior. In the case of

AIDS research, identity and behavior have been confounded in analyses of HIV-risk behavior (Schiller, Crystal, and Lewellen 1994), this is particularly true for African Americans who have historically been cast as having deficits in behavior. There is a tendency for some to associate AIDS with "black cultural" cognitive or behavioral style. Conners (1996, 120) notes the "troubling examples of how researchers have collapsed 'culture into AIDS' with such terms as 'black resistance' and 'HIV risk denial' when referring to the escalating AIDS cases among African Americans." This approach fails to acknowledge the structural issues—poverty, institutional racism, economic vulnerability, legislation, isolation—that support the disproportionate number of AIDS cases among African Americans. Moreover, gender plays a crucial role in the escalating rate of HIV-infection among women who are relatively more vulnerable because of sexism and gender inequality in personal and sexual relationships. African American women are said to be "triple burdened" by race, gender, and class (Quinn 1993). Rather, their ability to respond to the risk of contracting HIV is shaped by sexism, racism, and, to a great extent, socioeconomic oppression.

Although the literature has acknowledged the vicissitudes of poverty and gender inequality as risk factors, rather than inherent racial or ethnic factors, there is still a need to examine the complexity and inextricably intertwined sociocultural factors that place African Americans, particularly African American women, at increased risk for HIV-infection. This chapter examines HIV-infection among African American women by situating the disease within a sociocultural context and delineating the interrelatedness of the many sociocultural factors that underlie the alarming rates of HIV-infection among distinct, yet connected, African American subgroups. The discussion aims to explain "risky HIV behavior" within the context of formidable structural impediments.

STRUCTURAL IMPEDIMENTS IN THE LIVES OF AFRICAN AMERICAN WOMEN

Structural impediments refer to those social, political, and economic forces in our society that establish and define the reality of certain populations and restrict the options that people can choose as a means of survival. Lifestyle choices can be said to be dependent on the extent to which individuals have access and personal agency to obtain crucial societal resources such as food, shelter, education, housing, and appropriate mental and physical health care—all of which are limited by poverty and social inequality, which, in turn, impact the effectiveness of AIDS prevention messages. Structural impediments also place people in "high risk situations" (Zwi and Cabral 1992), where sociocultural forces act in ways to increase individual or group vulnerability to HIV-infection.

In retrospect, HIV/AIDS researchers and policy makers agree that early prevention strategies have failed to influence African American communities for two major reasons. First, initial prevention messages were not targeted in culturally specific ways to reach ethnic minority communities. Initial prevention efforts were targeted primarily to White, gay males. As Patton (1994, 167) explains, "The collective social identity supported by an elaborate economy of bookstores, bars, and newspapers of urban gay men made it relatively easy to 'sell' safe sex through marketing-style risk-reduction education campaigns."

Second, for African Americans, AIDS is much more embedded in societal ills such as poverty, chemical dependency, lack of accessible and affordable health care, mistrust of medical and other institutions, isolation, institutionalized racism, and internalized oppression. Thus, African American women's vulnerability to HIV-infection includes the entire spectrum of issues that impact their lives and place them in "high-risk situations." This chapter addresses the intersection of poverty, drug use, racial inequality, gender inequality and sexuality, health and mental health, and social isolation in helping to explain the startling high rates of HIV-infection among African American women. The analysis also incorporates social-psychological explanations, under the assumption that these are shaped by a person's social context. More specifically, the discussion addresses the relationship between social impediments and increased vulnerability to HIV-infection by considering the ways in which people adapt psychologically and behaviorally to their environment.

Poverty: Creating an Environment of Risk

Poverty is a major underlying factor in HIV-infection among African Americans, who are disproportionately poor in our society. Rank and Hirschl (1999) estimated the likelihood of poverty across the lifespan (age twenty to eighty-five) and found that by age thirty-five nearly one-third of the U.S. population will have experienced a year in poverty. However, the researchers' analysis revealed that "nearly every black American adult in this country will at some point experience a year below the poverty line" (1999, 212). More specifically, the authors note that by age seventy-five, 91 percent of Black Americans will have experienced at least one year in poverty, and 68 percent will have encountered the stark experience of extreme poverty. Unemployment is a large part of that equation, with the unemployment rate for African Americans remaining twice as high as that of White Americans for more than three decades (Tienda and Stier 1996; Wilson 1996), and consequently, African Americans continue to lag behind Whites in adequate housing and educational opportunities. In addition, African American populations in the United States are more concentrated in poor, urban areas as a result of residential discrimination rooted in the legacies of slavery, segregation, and individual and institutionalized discrimination. In addition, many poor urban environments are characterized by deteriorating housing, extreme isolation, and a decaying sense of community. Between 1955 and 1972, poverty rates lessened for African Americans, but this economic growth slowed dramatically in the late 1970s and 1980s, a period of political conservatism. This period also correlates highly with sharp rises in drug use and in sexually transmitted disease (STD) rates among the African

American population, problems that, as explored later, link poverty with HIV infection.

Across racial and ethnic lines, women continue to be concentrated in occupations where they receive lower wages and fewer benefits on average than men, yet single African American women with children are among the poorest of women. In 1995, households headed by African American women with children had median earnings of $13,608 or 28 percent of the median for married-couple African American families with children (U.S. Bureau of Census 1999). Thus, African American women with children are overrepresented among poor populations, and this is reflected in the majority of African American women living with HIV (Conners, 1996; Schable et al. 1995).

Demographics of HIV-positive African American women indicate that a disproportionate number are poor and from urban environments. They are usually the sole supporter of themselves and their children (Conners 1996; Schable et al. 1995), in some cases due to the death of a husband or male partner from AIDS. These women are usually faced with tragedies associated with impoverished living: inadequate housing, poor health, violence, isolation, discrimination, and substance abuse that predated their HIV-infection. Poor African American women tend to be overwhelmed by life's circumstances, even before HIV became a threat to them. In a study of 817 HIV-infected and 439 uninfected women from socially and economically disadvantaged environments, researchers found that the two groups did not differ on the number of severe adverse life events (e.g., insufficient money for necessities, physical attack or rape, death of a person close to them) and levels of depression (Moore et al. 1999). For both groups, low socioeconomic status, intravenous drug or crack-cocaine use, and high-risk sexual activity were related to reports of more adverse events and depression. The study highlights that regardless of HIV status, poor women must deal with many social and psychological adversities that may make it difficult for them to practice healthy behaviors; they exist and adapt to survival in environments where situational risks for HIV and other social ills are pervasive.

Drug Use: Gender Disparities Within the Drug Culture

Overall, relative risks for AIDS associated with poverty and intravenous drug use (IVDU) are much higher for ethnic minorities than for White populations (Singer 1992). Substance abuse among African Americans has been linked to hopelessness, deteriorating communities, and self-destructive behavior associated with poverty and isolation (Bowser, Fullilove, and Fullilove 1990; Kim, Marmor, Dubin, and Wolfe 1993). As a twin epidemic, substance abuse has existed in tandem with HIV infection.

Within the drug-using population, women appear to suffer greater negative life events than men due to a number of gender-related factors. Drug-using women experience extremely high levels of stress as compared with male drug users or nondrug-using women due to their responsibility to children, living alone, low level of education, lack of financial resources, and partners who are more likely to use drugs (Mondanaro 1990). Compared with men, women who use drugs also experience more dysfunction and pathology in family of origin, higher levels of depression and anxiety, and lower levels of self-esteem; they usually experience more medical problems than their male counterparts, possibly because drugs exert a more toxic influence on women (Mondanaro 1990); at the same time, women are underrepresented in traditional drug treatment programs and receive relatively less help for their addiction than men (Mondanaro 1990).

Other gender and drug-related factors place women at increased risk for HIV-infection. Intravenous Drug Use (IVDU) accounts for the greater percentage of African American women's exposure to HIV-infection, either through their own use or through sexual relationships with IV-drug using men. Thus, even when women do not use drugs, they are at great risk because of the disproportionate number of African American men who are drug users. It has been reported that 80 percent of male IV drug users have their primary relationships with women who do not themselves use such drugs (Mondanaro 1990). Women's unawareness of their partner's drug use played a key role in infection rates in the beginning of the epidemic (Des Jarlais et al. 1984) and perhaps continues to do so. Because of the stigma associated with drug use, it appears fairly common for individuals to conceal their drug use, especially IVDU and crack-cocaine use, from spouses and intimate partners (Des Jarlais et al. 1984; Maher, Dunlap, Johnson, and Hamid 1996).

The greatest risk of HIV-infection among the African American drug-using population appears to be among those who both inject drugs and use crack cocaine. Like IVDU, crack has played a huge part in HIV-infection rates in African American communities across the country (Warner and Leukefeld 1999; Wingwood and DiClemente 1998). African Americans represent a disproportionate number of crack users (Bencivengo and Cutler 1993; Edlin et al. 1994). The typical crack-cocaine users have been described as disproportionately inner city, ethnic-minority males, high school dropouts, unmarried, unemployed, and with little or no legal income (Lewis, Johnson, Golub, and Dunlap 1992), although one multistate study reported that more women than men had used crack (Wechsberg et al. 1998). Overall, young African American teens living in disintegrated communities have been especially affected in situations where the deteriorating conditions of public housing projects acted as virtual breeding grounds for the crack-cocaine epidemic and crack trafficking created an "underworld" economy (Bowser, Fullilove, and Fullilove 1990). At the same time, individuals who became quickly addicted to crack also developed extraordinarily high risks for HIV-infection (Bowser, Fullilove, and Fullilove 1990). Several studies have shown crack smokers to be more likely than noncrack smokers to have unprotected sex, exchange sex for money or drugs, have a higher number of sexual partners, and have sex while using drugs (Booth, Watters, and Chitwood 1993; Cohen, Navaline, and Metzger 1994; Edlin et al. 1994; Fullilove, Lown, and Fullilove 1992; Longshore and Anglin 1995; Wingood and DiClemente 1998).

The inner-city drug culture associated with crack cocaine resulted in a high frequency of street-level sexual acts for monetary and drug gain by crack-addicted women (Carlson and Siegel 1991; Edlin et al. 1992; Fullilove and Fullilove 1989; Fullilove, Lown, and Fullilove 1992). Although these transactions were different from the oppressive pimp-prostitute structure predating the crack epidemic, the crack industry and women's dependency on crack has placed women in lowly confined roles as prostitutes or "skeezers" in "freakhouses" or as street-level runners with extensive reliance on men for shelter, drugs, and other commodities. Such women have suffered extensive degradation in the process (Fullilove, Lown and Fullilove 1992; Maher et al. 1996). Maher et al. (1996) state, "The cumulative effect of these influences was a large number of crack-abusing women who had no legal income, expended all of their illegal income on crack, had no relatives or friends who allowed them into their households, and were excluded by male crack sellers who dominated them sexually or as women employees" (183).

Implementing HIV/AIDS prevention programs for chemically dependent women can be extremely challenging because of the complexity of their high-risk situations. Specifically, these programs demand that women change both their drug-taking behaviors and their sexual risk behavior. Mondanaro (1990) explains that often debilitating situations (e.g., sense of hopelessness and stress, lack of financial resources, low income, instability, higher levels of depression) force a woman into a psychological suppression of vulnerability; the woman assumes a "fatalistic attitude that she will contract the disease no matter what precautions she takes [and this] may be the woman's only defenses" (73).

Health Disparities: The Sexually Transmitted Disease Epidemic

Twenty-one percent of African Americans often report no usual source of medical care, and clinic or emergency room care is used even after controlling for demographic factors such as income and insurance coverage (Flack 1996). Discrimination in the health care system against African Americans supports the belief among people of color that health and medical care providers are not genuinely interested in them or their health (Blendon, Aiken, and Freeman 1989; Dalton 1989; Telfair and Nash 1996). Although Black women are more likely to receive medical and mental health care than their male counterparts, poverty is a barrier to adequate health care for Black women (Gaston, Johnson, and Epstein 1998; Weiss, 1997). Among the most serious health issues facing African Americans, STDs rank high. As mentioned earlier, STDs are linked to poverty rates. "The association between declining socioeconomic conditions for some members of racial/ethnic minorities and increasing race/ethnicity differentials in STD rates in the 1980s is remarkable" (Aral and Wasserheit 1995, 21). Johnson (1993) notes that "there has been a sexually transmitted disease epidemic among

African-Americans long before HIV/AIDS came on the scene," with subs₄ tially higher rates of syphilis and gonorrhea for the past ten to twenty years, and, unfortunately public health officials directed very little attention toward this epidemic.

Persons with STDs have been found to be more susceptible to HIV infection (Aral and Wasserheit, 1995). Moreover a high rate of STDs among African Americans contributes to higher levels of HIV prevalence among Black women compared with White women. In general, inner-city African American women have been found to have relatively high rates of STDs, and Aral and Wasserheit (1995) discuss a number of factors that may help explain this.

First, compared with the age composition of the nonpoor population, the age composition of the poor population is substantially more youthful, and racial/ethnic minority populations below the poverty level have the most youthful age compositions—a characteristic of populations that is conducive to higher STD rates (Aral and Wasserheit 1995). Gender imbalance is another factor. The sex ratio (the number of men as compared with the number of women) of the Hispanic population is 1.00; the White ratio is .95, and the African American ratio is .88. The gender imbalance of the African American population in poverty is particularly marked, with a sex ratio of .69 creating a sizable excess of poor, young African American women over men (Aral and Wasserheit 1995). All societal factors that increase STD incidence, including youthful age composition, sex-ratio imbalance, and lower socioeconomic status of women, are observed to a greater extent in African American and Hispanic American populations and in the population below the poverty level.

Mental Health Disparities: Trauma and Violence

Trauma and violence are important but often overlooked aspects of risky behavior (Fullilove, Lown, and Fullilove 1992). Richie (1996) studied African American battered and incarcerated women and found that domestic violence was linked to a woman's involvement in illegal activity, drug use, and unsafe sex. A woman's history of childhood sexual abuse and involvement with an abusive partner have both been linked to a range of behaviors that lead to increased risk of HIV-infection. For example, abused women are more likely to experience early sexual initiation or teen pregnancy (Boyer and Fine 1992; Lodico and Di-Clemente 1994), dropping out of school (Bedimo, Kissinger, and Bessinger 1997; Zierler et al. 1991), and unstable or nonpermanent living situations (Bedimo, Kissinger, and Bessinger 1997). Also, abused women as compared with nonabused women have been found to have significantly more health problems, have had more operations, engaged in more risk behaviors, and reported more physical and mental symptoms (Springs and Friedrich 1992), including lower self-esteem (Beitchman et al. 1991; Rotheram-Borus, Mahler, Koopman, and Langabeer 1996), higher rates of STDs (Vermund, Alexander-Rodriguez, Macleod, and Kelly 1990), and HIV infection (Zierler et al. 1991). Furthermore a range of HIV-risk behaviors have been associated with previous child abuse, including early initiation of sexual activity; sex with casual or anonymous partners; sex with known risky partners; multiple sex partners; unprotected sex; prostitution; and coercive sex (Erickson and Rapkin 1991; Polit, White, and Morton 1990; Wyatt 1988).

Early childhood abuse has also been linked to drug use among women (Allers and Benjack 1991). Among substance-abusing women, those with a history of childhood sexual abuse have a higher risk for participation in commercial sex work than substance-abusing women with no history of sexual abuse (Paone et al. 1992). There is limited evidence of high rates of histories of sexual abuse among African American women who are HIV positive or at increased risk of HIV-infection. Bedimo, Kissinger, and Bessinger (1997) studied 238 HIV-infected women, predominantly (83 percent) African American, between the ages of fourteen and thirty-five, who were enrolled in the HIV Outpatient Clinic in New Orleans. Of these women, 76 percent reported a history of sexual abuse.

In many instances, sexual abuse is but one of a sequelae of traumatic events that occur in the lives of sexually assaulted women. Perez, Kennedy and Fullilove (1995) explain that a series of traumatic events beyond sexual abuse tends to shape the lives and decision making of women, including the woman's choice of safe partners, adoption of safe sexual behaviors, and recognition and prompt treatment of STDs. Thus, prevention messages to "choose safe sex" may not be very effective with women who have not healed from past traumatic events that tend to drive their current sexual relationships.

Racial Disparities: Incarceration, a Case in Point

In addition to racial disparities associated with income, employment, education, health care, geographic location, and drug use, biased law enforcement practices negatively impact African Americans. The disproportionate number of incarcerated Black men, for example, threatens family and relationship dynamics and also puts women at risk for HIV-infection.

For example in 1992, 42 percent of young African American men eighteen to thirty-five years of age in the District of Columbia were under criminal justice supervision—in prison or jail, on probation, parole, out on bond, or being sought on a warrant according to statistics from the National Center on Institutions and Alternatives (Miller 1992). In 1998, that figure had climbed to 50 percent although the population of African Americans in the District of Columbia had declined over that same period (Lotke 1998). In some geographical areas, these statistics are more alarming. Nationwide, one in three African American males between the ages of eighteen and forty are involved with the criminal justice system (Mayer 1999).

Miller (1996) estimated that including both jail time and prison, roughly eight out of ten African American men will spend time imprisoned during their lifetimes, typically before the age of forty. Since the early eighties, the increase in arrests associated with the "war on crime" and "war on drugs" has had a devastating impact on African American family life. The crack-cocaine phenomenon resulted in new laws, expanded police resources, and the building of new correctional facilities, but little attention was given to researching the nature and impact of the drug on individual and community health (Holden 1989). The institutionalization of African American males in prison has resulted in the destabilization of family life and relationships as men suffer loss of personal autonomy, negative health consequences, poor self-concept, and lifelong stigmatization due to imprisonment (King 1999). These men suffer mental health consequences, such as depression and suicide (Houston 1990), feelings of alienation (King 1999), and emerge from prison with few skills to survive as autonomous and independent individuals in society (King 1999; Lichenstein and Kroll 1990).

Within prisons, inmates are exposed to such dangerous and such life-threatening conditions as violence, drugs, rape, and HIV and AIDS. Mahon (1996) interviewed former male and female prisoners and city inmates in New York and found that a range of consensual and nonconsensual high-risk sexual behaviors occur among prisoners, and between prisoners and correctional personnel, and that male-on-male prisoner rape occurs with some frequency and involves men who do not identify themselves as homosexual. Although prisons may have some form of AIDS prevention education ranging from voluntary or mandatory testing and segregation and distribution of condoms (Hammett and Daugherty 1991), these programs are not necessarily available to every inmate, and we know little about their effectiveness, either in prison and after prisoners are released (Inciardi 1996). The increased incarceration rate of intravenous drug users, combined with homosexual acts occurring in prisons, by rape or otherwise, exposes a significant proportion of African American males to HIV-infection. In 1990, the national AIDS incidence rate was 17 cases per 100,000 residents; whereas the AIDS incidence rate for that same year was 181 per 100,000 inmates, a rate 18 times that of the general population (Hammett and Daugherty 1991). Inciardi (1996, 427) notes that the problem may be even more pronounced in city and county jails where "crowding and limited budgets, medical problems, and potential for disease transmission are considerable." Thus, the rate of AIDS in the prison population is indirectly a major source of spread of AIDS among African American women.

African American women in prison are also at risk. Since 1980, the number of women entering prisons in the United States has risen almost 400 percent, double the rate of men, and two-thirds of women in prison are women of color (Bureau of Justice Statistics 2000). This trend has much to do with the worsening economic conditions for women, which often places them in compromising situations that lead to criminal activity. The majority of women imprisoned in the past twenty years has been due to nonviolent crimes such as prostitution, fraud, and drug offenses. In discussing her findings related to African American female inmates, Richie (1996) argues that her theory of gender entrapment, "a circumstance whereby an individual is lured into a compromising act" (120), explains women's forced involvement in illegal activities as a result of violence in their intimate relationships. In prison, women face similar risks of HIV-infection, as well as loss of autonomy, self-esteem, and sense of connectedness (Mahon 1996).

Once outside, the economic hardships, emotional distress, and strained interpersonal relationships faced by African American men and women and their families are inadequately addressed due to a lack of effective services and programs in place to meet the unique needs of inmates, former inmates, and their families (King 1999). King (1999, 13) notes that "if a significant percentage of African-American males continue to be subjected to the emotional, psychological, and health-related risks associated with prison environment then the supply of able-bodied African-American males will continue to dwindle."

Lack of Perceived Susceptibility: Denial or Adaptive Responses to Mistrust and Stigma

Current and historical racism plays a significant role in African American health, including knowledge and beliefs about HIV and AIDS (Dalton 1989). The notion of "AIDS denial" among African Americans has been discussed in connection to both the lack of knowledge and rejection of mainstream HIV/AIDS knowledge, as well as the documented lack of susceptibility of HIV-infection among some groups of African American men and women. Klonoff and Landrine (1997) studied relationships among acculturation, distrust of Whites, and AIDS knowledge for African Americans. The results revealed that African Americans who had high knowledge of the behaviors that spread AIDS were more acculturated than those with low knowledge and also the former group scored significantly lower on the cultural mistrust scale, a scale that measures distrust of Whites, if they had high knowledge about AIDS. Specifically, those who knew the least about AIDS were the most distrustful of White mainstream society.

This research helped to clarify the hypothesis that African Americans' knowledge of and openness to AIDS prevention messages is affected by their distrust of Whites. These findings are consistent with similar findings among Latinos related to acculturation and AIDS knowledge (Epstein, Dusenbury, Botvin, and Diaz 1994). This research may also explain which groups of African Americans have stronger tendencies to believe conspiracy theories or the rumors that circulate within various African American communities that AIDS is a plot to kill African Americans. In 1996, the Kaiser Family Foundation Survey found that 27 percent of African Americans believe that "AIDS is a form of systematic destruction of minorities" compared with only 13 percent of Whites who believed this. Ironically, prevention messages regarding condom use are construed as further evidence of theories such as genocidal conspiracy, that is, the view that AIDS is a man-made virus that is being employed against Blacks (Thomas and Quinn 1991). Klonoff and Landrine's (1997) findings suggest that rather than simply lacking AIDS knowledge, some African Americans consciously reject health information which they perceive as untrustworthy. This may have direct implications for condom-use behavior. Those who equate condom use with "killing off the race" may be resistant to condom-use prevention messages.

Studies have documented that African Americans have a tendency to underestimate personal risks or personal susceptibility to AIDS as compared with other groups (Johnson 1993; Kalichman et al. 1993; Neff and Crawford 1998). Johnson (1993) studied high- moderate- and low-risk (based in a distribution of scores on the Perceived Risk Scale) African American male and female college students and reported the puzzling finding that there were no significant differences in the personal perception of risk for contracting AIDS among the three groups. Rather, high-risk engagers tended to believe they were not at risk for being exposed to HIV/AIDS; they were "not worried" or reported that they "do not consider themselves the kind of person to get AIDS" even though they had engaged in high-risk behavior. Indeed, higher risk behaviors were associated with lower perceived susceptibility. Although one may label this "denial," another explanation is the psychological need for socially stigmatized individuals to minimize further stigma. AIDS is arguably the most stigmatizing disease in U.S. history, and the role that stigma plays recognizing one's probability of taking on additional stigma for highly stigmatized populations has largely gone unstudied. The experience of gay, White males is substantially different from drug-using African American men and women who face societal stigma, as well as stigma from within their own communities.

Studies investigating women's negotiation of condom use and sense of control around HIV susceptibility have also shown that despite all indications that a potential risk exists, some African American women tend to believe they can, and do adequately, assess risk based on their "wisdom to choose a clean man" (Sobo 1993) or where the sexual encounter happens. A Barker et al. study of low-income, nondrug-using African American women reports that "during a session discussing risky situations, such as having sex with a stranger, one woman adamantly advanced the view that she would not be at risk were she to engage in sexual intercourse with a (male) stranger/casual partner while intoxicated as long as she was in her own house" (1998, 277). The authors note that although the training emphasized that regardless of an individual's whereabouts, she places herself at risk if her judgment is impaired as a result of drugs or alcohol, more than half the participants found this unconvincing, feeling that a woman, intoxicated or not, was always capable of being—and indeed was—in control as long as she was in her home. On the other hand, drinking or doing drugs away from home was "risky." Barker and colleagues (1998) offer as an explanation that home as a "safeplace" was a pervasive but potentially harmful value.

Another explanation would involve a closer look at stigma and, specifically, highly stigmatized individuals within the African American community. In his study of African Americans and HIV risk behavior among college students, Johnson (1993) found that 28 percent of the participants believed that "AIDS existed as God's punishment for homosexual people who sin," (151) a group perceived as further stigmatizing the Black community. Managing one's actual or perceived stigma can be a powerful cognitive-behavioral motivator. Similarly, the women who are "out in the streets doing drugs (i.e., crack-addicted prostitutes) are also highly stigmatized within the Black community. In order to minimize their own stigma, nondrug-using women may view themselves as "safe" just by virtue of the fact that they are having sexual encounters at home, not "out there" in the "streets." This explanation would be consistent with an attribution theory that predicts that people search for understanding and seek to explain events in their lives, particularly when they need to gain or maintain control over their environment (Kelley 1971). Consistent with this attribution theory, women may create their own hierarchy of values to justify or explain their behavior, such that they can distinguish their sexual behavior from that of women perceived to be the most deviant within their community. However, such findings clearly warrant further ethnographic research. The psychological vulnerability that African Americans experience as a result of enduring daily social stigma has primarily been studied in cross-cultural situations (Crocker and Major 1989; Gilbert 1998). We know very little about how severely marginalized African American women manage stigma (e.g., extreme poverty, sexism, racism).

The Intersection of Gender and Racism and Sexuality: More on Stigma and Horizontal Oppression

A large part of why AIDS prevention messages have failed is our lack of knowledge about Black sexuality (Barker, Battle, Cummings, and Bancroft 1998; Johnson 1993). More importantly, Black sexuality has been defined primarily through distorted historical and current mainstream depictions of African Americans. Although all women in our society are subjected to stereotypical depictions of oversexualized images and objectification, African American women tend to suffer the most extreme images of sexualized, deviant exotic, and dehumanized behavior in the media, which is both perpetuated by Black males and supported by the larger media culture. hooks (1994) states that, without a doubt Black males, young and old, must be held politically accountable for their sexism, yet the broader accountability for the commodification of perverse Black sexuality rests with larger structures of domination (sexism, racism, class elitism). Television and films often stigmatize and demonize the young African American woman by depicting her as a welfare mother, drug addict, sex object, and/or prostitute (Gray 1995). The correlate of the oversexualized African American female is the depiction of African American males as criminals, rappers, pimps, and drug dealers (Gray 1995; Kivel 1996). The damaging media images of African American men have resulted in the commodification and aggressive marketing of sports figures and gangster rap artists, which has created a stereotype of the "black male persona [in which] criminality, real or imagined, is an essential ingredient of this charismatic black persona" (Hoberman 1997, xix). Sadly, many African Americans fall prey to these distorted gender images as a way to establish their identity. As a result, the legacy of racism becomes embedded in the dynamics of Black sexuality.

In speaking about the etiology of AIDS among African American women, Dicks (1994) explains that the historical assault on the Black male's ego through history of castrations, lynchings, and discrimination in employment has had the effect of causing women to compromise themselves to aid in reducing the consequences of the social and psychological assaults on the men. Within the context of sexual activity, that amounts to upholding men's "superstud" role, including buying into men's resistance to condoms based on the explanation that condoms undermine their masculinity and virility (Dicks 1994).

To the extent that Black males and females internalize these images of themselves, there are two outcomes. First, heterosexism and sexual conquests become avenues through which Black men can overcome the historical emasculation they have suffered. Second, all those within the group who do not adhere to such behavior become stigmatized as "shaming the race," an outcome that supports homophobia within the Black community. Although some studies have found no direct evidence of disproportionately high homophobia among African Americans (Herek and Capitanio 1995), other literature has linked strong antigay attitudes within the African American community to strong religiosity (Icard 1986); distortions of black masculinity (Julien and Mercer 1991); strong heterosexist attitudes (Gomez and Smith 1990), and the shortage of available men to African American women (Ernst et al. 1991; Poussaint 1991). With regard to lesbian women, Lorde (1984) explained part of the need to misname and ignore Black lesbians comes from a fear that openly women-identified Black women who are no longer dependent on Black men for their self-definition may well reorder the whole concept of social relationships in Black communities.

Ethnic-minority gay men and lesbians frequently experience a sense of alienation because of the double-stigma they face from the larger White society and within the White dominant gay society, as well as within the African American community (Gilbert-Martinez and Sullivan 1998; Greene 1994). This alienation leaves them at greater risk for isolation, feelings of estrangement, and increased psychological vulnerability (Greene 1994). The Black church has played an active role in alienating gay males based on biblical beliefs that homosexuality is a sin, while simultaneously embracing them, albeit in a secretive manner, as the "archetypal gay male in the church, usually involved in music production and singing" (Boykin 1996). Fullilove and Fullilove (1999) refer to this phenomenon as the "paradox of the open closet" (1114): that gays have a creative role in the church is widely known yet they are denounced from the pulpit with harsh, degrading condemnation. They argue that this has resulted in traumatic losses for gay men, including loss of peace through spiritual renewal and loss of self-esteem, in addition to their increased involvement in heterosexual relationships to maintain status within the community.

Because of their need to remain connected to family and community, African American gay men and lesbians may be more inclined to engage in heterosexual relationships and/or identify as bisexual. A higher proportion of HIV-positive African American men with AIDS were bisexual compared with their hite counterparts (Rogers and Williams 1987). In the first decade of AIDS, Mays (1989, 266) noted that among bisexuals with AIDS, Black men are "dramatically overrepresented," accounting for 28 percent of all cases. At the same time, heterosexual women are at increased risk due to the stigma that hinders gay Black males from fully claiming a gay identity. When African American gay males, who engage in unprotected sex with men, keep their homosexual activity a secret and also engage in heterosexual activity, they could place African American women at increased risk. In addition, Black gay males may maintain heterosexual relationships to protect their image in the Black community. Thus, stigma and sanctions against homosexuality in the African American community can force Black men to hide their sexual preferences and they may engage in secret homosexual activity. (Dicks 1994; Fullilove and Fullilove 1999).

Similarly, compared with their White counterparts, African American lesbians are reported to have had extensive heterosexual relationships, to have been married, and to have had children (Bell and Weinberg 1978; Mays and Cochran 1988). Yet lesbian women tend not to consider themselves at risk even though they engage in sexual activity, whereby HIV can be transmitted due to early hierarchial categorization of risk groups, which virtually ignored sexual risks to women who have sex with women (Morrow 1995). For example, in one study, more than 10 percent of black female intravenous drag users reported engaging in sex with women (Feucht, Stephens, and Roman 1990).

Gender Imbalance: African American Women at Heightened Risk

The role that gender imbalance plays in the high HIV-infection rates among African American women is an issue that warrants full attention. The gender imbalance ratio, whereby there simply exists more African American men than African American women, is one part of the issue; but this phenomenon is compounded by the relative scarcity of economically, self-sufficient young men, referred to as "the male marriageable pool index" (Wilson 1987). Considering the high rates of incarceration, unemployment, and drug abuse among African American men, combined with the male homosexual population, this pool shrinks further. This dimensioned male pool index creates heightened risk for African American women in three ways: men's multiple relationships, women's tolerance of less than desirable relationship dynamics, and women's perceived need for multiple male relationships for financial stability.

Social exchange theory predicts that when one gender is in short supply, this results in relatively less power for the larger gender group (Guttentag and Secord 1983), namely, African American women in this case. This imbalance of power leads to men demonstrating less commitment to relationships (Guttentag and Secord 1983; Jemmott, Ashby, and Lindenfeld 1989), and having relatively greater numbers of female partners (Wilson 1987). One estimate is that nearly

40 percent of unmarried African-American males between the age of eighteen and forty-five have multiple partners (Bower 1991).

Thus, a diminished pool of men having multiple partners can place a great number of women at risk. This has been shown to be the case with the incidence of STDs among African American women, whereby the probability of exposure to a sexually transmitted pathogen per sexual encounter is higher among African American women than among White women. Aral and Wasserheit (1995) point out that African American women who have two to three lifetime sex partners have a 100 percent increased likelihood of developing acute pelvic inflamatory disease, compared to those with one lifetime sex partner; however the increased risk is only 50 percent among White women.

Thus, even when African American women have few lifetime sexual partners, they may be especially at risk for STDs due to the high prevalence of infection among sex partners, largely African American men (Seidman and Aral 1992, as cited in Aral and Wasserheit 1995). This phenomenon is compounded by the diminished pool of men, their tendency to have multiple relationships, and the concentration of poor African Americans in urban areas where geography also determines one's choice of intimate partnerships.

At the same time, the fact that men are in short supply means that women may be more tolerant of their male partner's multiple relationships. This may occur both because of a woman's perceived need to have a man in her life based on societal standards and also because having a man, a scarce resource, may now afford the woman higher status in her immediate environment. Women who perceive they have limited chances of finding a new man if they alienate or displease their current partner may choose to accept whatever social situation they are in (e.g., domestic violence, partner's infidelity, etc.). Based on interviews with low-income women attending an STD clinic, Sobo (1993) offers two explanations for why women engage in unsafe sex based on emotional and social dependence on men. Based on a "wisdom narrative," a woman may engage in self-talk to convince herself of the belief that she has the ability to judge men and that her standards for partners are high. In the "monogamy narrative," a woman may idealize that a monogamous relationship exists between her and her man. Refusing to acknowledge the possibility that her partner may have sex with other women (or men) supports the woman's monogamy idealization. Unsafe sex is paramount in maintaining both narratives as conceptualized by the women. Through unsafe sex, the woman "qualifies" the man as deemed worthy of a committed, monogamous relationship, and the woman can feel assured that she has the ability to "tell a 'good' man from a 'bad' one" (Sobo 1995, 114). With the context of poverty and other life circumstances that limit lifestyle choices, "having a man" takes on a higher status, and with such perceived improved life opportunities, women will likely reframe their decisions.

Although some HIV prevention programs have shown effectiveness with poor African American women, the need for this population of women to find and establish a relationship with a suitable male—a scarce resource, oftentimes in an otherwise deprived environment—may drive sexual relationship dynamics more than HIV prevention messages. A high level of AIDS knowledge and a perception of being at risk do not necessarily correlate with behavior changes that reduce a woman's risk. In one HIV prevention study of low-income African American mothers in Oakland, California, findings after the three-month follow-up revealed that only 42 percent of participants benefited by developing increased trust in and the resolution to use condoms to reduce the risk of HIV-infection. Those not positively influenced by the intervention tended to prioritize short-term goals of establishing a sexual relationship, fulfilling emotional needs, and providing for children over the long-term goal of avoiding HIV-infection (Barker, Battle, Cummings, and Bancroft 1998). Several other studies support the notion that women can reduce their risk when they perceive that there are enough men for women and sufficient choices for partners (Gielen et al. 1994; Wingwood and DiClemente 1998; Wyatt, Forge, and Guthrie 1998) and that women and men are "acting/reacting" sexually to their social context (Fullilove, Fullilove, Haynes, and Gross 1990).

A third way that women are at risk due to the diminished male pool is women's perceived or real need for multiple male relationships for financial stability. Wyatt, Forge, and Guthrie (1998) studied family constellation and ethnicity as these relate to HIV risk taking. African American women in the sample were more likely to live alone, be single with a child, or live in a single extended family household or with roommates. Compared with White and Hispanic women, African American women were more likely to accept money for sex and to have a sexual relationship with someone other than their primary partner. However, as Wyatt and colleagues (98) note, "a closer look at their demographic characteristics may help explain further these relationships," which, rather than reflecting promiscuity, bartering, and financial stress, seemed to be the underlying reasons. In other words, African American women were more likely to engage in outside relationships as a way to seek out the most eligible and likely partner to commit to relationships and family stability, whereas for White women in the sample, relationships outside primary partners appeared to be related to recreational sex for pleasure (Wyatt 1988). Although across ethnic groups single women with a child experienced similar patterns of risk taking through sexual relationships with casual in addition to primary partners, the insufficient availability of African American men who have high rates of unemployment may increase African American women's risk taking in their quest to find financial and familial stability. Ironically, when women accept the belief that "half a man is better than none," this leads them to be willing to share a man, which reduces the social, emotional, and financial resources available to each woman, and, in turn, leads women to take multiple partners as well (Sobo 1995, 17), thus increasing their risk of HIV-infection if unsafe sex is fractured.

CONCLUSION

This discussion examined the social context of the lives of African American women, particularly poor African American women, and the intersecting sociocultural forces that place them at increased risk for HIV-infection. Taken together, the analyses appear to have several important implications. First, as we are finding out now, as we enter the third decade of AIDS, prevention cannot be effective until we have a good understanding of the reasons why people have increased risks for HIV-infection. The discussion suggests that removal of structural barriers to healthy living, good self-esteem, and improved life circumstances must occur, together with prevention messages. Intervention or prevention programs cannot be effective if there is no change, or even an attempt to change or address the underlying causes that move people to engage in the risk in the first place.

For the past two decades, prevention programs have been crippled by a lack of knowledge about the sociocultural context of the lives of African American women, specifically those that have been at highest risk for HIV-infection. The research reviewed here should serve as a basis for continued exploration of how to best achieve effective prevention. Interestingly, we are just beginning to have a full picture of precisely how African American women are experiencing such high rates of HIV-infection.

The challenge is to act on multiple levels. National, community, and individual responses are required. For example, HIV prevention strategies should include advocacy for policies that stress intervention and treatment for substance abuse problems, and not simply incarceration. It is also critical to work toward improving life circumstances for poor, isolated African Americans. Moreover, a tremendous healing must take place within and across African American communities to heal the kind of horizontal oppression that alienates gay and lesbian African Americans from their community, that creates violence in our communities, and that supports the systems whereby Black men degrade Black women. In addition, we have to find ways to help individuals heal through traumatic experiences, including the trauma experienced in decaying communities, while at the same time working to better their communities. Finally, there needs to be a dramatic increase in consolidated efforts to reach diverse groups of African Americans and to have a stronger presence in legislation. Much is being accomplished to date to develop effective prevention programs through studies and intervention trials. So much more is needed.

ACKNOWLEDGMENT

The author would like to thank Lisa Bowleg, Ph.D., Department of Psychology, University of Rhode Island, for her review and feedback on an earlier draft of this chapter, and Amy Doleys for her assistance with the research for this chapter.

REFERENCES

Allers, C.T., and Benjack, K.J. (1991). Connections between childhood abuse and HIV infection. *Journal of Counseling Development*, 70 309–319.

Aral, S.O., Mosher, W.D., and Cates, W. Jr. (1991). Self-reported pelvic inflammatory disease among women of reproductive age: United States 1982–1988. *JAMA*, 266 (18), 2570–2573.

Aral, S.O., Soskolne, V., Joesoef, R.M., and O'Reilly, K.R. (1991). Sex partner selection as risk factor for STD: Clustering of risky modes. *Sexually Transmitted Diseases*, 18 (1), 10–17.

Aral S.O., and Wasserheit, J.N. (1995). Interactions among other HIV, other sexually transmitted diseases, socioeconomic status, and poverty in women. In A. O'Leary and L.S. Jemmott (Eds.), *Women at risk: Issues in the primary prevention of AIDS* (pp. 13–41). New York: Plenum Press.

Barker, J.C., Battle, R.S., Cummings, G.L., and Bancroft, K.N. (1998) *Condoms and Consequences: HIV/AIDS Education and African American Women. Human Organization*, 57 (3), 273–283.

Bedimo, A.L., Kissinger, P., and Bessinger, R. (1997). History of sexual abuse among HIV-infected women. *International Journal of STD & AIDS*, (8), 332–335.

Beitchman, J.H., Zucker, K., Hood, J.E., DaCosta, G.A., et al. (1991). A review of the short-term effects of child sexual abuse. *Child Abuse and Neglect*, 15 537–556.

Bell, A.P., and Weinberg, M.S. (1978). *Homosexualities: A study of human diversity among men and women*. New York: Simon & Schuster.

Bencivengo, M.R., and Cutler, S.J. (1993). Drug use in Philadelphia, Pennsylvania. In *Epidemiologic trends in drug abuse*. Rockville, MD: National Institute of Drug Abuse.

Blendon, R.J., Aiken, L.H., Freeman, H.E. (1989). Access to medical care for black and white Americans: A matter of concern. *JAMA*, 261, (2), 278–81.

Booth, R.E., Watters, J.K., and Chitwood, D.D. (1993). HIV risk-related sex behaviors among injection drug users, crack smokers, and injection drug users who smoke crack. *The American Journal of Public Health*, 83 1144–1149.

Bower, B. (1991). Risky sex and AIDS. *Science News*, 140 (9) (8/31) 41.

Bowser, B.P., Fullilove, M.T., and Fullilove, R.E. (1990). African-American youth and AIDS high risk behavior: The social context and barriers to prevention. *Youth and Society*, 22 (1), 54–66.

Boyer, D., and Fine, D. (1992). Sexual abuse as a factor in adolescent pregnancy and child maltreatment. *Family Planning Perspective*, 24 4–11.

Boykin, K. (1996). *One more river to cross: Black and gay in America*. New York: Anchor Books.

Bureau of Justice Statistics, U.S. Department of Justice. (March 2000). Women in Prison Fact Sheet.

Carlson, R.G., and Siegel, H.A. (1991). The crack life: An ethnographic overview of crack use and sexual behavior among African-Americans in Midwest metropolitan cities. *Journal of Psychoactive Drugs*, 23 11–20.

Centers for Disease Control and Prevention (2000). HIV/AIDS Among African American Fact Sheet.

Centers for Disease Control and Prevention (2001a) HIV/AIDS Among African Americans Fact Sheet.

Centers for Disease Control and Prevention. (2001b.). HIV/AIDS Surveillance Report. June 13(1), Midyear Report.

Cochran, S.D. & Mays, V.M. (1988a). Epidemiologic and sociocultural factors in the transmission of HIV infection in Black gay and bisexual men. In M. Shernoff & W.A. Scott (Eds.), *A sourcebook of gay/lesbian health care* (pp. 202–211). Washington, DC: National Gay and Lesbian Health Foundation, 2nd Edition.

Cochran, S.D. & Mays, V.M. (1988b). Disclosure of sexual preference to physician by Black lesbian and bisexual women. *Western Journal of Medicine*, 149 616–619.

Conners, M. (1996). Sex, drugs and structured violence. In P. Farmer, M. Conners, and J. Simmons (Eds.), *Women, poverty, and AIDS: Sex, drugs and structured violence* (pp. 94–124). Monroe, MA: Common Courage Press.

Crocker, J., and Major, B. (1989). Social stigma and self-esteem. The self-protective properties of stigma. *Psychological Review*, 96 608–630.

Dalton, H.L. (1989). AIDS in blackface. *Daedalus*, 118 (3), 205–227.

Des Jarlais, D.C., Chamberland, M.E., Yancovitz, S.R., Weinburg, P., and Friedman, S.R. (1984). Heterosexual partners: A large risk group for AIDS. *Lancet*, 2 (8415), 1346–1347.

Dicks, B.A. (1994). African American women and AIDS: A public health/social work challenge. *Social Work in Health Care*, 19 (3/4), 123–143.

Edlin, B.R., Irwin, K.L., Ludwig, H.V., Faruque, S., et al. (1994). Intersecting epidemics—crack cocaine use and HIV infection among inner city young adults. *New England Journal of Medicine*, 331 1422–1427.

Edlin, B.R., Irwin, K.L., Ludwig, H.V., McCoy, H.V., et al. (1992). High-risk sex behavior among young street-recruited crack cocaine smokers in three American cities: An interim report. *Journal of Psychoactive Drugs*, 24 363–371.

Epstein, J.A., Dusenbury, L., Botvin, G.J., and Diaz, T. (1994). Acculturation, beliefs about AIDS, and AIDS education among New York City Hispanic parents *Hispanic Journal of Behavioral Sciences*, 16 342–354.

Erickson, P.I., and Rapkin, A.J. (1991). Unwanted sexual experiences among middle and high school youth. *Journal of Adolescent Health*, 12 319–325.

Ernst, F.A., Francis, R.A., Nevels, H., & Lemeh, C.A. (1991). Condemnation of homosexuality in the Black community: A gender specific phenomenon?: *Archives of Sexual Behavior*, 20 579–585.

Feucht, T.E., Stephens, R.C., and Roman, S.W. (1990). The sexual behavior of intravenous drug users: Assessing the risk of sexual transmission of HIV. *Journal of Drug Issues*, 20 195–213.

Flack, J.M. (1996). Panel I: Epidemiology of minority health. *Health Psychology*, 14 (7), 592–600.

Fullilove, M.T., and Fullilove, R.E. (1989). Intersecting epidemics: Black teen crack use and sexually transmitted diseases. *Journal of the American Medical Association*, 44 146–153.

Fullilove, M.T., and Fullilove, R.E. (1999). Stigma as an obstacle to AIDS action: The case of the African American community. *American Behavioral Scientist*, 42 (7), 1113–1125.

Fullilove, R.E., Fullilove, M.T., Bowser, B., and Gross, S. (1990). Risk of sexually transmitted disease among black adolescent crack users in Oakland and San Francisco, Calif. *JAMA*, 263 851–855.

Fullilove, M.T., Fullilove, R.E., Haynes, K., and Gross, S. (1990). Black women and AIDS prevention: A view towards understanding the gender rules. *Journal of Sex Research*, 27 (1), 47–64.

Fullilove, M.T., Lown, E.A., and Fullilove, R.E. (1992). Crack 'hos and skeezers: Traumatic experiences of women crack users. *Journal of Sex Research*, 29 275–287.

Gaston, M.H., Barrett, S.E., Johnson, T.L., and Epstein, L. (1998). Health care needs of medically undeserved women of color: The role of the Bureau of Primary Health Care. *Health and Social Work*, 23 (2), 86–95.

Gielen, A.C., Faden, R.R., O'Campo, P., Kass, N., and Anderson, J. (1994). Women's protective sexual behaviors: A test of the Health Belief Model. *AIDS Education and Prevention*, 6 1–11.

Gilbert, D.J. (1998). The Prejudice Perception Assessment Scale: Measuring stigma vulnerability among African American students at predominantly Euro-American universities. *Journal of Black Psychology*, 24 (3), 305–321.

Gilbert-Martinez, D.J., and Sullivan, S.C. (1998). African-American gay men and lesbians: Examining the complexity of gay identity development. In L.A. See (Ed.), Human behavior in the social environment: An African-American perspective (pp. 243–264). Binghamton, NY: Haworth Press.

Gomez, J. & Smith, B. (1990). Taking the home out of homophobia: Black lesbian health. In E.C. White (Ed.), *The Black women's health book: Speaking for ourselves* (pp. 198–213). Seattle, WA: Seal Press.

Gray, H. (1995). *Watching race: Television and the struggle for "Blackness."* Minneapolis: University of Minnesota Press.

Greene, B. (1994). Ethnic-minority lesbians and gay men: Mental health and treatment issues. *Journal of Consulting and Clinical Psychology*, 62 (2), 243–251.

Guttentag, M., and Secord, P. (1983). *Too many women?* Beverly Hills, CA: Sage Publications.

Hammett, T.M., and Daugherty, A.L. (1991). *AIDS in correctional facilities: Issues and options*. Washington, D.C.: U.S. Government Printing Office, National Institute of Justice.

Herek, G.M., & Capitanio, J.P. (1995). Black heterosexuals' attitudes toward lesbians and gay men in the United States. *Journal of Sex Research*, 32 (2), 95–105.

Hoberman, J. (1997). *Darwin's athletes: How sport has damaged black America and preserved the myth of race*. New York, NY: Houghton Mifflin Company

Holden, C. (1989). Street-wise crack research. *Science*, 24 (6), 1376–1381.

hooks, b. (1994). *Outlaw Culture; resisting representations*. New York: Routledge.

Houston, L.N. (1990). *Psychological principles and the black experience*. Lanham, MD.: University Press of America.

Icard, L. (1986). Black gay men and conflicting social identities: Sexual orientation versus racial identity. *Journal of Social Work and Human Sexuality*, 4, 83–93.

Inciardi, J.A. (1996). HIV risk reduction and service delivery strategies in criminal justice settings. *Journal of Substance Abuse and Treatment*, 13(5), 421–428.

Jemmott, J.B. III, Ashby, K.L., and Lindenfild, K. (1989). Romantic commitment and the perceived availability of opposite sex persons. On loving the one you're with. *Journal of Applied Social Psychology*, 19 1198–1216.

Johnson, E.H. (1993). Risky sexual behavior among African-Americans. Westport, CT: Praeger Publications.

Julien, I., & Mercer, K. (1991). True confessions: A discourse on images of black male sexuality. In E. Hemphill (Ed.), *Brother to Brother: New writings by Black gay men* (pp. 167–173). Boston: Alyson Publication.

Kalichman, S.C., Kelly, J., Hunter, T.L., Murphy, D.A., et al. (1993). Culturally-tailored HIV-AIDS risk-reduction messages targeted to urban women: Impact on risk sensitization and risk reduction. *Journal of Consulting and Clinical Psychology*, 61 291–295.

Kelley, H.H. (1971). Attribution theory in social interaction. In E.E. Jones, D.E. Kanouse, H.H. Kelley, R.E. Nisbett, et al. (Eds.), *Attribution: Perceiving the causes of behavior* (pp. 1–26). New York: General Learning Press.

Kim, M.Y., Marmor, M., Dubin, N., and Wolfe, H. (1993). HIV risk-related sexual behaviors among heterosexuals in New York City: Associations with race, sex, and intravenous drug use. *AIDS*, 7 409–414.

King, A.E.O. (1999). African-American males in prison: Are they doing time or is the time doing them? *Journal of Sociology and Social Welfare*, 9–27.

Kivel, P. (1996). *Uprooting Racism: How White People Can Work for Racial Justice*. Philadelphia: New Society Publisher.

Klonoff, E.A., and Landrine, H. (1997). Distrust of Whites, acculturation, and AIDS knowledge among African Americans. *Journal of Black Psychology*, 23 (19), 50–57.

Levin, C. (1990). AIDS and changing concepts of family. *Milbank Quarterly*, 68, 33–58.

Lewis, C., Johnson, B.D., Golub, A., and Dunlap, E. (1992). Studying crack abusers: Strategies for recruiting the right tail of an ill-defined population. *Journal of Psychoactive Drugs*, 24 (4), 323–336.

Lichtenstein, A.C., and Kroll, M.A. (1990). The fortress economy: The economic role of the U.S. prison system. Philadelphia, PA: American Friends Service Committee.

Lodico, M.A., and DiClemente, R.J. (1994). The association between childhood sexual abuse and prevalence of HIV-related risk behaviors. *Clinical Pediatrics*, 33 498–502.

Lorde, A. (1984). *Sister Outsider*. Freedom, CA: Crossing Press.

Lotke, E. (1998). Hobbling a generation: Young African American men in Washington, D.C.'s criminal justice system—five years later. *Crime and Delinquency*, 44 (3), 355–366.

Longshore, D., and Anglin, M.D. (1995). Number of sex partners and crack cocaine use: Is crack an independent marker for HIV risk behavior? *Journal of Drug Issues*, 25 1–10.

Maher, L, Dunlap, E., Johnson, B.D., and Hamid, A. (1996). Gender, power, and alternative living arrangements in the inner-city crack culture. *Journal of Research in Crime and Delinquency*, 33 (2), 181–205.

Mahon, N. (1996). New York inmates' HIV risk behaviors: The implications for prevention policy and programs. *American Journal of Public Health*, 86 (9), 1211–1215.

Maver, Marc (1999). *Race to incarcerate: The Sentencing Project*. New York: The New Press.

Mays, V. (1989). AIDS prevention in Black populations: Prevention of a safer kind. In V. Mays, G. Albee, and S. Schneider (Eds.), *Primary prevention of AIDS: Psychological approaches* (pp. 264–279). Newbury Park, CA: Sage Publications.

Mays, V.M., and Cochran, S. (1988). Issues in the perception of AIDS risk and risk reduction activities by Black and Hispanic/Latina women. *American Psychologist*, 43 949–957.

Miller, J.G. (1992). *Hobbling a generation: African American males in the District of Columbia's criminal justice system*. Washington, DC: National Center on Institutions and Alternatives.

Miller, J.G. (1996). *Search and destroy: African American males in the criminal justice system*. Cambridge, UK: Cambridge University Press.

Mondanaro, J. (1990). Community-based AIDS prevention interventions: Special issues of women intravenous drug users. In *AIDS and intravenous drug: Future Directions for Community-based prevention research*. NIDA Research Monograph 93. U.S. Dept. of Health and Human Services.

Moore, J., Schuman, P., Schoenbaum, E., Boland, B., et al. (1999). Severe adverse life events and depressive symptoms among women with, or at risk for, HIV infection in four cities in the United States of America. *AIDS*, 13 2459–2468.

Morrow, K.M. (1995). Lesbian women and HIV/AIDS: An appeal for inclusion. In A. O'Leary and L.S. Jemmott (Eds.), *Women at risk: Issues in the primary prevention of AIDS* (pp. 237–256). New York: Plenum Press.

Neff, J.A., and Crawford, S.L. (1998). The health belief model and HIV risk behaviors: A causal model analysis among Anglos, African-Americans, and Mexican-Americans. *Ethnicity and Health*, 3 (4), 283–299.

Paone, D., Chavkin, W., Willets, I., Friedman, P., & Des Jarlais, D. (1992). The impact of sexual abuse: Implications for drug treatment. *Journal of Women's Health*, 1, 149–153.

Patton, C. (1994). *Last served? Gendering the HIV pandemic*. Bristol, PA: Taylor & Francis.

Perez, B., Kennedy, G., and Fullilove, M.T. (1995). In A. O'Leary and L.S. Jemmott (Eds.), *Women at risk: Issues in the primary prevention of AIDS* (pp. 83–101). New York: Plenum Press.

Polit, D.F., White, C.M., and Morton, T.D. (1990). Child sexual abuse and premarital intercourse among high risk adolescents. *Journal of Adolescent Health Care*, 11 231–234.

Poussaint, A. (1991, September). An honest look at Black gays and lesbians. *Ebony*, pp. 124, 126, 130–131.

Quinn, S.C. (1993). AIDS and the African American woman: The triple burden of race, class, and gender. *Health Education Quarterly*, 20 (3), 305–320.

Rank, M.R., and Hirschl, T.A. (1999). The likelihood of poverty across the American adult life span. *Social Work*, 44 (3), 201–216.

Richie, B.E. (1996). Gender entrapment: An exploratory study. In A. Dan (Ed.), *Reframing women's health: Multidisciplinary research and practice* (pp. 219–232). Thousand Oaks, CA: Sage Publications.

Rogers, M.F., and Williams, W.W. (1987). AIDS in Blacks and Hispanics: Implications for prevention. *Issues in Science and Technology*, 89–94.

Rotheram-Borus, M.J., Mahler, K.A., Koopman, C., and Langabeer, K. (1996). Sexual abuse history and associated multiple risk behavior in adolescent runaways. *American Journal of Orthopsychiatry*, 66 (3), 390–400.

Schable, B., Diaz, T., Chu, S.Y., Caldwell, M.B., et al. (1995). Who are the primary caretakers of children born to HIV-infected mothers? Results from a multistate surveillance report. *Pediatrics*, 95 511–515.

Schiller, N.G., Crystal, S., and Lewellen, D. (1994). Risky business: The cultural construction of AIDS risk groups. *Soc. Sci. Med*, 10 1337–1346.

Seidman, S.N., Mosher, W.D., and Aral, S.O. (1992). Women with multiple sexual partners: USA, 1988. *American Journal of Public Health*, 82 1388–1394.

Singer, M. (1992). AIDS and U.S. minorities: The crisis and alternative anthropological responses. *Human Organization*, 51 (1), 89–95.

Sobo, E.J. (1993). Inner-city women and AIDS: The psycho-social benefits of unsafe sex. *Culture, medicine, and Psychiatry*, 17 (4), 455–485.

Sobo, E.J. (1995). *Choosing unsafe sex*. Philadelphia: University of Pennsylvania Press.

Springs, F.E., & Friedrich, W.N. (1992). Health risk behaviors and medical sequelae of childhood sexual abuse. *Mayo Clinic Proceedings*, 67, 527–532.

Stanton, Li Xiannian, B.S., Black M., Ricardo, I., Galbraith, J., Kaljee, L., Feigelman, S. (1994). Sexual practices and intentions among preadolescent and early adolescent low-income urban African-Americans. *Pediatrics*, 93, 966–974.

Telfair, J., and Nash, K.B. (1996). African American culture. In N.L. Fischer (Ed.), *Cultural and ethnic diversity: A guide for genetics professionals*. Baltimore, MD: Johns Hopkins University Press.

Thomas, S.B., and Quinn, S.C. (1991). The Tuskegee syphilis study, 1932 to 1972: Implications for HIV education and AIDS risk education programs in the Black community. *American Journal of Public Health*, 81 (1), 1498–1505.

Tienda, M., and Stier, H. (1996). Generating labor market inequality: Employment opportunities and the accumulation of disadvantage. *Social Problems*, 43 (2), 147–165.

U.S. Bureau of the Census. (1999). Statistical abstract of the United States. Washington, DC: U.S. Government Printing Office.

Vermund, S.H., Alexander-Rodriguez, T., Macleod, S., and Kelly, K.F. (1990). History of sexual abuse in incarcerated adolescents with gonorrhea or syphilis. *Journal of Adolescent Health Care*, 11 449–452.

Warner, B.D., and Leukefeld, C.G. (1999). Racial differences in HIV infection and risk behaviors among drug users in a low seroprevalence area. *Journal of Drug Issues*, 29 (2), 423–441.

Wechsberg, W.M., Desmond, D., Inciardi, J.A., Leukefeld, C.G., et al. (1998). HIV prevention protocols: Adaptation to evolving trends in drug use. *Journal of Psychoactive Drugs*, 30 (3), 291–298.

Weiss, L.D. (1997). *Private medicine and public health: Profit, politics, and prejudice in the American health care enterprise*. Boulder, CO: Westview Press.

Wilson, W.J. (1987). *The truly disadvantaged: The inner city, the underclass, and public policy*. Chicago: University of Chicago Press.

Wilson, W.J. (1996). *When work disappears: The world of the new urban poor*. New York: Knopf.

Wingood, G.M., and DiClemente, R.J. (1996). And sex research. Challenges for the 1990s and beyond. *American Psychologist*, 49 748–754.

Wingood, G.M., and DiClemente, R.J. (1998). The influence of psychosocial factors, alcohol, drug use and African-American women's high-risk sexual behavior. *American Journal of Preventive Medicine*, 15 (1), 54–59.

Wyatt, G.E. (1988). The relationship between child sexual abuse and adolescent sexual functioning in Afro-American and white American women. *Annals of the New York Academy of Sciences*, 528 111–122.

Wyatt, G.E., Forge, N.G., Guthrie, D. (1998). Family constellation and ethnicity: Current and lifetime HIV-related risk taking. *Journal of Family Psychology*, 12 (1), 93–101.

Zierler, S., Feingold, L., Laufer, D., Velentagas, P., et al. (1991). Adult survivors of childhood sexual abuse and subsequent risk of HIV-infection. *American Journal of Public Health*, 81 572–575.

Zwi, A., and Cabral, A. (1992). Identifying "high risk situations" for preventing AIDS. *British Medical Journal*, 303 1527.

2

Deep from Within the Well: Voices of African American Women Living with HIV/AIDS

Ednita M. Wright

REACTIONS TO THE DIAGNOSIS

> I went from feeling fine to no way I could have it to finding out two weeks before I left here [rehab] last year that I was HIV-positive. When they told me I just wanted to chop my head off.

Social construction theory assumes that social categories, such as gender, have been constructed through the historical and social processes of human activity (Berger and Luckman 1966). The societal construction of HIV-positive women has a profound impact on the ideological representation and institutional response to this population. Patton (1994, 3) suggests that "erasure of women's needs is systematic, grounded in a complex array of media representations of the HIV pandemic, cultural beliefs, and research and policy paradigms which are deeply gender biased and not easily changed." Furthermore, HIV-positive African American women are triple-burdened by race, gender, and, for most, class. Following the social constructionist paradigm, I suggest that the role of values, meanings, and intentions in understanding human behavior for women with HIV/AIDS can be richly captured only through qualitative approaches that allow those most involved to provide context and meaning to their situation.

In this chapter, you will meet eight of the many women[1] I have interviewed about their experiences with the disease. As reflected in the opening quote, the news of being diagnosed HIV-positive or having AIDS is traumatic and, for some, devastating. With those few words—"you are HIV positive" or "you have AIDS"—an individual's entire world changes. Each of the women I interviewed reacted to hearing the news of their diagnosis differently and in fact went through many subsequent changes which are discussed in the second half of this chapter. I begin by describing the women and their reactions to being diagnosed.

May

Reflected in the opening quote to this chapter, May's reaction to her diagnosis was one of shock and disbelief:

I thought about it for a long time. I really did. All I could say when she told me that, the tears was meeting me. I had this feeling she was going to come back and say it. I don't know why but the expression on her face. I can look right at a person and tell if they going to tell me some bad news. She said you all right and I said yeah, I'm all right. Then I started crying and she say you know what I'm going to say, and I said, I think so—she said, you got anybody to go home with you? I said I could go home by myself. Just don't beat around the bush, just tell me what is what, so she told me that I was sick. She said for me not to go anywhere, and I wanted to get up and walk right on out of there and keep on going.

May was a fifty-seven-year-old, small-framed, working-class woman who looked like she was in her late forties. She had requested that I conduct the interview in her home and that her group counselor accompany me. She lived in a housing project area on the corner of a busy main street in a city in New York. She greeted us in her housecoat with a smile and a hug for her counselor and a handshake for me. She offered us coffee and asked where did we want to talk, in the kitchen or living room. We opted for the living room. May's grandson was staying with her and she coaxed him and his friend to go upstairs so that we could talk. May's home is comfortable, but dark. There are windows, but the shades and curtains are drawn. There are pictures of children and other family members displayed on the walls.

May was the primary caretaker of her grandson. She continued to do some nurse's aide work with the elderly, which was her occupation prior to her diagnosis. She was raised in New York by her aunt and uncle, whom she calls mom and dad, although her people are from South Carolina. She had two daughters and a large family that lived close by, and only her eldest daughter knew about her diagnosis. May contracted the disease from her husband, who was a drug addict. It was after she persisted that he finally told her he was infected. Even though they were separated they still saw each other from time to time, and May took care of him until his death. May explained:

When he found out he had it, I still didn't know. So I figured something was wrong and I went to the doctor and the doctor wouldn't tell me nothing. I had asked my husband twice and he said it was just a virus. I never thought about AIDS. ... I said it can't be. I knew it was something and so I kept on and kept on. Finally, when we were at the doctor's office I said I am not going to move out of your office until somebody tells me something.

And when he told me that—all I could do is sit there. I went numb and I just started crying and crying and saying why didn't you tell me? My husband said I didn't want you to know and I didn't want you to get upset, see because you don't have nothing wrong with you, it's just me. I said are you sure about that. I told him, if you are sick, I will always be here for you—and I was—until the end. So, I went and got tested. Although I still didn't pay that [results] no attention [until I got real sick].

May decided to ignore the results of her test and go on with her life just as she had always done. It wasn't until May's husband died that she became really scared and resorted to a strategy that had worked in the past: "So, I just went to drinking. Woo—I had me a fifth of liquor and I would drink the whole fifth in a day and turn around and buy me another and drink half of that and on and on. That's the only bad thing I did."

May utilized alcohol in an effort to relieve the anxiety associated with her diagnosis. The alcohol also provided a means by which May could deny the impact that the news of her diagnosis would mean to her life until the reality of the situation could not be denied any longer.

I got serious there [for a while with the drinking]. But then the thing about it was I didn't get drunk [after a bit]. I didn't feel it. I couldn't sleep or nothing. That was the only way it [began] to affect me. And it made me sick. I think [it was on a day] the house was full of people and I had poured me a big glass full, I couldn't drink it, I had to pour it out. That was about four years ago and I have not drank any liquor since.

Even though May admitted that she felt that she was physically weakening, she didn't admit she had AIDS, only that she was HIV-positive, although she had been medically diagnosed with full-blown AIDS.

Glow

The rapport that I developed with Glow prior to the interview took place over nine months. She was quite fearful of talking to anyone except those within her support group about being diagnosed with AIDS. She exposed this feeling within the first few minutes of our interview:

I work in a small town, which is predominantly populated by White people and there are very few Blacks who hold any occupational status close to mine. That is why for the first six months after diagnosis I was real paranoid. The only reason I am getting less paranoid now is because I am thinking of going on disability. Now my fear about [the disease] hasn't changed, but because my lifestyle will change I can be a little less obnoxious about where I live.

Glow was forty years old, a chestnut-brown woman with corn-rolled hair, wearing jeans and a sweater. Glow introduced herself with a broad smile and extended hand which I met with my own. Her skin looked dry and broken. She had recently completed her Ph.D. and had an administrative position in a state college. The reason that she made contact with me to be interviewed was that she had recently come to the conclusion that there is a need for other African American women in her situation to know what it is like to be living with AIDS. As she communicates:

I realized yesterday somebody needs to do something in terms of a support group or some kind of news article or something that talks about professional, single Black women who are not drug addicts and aren't ill yet. [In terms of] what it is like to go through [this] without having a whole lot of peers. I have no peers, except for some White women in the group. I don't know of any other Black women, like me, in my situation.

This was Glow's biggest difficulty with being diagnosed—feeling that she was all alone, without any peers for support or with whom she could discuss the implications of the disease.

I had never been up here before a year ago and the only reason I came is because I had a grant position that was going to expire and in the middle of a recession you take what you can and the title and salary wasn't bad. I have absolutely no one up here, no other blood relative or friend that is long term—I am up here by myself. But I am a military brat and so you get used to stupid stuff like that.

I revealed to Glow that I was also a military brat, and this piece of information seemed to open her up. It was the first time I heard any real emotion in her voice.
   Upon the urging of a friend, Glow decided to get tested when she returned from an extended stay in Africa:

I had gone to West Africa for a year and came back and was very pleased that I had lost a lot of weight. I was just delirious and a friend of mine said that may be cute but it still doesn't make sense to me. She said you have gone out with men whose lives have been a little bit mysterious. I was very defensive and very angry with her but finally decided, oh, I will go get tested, thinking that it is not—[it would] not ever happen to me.

As Glow awaited the results she was admitted to the hospital.

I got the diagnosis in the hospital last fall. I was told that I had PCP pneumonia and I said you mean *the* pneumonia. I was right and within twenty-four hours the [personnel] from the health clinic where I had been tested came and said you are HIV-positive. So, even though I was thinking that this will never happen to me, it was not a shock by the time I was laying in the hospital. It was devastating, but it wasn't a shock.

   Glow's initial anger at her friend protected her from confronting the fact that she had placed herself in a compromising position. She came to realize that her anger at her friend was due to the fact that regardless of how much she controlled her world, once infected she had no control over the virus. "I think part of it's the military and part of it is that I have never had to compromise which meant I was generally in control and when you have to give up control, that is very different. I have tried to force the world to be what Glow wants and now I am realizing at forty that with or without this [disease] you can't do it." The inability to keep the diagnosis secret because of the need to talk to others, coupled with the anticipation of the loss of control, was the most difficult change that Glow had to adapt to, although through these changes she felt came some of her most significant learnings.

Wind

My first interview with Wind was postponed when she was hospitalized due to an abscess on her leg. I had met Wind through counseling her sister some years before and was asked by her family to assist her in securing some addiction treatment. Wind had been a drug addict for over twenty years and had been a prostitute and homeless due to her addiction. She was thirty-nine years old when I first interviewed her and had lived with the diagnosis for a year.

After Wind got discharged from the hospital, she called and said that we should meet soon. Wind greeted me with a big hug and ushered me into her apartment. The door from the hallway opened right into her living/dining room area, which was cluttered with papers, books, and magazines, most of which had to do with AIDS. The wall was filled with pictures of family and friends, awards she had received, newspaper clippings, and her prized possession—a framed note from Angela Davis.

Wind spoke to me from the kitchen as she mixed some Kool-Aid for us to drink. She was wearing silver hoop earrings and two gold necklaces—one said TRY GOD and the other was a bust of Nefertiti.

Wind was diagnosed in February 1990—one month after her partner tested positive—while receiving routine tests for a hysterectomy. She had been sober since July the year before and felt that she knew her tests results would return positive. Wind explained her initial reaction and her feelings during the first six months:

So when they told me it wasn't like I was that surprised. First of all being sober I realized that all of the deaths of my friends had been AIDS-related deaths for years. I guess the first six months of this year was just the process of accepting that I really had AIDS and what does that mean and what was I going to let it mean to my life. Because at first I was really buying into it because I was afraid. I was afraid that I was going to sit here and literally begin to die from that point.

[It] was scary because I didn't know what was going to happen to me. You know a lot of stuff in the medical booklet really was scary. I mean, I didn't have a lot of medical background and when I would read up on what these things meant I was like, my God, no one can take all this.

It was of particular importance to Wind that the African American community would acknowledge persons with HIV/AIDS, and making herself visible was one way she saw to work toward that. She was the first African American person within her community to speak openly about her life before her diagnosis and about health issues related to AIDS. Although Wind readily admitted that she was unsure about what she was supposed to do, she also felt there was a purpose in being diagnosed with AIDS. As she revealed:

And when I got my diagnosis, every single thing made sense to me. The ways that things happen made perfect sense, that God had kept me through the addiction and the attempted suicides. It just all made sense that—my godmother used to always say that God has something for you to do and you don't know what it is but God has something for you. So when the diagnosis came I just instinctively said okay—I lived through this, I'm supposed to do something about this AIDS thing.

Wind's first reaction to her diagnosis was fear. Her acceptance of the disease and the changes it would make upon her life came later. The acceptance was strengthened by her belief that she was doing "God's work," and it was what supported Wind as she spoke out, advocating for persons with AIDS.

Angel

Angel was forty-three years old and was an international model. She returned to the United States after being diagnosed six years before our interview. She wanted to be closer to her daughter, who was in college in a city a few hours away. She readily admitted that she knew that she probably had AIDS a long time before she was diagnosed, mainly because of her "risky" behavior, primarily involving drugs.

I was diagnosed in 1986 and I knew it. I knew I was HIV-positive at least four years before that because of the people I was messing with and I also had an anonymous test four years before and the results were definitely positive, but I didn't pursue anything. I was an IV drug user. I lived a very fashionable life and I was twenty-one. I didn't see what I was doing as bad. I never thought of it as shooting drugs or smoking crack. I saw it as being glamorous. And once I found out I had AIDS, I didn't stop—I had a habit.

Angel has since quit using drugs, and she says that it was a gradual process: "I stopped gradually. I liked it less and less and I was getting sicker and I said I need all this body's got left in it—whatever is left in here I really need it. I can't be messing with my heart and all that stuff and eventually I just didn't do it anymore and also disassociated with the people."

Angel confided in me that the most difficult part of this situation for her would be disclosing her diagnosis to her daughter. Even though she believed her daughter knew, she had not said the words to her and felt that doing so was important.

I can't just look at her and say it. I just can't, I don't know why. She is taking a semester off right now because she knows that I am sick and lately I have been really sick. My daughter has gone with me to the hospital because they had to treat my abscess which had become really big and swollen and she held my hand. I said everything except that [I have AIDS] and she was looking at me and her eyes was saying—yes, mommie I do [know]—but the words wouldn't come out of my mouth. It is so frustrating. I am going to do it—I will, I will.

The inability to share this information with her daughter was especially arduous for Angel because she had always shared other important events with her. Even though she remained silent with herself for four years after her first positive test results, and with her daughter, Angel felt it was deeply important to share this information with me because she felt that other African American women needed to know just what they are going to be up against living with AIDS.

Dell

I arrived at Dell's apartment and she greeted me with a warm but hesitant smile and led me up the stairs to her apartment. As I climbed the stairs, two young boys were putting on their coats and boots as they talked about going outside to play. Dell lived in a second-floor flat on the west side in New York. Dell's apartment is very neat and homey. Upon entering the apartment, I saw another young boy in the doorway of the kitchen. Dell told him that if he finished washing the dishes he could join the other two boys outside. Dell told me that the boy in the kitchen and the oldest boy in the hall were her sons. Dell formally welcomed me with a smile that brightened the room, and we exchanged handshakes. She took my coat and motioned for me to have a seat. She had dark chocolate skin, short-cropped black hair, deep dark brown eyes, and was slightly overweight. She was wearing jeans with a white turtleneck and small gold earrings.

She engaged the boys in light conversation as they waited for her other son to finish his chore. The walls in the living room and in the dining room were adorned with bamboo fans and flowerlike pieces. In front of the sofa was a large cabinet that held a television, stereo system, and VCR. The apartment was lit with rays from the sun coming through the window, and it felt warm once the hall door was closed. A bamboo shelf to the left of the sofa held individual portraits of children.

The boys left, and Dell sat in a large overstuffed chair. She said that she has never done anything like this and didn't know where to begin. She began with saying that the children knew about her diagnosis and that they were dealing with that as best they can. She added that her "coming out" (acknowledging that she was a lesbian) to them was more on their minds than her diagnosis. Dell explained: "Well I am thirty-three years old. I am an alcoholic and drug addict, too. And so [my oldest son] is having problems. He holds it in, but we can see it."

Dell was diagnosed as HIV-positive in 1988. The man she had been with for about four years became sick, and they found a lump under his arm. The hospital found that he was HIV-positive and so they asked to test her. It wasn't until then that Dell found out that he "went both ways"—he was bisexual. She explained:

I asked him about being gay and whether he had AIDS, and he said no—he denied it. But after [he went into the hospital] I found out he was positive. That was one of the most painful things, finding out that he had the virus and I didn't have anybody to turn to. So, when I found out that I was positive I just told my mother and left it like that.

Dell didn't explain to her mother or the rest of her family what being positive meant and in truth Dell didn't really understand it herself until later.

Dell didn't have to just contend with her own HIV status. It was also at this time that her boyfriend admitted that he had sexually abused her daughter and that she was probably infected. Dell states that she didn't want to believe that her daughter could be infected, so it wasn't until after her lover died that she took her daughter to be tested, along with her other children.

I thought sure that all three of my kids had it, so I wanted to have them checked, mainly her, since he had touched her. Her results came back in June and they were positive. She was probably five or six when he did this to her and she was eight when she was diagnosed. She was almost twelve when she died. She was my only daughter.

Dell had lost one son already to suicide.

Rose

Rose's house seemed out of place in the midst of the huge projects and the apartment buildings that surrounded it. Here sat this sweet-looking, fenced-in, one-family house with a well-kept lawn and a garden in the back in one of the toughest boroughs in New York City. Rose greeted me in a cool manner and showed me into the living room. The house was nicely furnished, and I could smell okra cooking. The sofa and chairs were covered in plastic, and she motioned for me to sit on the sofa. She seated herself in a lounge chair opposite me; there was a television table in front of the lounge with papers on it.

She started by saying that she really didn't understand why I wanted to talk to her and that she was still somewhat in the closet about having AIDS, although she did have her picture taken for an art gallery exhibit featuring persons with AIDS.

Sometime around 1984 I stopped getting high because I am a recovering addict. In July of 1987 I got married again. My first husband died of AIDS. Later that year my husband starting having headaches and then he was admitted to the hospital with some unknown virus. So he was in and out several times—well somewhere around November a nurse called me in and said your husband has all the symptoms of AIDS and you should think about being tested.

So I went and got tested and you know one thing, even when you know that you was on drugs and out there having all this here sex—time passes and I had cleaned myself up and my life had changed and you don't think that stuff will catch up with you.

Rose was forty-one years old, born in Harlem in a family of lower socio-economic status, and raised in Brooklyn except for a few years when she went down South to live with her grandmother. She was a tall, thin woman with coffee-cream-colored skin and soulful brown eyes. Rose had one daughter who was married and expecting a child soon. Her days were filled with caring for her husband who had AIDS and was bedridden. She participated in a group for women that were HIV-positive or have AIDS. She was the last of the original group and she was proud of the work that she had done in the group.

Each year up to now, two and three at a time were dropping back to back. I mean my very close good friends. I mean very close, you know. My daughter she said the other day she said, "Mommy, you don't get very many calls." And I guess we both were thinking the same thing—you know—that is because all my friends are dead. But I am happy that they are at peace now because I know that when they were here I was there for them.

Rose really warmed up as our conversation progressed and asked if I didn't want to meet her daughter. I did, and as her daughter came downstairs, she said that once her mother got started she could be up all night running her mouth. We all laughed. My ride had come, and as I was getting ready to leave, Rose said, "I don't talk to everyone about having the virus. I don't feel I need to tell everybody, only to help them." I told her that she had helped me and I was thankful.

Shell

Shell and I met in an office of the agency where she came for group. The office was dark and bare, lit only by a lamp. Shell was already there when I arrived. She was dressed in jeans and a T-shirt with short sleeves rolled up showing the top of her shoulders. She wore untied sneakers and sat slouched in the chair until we were being introduced. Although she stood during the introduction, her eyes were downcast and her handshake limp. We were asked if we wanted any coffee. As we sat waiting for the coffee, I asked if she had been waiting long and she said that she had come early because she was a little nervous. Our coffee came and we got started.

Shell was a tall woman with deep-set brown eyes. She was twenty-six years old, born and raised in New York. She was adopted by an upper-middle-class family when she was five. She had two brothers and one sister. Her father had recently died, and her mother had since relocated to the South. Shell was diagnosed as HIV-positive last year while she was in rehab. Shell describes the situation leading up to her diagnosis:

I was diagnosed with being HIV-positive last year when I was in rehab. I had been an IV drug user but had stopped using drugs but had continued drinking. It was my first time in the rehab and when I got out I was sober for six weeks and at that time I was raped. I became pregnant and I became HIV-positive.

So I went back to binge drinking at that time, not knowing that I was HIV-positive. I had been tested before this and had been negative, so May of 1992 I gave birth to a daughter. I didn't know how to take care of myself so I knew I couldn't take care of my daughter, so I gave her up for adoption. I then went into rehab last year. At the end of September I took the AIDS test, and three days before I was supposed to leave rehab I was told I was HIV-positive.

Shell had completed her GED and would be starting some volunteer work soon. She lived in a community residence for addicts and wanted to be there until the end of the program; she felt her sobriety depended on it. Shell felt really lucky because she had not had any opportunistic diseases yet, which helps keep her status in the background of her life. "I don't think about it unless—I mean there are days that I don't think about it. But as soon as I get a slight pain or something, it is oh my God I'm dying. That is the only time, or if someone coughs around me—I don't think about it."

For Shell, being diagnosed was the beginning of her coming back to life from addiction. "This happened [being diagnosed HIV-positive] to me to save my ass. There was nothing else that could possibly [have] stopped me from drinking. Now I can do something positive with my life and not just stand on a corner and drink. I can do positive things."

Dar

Dar was thirty-five years old and had been doing drugs, mainly crack and alcohol, since she was thirty. She was born and raised in a poor family that continued to live in the housing projects of a city in central New York. She had suffered seizures most of her adult life. She had been married and had four children and two grandchildren. Dar mentioned how difficult it was for her to talk about her diagnosis because of still being unable to pinpoint how she contracted the disease.

I haven't gotten past the point where I can talk about it and not cry. I will probably start crying while we are talking. I just don't understand nothing about it. I went from feeling fine to no way I could have it to—finding out two weeks before I left here [the rehab] last year that I was HIV-positive. When they told me that I just wanted to chop my head off. I didn't believe that it could happen to me because I didn't mess around a lot in the streets. Since I left my husband, I lived with three different guys and that was nine years ago.

Dar had been doing cocaine for the last couple of years. Although she recognized that since she had been doing drugs her ability to recall events was compromised, she maintained that in all her sexual encounters she was protected. She related her anger: "It always come back to where the fuck did it come from. [The persons] I did have sex with wore protection. I have never been a promiscuous person. I know people that will fuck anything walking and there ain't shit wrong with them. That makes me mad, you know—it makes me real mad." At the time of this interview, Dar's feeling, although unsubstantiated, was that she had contracted the disease from her female lover.

Dar believed there was something that she was here to do. She explained:

I have a feeling that there is somebody to come in my life that is going to need me as far as the HIV goes. I don't know who or what, I hope that it is not one of my children but I have a feeling that it is going to be somebody that is going to need me and is going to survive. Because it is a hell of a thing—because it has been exactly a year since I have known and within this year I have done died and went to hell and I'm back on my way to heaven. That is just the way I feel about it.

Summary

In this section I have introduced the women and what they recounted as their initial reactions to their diagnosis. Each woman had a different reaction: for May, it was flight; for Glow, secrecy; for Angel, silence; for Dell, blame; and for Rose and Shell, denial. In the remainder of this chapter, I discuss the changes that the women related to me concerning how they moved from their initial reactions and what that meant for their relationships in depth: from taking care of others to needing others; from a stigmatized identity to that of managing the stigma; and from perceiving themselves as dying to that of living with HIV/AIDS.

TRANSITIONS IN RELATIONSHIPS

> I said I didn't want to [ask for help]. I said, listen, my daughter just passed away with AIDS. I have the virus. My son is giving me problems. I'm an alcoholic and a drug addict and I need help.

In our culture women are expected to be primary caretakers. Even though taking care of children, in recent years, has become more of a shared experience between women and men, the role of caretaker is still seen as the domain of women. Within the context of the AIDS pandemic, women have assumed this traditional role. Assuming the relegated responsibility of caring for an incapacitated family member, friend, or lover has left women outside of the conversation, as it relates to care for themselves. African American women are even further removed from this conversation, as many of them are already marginalized due to poverty, race, and gender discrimination. Within the African American community, caring for others is seen as a primary duty, and women "learn from an early age that they must sacrifice their own needs and take care of others" (Moore 1994, 24).

This learned behavior is not forsaken just because a woman is an African American woman who has AIDS. As Rose explains,

I said I have to go home. I said let me go home first and make sure that I have everything taken care of and he [doctor] said, I can't let you go home. And I started crying because—I always felt like [my husband] came first because he couldn't help himself and stuff like that. See, I will be all right, but you know that is how women think. When they say women die faster, it is because they busy taking care of the kids and the husband and saying, oh I will get to myself one day.

As with other women with AIDS, Rose found that relinquishing, or abandoning in some cases, the role of primary caretaker was difficult. Women who must give up control of their resources and bodies feel they have little left of their own, leaving them to feel powerless, ineffective, and incompetent (Bartlett and Finkbeiner 1991). The relationship to others is very important to women, particularly as it relates to family and other loved ones. Another woman echoed Rose's words, and suggested that women need to care for others: "Can I talk a little about us African-American women? We identify ourselves by the relationship we are in—we are somebody's mother, daughter, sister, aunt. Women don't function well as self-contained entities—men can and do, women don't do this well." Because of this role of taking care of others, receiving care is some-times delayed for women who are HIV-infected or have AIDS. Simpson and Williams (1993) suggest that the caretaking role is central to women's experi-ences with their illness. "Because more than 99% of women with AIDS are het-erosexual and usually of childbearing age, the needs of many HIV-infected women are inextricably linked to motherhood and family responsibilities" (202).

The movement from taking care of others to needing others seems to follow a pattern that initially begins with denial. Even though Kübler-Ross's (1969) stages focus on death and dying, they can also be applied to the fear associated with the loss of one's position or role as a woman knows it. The women lessen the impact of their illness by continuing to keep busy in their routine affairs of caretaking and not permitting the diagnosis to "rent space"[2] in their heads. Hid-ing their illness in this way had a dual purpose: it provided a means to protect the women's role as primary caretakers and protected them from possible neg-ative reactions from family and friends. For example, May told about postpon-ing her own care in order to fulfill her commitments to another. "I was seriously anemic. I didn't feel good. When [the nurse] called that day, on the job, and told me I had to come to the hospital to be admitted—I didn't go right away. I went to the store and got some groceries for the lady [I was working for]." And Angel explained that protecting her daughter was one reason to keep the news of her diagnosis a secret. "I am ashamed to say it [tell of her diagnosis] to her [daugh-ter]. I am afraid to say it to her. I am afraid of her response." It seems that the ability to continue to care for others was a strategy the women employed to give themselves time to come to terms with their diagnosis. By using this strategy, the women were able to remain autonomous, prepare themselves to handle the reactions of others, and gain the strength they needed to face the impact of the diagnosis.

In assessing the degree and extent of the impact of the diagnosis, the women had to redefine what needing others meant. As Levine points out in *Who Dies?* there are no real stages (referring to Kübler-Ross), just changes of mind. He de-scribes an uneven process of change: "A moment of denial or anger opening into acceptance until a moment later the mind curls back on itself in depression and fear, trepidation and confusion" (1982, 234). This aptly describes what the women related to me as they moved from the initial stage of denial through anger and depression—the need to maintain independence. Independence was viewed as the ability to conduct your own affairs without outside assistance from family, friends, or medical and social services. Independence was so treasured by the women that one woman stated that she was not willing to let people know she was feeling ill. "I find myself, always, even with my friends that I am not willing to admit when I don't feel good, and even being on [performing] when I am with them." And May explained that even when she knew she was sick, she waited to get treatment. "I never went to the doctor at that time [before di-agnosis], until I really got sick and then I didn't know what was wrong with me. By the time I got to the doctor I needed four pints of blood. I stayed in the hos-pital almost two weeks, that is how sick I was and I didn't want to go then."

It was hard for these women to show their fear about the diagnosis to their families and friends. Showing fear was not within their own established behavior patterns or what others had come to know of them. They became angry as they came to recognize that their diagnosis would interfere with their lives. For some of them, this meant repressing their feelings and appearing to be in total control, even more so than usual. They could not allow themselves to "fall apart," a phrase that meant illness, frustration, being tired, having depression rendering them incapable of fulfilling their traditional role. Moore points out that this is a characteristic response. "Black women often say that they don't have the luxury to fall apart because they are responsible for bringing home the paycheck, raising the kids, often taking care of an aging relative" (Moore 1994, 24). When the anger subsided, the concern and subsequent depression focused on what would happen as the disease progressed. As she absorbed the impact of the diagnosis, Rose kept her feelings to herself out of concern for her daughter. "What I believe is if I was to get sick I don't think [my daughter] would be doing all right, really, but as long as I am doing all right. . . . That is why a lot of times a lot of things is going on with me I keep it to myself."

Finally the women began to accept, at least partially, that they must get help. In so doing they had to allow themselves to "fall apart" so that others could see that they needed help. All the women spoke of how it felt to give up doing things by themselves and the changes they had to make in their relationships to others, as they allowed themselves to receive emotional and practical support from their families, friends, and institutions. In most instances it was a critical situation that forced them to get assistance. For Dar it was returning to drug abuse after some time of abstinence that made her realize that she needed some help to deal with the changes that living with AIDS was having on her life. "I went there and I told them I need some help. I was scared to go back out [home or community] because if I went back out I was scared that I was going to die. Or I might get enough courage to maybe kill myself."

In the following pages several changes in women's relationships with others are explored. First, I discuss their concern with not allowing the diagnosis to "rent space" in their heads; their refusal to be a "fall apart" person; their concern for their children and families; and finally their coming to terms with giving up some independence. These adjustments or changes came with great difficulty, but they developed from the women's existing strategies and strengths. As Andre Lorde explains, referring to her own experience with cancer, the need for "survival [wasn't] some theory operating in a vacuum. It [was] a matter of [their] everyday living and making decisions" (Lorde 1990, 28).

"I Am Not Going to Allow It to Rent Space in My Head"

African American women have long been seen as strong, independent women and have attempted to live up to that perception. We are heralded as individuals who require no assistance as we go about our daily lives of work, family, crises, raising children, maintaining relationships, and attempting to keep a small portion of life for ourselves. It was not that the women interviewed did not understand what was being said to them regarding their diagnosis, but that they did not have time for it. They could not and would not let it interfere with their lives, at least for a time. For example, Shell realized that she was HIV-infected but chose not to give it power over her life until the reality was inescapable: "I don't know—I'm not in denial about it. I don't think about [the diagnosis], I try not to think about that, I push that to the side. Because when it [getting sick] happens then I will deal with it. But until then I am not going to allow it to rent space in my head. I don't have time for that crap right now, when it [getting sick] happens, it happens."

Not allowing the diagnosis to "rent space in her head" meant that Shell could continue her life as usual and could delay the impending assault the diagnosis would eventually have on her plans for the future, the principles by which she makes decisions, and her vision of herself (Bartlett and Finkbeiner 1991). This strategy enabled Shell to maintain her sense of self and protect her family from the news. As long as she could hold out, as it were, from acknowledging the ramifications the diagnosis would have on her life, she could maintain her personal identity. Personal identity in general is both a reflection of a person's sense of relationship to others and a recognition of past relationships and roles (Charmaz 1987). The women's strategies show how they try to balance their previous relationships with the new ones that they must accept.

Although Shell didn't allow the diagnosis to rent space in her head, other women allowed it some space, but not enough to interfere with their ability to take care of themselves or others. May explained, "I am not going to let nothing get me down and I am going to push until every strength is out of my body and I said to myself I think I can do it. Now like I can't walk up that hill [to the hospital] sometime, [but] I will make myself do it and then I come back home and lay down and take a cat nap." Even though May knew that she was ill and had to make routine visits to the hospital, it was important to her that she get there and back on her own strength. Rose, on the other hand, had no choice in being admitted to the hospital but still continued her caretaking role from her hospital bed:

So what I did, they admitted me in the hospital and after they had given me the phone I started making calls. I called the church and the lady next door to me. So [my husband] had plenty of food and then my daughter came from school, plus I had home care [for my husband] up until noon everyday. So he was really taken care of [although] I worried those two weeks like a dog in that hospital. He had to go to his clinic appointment and I called his doctor and says [to his doctor] to give him this type of medicine and not that other kind. Oh, I was on the case. So everything was taken care of while I was gone. I stayed in there two weeks and when I came home the house was nice and clean and the yard and everything was so nice. I said [to myself], Rose, you worried yourself for nothing.

The behavior of taking care of others also served to protect the women's families, friends, and other significant individuals from both the news of their diagnosis and its effects. For example, Shell talked about protecting her family—her mother in particular—from the information that she is HIV-positive: "Part of me really wants to tell someone in the family, but then part of me doesn't because I don't want my mother to worry about me. She worries about me enough and I don't want to put her through this. I am not sick—yet—you know. And when that day comes, that I do become sick, then, if she has to know, then I have no problems telling her—or someone else telling her." She made it clear that this was to keep her mother from worrying about her. Because she has not experienced any "sickness" she feels that divulging the information now would not be useful. For Shell, "sickness" means that she can no longer be self-sufficient and therefore would require assistance. The inability to take care of others, and the eventual need for others' help, adds to the stigma of having HIV/AIDS for these women because requiring assistance is so foreign to their sense of themselves.

Even after some months, during our second interview, Shell maintained that she should delay telling her mother: "No, it hasn't changed—because she would worry and my mother has done enough worrying about me. There really isn't any real reason for her to know. When the time comes that—when I become sick, then I will notify her and whatever else needs to be done, but until then I really just don't see it." When asked what she felt her mother's reaction would be once she did tell her, Shell thought the reaction would not be negative. She felt that her mother would understand her need to keep the information from her. By holding onto the information, she illustrated another way in which these women took care of their loved ones and maintained their self-image for as long as possible.

For some of the women their relationships with others seemed to survive the news of the diagnosis. But they felt that for it not to rent space in their heads or their families, the news should not be discussed. During our interview, Angel spent a great deal of time talking with me about the dilemma she felt regarding whether to discuss with her daughter the relevance that living with AIDS would have for their relationship. Angel was attempting to understand her resistance, but it also seemed that the lack of discussion was providing some comfort. It seemed as if the avoidance of the topic sustained the illusion that the diagnosis was not real, and thus had no power.

Yes, she knows. There is no question that she knows but I haven't actually sat my daughter down and said look—I really can't say why I haven't done that, I can name a million excuses but none of them are any good.

Shame—just shame—just thinking that she might break down from actually the words coming out. You know she knows, the knowledge is there—it is. If I tell her she isn't going to be able to function and here she is functioning for six years knowing that—but I just haven't said it yet. It is just a thing we do in my family, we know things but we don't say them, we don't talk about them and this is one of those things.

Everyone knew that Angel had AIDS, but without any discussion they never really knew the effect living with AIDS was having on Angel. The struggle that

Angel was having left her alone to deal with her fears, anger, pain, needs, and wants. Because of her need to be the caretaker, Angel wished she could talk with her daughter about all that was really bothering her without hurting her daughter. It would also appear that not discussing it was another form of denial. As Angel pointed out, she came from a family that did not discuss "those things." This family pattern mirrors what is occurring in the African American community—an inability to name AIDS as a disease that is killing us.

The women often believed they needed to maintain the secret of their illness. They worried that family would count them out just because they were sick, and especially if they knew that they had AIDS. Other researchers have found similar patterns, in that people with HIV-infection protect their caregivers by keeping worrisome information to themselves or minimizing their symptoms and pains (Bartlett and Finkbeiner 1991). As their ability to care for others changed—whether that be cooking, baby-sitting, looking after the family—the women experienced the conflict of relinquishing control as caretaker but still asserting their autonomy as they attempted to fit this change into their lives.

"I'm Not One of Them Fall Apart People"

Everybody needs help. The paradox for these women is that, traditionally, African American women have been encouraged not to recognize their needs for help, whereas White women (or privileged White women) have been encouraged to overemphasize their dependence. Angel continued to deny that she needed help. "I don't—I am not one of them fall apart people. I don't fall apart. I may have a day where I cry all day but once I get it out, you know, give me something to eat or do my laundry, if I can. Whatever had to be done I try to do it." Angel credited herself with being able to fulfill her own needs. Falling apart for Angel is equal to succumbing to the disease and therefore giving it control over her life. Even though Angel did allow herself to break down sometimes, she refused to remain there for long. "You know, I am not a superwoman. I break down, not for long, it is not my nature. It's just not like me to stay down and crying all the time."

Like Angel, May felt it was important for her to continue doing as she had always done in her work and with her family, and that this focus off self took away the anxiety associated with being sick. It was also evident that even though May was sick, her role of caretaker did not disappear. "Well, like I have some older ladies that I visit, that I used to work for, and I do these things for them. I [also] keep my grands and that takes away everything that I have wrong with me. I don't know why I don't focus on me, I can't focus on me and never could focus on me, if I was feeling sick." Although the disease had progressed to the point that May could not work anymore, she made it clear that she worked until she just could not. It was important to her self-definition that she was able to do for others.

The ability to keep busy was a way for May to put distance between her and the illness. Falling apart for May meant that she would be unable to fulfill her role, thus separating her from her family, which had the potential for eventual isolation. "I don't want them to know that I am sick. Because, it is like when we had that cookout last week for my mother's birthday. They didn't want me to bring anything. [They said] oh you are sick, you can't afford it, so we just invited you to come and never did want you to fix anything. I said don't leave me out. I can do things."

Most of these women were not used to being seen in a way that would be considered weak or unable to contribute. So as not to be seen in this way, there were times when the women jeopardized their health. As May explained,

[My daughter] made an appointment and said she was taking me to the doctor. And I said, why I'm okay and she said, no you not. So [we went to the doctor]. I don't like to go to the doctor, cause I know what he is going to tell me—that I [would have] to go to the hospital. Stay[ing] in the hospital [is what] made me [feel] worse. The only reason I went to that hospital was because I didn't have no blood and that is the only reason. I wouldn't have gone, in fact, I would have been dead.

The women had to strike a balance between maintaining a sense of self and letting those close to them know that they were in need without being viewed as falling apart. It was also within themselves that the women had to remain vigilant against a feeling of instability. For example, Rose explained, "It is always there [living with AIDS]. I could put myself in a position that I could start getting depressed and start really thinking about it and stuff like that but I refused to get like that because you know in order to stay healthy you have to be mentally well." Rose believed that controlling her thoughts about the disease would help her preserve her self-image as a capable woman.

Finally, Weitz (1991) found that the process of becoming a person with AIDS and balancing our relationships with others centers around coming to terms with uncertainty. The distress associated with the possibility of being left out is surpassed only by the loss of control over the disease and its effect on the body and self-identity. The women in this study struggled with learning to deal with uncertainty by not becoming a "fall apart person." As the body's response to the disease became more inconsistent, they found that one day they might be feeling fine and the next day they might be literally incapacitated. Angel reported: "Some days I feel like, wow, I don't even have AIDS. That is how I feel some days and then there are others that I feel I am going to die today, right now, right here, today. [Those are the days] I couldn't even get out of bed. For the first time I had a terrible accident, in the bed, and I was so frustrated cause I just couldn't get up, I just couldn't." This description is similar to the effects of chronic illness on the self conveyed in Charmaz's work *Good Days, Bad Days*. A good day is defined as one with minimal intrusions of the illness and maximal control over the mind and body, and a bad day is described by less control over the mind and body, due to the intensity of the intrusion of illness. Glow's comments illustrate how the loss of self was attached to the inability to do for oneself, and exposed her fear of the potential inability to recognize herself altogether. "I guess with the infections, which I haven't had yet, except for the pneumonia, I don't want to be in pain and I would like to be relatively lucid, in terms of who I am."

The ability to maintain the image of self as the same and as capable for as long as possible was critical. This stance did not appear to be a denial of illness; rather, the women were unwilling to give up a familiar identity for one as an invalid. Dying was not seen as merely a physical process, but the inability to identify themselves.

"I'm Not Sure Where They Are Going"

Four of the women interviewed had children, and all spoke about their anguish over how, or if, to tell them about their situations. This decision was usually based on considering which action would best protect their children from the reactions of others. Although telling the children, particularly young children, was an important issue, the women's greatest concern and what caused the most stress was who would care for their children as the disease progressed.

Prior to any hospitalizations, Dell was being encouraged to prepare for the care of her children when that did occur. As Dell describes it,

I wouldn't want neither one of them to go to their father, really. I want them to be with somebody who will treat them like I would treat them. Take care of them like I'm taking care of them. The closest one is my mother or my sister and I know they might take one, but they won't take both. And then again, they might not take neither one of them. That's where I am at with that [right now] Just trying to get somebody that is open.

Dell really wanted her children to be with family, if at all possible, but what was more important is that her sons were taken care of like she would care for them, by someone who would have the same hopes and dreams for them.

If I become sick, that I don't suffer and that my kids get taken care of—mainly my kids. I hope that they get taken care of and grow up to be good people for themselves and that they live happy and to treat others like they would want to be treated. I really pray that they don't turn out to be violent or use drugs and things like that and that they don't have kids by different women. I try to tell them that when we do talk about what I hope for them. So I am hoping that they will have a better life.

A difficult reality for Dell was that her mother was not willing to take both of her sons because of her younger son's violent behavior. "I would want my mother, but my mother, I don't believe ... well, my mother would take my oldest son, but she wouldn't take my youngest son, because they are scared of him. You know, they think he is dangerous." An opportunity arose where Dell's sister was willing to take her sons if their airfare could be arranged when she was in town on a visit. Unfortunately, Dell could not raise the money, and she felt that to pursue it through social services would be much too time-consuming. "I was all crazy because I wanted him to go with my sister, but I didn't have the money and she didn't have the money either. I wanted to do all that before we went to court cause he was already in foster care. [Social services] said the only way we could do it was to do all this red tape and my sister didn't want to go through that."

The optimum situation, as Dell saw it, was for her sons to be together. The only alternative that remained was to pursue foster care through social services before she became too ill to have any power over where they would be placed. "Do I think about dying? Yes, I do, and it scares me because I don't know where I'm going to go. It also scares me because I don't want to leave my kids. I'm not sure where they are going to go." Bartlett and Finkbeiner also found these concerns in their study. "They worry that their own health may prevent them from caring for their young children, and they feel a moral obligation to provide for that possibility. They are intensely worried, and they are often more distressed about this than about their own health" (1991, 109).

Several months later, when I spoke with Dell again, both sons had been placed in foster care. Even though her oldest son had to be moved to another home due to mistreatment, later he seemed well taken care of and comfortable. Dell was so glad that she was still well enough to advocate for her sons. "The boys are doing pretty good. [My oldest son] is in foster care and he seems to have adapted pretty well. I get to see him every other weekend or if something comes up and we have the money I can get to see him on that day unless he is doing something else." Dell fulfilled her caretaker role by securing arrangements for her sons. For any woman with children, arranging for the care of them is a huge issue even if a woman is healthy. In addition to the use of family or foster care for the provision of child care, an increase in another option, promoted by child welfare agencies, is becoming more visible—"permanency planning." Although "permanency planning" would seem like a rational and reasonable choice for a parent to make given the circumstances of AIDS, appropriate timing with regard to the initial discussion of this option is critical.

"It Hasn't Been Easy Giving Up Stuff on My Own"

Historically, African American women have been seen, as Zora Neale Hurston (1937) aptly put it, as "the mules of the world." As stated earlier, they are expected to care for everyone, and to a large extent their very identity is based on that ability. The women interviewed illustrated the process involved in coming to the realization that they needed assistance. Besides their self-perceptions, the perceptions of others were key to the decision to request help. This seemed to coincide with the increasing debilitation of the disease itself, so that it was almost all right to ask for help. One woman said,

They want me to get a health aide for when I go home and I have been fighting them on that but I think I may have to have one. I just haven't wanted anyone in my house and, well I felt I could do it all, but I just get so tired especially when I have to do laundry which is downstairs. But it has been too many hospitalizations and I guess I am just going to have to have some other people to do some things for me—but that is hard.

The inability to do the most routine tasks weakens the way in which a woman perceives herself as a functioning adult. According to literature on chronic illness, as a person suffers "losses of self from the consequences of chronic illness and experiences diminished control over their lives and their futures, affected individuals commonly not only lose self-esteem, but even self-identity" (Charmaz 1983, 169). One woman explained, "I mean I was so sick first off it started here and I thought I was going to die and I wanted to die because the suffering was getting me. The being incapacitated was and is what I can't and couldn't handle and I was here when it started. I lost control of my bowels and my eyes turned all red and my leg, there was no definition between my leg and my thigh."

The invasion of the disease coupled with the subsequent and inevitable need for help weighs heavily on those who value their independence. In our society, dependence is considered to be acceptable for children and those who are ill, but only if the care does not last too long or take too much from those providing assistance. Given the stigma of AIDS, the request for help at times has a price attached that is too high—the loss of self-respect. Even for those women who had not yet experienced any opportunistic diseases, becoming dependent or losing the ability to do for oneself was their greatest fear. Glow illustrated this point: "I guess with the infections, which I haven't had yet except for the pneumonia, I don't want to be in pain, I would like to be relatively lucid in terms of who I am, I am just afraid of losing control and not being able to help myself."

At times, society interprets needing help as weakness. Some of us do not see a reason to ask for help if we can do it for ourselves, and some of us have asked for help in the past and have been met with attitudes of condescension or resistance. May believed it was a waste of time to ask and/or wait for something that you can do for yourself. "I don't see no sense in going up to the hospital waiting on a nurse for half a day to give you a shot, when you could give yourself shot at home like I do." May felt that until she was unable to do for herself there was no need to create a dependence. Additionally, by doing for herself, May was able to manage the stigma associated with being "sick," and she felt more in control of her care.

Boyd (1993) asserts, "Being strong all the time is a burden and doesn't leave us much room to be human. When we can't live up to everybody's idea or expectation of a strong Black woman, we feel like a failure, and feeling like a failure only leads to big-time depression. It would be nice to have some room for emotional flexibility, but often we don't have a clue as to what emotional flexibility looks like for ourselves" (15). One of the most difficult challenges for us is to acknowledge when we need help. This general pattern contributed to problems experienced by the women in the study as they struggled to ask for help. For example, one woman described how she avoided depending on the members of her support group until she was so tearful that she confronted them. "I said all of you look to me for strength all the time and even though I have been a part of this group I haven't been a part of this group cause I have never talked about me. It is always been about trying to help you all out and I started crying and I said I am scared."

Another part of this state of needing help is what it does to self-perception. This perception is not just based on how one has lived her life thus far. As the body's response to the disease becomes more inconsistent, where one day you are feeling fine and the next you are incapacitated, people notice the changes. It seemed that some of the women felt more at ease requesting help from their younger children or grandchildren. For example, May explained:

He always trying to fix food for me. He is six years old. So I tell him what you can do is you get the forks and plates and I will get the food and we will fix it together and he would say okay. Then we [would] eat and he [would] collect the trash and we will sit together and then he say grandma you can take your cat nap now. I will close the door and lock it and I won't open for nobody. Yeah, he is a big help. He will go get me some water and he will say, You took your medicine? I say yeah, I took my medicine.

In fact, receiving help from children appeared to make it easier for the women to request assistance from others. "I try to always have somebody with me and I tell my grandson you are going to walk up to the hospital with me today. I say if anything happens to grandma you know what to do and he says yes grandma I know what to do. I will call 911 and then I will call [your oldest daughter]."

Children were also helpful in encouraging their mothers to remain in treatment where they could get the help they needed. In Dar's situation, her nine-year-old son felt it was important for his mother to stay in treatment for her addiction even though she would have to be away from him. Dar states that his letter gave her hope and strength. The following is what she read to me:

Dear Mom—how are you doing? I have been fine and the other kids are doing good. We all miss you very much and I hope to hear from you and see you as soon as possible in the best condition that you can get in. Don't come back to us less you know you are ready because we want you back home for good this time. We miss you and love you very much. The kids say Hi and hope you get better. Mom I know that it may be hard what you are doing or going through but you must be strong and take one day at a time. I know you can do it if you just believe in yourself and say I am not going to do drugs anymore. If you love us you will not do it. I want you back here with us cause when you are not here it is hard for me to do things cause you are a missing part of my heart. I love you.

When I asked her what did she mean that the letter gave her hope, she responded with, "Hope is like—like I have the courage in myself that I don't want to do anymore drugs, I have faith in myself knowing that one day soon I will be able to accept this HIV and live with it. And maybe I will just save somebody else with it. This here letter makes me feel like I can because I got three young lives rooting for me."

For these women, the movement from taking care of others to needing others marks the process of coming to terms with having HIV/AIDS. The women accepted that something significant had happened to change their lives. Practicing denial by keeping busy through taking care of others could only last for a time. Then the women were forced to begin to reconstruct their identities. Each woman came to realize that her relationships with others would never be the same as they were before the diagnosis of HIV/AIDS.

NOTES

1. The names of the interviewees were changed to protect their identity.
2. The term "rent space" was used by Shell in her interview.

REFERENCES

Bartlett, J.G., and Finkbeiner, A.K. (1991). *The guide to living with HIV infection*. Baltimore: Johns Hopkins University Press.

Berger, P.L. and Luckman, T.L. (1966). *The social construction of reality*. Garden City, NY: Doubleday.

Boyd, J.A. (1993). *In the company of my sisters: Black women and self-esteem*. New York: Dutton.

Charmaz, K. (1983). Loss of self: A fundamental form of suffering in the chronically ill. *Sociology of Health and Illness*, 5 (2), 169–195.

———. (1987). Struggling for a self: Identity levels of the chronically ill. *Research in the Sociology of Health Care*, 6, 283–321.

———. (1991). *Good days, bad days: The self in chronic illness and fine*. New Brunswick, NJ: Rutgers University Press.

Hurston, Z.N. (1937). *Their eyes were watching God*. Chicago: University of Illinois Press.

Kübler-Ross, E. (1969). *On death and dying*. New York: Collier Books.

Levine, S. (1982). *Who dies? An investigation of conscious living and conscious dying*. New York: Anchor Books.

Lorde, A. (1990). Living with cancer. In E. C. White (Ed.), *The black woman's health book: Speaking for ourselves* (pp. 27–37). Seattle, WA: Seal Press.

Moore, T. (1994). Divorcing with grace. *The Family Therapy Networker*. May/June, 24–25.

Patton, C. (1994). *Last Served: Gendering the HIV pandemic*. Bristol, PA: Taylor and Francis.

Simpson, J.B., and Williams, A. (1993). Caregiving: A matriarchal tradition continues. In A. Kurth (Ed.), *Until the cure: Caring for women with HIV* (pp. 200–211). New Haven, CT: Yale University Press.

Weitz, R. (1991). *Life with AIDS*. New Brunswick, NJ: Rutgers University Press.

3

Substance Abuse and African Americans: The Need for Africentric-Based Substance Abuse Treatment Models

Cheryl Tawede Grills

Ethnic patterns in utilization of drug abuse treatment have not been studied systematically. The limited research to date suggests that African American drug users may be less likely than White users to receive treatment for illegal drug use (Jones, Lewis, and Shorty 1993; Little 1981; Longshore, Hsieh, Anglin, and Annon 1992; Rounsaville and Kleber 1985) and less likely than either White or Hispanic users to believe they would benefit from it (Longshore, Hsieh, and Anglin 1993). There are at least three explanations for these possible differences. First, few treatment programs specifically address social, cultural, and individual factors associated with drug use by African Americans (Rowe and Grills 1993). Second, many African Americans view mainstream social service programs, including drug abuse treatment, as intrusive, punitive, and untrustworthy (Aponte and Barnes 1995; Finn 1994; Pakov, McGovern, and Geffner 1993; Taha-Cisse 1991). Finally, the expected benefit of treatment may be a particularly important determinant of treatment motivation among African Americans (Longshore, Grills, Anglin, and Annon 1998) that can mitigate against seeking treatment.

In recent years, researchers and community advocates have cited a need for drug use interventions that build on cultural resources in the African American community. Interventions of this sort are said to be "culturally congruent" (Singer 1991). The expectation is that treatment can be more effective if provided in a manner congruent with the health beliefs, worldviews, values, and culture of the individuals, families, and communities they serve. In other words, treatment would be African-centered. Problem definition, conceptualization of the client, appreciation of the client's ecological reality, and history are understood from an African cultural reality and worldview. Congruence with African

American culture would mean, for example, delivering an intervention in ways that affirm the heritage, rights, and responsibilities of African Americans and that use interaction styles, symbols, and values shared by members of that group (Amuleru-Marshall 1991; Asante 1987; Kambon 1992). The significance of constructing such interventions congruent with African American culture has been described in drug use prevention and treatment, HIV-preventive education, and psychotherapy (e.g., Jackson 1983; Jackson 1995; Grills and Rowe 1999; Longshore, Grills, and Annon 1999; Nobles and Goddard 1993; Parham, White and Ajamu 1999; Phillips 1990; Rowe and Grills 1993; Saulnier 1996).

The first step in the adoption of a truly African-centered approach is conceptual. The program and therapist must make a paradigm shift to an African frame of reference. Here the clinician develops an appreciation for important distinctions in worldview and the consequent impact of worldview on thoughts, behavior, emotions, and interpersonal relations. Cultural differences are not primarily differences in behavior, but rather in the meanings attached and attributed to "the same behaviors" (Landrine 1992). Culturally congruent approaches help us to appreciate that people differ in:

• Their experience of pain

• What they label as a symptom

• How they communicate about their pain or symptoms

• Their beliefs about its cause

• Their attitudes toward helpers

• The treatment they desire or expect (McGoldrick and Giordano 1996)

Understanding these dimensions of meaning can contribute to more culturally congruent, African-centered treatment.

This chapter describes the basic principles in African-centered psychology and how these principles are used in the development of Africentric treatment models, as well as the measurement of Africentrism among African Americans. Research findings are presented of the culturally congruent African-centered treatment engagement project in which potential factors associated with treatment motivation among African Americans were studied in addition to testing whether an African-centered drug treatment intervention was more effective than a standard treatment with African American substance users. Based on Africentric theories and research, the chapter concludes with recommendations for establishing culturally based African-centered programs and intervention strategies to enhance substance abuse treatment motivation and recovery for African Americans. Finally, a focus on solutions section is included that describes the principles and methods that form the basis of a brief African-centered drug treatment engagement with African Americans in Los Angeles.

BASIC PRINCIPLES IN AFRICAN-CENTERED PSYCHOLOGY

Grounded in African cultural tradition, the way in which people of African descent come to acquire knowledge and information is fluid and inclusive. Although western practice tends to limit knowledge to that which is acquired through the intellect, the senses, and the conscious mind, African epistemology (ways of knowing) utilizes these methods and nonconscious, nonmaterial, nonrational, and affective faculties. Further, the story of African survival in the United States is a story of transformation—the capacity to transform through experiencing all that initially was foreign while maintaining the essential African core. It has been that capacity to "make a way out of no way" which characterizes how Africans in America have approached and maintained mental health. Psychotherapeutic work with an African American client requires the therapist to understand the cultural thrust that contributes to the client's greater emphasis on (a) consciously or unconsciously being African in his or her orientation to life; (b) the spiritual meaning of life, (c) metaphysical ways of knowing, and (d) maneuvering the dynamics of race and social class in daily life. African-centered psychology provides a framework for understanding this culturally derived orientation to existence and the resulting culturally based models of health.

The Association of Black Psychologists (Nobles, King, and James, 1995) defines health as a dynamic process resulting in the capacity to maintain, adapt, and creatively refine (change, integrate, evolve, correct) one's quality of life, at least to the status of effective, if not to optimal and maximal functioning. Nobles and colleagues (1995) assert that health is the ever-present ability to adapt and evolve toward a more complex, integrated, and creative structure or being. Consistent with an African-centered conceptualization, they argue that health is connected to the spirit, the energy, force, or power that is both the inner essence and outer envelope of human beingness. In this schema, persons are unified wholes consisting of spiritual/cultural, physiological, emotional, and social/behavioral elements in continuous relation with each other. Any effort to improve health and health behaviors that are inclusive of indigenous practices and models must be attentive to the dynamic interactions that occur within each of these dimensions.

African-Centered Psychology: A Basic Definition

African-centered psychology is concerned with defining African psychological experiences from an African perspective—a perspective that reflects an African orientation to the meaning of life, the world, and relationships with others and one's self. The Association of Black Psychologists defines African-centered psychology as:

the dynamic manifestation of the unifying African principles, values and traditions. It is the self-conscious "centering" of psychological analysis and applications in African reality, culture and epistemology. African-centered Psychology examines the process that allows for the illumination and liberation of the spirit. Relying on the principles of harmony within the universe as a natural order of existence, African-centered Psychology recognizes: the Spirit that permeates everything that is; the notion that everything in the universe is interconnected; the value that the collective is the most salient element of existence; and the idea that communal self-knowledge is the key to mental health.

African-centered Psychology is ultimately concerned with understanding the systems of meaning of human beingness, the features of human functioning, and the restoration of normal/natural order to human development. As such, it is used to resolve personal and social problems and to promote optimal functioning. (African Psychology Institute 1995)

The essential features of African-centered psychology presented in this definition include self-definition, spiritness, connection to nature, metaphysical interconnectedness, communal order, and self-knowledge.

Self-Definition

Africans in the diaspora have been other defined, other defended, and other reliant under the wake of European exploration, enslavement, and colonialism at great cost to their humanity, health, and identity as a people. As Ani (1980, 1) aptly notes: "We, as Black people, have been told that we are not African for so long and with such social scientific 'expertise' that we have great difficulty believing otherwise." This comes with some consequence to identity, affiliative ties, and sense of historical continuity. A critical task facing African Americans, individually and collectively, is definition of self using constructs, models, and knowledge derived from an African-centered perspective.

Spirit

Spirit is as important as the physical manifestation of the self. In the African cultural worldview, the essential ingredient and essence of everything, including humans, is spirit. To have spirit is to be imbued with life, a mind and soul, energy, force, passion, allegiances, and a guardian presence. It involves the condition of *being* spirit, not merely practicing spirituality. In other words, the human being not only *has* spirit; s/he *is* spirit. In the African worldview, spirit has both real and symbolic meaning. "As energy, spirit becomes 'Spiritness' and therein serves to ignite and enliven the human state of being" (Nobles 1998, 193).

Nature and Metaphysical Interconnectedness

We as human beings do not exist alone in the universe but are always interacting with and under the influence of the rhythms and forces of life (Dukor 1993). Nature provides rules for living peacefully in society. There are metaphysical components to the person that connects her to rituals (rhythms in life). Further, in contrast to western epistemology within the African schema of knowledge acquisition, knowing includes and extends beyond linear reasoning. It includes and extends beyond the boundaries of space and time. The senses, cognition, and tangible verification or control is not the only pathway to knowledge. The spiritual basis of all there is to know makes African epistemology admit realities that western epistemology will dismiss. In the pursuit of knowledge, the African willingness to engage and include that which is empirically, tangibly verifiable and that which is not makes this an inclusive epistemology. Within the venue of Euro-American clinical praxis, therapist and client are socialized to remain within the confines of linear reasoning and materialist explanations of knowledge acquisition. This is not without consequence to clinical practice and the needs of the African American client. In treatment, to what extent do we negate the existence and experience of an inclusive epistemology? To what extent do clients silence their internal experience of preter-sentient knowledge (knowledge that is derived without the agency of the sensory system), nonlinear reasoning, and unverifiable intuitive data? What validity is given to intuition as a real and legitimate source of information? As Bergson (1889) notes, "Intuition is the direct vision of the spirit by the spirit. Intuition, therefore means first and foremost an immediate consciousness, a vision barely distinguishable from the object, a knowledge that is consciousness and even coincidence." This definition of intuition complements the African-centered paradigm of the centrality and function of spirit in human functioning and consciousness. Within the African-centered model, an inclusive epistemology is not only germane to understanding all knowledge production, but also is an integral part of praxis.

Communal Order and Self-Knowledge

We come to know ourselves through our relationships with others. In the African world, there is no "I" without a "we." In fact, in several African languages there is no equivalent for the English term "I." "To be human is to belong to the whole community" (Mbiti 1990, 2). Individuals exist because of the community, and the community is responsible for the conduct of its individual members (Kamalu 1998). In this African schema, the corporate or collective reality predominates.

The resulting African-centered paradigm contains distinctly African values and ways of defining reality, governing/interpreting behavior and social relations, and designing environments to sustain healthy, adaptive development and functioning within a communal context. In this framework, the life experiences, history, and traditions of the community are at the center of one's sense of self and agency. In fact, in this communal order, individual destinies are interconnected through the unity of purpose for the common good characteristic of communal existence (Ladner 1998).

As we can see, African-centered approaches to psychology contain many principles and concepts eschewed by western psychology. In fact, these principles were consciously removed from the western paradigm (Lindskoog 1998). These include introspection and inclusion of constructs related to the soul and spirit and the centrality of such cultural constructs as interdependence, connection to nature, and social collectivity in defining human functioning. Regardless of western psychology's decision to extract certain phenomenon in its aim to define human psychological reality, these concepts continue to manifest themselves in the daily practice of diasporan African life and psychology (e.g., extended family; religious expression and practices; music, song, and dance; shared participation; social-affiliative emphasis; phenomenal time).[1] These concepts have also been applied to various Africentric treatment and prevention models (see Longshore and Grills 2000; Nobles and Goddard 1993; Phillips 1990; and Rowe and Grills 1993).

Guiding Principles of an African-Centered Treatment Model

Certain principles in African and African American culture have been termed Africentric (Ani 1994; Asante 1987; Karenga 1993; Nobles and Goddard 1993; Perkins 1992) and have been cited as an appropriate basis on which to develop services for African Americans (e.g., Amuleru-Marshall 1991; Kambon 1992; Kunjufu 1986; Rowe and Grills 1993; Wilson and Stith 1993). Current formulations of Africentrism differ in some important respects (Cress-Welsing 1991; Cross 1991; Kambon 1992; Myers 1988; Wilson 1993). In the construction of the culturally congruent, African-centered treatment engagement project, our working definition of Africentrism was based on the *Nguzo Saba*; the seven principles. They are:

1. *Umoja* (Unity)—to strive for and maintain unity in the family, community, nation, and race
2. *Kujichagulia* (Self-determination)—to define ourselves, name ourselves, create for ourselves, and speak for ourselves instead of being defined, named, created for, and spoken for by others
3. *Ujima* (Collective work and responsibility)—to build and maintain our community together and make our sisters' and brothers' problems our problems and to solve them together
4. *Ujamaa* (Cooperative economics)—to build and maintain our own stores, shops, and other businesses and to profit from them together
5. *Nia* (Purpose)—to make our collective vocation the building and developing of our community to restore our people to their traditional greatness
6. *Kuumba* (Creativity)—to do always as much as we can, in the way we can, to leave our community more beautiful and beneficial than we inherited it
7. *Imani* (Faith)—to believe with all our heart in our people, our parents, our teachers, and the righteousness and victory of our struggle.

These principles are grounded in Kawaida theory, a synthesis of tradition and reason in nationalist, Pan-Africanist, and socialist thought (Karenga 1980). They represent the "minimum set of values [that] African Americans need to build and sustain an Afrocentric family, community and culture" (Karenga 1988, 43). When applied as codes of conduct for daily life, the *Nguzo Saba* are believed to represent guidelines for healthy living (Madhubuti 1972; Phillips 1990). For example, adherence to the value of *Ujima* might be manifested in daily life through volunteer service to the community.

Rowe and Grills (1993) offered a behaviorally anchored version of the *Nguzo Saba* called the *Kusudi Saba* (the seven behavioral intentions). The *Kusudi Saba* and the *Nguzo Saba* can be linked to traditional African value systems identified in Africa, as well as African American articulations of basic African-centered values and precepts. Examples are presented in Table 3.1.

Table 3.1
**Linking the Kusudi Saba and the Nguzo Saba to Traditional African Value
Systems and African American Values and Precepts**

Nguzo Saba (Karenga 1988)	Kusudi Saba (Rowe and Grills 1993)	African Cultural Values (Gyekye 1998)	African American Values (Ladner 1998)	African-Centered Prevention (Nobles and Goddard 1993)	African/Black Psychology (Kambon 1999)
Unity	Consciousness	Humanity	Sense of Identity	Consubstantiation	Oneness/ Harmony with Nature
Self-Determination	Character	Brotherhood	Faith in God	Interdependence	Survival of the Group
Collective Work and Responsibility	Conduct	Morality/ Character	Respect for Others	Egalitarianism	Inclusiveness/ Synthesis
Cooperative Economics	Collectivity	Responsibility	Honesty and Sense of Responsibility	Collectivism	Cooperation Collective Responsibility
Purpose	Competence	Truthfulness	Self-Reliance and Respect for Hard Work	Transformation	Interdependence
Creativity	Caring	Family	Resourcefulness Resilience	Cooperation	Spiritualism/ Circularity
Faith	Creed	Work	Belief in Education	Humaneness	Complementarity/ Understanding
		Knowledge/ Wisdom	Courage Integrity	Synergism	

These principles reflect fundamental African wisdom, retained to varying de-
grees by Africans wherever they might find themselves in the world. Providing
a blueprint for good conduct, ethical existence, and generativity, they are designed to guide human development, promote harmonious relations, and advance sustainable, life-affirming communities. These principles, ultimately help
the individual to experience congruity between the supra-, inter-, and inner-
realms (Nobles 1998) of their spiritual, communal, and individuated essence,
achieving a sense of human integrity and the "unlimited and total expression
of energy and power that represents human possibility, probability, and potential" (Nobles 1998, 195). Of course there will be individual differences across
African Americans to the extent that these principles are a conscious or opera-
tive part of their ethnic identity and behavior. In other words, African Americans, like any ethnocultural group, exist within a range of levels of ethnic
identity and conscious subscription to their cultural heritage. We can expect to
find individual differences in the degree to which they operate, consciously and
unconsciously, by these principles.

Developing a Measure of Africentrism

As the field develops African-centered strategies for service delivery, tools
will be needed for client assessment and targeting services. If, for example, the
drug-treatment system in a community includes but a few African-centered

programs, overall system effectiveness may be enhanced if referral agencies (e.g., walk-in community centers and central intake) are able to consider the suitability of individual clients for those programs. Similarly, if a program has only a few counselors trained in African-centered approaches, the program may wish to identify the clients most likely to benefit from working with those counselors.

Efforts to assess the effectiveness of culture-based services will require tools by which the cultural characteristics of groups and individuals can be measured. If practitioners know the status of their clients on cultural characteristics considered relevant to effectiveness, culture-based services can be targeted more wisely. If individual-level variability in cultural characteristics can be measured, providers will be able to evaluate the value added of culture-based services.

One initial instrument developed in this regard was a self-report measure of *Africentrism* (Grills and Longshore 1996). Africentrism was operationalized based on the degree to which a person subscribed to the *Nguzo Saba*. In a series of four studies involving African Americans and Whites, Africentric values (commitment to ethnic identity, involvement in group activities and traditions, group attachment, and pride, etc.) were conceptually related to aspects of ethnic identity that are widely viewed as important to a healthy sense of self. We also found that Africentrism was an integral part of ethnic identity for the African Americans but not so for Whites. Culture is a unified field, not just a laundry list of beliefs, behaviors, rituals, and customs. It is "one whole fabric ... rather than split sheets or bits and pieces" (Asante 1993). The lack of coherence in the item scores on the Africentrism measure administered to Whites reflects this. Whites who scored high on one item failed to score high on others because the items did not represent a unified cognitive set for them whereas the items did represent a unified cognitive set for African Americans.

Our research suggests that Africentric values are an integral yet distinguishable aspect of ethnic identity for African Americans. It may therefore be important to include a measure of Africentrism among the outcome indicators when evaluating interventions designed to affect ethnic self-perceptions. More broadly, measuring Africentrism may be important in evaluating any intervention that is African-centered, regardless of its intended outcome. There are two hypotheses regarding its relevance. One is that African Americans who score high on Africentrism at treatment entry may respond more readily to an intervention that is African-centered. On the other hand, African Americans who score low on Africentrism at treatment entry may gain more from an African-centered intervention because they acquire a healthier ethnic identity through exposure to African-centered material.

Simple ethnic group membership serves as a crude proxy for factors known or thought to be correlated with ethnicity. Underlying correlates of ethnicity tend to include ethnic identity, acculturation, and related attitudes, norms, and values; experience or expectation of discrimination; socioeconomic status; health and risk indicators; community conditions and institutions; and social and personal resources. These factors can play an important role in the recovery process for clients from the point of problem recognition to aftercare and maintenance. In decisions to seek help for example, people of color who identify more strongly with their own culture may see drug dependence as a spiritual problem or an error in judgment, not as a problem appropriate for professional treatment. They also may be more likely to expect discrimination from mainstream health care providers and therefore less motivated to seek care from them (e.g., Bailey 1991; Jones, Harrell, Morris-Prather, Thomas, et al. 1996; Landrine and Klonoff 1994). An alternative hypothesis may also be plausible. Identification with one's own culture and perceived discrimination are positively related to physical health, self-esteem, and effective coping (e.g., Cross 1991; Jackson et al. 1996; Oysterman, Grant, and Ager 1995; Williams, Lavizzo-Mourney, and Warren 1994). It is important, however, not to assume. As practitioners, we should not assume the client's level of ethnic identity, its relevance to their drug use and recovery, and its effect on problem recognition or treatment motivation.

Africentrism and Motivation for Treatment among African American Users

In our research on treatment motivation (Longshore, Grills, Anglin, and Annon 1998) we found that as Africentrism increased, the relationship between problem recognition and treatment motivation became stronger. Thus, motivation to seek care may be higher among people whose ethnic identity is strong. Most highly related to treatment motivation was problem recognition. To the extent that African American drug abusers recognize their drug use as problematic on some level, the more likely were they to be motivated for treatment.

The strong association between problem recognition and treatment motivation may reflect a link between the occurrence of problems in one or more interpersonal areas (work, family, etc.) and African American drug users' interest in treatment (Longshore, Grills, Anglin, and Annon 1998). Notably, typical drug-use indicators (e.g., frequency of use and years of use) had no direct bearing on treatment motivation in our studies. This finding is congruent with some prior research in which patterns of drug/alcohol use, as distinct from their interpersonal consequences, have not predicted treatment entry (Carroll and Rounsaville 1992; Tucker and Gladsjo 1993). Drug-use indicators cannot be ruled out, however, as factors that may influence treatment perceptions.

Perceptions of treatment have a particular bearing on decisions to seek treatment among African American drug users. Following problem recognition, additional factors such as perceived treatment benefit affect treatment motivation. Despite prior research on the antipathy of African Americans toward drug-use treatment, most African Americans believed they could benefit from treatment in at least one of five major modalities (outpatient drug-free, methadone maintenance, methadone detoxification, inpatient, and residential or therapeutic community), and those who expressed this belief were motivated for treatment.

Although conventional moral beliefs did not predict treatment motivation in our research, there may nevertheless be an important link between the two. Recognizing one's drug use as a problem and deciding to seek treatment depends, in part, on whether the user wishes to claim or reclaim moral standing in a community of conventional others (Biernacki 1986; Shaffer and Jones 1989; Waldorf, Reinarman, and Murphy 1991). This motive may loom especially large in African American and other communities of color because of the value placed on collective identity and connectedness to others (Crocker, Luhtanen, Blaine, and Broadnax 1994; McCombs 1985; Nobles, 1973). In addition, although some users in our study reported that fear of social stigma had previously been a barrier to treatment, it did not appear to undermine their motivation for treatment. On the contrary, those showing more motivation for treatment were *more* likely to say they had feared being stigmatized. Endorsement of conventional morality and concern about one's reputation (stigma) both reflect the drug user's stake in conformity, which may, in turn, be an important determinant of treatment seeking and recovery. This is consistent with the African cultural precept of communalism. The basic human unit is the group, not the individual (Parham, White, and Ajamu 1999). The resulting culturally centered identity includes a sense of self that is collective or extended, a sense of mutual responsibility (Nobles 1986), and the need to adhere to or bond with others (Grills in press; Grills and Ajei in press). This dynamic is an outgrowth of African and African American cultural patterns. In extended families, African Americans developed an early sense of human conduct, social responsibility, moral character (Nobles and Goddard 1993), and accountability (Ladner 1998) to many significant others.

Finally, to understand what factors influence motivation for treatment among African American drug users, we tested a range of attitudes, perceptions, and experiences regarding ethnic group membership. Perceived racism was the only ethnicity-related factor associated with treatment motivation. The relationship between problem recognition and treatment motivation, where treatment motivation was higher for those who recognized they had a drug use problem, was stronger among people who more strongly endorsed Africentric values. This finding is consistent with previous research documenting a positive association between ethnic identity on one hand and physical health, self-esteem, and effective coping on the other (e.g., Jackson et al. 1996; Oysterman, Grant, and Ager 1995; Williams, Lavizzo-Mourney, and Warren 1994). Research has also found that physical health is worse among African Americans who downplay, deny, or internalize racism (Taylor and Jackson 1990; Williams, Lavizzo-Mourney, and Warren 1994). Thus, African American drug users most motivated for treatment may be those who are wary of the treatment experience yet also confident of their ability to derive its benefit on their own terms. The need for replication and further study is evident. Nonetheless, these preliminary findings offer some new points for consideration regarding how to engage African American users into the treatment process. In a sense, the benefit of an African-centered value system and identity is the increased ability to engage in critical reflection and action that can lead to transformation.

FOCUS ON SOLUTIONS

The Culturally Congruent African Centered Treatment Engagement Project: Treatment Applications

Culture can be defined as those elements of a group's history, values, knowledge, and behavioral norms that become implicitly or explicitly meaningful in social interaction (Betancourt and Lopez 1993; Green 1982). At the group level, culture is analyzed as a constant; it is a unitary attribute of the group as a whole. At the individual level, however, culture is variable. Group members may vary widely in the degree to which their personal characteristics reflect group-level patterns. It is necessary that clinicians and researchers move beyond the ethnic gloss of prior assessments and research by including ethnicity-related attitudes, perceptions, and experiences among the factors tested (Grills and Longshore 1996) and considered in treatment.

The Culturally Congruent African Centered Treatment Engagement Project was developed as an attempt to translate African-centered principles into concrete praxis in the treatment of substance abuse. It was important that the intervention be *congruent* with the cultural precepts noted earlier. The purpose of the research study was to test the relative effectiveness of this African-centered treatment intervention compared with a standard assessment-referral protocol to promote recovery from illegal drug use among African Americans (Longshore and Grills 2000). African and African American values were integral to the content and format of the intervention. The model was tested in a study consisting of 364 African American drug users recruited to participate in the study via outreach to community service providers, jails, and the streets. Participants ranged in age from nineteen to seventy-four with a mean age of forty-one. Thirty-six percent were women. Participants tended to be unmarried (87 percent), unemployed (91 percent), and high school educated (62 percent). Seventy-four percent had used cocaine regularly, and 37 percent had used heroin regularly.

Philosophy of Treatment

In the African-centered model, the primary treatment issue is not one of merely changing individual attitudes, beliefs, and narrowly defined interpersonal relationships or behaviors. Rather, the central treatment issues involve empowering African Americans:

• To create a critical consciousness through dialogue, reflection, and action upon their current oppression of addiction in order to bring about fundamental transformation of self and circumstance[2]

- To enter more fully into the reality of the conditions of life and their life so that knowing it better, they can better recognize the contradictions and transform their reality[3]

- To understand the fundamental cultural-economic-political power imbalance that informs class and racial differences in the United States (institutionally, ideologically, and structurally)

- To emphasize African-centered ideas, methods, and values in the development of drug abuse treatment and recovery

The goal is to provide African Americans clients with sufficient knowledge, power, and support to choose drug-free lives and to recognize those forces (personal, proximal and distal) mitigating against a drug-free lifestyle. In other words, they gain the critical consciousness necessary for substantive transformation and liberation (Freire 1970). Further, with communal support the individual is not afraid to confront, to listen, to see the world unveiled. Equipped with insight into what is (including the myriad personal and social contradictions) and a vision of what could be (a life consistent with their culture, aspirations, and principles), they embrace a commitment to authentic existence for themselves and others.

In this approach, the conceptualization of drug abuse and recovery issues is expanded from an individual affliction to a cultural-political disorder for African American communities whose effect, among others, maintains the social class and racial divide in America (Rowe and Grills 1993). Effective drug abuse treatment and recovery must emphasize the acquisition of power (spiritual, personal, familial, communal, institutional, and cultural) that emanates from an awareness of the essential interrelatedness of humans with the Supreme Being (Nobles 1984) and with the peculiar socioeconomic, historical, and political reality within which they find themselves. Critical questions in the recovery process become Who am I? Where am I? How in the world did I get here?

Empowering African Americans within the African-centered approach facilitates their ability to define, decide, and determine the direction and course of their individuated and collective lives. Thus, intervention systems that require African Americans to further relinquish power (personally, spiritually, culturally) are not considered particularly useful to transformation. In the scheme of history, the travesty of African enslavement was only yesterday and the dehumanization and injustices of postenslavement were just last night.[4] Have we adequately accounted for the effects of this African American holocaust, or *maafa* (Kiswahili for "holocaust")?

To be effective, drug abuse treatment and recovery must adopt African-centered precepts that address the totality of life experiences and development of African Americans. Central to this assumption are beliefs in the essentialness of spirit, interdependence, transformative development, and sociopolitical consciousness. Here effective drug abuse treatment and recovery must emphasize the positive potential of human behavior, based on a value system and sense of order committed to the greater good of humankind. Treatment strategies that simply emphasize the cessation of addictive behaviors without refocusing individuals toward the production of life-sustaining activities for self and others are considered insufficient.

Effective drug abuse treatment and recovery must be long term and multidimensional in scope. Treatment must focus on total development that is directed toward reproducing the best in Africans (Nobles 1998). Such an approach reflects what may be termed a psychocultural transformation. In order to render the influences of alcohol and other drugs irrelevant, African Americans must become directly involved in meeting their required life-sustaining needs. They must develop ongoing rituals, traditions, practices, and disciplines that operate against the use of alcohol and other drugs.

The approach involved requires a conceptualization of treatment based on a "human-to-human" versus a "human-to-object" orientation (Dixon 1976). In other words, the treatment relationship is based on reciprocity, equality, and respect. Rather than being objective, distant, and removed, counselors are engaged, familiar, personal, and affective. The relationship is egalitarian, and the objective is dialogue that leads to critical consciousness that can propel the client into action. In this dialogue, the therapist is no longer the one who teaches and guides the evolution of insight, understanding, and behavior change. The therapist is taught in the dialogue with the client, brought to insights and understanding, and engages in behavior change relative to the behavior change process of the client. Client and therapist both become cotherapists. Consistent with the Freirian critique of the "banking model of education," the therapist presents material for the client to consider and revisits earlier conceptualizations of the client as the client expresses her own perspective and lived experience. This approach is intended to stimulate the client's self-healing, creative, and analytic capacities, bringing to the client a problem-posing therapeutic process that involves a constant unveiling of reality. To alienate clients from their own self-healing, reflective, and decision-making processes is to change them into objects rather than supporting them to be subjects of their own recovery. This requires a fundamental faith in humankind and their ability "to make and remake, create and re-create, faith in their vocation to be more fully human" (Freire 1970, 126).

This African-centered process poses a cyclic model of human dynamism that focuses on centeredness: (e.g., *relationship* between the counselor and the client is important rather than on the respective positions of either). The transformative power derives from the relationship between the two, guided by

- The realization that the clients' view of the world, manifested variously in their action and perceptions, reflects their situation in the world. This brings important insights and tools that can be used to assist clients in the construction of their plans for recovery.

- The principles of Maat, the ancient Egyptian value system that emphasizes truth, justice, propriety, balance, harmony, reciprocity, and order (Karenga 1986; Parham, White, and Ajamu 1999).

Finally, mindful of the principle of communalism, individual drug abuse treatment and recovery is reframed as a healing of the African American community. Recovery reflects community healing because of the essential interdependent characteristic of African American communities. "I am because we are, since we are therefore I am." The philosophical assumption of interdependence is indicative of a crucial issue contrasting the theories and techniques of traditional western clinical/counseling psychology and the culturally driven service needs of many African Americans.

Communalism is one of the central values in African American culture contributing to a collective identity and ultimately influencing an African-centered approach to treatment. This value is distinguishable from the White European emphasis on an individual's separate identity and self-actualization (Dana 1993; Grills and Longshore 1996; Karenga 1988). Although there is variability in the degree to which members of any ethnic group subscribe to and act on these values, communalism appears more salient as a value for African Americans overall. For example, research has shown that the relationship between group perceptions and self-perceptions is closer for African Americans (and for other non-Whites) than for Whites (Crocker, Luhtanen, Blaine, and Broadnax 1994; Kim et al. 1994; Oyserman 1993; Oyserman, Grant, and Ager 1995). In accord with communalism in African American culture, perceptions of reality (judging the credibility of information, interpreting behavior and events, etc.) are based on group process, as well as individual cognition (Asante 1987). A concrete example is the African American vocal tradition ("call and response" in church settings) based on the presence of others who actively affirm the thoughts, feelings, and experiences evoked by a speaker.

Communalism and group process represent the cultural base of the African-centered treatment approach. First, in the treatment model, we depicted drug dependence both as an individual affliction *and* a community disorder rooted in cultural and power disparities between African Americans and dominant Euro-American institutions and public policies. Second, we defined recovery as a holistic process that entails acquisition of power in the form of knowledge, spiritual insight, alignment with personal and communal destiny, and community health. Third, we framed discussion of the client's drug use and recovery in a context that acknowledged the totality of life experiences faced by the client as an African American (e.g., racial prejudice, possibly poor self-image, and low job opportunity). Fourth, we emphasized that changing one's behavior is important not just for the individual but also for the greater good. Fifth, we discussed drug-use alternatives with particular meaning given to expectations of treatment, the recovery process, and reintegration back into the community.

Treatment Effect

A comparison of the relative effect of a culturally congruent assessment-referral protocol and a standard protocol in promoting recovery among African

American drug users yielded significant differences between the two approaches. We found that study participants assigned to a culturally congruent assessment-referral protocol were significantly more likely than those assigned to a standard assessment-referral to report being drug abstinent one year later. These findings were not attributable to differences in the willingness of participants to self-report drug use. Urine specimens taken from a random subsample of participants confirmed the reliability of self-reported drug use or nonuse.

We operationalized cultural congruence as follows. First, addition of a peer (former drug user) to the counseling team converted the typical one-on-one format to a communal process in which identification of drug problems and goals and/or values was interactive. The peer encouraged and modeled disclosure of drug use and honest expression of ambivalence regarding recovery. Second, drug use was depicted as both a personal problem and a community problem rooted in cultural and power disparities between the African American community and dominant institutions. Third, we placed issues in a context that acknowledged the totality of a participant's life experience, not only as an individual but also as an African American. Fourth, we emphasized that change is important not only for the individual but also for the collective good. Finally, change processes in the trans-theoretical model were articulated in terms consistent with African American cultural values.

Like many other interventions, the treatment approach was multifaceted. Cultural congruence was operationalized in multiple ways and blended into a motivational intervention based on the transtheoretical stage-of-change framework. Apart from the content of counseling, the intervention also differed from standard practice in its use of a two-person team (counselor and peer), a video containing images, symbols and messages designed to raise consciousness, and a meal intended to evoke a more familiar family/communal atmosphere.

Motivational Intervention and the Transtheoretical Stages of Change

Motivational intervention (MI) (also known as motivation interviewing) is an approach and a style of counseling that can be used throughout the therapeutic process. Specific MI strategies are thought to be particularly useful during the initial stages of treatment, especially with clients who are at the precontemplation or contemplation stages of change with marked ambivalence about their drinking or drug use. The goal of MI is to have the client talk herself into changing their drug use behavior. This approach emphasizes the client's right to *choose* abstinence or not and to accept responsibility for her decision. MI strategies avoid traditional substance abuse techniques such as confrontation and argumentation because these offensive tactics (*"You* have a *problem."*) naturally lead to defensive reactions (*"I* don't have a *problem."*). This form of confrontation is both unhelpful and counterproductive when the aim is to get the client to present the arguments for change. MI is a directive, client-centered style of counseling (Miller and Rollnick 1991) for eliciting behavior change by helping clients to explore and resolve ambivalence. It is most centrally defined *not* by technique, but by the *philosophy and spirit* of the approach as a facilitative style for interpersonal relationships. This philosophy and approach to counseling engages clients to examine and commit to change in areas of concern to them (and/or to others). The approach recognizes differential levels of readiness change, skills for change, and support for change. The approach respects the integrity of the individual and attempts to solicit the client's own definition of the issues and strategies for resolution that include a repertoire of options. As an approach to counseling, MI is intended to promote behavior change by starting "where the client is at" and using a specific set of strategies and skills to move the client forward in the behavior change process.

Targeting drug users who had never been in treatment, the African-centered culturally congruent treatment engagement model used the techniques and philosophy of motivational interviewing and the foundation of African American cultural values as a source of motivation. The model was designed to move people from one stage of nonreadiness for change to readiness and action for recovery. In the stages of change model, the relevant processes to move people from precontemplation to contemplation or contemplation to action include consciousness raising, self-reevaluation, dramatic relief, and environmental reevaluation. To maintain cultural congruence, these processes were articulated in terms consistent with the *Nguzo Saba*. For example, raising consciousness was approached using principles such as purpose (*nia*). We explored the effects of racism on personal and community behavior. Self-reevaluation may have been approached from the principle of self-determination (*kujichagulia*). To stimulate dramatic relief, we used several charged scenes in the video segment of the counseling process that poignantly displayed the consequences of drug use for self, family, and community and clearly displayed the deep emotional bonds between self, family, and community.

IMPLICATIONS AND CONCLUSIONS

The single most critical issue facing the science and profession of psychology is how to address the cultural, spiritual, economic, social, historical, and political factors that influence conceptions of human beingness, features of human functioning, and methods for restoring healthy order to humans throughout the world. African American mental health specialists have relied on the systems of meaning emerging out of the cultural traditions of Europeans. These systems have been used as the philosophical, methodological, and ethical standards to direct and inform the majority of work relating to the promotion, prevention, and intervention of health concerns for African persons throughout the diaspora.

Motivation and recovery can be enhanced through culturally based African-centered programs and intervention strategies. Critical cultural principles such as interdependence, spirituality, courage, integrity, character, and collective work and responsibility can and should guide the philosophy, development, and implementation of treatment. For example, conventional moral beliefs and concern about reputation (stigma) may reflect African Americans stake in conformity and be an important determinant in seeking treatment and recovery. Among African American adults, self-concept and subjective well-being appear to be collective as well as personal (Crocker, Luhtanen, Blaine, and Broadnax 1994; McCombs 1985; Nobles 1973). Thus, stake in conformity, as a motivating factor for African Americans, may be best understood as the desire to enter or reenter a moral community with culturally defined principles of conduct. Conformity with African American values and behavioral norms would entail active engagement in the community, spirituality, strong collective self-esteem, and assumption or reassumption of conventional roles in one's nuclear and extended families.

Understood this way, the stake in conformity may be a valuable but underused source of leverage in treatment outreach and counseling. For example, many African American drug users may overcome their ambivalence about treatment/recovery more readily if the initial focus is on prosocial reasons for drug abstinence rather than on forcing users to self-label as addicts, breaking down defense mechanisms, and emphasizing the "cons" of continued use (Miller 1995). It is important that these prosocial reasons be expressed in culturally specific terms, such as those cited earlier: entry or reentry in a moral community, renewed spirituality, collective as well as personal grounds for self-esteem, and assumption or reassumption of conventional roles in the community and in nuclear and extended families.

Second, racism, as both a personal experience and a systemic problem, often goes unaddressed during the treatment of African American clients (Rowe and Grills 1993), perhaps because treatment staff view racism as a topic too far afield or too awkward to deal with. However, outreach, intake, and counseling may be more effective if the review of clients' needs and expectations explicitly addresses their concerns regarding equity, respect, and understanding and if outreach/intake staff work to reinforce the client resolve to deal with these concerns constructively (e.g., to extract the benefits of treatment despite the possibility of encountering discrimination in the process).

Finally, the interaction of Africentric values with problem recognition suggests that treatment outreach and counseling might be more effective with African Americans if delivered in ways congruent with African American culture (see also Longshore, Grills, Annon, and Grady 1998). Culturally congruent treatment would mean:

- Including extended family members when family counseling is part of the treatment protocol

- Framing recovery as a process involving and benefiting the whole community

- Contextualizing substance use as an issue that occurs within a specific social, ecological, and historical context

• Building self-esteem in collective as well as personal terms

• Integrating cultural awareness and spiritual growth into a holistic psychotherapeutic approach

• Adapting therapist techniques for congruence with Africentric values and behavioral norms (Rowe & Grills 1993)

It remains essential to recognize that moral beliefs, perceived racism, and Africentrism are variables, not constants, in the African American population. As outreach and counseling procedures are adapted to address these group-based issues, each individual must be understood in terms of her or his own ethnic identity needs and perceptions.

NOTES

1. See Barrett 1974; Hilliard 1997; Holloway 1991; Kambon 1999; Noll 1992; Pinckney 1998; and Smith 1994 for a more complete discussion of cultural retentions.

2. "Liberating action necessarily involves a moment of perception and volition" (Freire 1970, 51).

3. "This person is not afraid to meet the people or to enter into dialogue with them" (Freire, 1970, 39). This Freirien ideology helps us to see the liberating potential of psychology where clients are aided in the discovery of both their personal and contextual conditions and where treatment does not teach people how to accommodate to unhealthy realities but become empowered to bring about personal and social transformation. This African-centered psychology, then, becomes a form of what I refer to as "Liberation Psychology."

4. African Americans have spent more time in the United States in the condition of enslavement and second-class citizenship than free, equal and valued members of the society. From approximately 1619 to 1865, a period of 246 years , Africans in America were bought and sold like chattel. From 1865 to 2001 they have had only 136 years out of the condition of enslavement. In other words, Africans in America have a longer history in this society in the state of enslavement than in freedom. From 1865 to 1964, 99 of those 136 years, basic civil rights that affected their education, housing, health, social life, ability to vote, and incomes were denied. From 1964 to the 2001, a period of only 37 years Africans in America have had a tenuous hold on legally defined civil rights and equality, continue to face incredible conditions of racism and have yet to achieve equal status on all basic measures of health, well-being, and social status.

REFERENCES

Amuleru-Marshall, O. (1991). African Americans. In J. Kinney (Ed.), *Clinical manual of substance abuse* (pp. 5–31). St. Louis, MO: C.V. Mosby.

Ani, M. (formerly Richards) (1980). *Let the circle be unbroken: The implications of African spirituality in the diaspora*. Trenton, NJ: Red Sea Press.

———. (1994). *Yurugu: An African centered critique of European cultural thought and behavior*. Trenton, NJ: Africa World Press.

Aponte, J.F., and Barnes, J.M. (1995). Impact of acculturation and moderator variables on the intervention and treatment of ethnic groups. In J.F. Aponte, R.Y. Rivers, and J. Wohl (Eds.), *Psychological interventions and cultural diversity.* Needham Heights, MA: Allyn & Bacon.

Asante, M.K. (1987). *The Afrocentric idea.* Philadelphia: Temple University Press.

———. (1993). Racism, consciousness, and Afrocentricity. In G. Early (Ed.), *Lure and loathing: Essays on race, identity, and the ambivalence of assimilation.* New York: Penguin Books.

Association of Black Psychologists. (1995). *Convening of the African Psychology Institute in Laguna Beach, CA.* Washington, DC:

Bailey, E. (1991). *Urban African American health care.* Lanham, MD: University Press of America.

Barrett, L.E. (1974). *Soul-force: African heritage in Afro-American religion.* Garden City, NY: Anchor Books.

Bentacourt, H., and Lopez, S.R. (1993). The study of culture, ethnicity, and race in American psychology. *American Psychologist,* 48 629–637.

Biernacki, P. (1986). *Pathways from heroin addiction: Recovery without treatment.* Philadelphia: Temple University Press.

Carroll, K.M., and Rounsaville, B.J. (1992). Contrast of treatment-seeking and untreated cocaine abusers. *Archives of General Psychiatry,* 49 464–471.

Cress-Welsing, F. (1991). *The Isis papers: The keys to the colors.* Chicago: Third World Press.

Crocker, J., Luhtanen, R., Blaine, B., and Broadnax, S. (1994). Collective self-esteem and psychological well-being among White, Black, and Asian college students. *Personality and Social Psychology Bulletin,* 20 503–513.

Cross, W.E., Jr. (1991). *Shades of Black: Diversity in African-American identity.* Philadelphia: Temple University.

Dana, R.H. (1993). *Multicultural assessment perspectives for professional psychology.* Boston: Allyn & Bacon.

Dixon, V. (1976). Worldviews and research methodology. In L. King (Ed.), *African philosophy: Assumptions and paradigms for research on Black persons.* Los Angeles: Fanon Research & Development Center.

Dukor, M. (1993). African concept of man. *Orunmilism,* 2 27–34.

Finn, P. (1994). Addressing the needs of cultural minorities in drug treatment. *Journal of Substance Abuse Treatment,* 11 (4), 325–337.

Freire, P. (1970). *Pedagogy of the oppressed.* New York: Seabury Press.

Green, J.W. (1982). *Cultural awareness in the human services.* Englewood Cliffs, NJ: Prentice-Hall.

Grills, C. (in press). African psychology. In R.L. Jones (Ed.), *Black psychology, fourth edition.* Hampton, VA: Cobb & Henry.

Grills, C., and Ajei, M. (in press). African centered conceptualizations of self and consciousness: The Akan model. In T.A. Parham (Ed.), *Therapeutic approaches with African American populations: Raising the bar of what passes for competence.* Thousand Oaks, CA: Sage.

Grills, C., and Longshore, D. (1996). Africentrism: Psychometric analyses of a self-report measure. *Journal of Black Psychology,* 22 (1) 86–106.

Grills, C., and Rowe, D. (1998). African traditional medicine: Implications for African-centered approaches to healing. In R. Jones (Ed.), *African American Mental Health.* Hampton, VA: Cobb & Henry.

Gyeke, K. (1996). African cultural values. An Introduction. Philadelphia, PA and Accra, Ghana: Sanleaf.

Hilliard, A.G. (1997). *Sba: The reawakening of the African mind*. Gainsville, FL: Makare Publishing Co.

Holloway, J.E. (Ed.) (1991). *Africanisms in American culture*. Bloomington: Indiana University Press.

Jackson, A.M. (1983). Treatment issues for Black patients. *Psychotherapy: Theory, Research, and Practice*, 20 143–151.

Jackson, J.S., Brown, T.N., Williams, D.R., Torres, M., et al. (1996). Racism and the physical and mental health status of African Americans: A 13-year national panel study. *Ethnicity and Disease*, 6 132–147.

Jackson, M.S. (1995). Afrocentric treatment of African American women and their children in a residential chemical dependency program. *Journal of Black Studies*, 26 17–30.

Jones, A., Lewis, C., and Shorty, V. (1993). African American women injection drug users. In B. Brown and G. Beschner (Eds.), *Handbook on risk of AIDS: Injection drug users and sexual partners* (pp. 275–296). Westport, CT: Greenwood.

Jones, D.R., Harrell, J.P., Morris-Prather, C.E., Thomas, J., et al. (1996). Affective and physiological responses to racism: The roles of Afrocentrism and mode of presentation. *Ethnicity and Disease*, 6 109–122.

Kamalu, C. (1998). *Person, divinity & nature: A modern view of the person & the cosmos in African thought*. London: Karnak House.

Kambon, K. (1992). *The African personality in America: An African centered framework*. Tallahassee, FL: Nubian National Publications.

Kambon, K.K.K. (1999). *African/Black psychology in the American context: An African-centered approach*. Tallahassee, FI: Nubian Nation Publications.

Karenga, M. (1980). *Kawaida theory: An introductory outline*. Los Angeles: University of Sankore Press.

———. (1986). Restoration of the Husia: Reviving a sacred legacy. In M. Karenga and L. Carruthers (Eds.), *Kemet and the African worldview: Research, rescue and restoration*. Los Angeles: University of Sankore Press.

———. (1988). *The African American holiday of Kwanzaa: A celebration of family, community, and culture*. Los Angeles: University of Sankore Press.

———. (1993). *Introduction to Black studies*. Los Angeles: University of Sankore Press.

Kim, U., Triandis, H.C., Kagitcibasi, C., Choi, S., et al. (Eds.) (1994). *Individualism and collectivism*. Thousand Oaks, CA: Sage.

Kunjufu, J. (1986). Behavior and its value base. *Black Books Bulletin*, 4 (2) 40–43.

Ladner, J.A. (1998). *The ties that bind: Timeless values for African American families*. New York: John Wiley and Sons.

Landrine, H. (1992). Clinical implications of cultural differences: The referential versus the indexical self. *Clinical Psychology Review*, 12 401–415.

Landrine, H., and Klonoff, E.A. (1994). Cultural diversity in casual attributions for illness: The role of the supernatural. *Journal of Behavioral Medicine*, 17 (2) 181–193.

Lindskoog, D.P. (1998). *The idea of psychology: Reclaiming the discipline's identity*. Washington, DC: Howard University Press.

Little, G.L. (1981). Relationship of drug of choice, race, and crime to entry into drug abuse treatment. *Psychological Reports*, 48 486.

Longshore, D., and Grills, C. (2000). Motivating illegal drug use recovery: Evidence for a culturally congruent intervention. *Journal of Black Studies*, 26 (3), 288–301.

Longshore, D., Grills, C., Anglin, M.D., and Annon, K. (1998). Desire for help among African-American drug users. *Journal of Drug Issues*, 27 (4), 755–770.

Longshore, D., Grills, C., and Annon, K. (1999). Effects of a culturally congruent intervention on cognitive factors related to drug-use recovery. *Substance Use and Misuse*, 34 (9), 1223–1241.

Longshore, D., Grills, C., Annon, K., and Grady, R. (1998). Promoting recovery from drug abuse: An Africentric intervention. *Journal of Black Studies*, 28 (3), 319–333.

Longshore, D.L., Hsieh, S., and Anglin, M.D. (1993). Ethnic and gender differences in drug users' perceived need for treatment. *International Journal of the Addictions*, 28 539–588.

Longshore, D.L., Hsieh, S., Anglin M.D., and Annon, T.K. (1992). Ethnic patterns in drug abuse treatment utilization. *Journal of Mental Health Administration*, 19 268–277.

Madhubuti, H.R. (1972). *Kwanzaa: A progressive and uplifting African American holiday*. Chicago: Third World Press.

Mbiti, J.S. (1990). *African religions and philosophy*. 2nd ed., revised and enlarged. Portsmouth, NH: Heinemann Educational Books.

McCombs, H.G. (1985). Black self-concept: An individual/collective analysis. *International Journal of Intercultural Relations*, 9 1–18.

McGoldrick, M., and Giordano, J. (1996). Overview: Ethnicity and family therapy. In M. McGoldrick, J. Giordano, and J.K. Pearce (Eds.), *Ethnicity and family therapy*, 2nd ed. (pp. 1–27). New York: Guilford Press.

Miller, W.R. (1995). Increasing motivation for change. In R.K. Hester and W.R. Miller (Eds.), *Handbook of alcoholism treatment approaches: Effective alternatives*, 2nd ed. Needham Heights, MA: Allyn & Bacon.

Miller, W.R., and Rollnick, S. (1991). *Motivational interviewing: Preparing people to change addictive behavior*. New York: Guilford Press.

Myers, L. (1988). *Understanding an Africentric worldview: Introduction to an optimal psychology*. Dubuque, IA: Kendall/Hunt.

Nobles, W.W. (1973). Psychological research and the Black self-concept: A critical review. *Journal of Social Issues*, 29 1–31.

———. (1984). Alienation, human transformation and adolescent drug use: Toward a reconceptualization of the problem. *Journal of Drug Issues*, 14 (2) 243–252.

———. (1986). *African Psychology: Towards its reclamation, reassencion and revitalization*. Oakland, CA: Black Family Institute.

———. (1998). To be African or not to be: The question of identity or authenticity—some preliminary thoughts. In R.L. Jones (Ed.), *African American identity development*. Hampton, VA: Cobb & Henry.

Nobles, W., and Goddard, L. (1993). An African-centered model of prevention for African American youth at high risk. In L. Goddard (Ed.), *An African-centered model of prevention for African-American youth at high risk*. Washington, DC: U.S. Government Printing Office.

Nobles, W.W., King, L., and James, C.B. (1995). *Health promotion and disease preventions: Strategies in the African American community*. African American professionals health promotion and disease prevention focus group report submitted to the Congress of National Black Churches. Washington, DC: Association of Black Psychologists.

Nole, J.E. (1992). *Company of prophets*. St. Paul, MN Llewellyn Publications.

Oysterman, D. (1993). The lens of personhood: Viewing the self and others in a multicultural society. *Journal of Personality and Social Psychology*, 65 993–1009.

Oysterman, D., Grant, L., and Ager, J. (1995). A socially contextualized model of African American identity: Possible selves and school persistence. *Journal of Personality and Social Psychology*, 69 1216–1232.

Parham, T.A., White, J.L., and Ajamu, A. (1999). *The psychology of Blacks: An African centered perspective*. Upper Saddle River, NJ: Prentice-Hall.

Pavkov, T.W., McGovern, M.P., and Geffner, E.S. (1993). Problem severity and symptomatology among substance misusers: Differences between African-Americans and Caucasians. *International Journal of the Addictions*, 28 (9), 909–922.

Perkins, U. (1992). *Afrocentric socialization paradigm for the positive development of Black males*. Chicago: Association for the Positive Development of African American Youth.

Phillips, F.B. (1990). NTU psychotherapy: An Africentric approach. *Journal of Black Psychology*, 17 55–74.

Pinckney, R. (1998). *Blue roots: African American folk magic of the Gullah people*. St. Paul, MN: Llewellyn Publications.

Rounsaville, B.J., and Kleber, H. (1985). Untreated opiate addicts. *Archives of General Psychiatry*, 42 1072–1077.

Rowe, D.M., and Grills, C.N. (1993). African-centered drug treatment: An alternative conceptual paradigm for drug counseling with African American clients. *Journal of Psychoactive Drugs*, 25 21–33.

Saulnier, C.F. (1996). African-American women in an alcohol intervention group: Addressing personal and political problems. *Substance Use and Misuse*, 31 1259–1278.

Schwaller de Lubicz, R.A. (1998). *The temple of man: Apet at the south of Luxor*. Rochester, VT: Inner Traditions International.

Shaffer, H.J., and Jones, S.B. (1989). *Quitting cocaine: The struggle against impulse*. Lexington, MA: Lexington Books.

Singer, M. (1991). Confronting the AIDS epidemic among IV drug users: Does ethnic culture matter? *AIDS Education and Prevention*, 3 258–283.

Smith, T.H. (1994). *Conjuring culture*. New York: Oxford University Press.

Taha-Cisse, A.H. (1991). Issues for African American women. In P. Roth (Ed.), *Alcohol and drugs are women's issues: Vol. 1. A review of the issues*. Metuchen, NJ: Scarecrow Press.

Taylor, J., and Jackson, B. (1990). Factors affecting alcohol consumption in Black women: Part II. *International Journal of the Addictions*, 25 (12), 1415–1427.

Tucker, J.A., and Gladsjo, J.A. (1993). Help-seeking and recovery by problem drinkers: Characteristics of drinkers who attended Alcoholics Anonymous of formal treatment or who recovered without assistance. *Addictive Behaviors*, 18 529–542.

Waldorf, D., Reinarman, C., and Murphy, S. (1991). Cocaine changes: *The experience of using and quitting*. Philadelphia: Temple University Press.

Williams, D.R., Lavizzo-Mourney, R., and Warren, R.C. (1994). The concept of race and health status in American. *Public Health Reports*, 109 (1), 26–41.

Wilson, A. (1993). *The falsification of Afrikan consciousness*. New York: Afrikan World Infosystems.

Wilson, A., and Stith, S.M. (1993). Culturally sensitive therapy with Black clients. In D.R. Atkinson, G. Morten, and Y.D. Sue (Eds.), *Counseling American minorities: A cross-cultural perspective*. Madison, WI: Brown & Benchmark.

II

The Collective Impact: Women, HIV-Affected Families, and Communities Impacted by and Responding to AIDS

The AIDS literature has focused on individual risk groups: intravenous drug users, gay men, women, and so on. The fact that these people are all part of families is obscured. Among African Americans, family is an incredibly important concept. Because many current problems of American Blacks can be traced to the historical trauma resulting from slavery and the persistent societal oppression, reliance on family and community, however these concepts are defined, provides emotional support and protection from outside forces of discrimination.

A major strength of African Americans is the ability to compete and survive in the face of oppressive mainstream forces and to act in collective ways that benefit the group. This is consistent with the Africentric worldview of interdependence and collectivist survival as contrasted to the mainstream Eurocentric emphasis on independence and individualism.

Thus, both the family and the construct of an African American community become paramount to healthy coping for most African Americans. Yet, social problems within the African American community (e.g., substance abuse, homophobia, and Black-on-Black crime) have challenged this notion of collectivity. For example, African American gay males and lesbians have been isolated and alienated by the African American community, especially by traditional Black churches. Black communities have been disrupted by substance abuse and violence, oftentimes causing further isolation in already marginalized neighborhoods. Family collectivism has been tested by substance-abusing family members, high incarceration rates, and extreme poverty that depletes family resources. And now AIDS, with its pervasive stigma, is placing even further burdens on family systems.

In Chapter 4, Williams addresses the barriers to effective coping and healthy survival for African American women by focusing on the overwhelming relationship dynamics some women experience. Although not discounting the strengths and resiliency of African American families, the chapter examines the outcomes for HIV-positive women who experience extreme family stressors within their immediate family and extended family networks. Chapter 5 examines the intersecting vulnerabilities that HIV-affected children face. Assumptions that all children are being taken care of adequately by an all-encompassing extended family or kinship network can further bury the needs of HIV-affected families. The *Focus on Solutions* piece, Chapter 6, highlights a Harlem family services agency and offers an opportunity to examine one agency's approach to providing culturally congruent, family-based community services for HIV-affected families. An agency case study illustrates the range of HIV/AIDS and family services provided to family members and the connection of agency services to the larger community.

Interventions based on empowerment and that build on the strengths that African Americans bring to the situation can be extremely effective in helping women cope effectively (Williams 1995), and many develop or rediscover new meaning in life. Williamson, in Chapter 7, presents findings from a study with African American women to distinguish characteristics that foster "transformative" healing for some women and not for others. These findings are important and point to both barriers and opportunities for women to work through a most difficult life event. Of particular importance is the desire for many of the women in the study to act in collective ways, to share their experiences of living with HIV as peer counselors or through advocacy work to help prevent other women from becoming infected.

Much has been written about the role of spirituality in the lives of African Americans, and prayer or spirituality has been shown to be relatively more important to coping for African American women living with HIV than their White or Hispanic counterparts (Kaplan, Marks, and Mertens 1997). In Chapter 8, Wright revists the theme of spirituality in the lives of the eight women initially introduced in Chapter 2. Spirituality, for many of the women, was defined in terms connecting them to "God," and a need to conceptualize their HIV infection into spriritual meaning. Accordingly, Chapter 9, a *Focus on Solutions* section, highlights the personal story of the development and expansion of the Balm in Gilead from a one-woman, door-to-door campaign to the mobilization of a national response to AIDS from Black churches as told by Pernessa Seele, founder and CEO of the Balm in Gilead. Through the Balm In Gilead, Black churches are beginning to "wake up" to the call that their presence is needed in the fight against AIDS. As the one, long-standing pillar across African American communities, it is increasingly apparent that a sense of collectivity in responding to AIDS as a community depends in part on the involvement of Black churches.

REFERENCES

Kaplan, M.S., Marks, G., and Mertens, S.B. (1997). Distress and coping among women with HIV infection: Preliminary findings from a multiethnic sample. *American Journal of Orthopsychiatry*, 67 (1), 80–91.

Williams, J.K. (1995). Afro-American women living with HIV infection: Special therapeutic interventions for a growing population. *Social Work in Health*, 21 (2), 41–53.

4

HIV-Positive African American Women and Their Families: Barriers to Effective Family Coping

Sharon E. Williams

AIDS has had a devastating effect on African American women and their families. A diagnosis of HIV/AIDS is much more than a medical situation; it has social, psychological, emotional, financial, and legal ramifications that affect the entire family constellation (Ward 1993). Women and their families are called upon to assume and adopt new roles if the family is to cope effectively, and the family's coping capabilities directly impact both psychosocial functioning and physical survival among women. Quality of life is significantly associated with HIV mortality. In general, AIDS-diagnosed women die sooner than their male counterparts (Cox 2000; O'Donnell 1996); yet women of color die nearly five times more quickly than their White counterparts (Land 1994). Further, the rate of progression from HIV-infection to AIDS among African American women is fifteen times greater than that of White HIV-positive women (Centers for Disease Control 1995). Obviously AIDS stigma, poverty, and other environmental barriers to effective coping play a large role in the quality of life and survival for African American women living with HIV and AIDS. Much has been written about the role of the African American family system as a resource to women; however, women and their families are challenged by stressful relationship dynamics. Although many family systems are coping effectively, this chapter focuses on the barriers to effective coping, barriers that must be addressed in order to assist HIV-positive women in their survival.

This chapter addresses the HIV/AIDS epidemic relative to African American women and their families from a family systems perspective with emphasis on challenges to effective coping within a family context. The author examines the impact of HIV disease on women's quality of life as caretakers, lack of readily accessible extended family support, and problems in intimate partner relationships. Finally, the chapter ends with implications for family interventions.

FAMILY SYSTEMS

Within our diverse society, various family forms and constellations are categorized under the broader concept of family. Family forms consist of dual parent, single parent, blended families, couples without children, extended, adoptive, and lesbian and gay families (Pequegnat and Szapocznik 2000). Any group whose bonds are based on trust, mutual support, and a common destiny may be regarded as family. Therefore, Cox (2000) argues that religious congregations, support groups, agencies, and associations may be seen as extended families within the overarching family of humankind. When defining approaches to working with families affected by HIV and AIDS, it is important to recognize the value of family mutual aid and the need for family support systems, especially in the African American community (Pequegnat and Bray 1997; Taylor and Roberts 1995). Because African Americans tend to call upon informal support systems before approaching more formal or external helping networks (Rothman 1998), it is crucial to consider both the coping mechanisms and risks associated with additional family stressors, especially when a family system is already burdened.

The family as a system seeks to perform the function of socializing and integrating its members into society. Primary to any system is the goal of equifinality, that is, the system's continuous struggle for balance and survival (Norlin and Wayne 1997). When family systems are confronted with a problem, medical or otherwise, that system utilizes its resources to adapt, accommodate, overcome, and survive the problem. The stigma and blame associated with AIDS often leaves families further victimized and without adequate interventions or appropriate social services.

The Burden of the Caretaking Role

Most HIV-positive women are the primary caregivers in families; they may care for spouses, children, and extended family members while contending with their own illness. Many women consider the caretaking role to be their first priority.

A woman's role as caretaker combined with other problems of living may be placed above her attention to her own health. Late diagnosis of HIV-positive status for women has been associated with low access to health care, uninformed professionals, and the woman's focus on the health situation of her child, partner, or some other family member. In some cases, women may decide to be HIV tested only when medical care is focused on another family member. Socially, women are expected to assume the role of caretaker in their families, and, at times, they neglect their own health care needs. For these women, emotional and physical exhaustion often accompany chronic illness.

Many HIV/AIDS infected women come from poor populations (O'Donnell 1996; Ward 1993), are inclined to get sicker faster, and have less resources for support (Farmer 1996; Ward 1993). As caretakers, women must deal with daily problems such as securing food, housing, jobs, and medical appointments for ill family members (Klein et al. 2000). Some women continue to progress in their illness with worsening symptoms while neglecting their own care (Cohen and Atwood 1994; O'Donnell 1996; Shelton et al. 1993). Other family members may be incapable of stepping in to assist these women, and they may also follow the societal trend that stresses reliance on the female family member to provide care despite her own care needs (O'Donnell 1996). Some women have buried spouses and children but are then left alone when they are terminally ill and require assistance with their own care.

Not being able to care for their children in a meaningful way adds to the incredible level of stress and guilt present for these women (Kotchick et al. 1999). HIV-positive mothers may become emotionally strained and may also feel guilty about not being able to parent their children because of illness or their impending death (Land 1994). Women who must keep their HIV status a secret may not be able to garner needed support, and, in such cases, women and their children suffer. HIV-positive mothers also face many challenges in making permanency plans for the care of their children. Such planning requires that helping professionals and child welfare workers utilize informal adoption and extended families as placement alternatives before a parent's death. Yet parents may be still struggling psychologically with the fact that someone will need to take care of their children after they die. Far too often, parents put off making these decisions until their ability to make decisions is compromised by AIDS-related dementia.

Burdens on Extended Family

Primary to the strengths operating in the Black family are strong kinship bonds existing among and across a variety of households, a high level of flexibility in family roles, a strong commitment to religious values and church participation, and communalism (Hill 1972). Such strengths inform us that the extended family unit which extends across many households in African American communities must be utilized to identify caretakers such as sisters, aunts, cousins, grandparents, and nonblood kin in seeking support and care for HIV-positive women.

African American women have always depended on one another for support, but the AIDS crisis has created a serious problem in this area. For many families, this "sisterhood network" and strong kinship bond of grandmothers, sisters, and aunts as caretakers has been debilitated and overburdened and can no longer provide support. In some cases, bonds were broken prior to a woman's HIV or AIDS diagnosis due to issues of substance abuse or other addictive behavior which strained extended family resources. Working with extended family members might first require healing and working through broken relationships. In some cases, HIV-positive women already have sufficient support systems in place. A critical issue will center around a woman's ability to disclose her HIV-positive status to family or to find a comfort level in maintaining her sense of privacy. When there are trusted others and sufficient social support, women are able to function more effectively.

However, these support systems may already be operational and need relief rather than more responsibility. Boyd-Franklin, Aleman, Jean-Gilles, and Lewis (1995) provide further insight into the role of extended family members as caretakers and the stressors they experience. These authors discuss how older caretakers in the extended family often serve a central role in their families as "switchboards" for all family communications. In some extreme cases, an extended family member may be responsible for multiple young members of the family (grandchildren, great-grandchildren, nieces, nephews, and younger siblings). Many of these family constellations experience devastation and disease in more than one family member. The added stress of multiple illnesses affects the capability of persons to otherwise assist with care.

The family myth that grandmothers and other extended family caretakers are "towers of strength" is true, but it does not allow the caretakers to protest when their burdens become too great (Boyd-Franklin et al. 1995). With a commitment to religious values as a strength and survival mechanism, they tend to bare their burdens from a religious perspective "God will make a way," "He will not put on me more than I can bear." Help from extended family members, as well as medical and social service systems, may not be available. Too often, no one discovers the degree of burden until a caretaker has become completely overwhelmed. In developing sensitive family interventions, we must be aware of this abiding desire among African Americans to hold on to spiritual faith and to try to hold together the extended family—sometimes at the cost of their own health.

Grandmothers are certainly among the heroines of the AIDS crisis, but they pay a high price. According to Joslin and Brouard (1995), stress associated with caregiving in later life compounded by the greater risk of poor health particularly among low-income African American elderly can potentially result in severe health risks for elderly surrogate parents. The needs of this population tend to be invisible. Grandparents raising grandchildren full time report psychosocial problems and deterioration in their psychological health due to isolation and stress from the demands of parenting. Mental health and health care providers are challenged to include preventive approaches with grandparents who are acting as social support and or surrogate parents for HIV-positive women. The task of service providers is twofold: to help grandparents open up and ask for assistance, and, more importantly, to help locate family members who can provide support or take over before the grandparents become overwhelmed. Some families have lost so many members to AIDS and other illnesses that there truly is no longer support available.

Culturally based intervention programs for caretakers of HIV-positive persons is crucial. Interventions based on culturally sensitive models of intervention which allow for flexibility in meanings attributed to existing concepts have been found to be effective as well. Boyle, Hodnicki, and Ferrell (1999) studied African American women caring for sons who were HIV-positive or had AIDS and found that allowing for flexibility in the meaning, interpretation, and operationalization of the term caretaker as observed by the mothers allowed for a more effective relationship between sons and mothers. Caretaking was reconceptualized as maintaining the relationship between both mother and son for as long as possible, as opposed to caring for someone else. The reconceptualization allowed for a mutual and reciprocal interaction between mother and son.

BARRIERS IN INTIMATE RELATIONSHIPS

Stewart (1998) and Gant (1995) provide some insight into the roles of African American men in the HIV/AIDS crisis. HIV/AIDS prevention in African American communities must acknowledge and include all members of the family, including African American men. The heterosexual male has become the invisible man. However, they are the fathers of children who are HIV-positive or who have AIDS, and the spouses and intimate partners of women who are HIV-positive or have AIDS. In many cases, men are supportive, become caretakers for ill women, and maintain responsibilities for children. Yet, intimate relationships may also place additional stress on women.

One serious relationship barrier to the well-being of HIV-positive women is domestic violence. Battering remains the primary cause of death and injury among women. Current literature regarding HIV/AIDS shows that there is a strong connection between HIV/AIDS and domestic violence (Morrill and Robbin 1997; Rice and Robbin 1995). For example, women with histories of childhood abuse or witnessing abuse of their mother have a higher risk of HIV contraction than those without such histories. Additionally, many facets of domestic violence, including control over sex, lack of power of women to engage in condom negotiation, and discomfort discussing issues related to sex contribute to the hindrance of proper care and treatment for women living with HIV and AIDS. For women, domestic violence is associated with being single or divorced, abuse of drugs, or having a partner who is a drug abuser, or obsessive or jealous. Thus, women who are living with domestic violence tend to have multiple problems, all of which interfere with their ability to cope effectively with their disease, including compliance to medical regimes.

For African American women who experience both race and gender oppression, domestic violence (also called intimate partner violence and spousal abuse) is an especially complex and multilayered demon. At the 2000 Annual Conference of the Institute on Domestic Violence in the African American community, Bylle Y. Avery, founding president of the National Black Women's Health Project, commented, "When sisters take their shoes off and start talking about what's happening, the first thing we cry about is violence-battering and sexual abuse." The widespread physical and emotional abuse that Black women suffer is a part of the secrecy that is pervasive in African American communities. The link between HIV/AIDS, sexual violence, and coercion within relationships is a significant barrier to women surviving with HIV disease. Some women do not reveal their HIV status to intimate partners or spouses because of a fear of violence, emotional abuse, or abandonment.

RELATIONSHIP-RELATED BARRIERS TO HIV-MEDICAL THERAPY COMPLIANCE

With the emergence of HAART (highly active antiretroviral therapy), we now have medical regimens that can lower death rates and allow HIV-positive persons to live with HIV as a chronic illness rather than as an immediate death sentence. In 1997, overall AIDS deaths declined for the first time, except for women (Cox 2000). HIV-infected women, particularly those who are pregnant, tend to adhere poorly to HAART (Laine et al. 2000). Even though there are advances in medicine for treatment of HIV and AIDS, compliance with treatment is a must if a patient is to receive the full benefits of such treatment. The daily experiences and responsibilities that are unique to women infected with HIV, such as home responsibilities, may hinder a woman's ability to adhere to medical regimens. Responsibilities to children, family, household chores, crises, and full- or part-time employment tend to have priority over following a treatment plan for women (Hurley and Ungvarski 1994).

Drug abuse and domestic violence are also factors associated with treatment noncompliance with HIV/AIDS treatment regimens (Stone 2000). The dynamics of violence and drug abuse need to be addressed in the provision of care to women who are HIV-positive and who have AIDS. Noncompliance with treatment due to violence and drug abuse compromises a woman's health and potential for survival.

CONCLUSION

Professionals must be cognizant of the various strengths operating in the African American community in general, and the African American family in particular, and how these strengths can be utilized in caring for a sick family member. Mobilizing and utilizing the family system can often be an effective strategy for intervening with HIV-positive women. This chapter has examined the family-relationship barriers to effective coping that women may experience. Although these barriers exist, intervention programs must begin by capitalizing on women's strengths and resources within a cultural context. Comprehensive family systems interventions are more likely to succeed when the family is treated as a whole, which helps to ensure positive outcomes for all family members.

Support groups for caregivers are needed to account for the enormous demands placed on the extended family and to prevent burnout. The issues facing heterosexual men must be addressed by including them in the service delivery system rather than excluding them and pretending that they do not exist. It is important that we continue to define and discuss the role of men and their issues and strategies for helping them to carry out their potential roles as a part of the larger informal support system for the African American female.

Many women are in need of church and community support and acceptance, whether extended family and other relationships are supportive. The Black church can therefore be an important resource for African American women and their families. The African American church as an extension of the African American family, however, must confront the issue of AIDS and understand that the disease affects all of us (Richardson 1996; Weatherford and Weatherford 1998).

HIV-affected families would benefit from policies developed at the national level to establish standards and provide resources that encourage structural permanency planning and allow mothers to keep and care for their children for as long as they can, utilizing kinship placements before a parent's death and foster care only after family resources have been explored and exhausted.

REFERENCES

Boyd-Franklin, N., Aleman, J.C., Jean-Gilles, M.M., and Lewis, S.Y. (1995). Cultural Sensitivity and Competence: African-American, Latino, and Haitian families with HIV/AIDS. In Nancy Boyd-Franklin, Gloria L. Steiner, and Mary G. Boland (Eds). *Children, families and HIV/AIDS: Psychosocial and therapeutic issues* (pp. 53–77). New York: Guilford Press.

Boyle, J.S., Hodnicki, D.R., and Ferrell, J.A. (1999). Patterns of resistance: African American mothers and adult children with HIV illness. *Scholarly Inquiry for Nursing Practice: An International Journal* 13 (2), 111–133.

Centers for Disease Control. (1995). *HIV/AIDS Surveillance Report.* 7 (1) 18.

Cohen, N., and Atwood, J.D. (1994). Women and AIDS: The social construction of gender and disease. *Family Systems and Medicine,* 12 (1), 5–20.

Cox, F.D. (2000). *The AIDS booklet.* Boston, MA: McGraw-Hill.

Farmer, P. (1996). Women, poverty and AIDS. In P. Farmer, M. Corners, and J. Simmons (Eds.), *Women, poverty and AIDS: Sex, drugs and structural violence.* Monroe, ME: Common Courage Press.

Gant, L.M. (1995). HIV/AIDS and men. In *Encyclopedia of Social Work,* 19th ed. (pp. 1306–1314). Washington, DC: NASW Press.

Hill, R.B. (1972). *The strengths of black families.* New York: Emerson Hall Publishers.

Hurley, P.M., and Ungvarski, P.J. (1994). Home healthcare needs of adults living with HIV disease/AIDS in New York City. *Journal of the Association of Nurses in AIDS Care,* 5 (2), 33–40.

Joslin, J., and Brouard, A. (1995). The prevalence of grandmothers as primary caregivers in a poor pediatric population. *Journal of Community Health,* 20 (5), 383–401.

Klein, K., Armistead, L., Devine, D., Kotchick, B., et al. (2000). Socioemotional support in African American families coping with maternal HIV: An examination of mothers' and children's psychosocial adjustment. *Behavior Therapy,* 31 1–26.

Kotchick, B.A., Forehand, R., Brody, G., Armistead, L., et al. (1999). The impact of maternal HIV infection on parenting in inner city African American families. *Journal of Family Psychology*, 11 461–557.

Laine, C., Newschaffer, C.J., Zhang, D., Coster, L., et al. (2000). Adherence to antiretroviral therapy by pregnant women infected with human immunodeficiency virus: A pharmacy based analysis. *Obstetrics and Gynecology*, 95 167–173.

Land, H. (1994). AIDS and women of color. *Families in Society*, 6 355–361.

Morrill, A.C., and Robbin, D. (1997). Violence against women and HIV risk: Implications for actions. Paper presented at the National Conference on Women and HIV, New England Research Institute.

Norlin, J.M., and Wayne, A.C. (1997). *Human behavior and the social environment: Social system theory*, 3rd ed. Boston: Allyn & Bacon.

O'Donnell, M. (1996). *HIV/AIDS: Loss, grief, challenge and hope*. Washington, DC: Taylor and Francis.

Pequegnat, W., and Bray, J. (1997). Families and HIV/AIDS: Introduction to special sections. *Journal of Family Psychology*, 11 (10), 3–10.

Pequegnat, W., and Szapocznik, J. (2000). *Working with families in the era of HIV/AIDS*. Thousand Oaks, CA: Sage.

Rice, L., and Robbin, D. (February 1995). When your relationship puts you at risk: A collaborative education campaign about the connection between HIV/AIDS and domestic violence. Paper presented at the HIV Infected Women Conference.

Richardson, W. (1996). *Reclaiming the urban family: How to mobolize the church as a family training center*. Grand Rapids, MI: Zondervan Publishing House.

Rothman, J. (1998). *Practice with highly vulnerable clients: Case management and community based services*. Englewood Cliffs, NJ: Prentice-Hall.

Shelton, D., Marconi, K., Pounds, M.B., Scopetta, M., et al. (1993). Medical adherence among prenatal HIV positive, African American women: Family issues. *Family Systems Medicine*, 11 (4), 343–356.

Stewart, P.A. (1998). Social work practice with African Americans with HIV/AIDS: Challenges to mind, body and spirit. In L.M. Gant and P.A. Stewart (Eds.), *Social workers speak out on the HIV/AIDS crisis: Voices from and to African American communities* (pp. 13–48). Westport, CT: Praeger.

Stone, V. (October, 2000). Treatment adherence and women. Paper presented at the conference on Treatment Adherence and Minorities: Opportunities for Minority Researchers. Arlington, VA.

Taylor, R., and Roberts, D. (1995). Kinship support and maternal and adolescent well-being in economically disadvantaged African American families. *Child Development*, 66 1585–1597.

Ward, M.C. (1993). A different disease: HIV/AIDS and health care for women in poverty. *Culture, Medicine and Psychiatry* 17 413–430.

Weatherford, C.B., and Weatherford, R.J. (1998). *Somebody's knocking at your door: AIDS and the African American church*. Binghamton, NY: Haworth Press.

5

African American HIV-Affected Children and Adolescents: Intersecting Vulnerabilities

Dorie J. Gilbert

Children and adolescents are considered HIV-affected if they have experienced the death or chronic illness of one or both parents from HIV disease. The majority of these children are healthy and may also lose one or more siblings to the disease. Micheals and Levine (1992) estimated that 80,000 HIV-infected women of childbearing age in the United States who were alive in 1992 would leave approximately 125,000 to 150,000 children orphaned. However, because many HIV-infected parents are living longer due to the increased prophylactic benefits of antiretroviral treatments, a growing number of HIV-affected children and adolescents are living with a chronically ill parent or sibling. We know that African Americans have been disproportionately affected by AIDS, accounting for nearly 50 percent of AIDS cases although they represent only 13 percent of the U.S. population, with African American women accounting for 63 percent of women with AIDS and African American children representing nearly two-thirds (65 percent) of pediatric AIDS cases (CDC 2002). Consequently, the vast majority HIV-affected children and adolescents are African American.

In general, HIV-affected children and adolescents are exposed to major psychological risk factors including "stigma, secrecy, exposure to acute and chronic illness, death of parents and/or siblings, separations, losses, orphanhood, and foster home placement—all of which are often experienced in an environment of poverty, drugs, alcohol, violence, abuse" (Lewis 1995, 50). Ironically, HIV-affected children and adolescents may themselves be at high risk for HIV-infection because, in some cases, unresolved trauma and ineffective coping may result in early and unsafe sexual practices and/or experimentation with drugs. Moreover, HIV-affected African American children and adolescents contend with the additional burden of racial inequality. Compounding their exposure to multiple losses associated with AIDS, stigma, and death, and parental chronic illness, it has been well documented that African American children and adolescents face social disadvantages, particularly within the child welfare system. Indeed, the variables that act collectively to support the disproportionate number of AIDS cases among African Americans—poverty, institutional racism, economic vulnerability, discrimination, and isolation—create broader barriers to effective coping with loss and result in a tangled array of intersecting vulnerabilities.

This chapter discusses how the intersection of AIDS, childhood trauma due to parental loss or chronic illness, and historical and current racial inequality create unique vulnerabilities for HIV-affected African American children and adolescents. First, concerns are delineated about African American AIDS orphans entering out-of-home, nonkinship placements given their already precarious status in the child welfare system. Next, the vulnerabilities of children within formal or informal kinship care systems are addressed because children absorbed into extended family or kinship placements may also remain at increased psychosocial risk due to a complex array of losses, the pervasive stigma of AIDS, and continued exposure to the vicissitudes of poverty and social isolation, which also impact the entire kinship family system. The chapter then outlines the experiences of children and adolescents living with a chronically ill, HIV-infected parent and the challenges they face. Finally, the author discusses the potential for resiliency among this group as a result of personal and environmental protective factors which can buffer trauma and adversity for this population. The summary highlights the need for community-based, family-oriented, and culturally sound interventions to HIV-affected families.

THE INTERACTION OF AIDS, PARENTAL LOSS, AND RACIAL INEQUALITY

Parental death during childhood may have enduring traumatic effects (Adams-Greenley and Moynihan 1983). Perry et al. (1995) found that relative to the length of time a child remains in trauma, emotional states are programmed into the developing nervous system. In essence, "childhood trauma, then, has the potential of influencing the emotional responses of human beings to various stimuli for a lifetime" (20–21). Bereaved children may experience increased risk for depression (Balk 1983; Bifulco, Brown, and Harris 1987; Raphael, Field, and Kvelde 1980; Rutter 1966; Saler and Skolnick 1992), conduct disturbance (Chiefetz, Stavrakakis, and Lester, 1989; Maddison and Raphael 1972; Raphael 1983), and suicide (Berlinksy and Biller 1982; Osterweis, Solomon, and Green 1984).

Much of the established literature on childhood bereavement has focused on parental death from cancer; however the nature of bereavement trauma changes significantly when death is due to AIDS. Parental death due to AIDS presents severe stress for HIV-affected families because AIDS is a stigmatized illness associated with preventability and lack of social support, unlike diseases such as cancer (Rando 1993). Bereavement reactions of children and adolescents are very strongly influenced by the dynamics of social attitudes prior to parental death and the grieving process, and for AIDS, we have no models or socially prescribed roles for AIDS mourners (Dane 1994). AIDS is also associated with disenfranchisement. Most HIV-affected children are living with poor single mothers of color with a history of their own or their partner's substance abuse (Land 1994). Rather than progressing through the bereavement process with empathic support and societal understanding, children and adolescents and their families are often forced to keep the nature of their loved one's death a secret. At the same time, they also lack needed resources. Due to multiple losses and family stressors, HIV-affected children and adolescents may be considered at developmental Risk (Brazdziunas, Roizen, Kohrman, and Smith, 1994).

Fears and separation anxieties that are normally present with childhood bereavement may be heightened for HIV-affected children, especially when children suffer multiple AIDS deaths within a family or among other people known to the child (Siegel and Freund 1994). When parents have acquired AIDS through drug use, children may internalize thoughts of death as a punishment for their own or others' bad behavior. The stigma surrounding AIDS may evoke a need for secrecy and hinder the child's ability to openly mourn or express feelings about the death. Behavior and self-concept changes may also be intensified by parental death from AIDS. Subtle behavioral changes such as withdrawn behavioral, disorganized play, or aggressive behavior often underlie a child's attempts to resolve the bereavement trauma. Research findings suggest that children's awareness of characteristics that set them apart from other children can potentially lead to low self-concept or negative self-evaluations (Kessler and Klein 1995; Moore and Polsgrove 1991). Potentially, children can experience hopelessness, emotional emptiness, worthlessness, fear of dependency on others, and a general sense of uncertainty about the world. Unresolved grief can result in personal, interpersonal, and social problems in the future.

For the most part, childhood bereavement literature discusses the impact of early losses for children under circumstances that would be considered favorable compared with the situation faced by most AIDS orphans. However, because the vast majority of children affected by AIDS are living with an HIV-positive mother in a single-mother household, parental loss almost invariably propels them into an orphanage status and displacement from their homes. When children are placed in out-of-home care, they may enter group homes, emergency shelters, residential treatment centers, kinship foster care, or nonkinship foster care. What does this mean for the African American AIDS orphans who enter an overburdened child welfare system already experiencing disproportionately high numbers of African American children? Furthermore, what does this mean for children absorbed into kinship care (both formal and informal child placement with relatives), among, in most cases, an already impoverished, overtaxed extended family system? Psychosocial concerns are prominent in both nonkin-ship and kinship care.

PSYCHOSOCIAL WELL-BEING IN NON-KINSHIP CARE

Both historically and currently, African American children experience dis-proportionately negative outcomes associated with the child welfare system (Hogan and Siu 1988; Taylor, Chatters, Tucker, and Lewis 1990). Historically, African American children have long been impacted by racism and insensitive policies within the child welfare system which have resulted in inequitable treatment and services. In the 1700s and early 1800s, evidence suggests that Black children who were placed in almshouses or indentured were treated more harshly than other children, and Black children were initially excluded from the developing foster care system during the late 1800s (Billingsley and Giovannoni 1972). Although the civil rights movement and growth of federal social welfare institutions in the 1960s spotlighted these inequities, exclu-sionary and discriminatory practices continued to negatively impact minority children in the child welfare system.

Over the past several decades, child welfare has maintained a critical presence in the lives of African American families, as a direct result of high rates of poverty, incarceration, and substance abuse, particularly the crack-cocaine epi-demic in the 1980s. The AIDS pandemic has placed the child welfare system even more visibly in the affairs of African American families. Currently, African American children are overrepresented in child abuse and neglect reporting and in the foster care system. The Child Welfare League of America (CWLA) 1997 statistical report indicates that African American children are overrepresented in both foster care (family and kinship relative care) and in group care (resi-dential treatment and group homes) compared with the entire U.S. child popu-lation (Petit and Curtis 1997). For example, African American children represent 52 percent of children in family foster care, although they comprise only 15 per-cent of children in the general population. Petit and Curtis (1997) note that an array of factors, "including discrimination, poverty, single parenthood, domes-tic violence, substance abuse, racism, staffing patterns, and staff decision mak-ing [are] all likely associated with this over presentation" (88).

Although most children and youths entering foster care will return home to their families or be adopted, it is estimated that one in four will remain in fos-ter care until late adolescence (Barth, Courtney, Berrick, and Albert 1994). In general, African American children wait longer on average for placement, enter at younger ages, remain in foster care for longer periods of time, and undergo more multiple placements relative to Caucasian children in the same system (Fein 1991; Taylor, Chatters, Tucker, and Lewis 1990). With the growing num-ber of AIDS orphans, this number would be expected to rise, particularly for African American foster children because they receive less in-home support ser-vices and have less likelihood of adoptive placements (Fein 1991). Significant obstacles in general undermine positive foster care outcomes for African American children due to differential treatment in the child welfare system. For instance, although African Americans are overrepresented in the child welfare system, they are underrepresented in the administration and vital decision-making positions that will impact their lives (Brown and Bailey-Etta 1997). One result of this discrepancy is that African American children may receive unfair evaluations, inappropriate placements, or damaging services (Gould 1991).

Children who are bereaved by AIDS present new and complex challenges to child welfare agencies. Clearly, if African American children lack a positive history with the child welfare system, the stigma associated with AIDS only exacerbates the situation for HIV-infected and HIV-affected children. For example, one study documented the prevalent fears and disruptions among foster parents of HIV-positive children. Among the greatest fears and doubts of foster parents were "fear of infection or transmission; child dying while in care; stigma [or] community opinion, or discrimination; and dealing with the natural family, especially those who are HIV-positive" (Cohen and Nehring 1994, 65). Of great concern are rejections of HIV-positive foster children by older natural siblings and the limited number of foster parents willing to accept HIV-positive children and/or sibling groups, the overwhelming majority of whom are African American (Cohen and Nehring 1994).

In essence, children who are already traumatized by a parental death due to AIDS will enter the child welfare system most likely displaying a number of emotional and behavioral responses to their grief. They may become quiet or withdrawn. Conversely, they may exhibit noncompliant and aggressive behavior that is symptomatic of grief and underlying feelings of fear, anxiety, anger, and resentment related to the loss of a loved one (Ormond and Charbonneau 1995). Both responses may place children at increased risk for abuse or mistreatment within foster care and other substitute placements. Aggressive and noncompliant behavior may increase the already strong likelihood that African American youths will be placed in more restrictive substitute care placements or referred to the juvenile justice system because of culturally biased services and decision making. While grappling with trauma and grief, AIDS orphans in nonrelative substitute care face vulnerability within the very system designed to help them.

Children in foster care approach developmental challenges with the added stress of being separated from their families of origin. In addition, separation and loss associated with AIDS adds another layer of complexity. Without strong interventions from within the child welfare system for these children, a lifetime of vulnerability will likely be set in motion. Early disruptions in attachment and stability can result in poor coping patterns that are established during childhood and remain part of personality functioning throughout life (Bowlby 1988). Although there is some debate about the long-term impact of foster care on children (see Lyman and Bird 1996 for a discussion on conflicting findings), studies have reported substantial social adjustment problems for children who have experienced multiple or lengthy placements in the foster care system. In writing about children in foster care, Toth (1997) comments that "once in the system, children have less chance of being adopted than they do of becoming homeless, getting pregnant as a teen, dropping out of school, or winding up in prison" (20). Others have noted problems with identity and self-esteem (Palmer 1990; Salahu-Din and Bollman 1994) and behavioral and psychosocial problems (Gil and Bogart 1982; McIntyre and Keesler 1986). Lyman and Bird (1996) investigated domains of self-image among male foster care adolescents and found that, contrary to other investigations, foster care youths did not have lower self-esteem than adolescents in the normative population. These researchers also discuss their unexpected findings that African American males in foster care did not have lower self-image scores compared with their White male counterparts. This finding conflicts with previous reports of low self-esteem among African American foster care youths due to prolonged stays and more frequent placements. Lyman and Bird (1996) offer two possible explanations. One explanation is that African American males may be more resilient than their White, male counterparts. However, a second explanation, referred to as the "creaming" effect, is that African American youths are held to higher standards; thus, only the most well functioning of the group are able to avoid the more restrictive foster care placements and/or referrals to the juvenile justice system (Festinger 1983). In either case, the adversity faced by African American youths in the foster care system cannot be minimized and must be factored into the concerns of the predominantly African American AIDS orphans.

PSYCHOSOCIAL WELL-BEING IN KINSHIP CARE

The term "kinship care" originated from the writings of Stack (1974), which emphasized the concept of extended family networks in the African American community. Heger and Scannapieco (1995) define kinship care as "the full-time nurturing and protection of children who must be separated from their parents by relatives, members of their tribes or clans, godparents, stepparents, or other adults who have a kinship bond with the child" (201). Historically, several federal child welfare policies have paved the way for a child's placement with relatives beginning with the Child Welfare Act of 1978, which required agencies to keep Native American children in kinship homes whenever possible. The practice of kinship caregiving includes both formal and informal child placement with relatives. Formal kinship care, where the child is in the legal custody of the state welfare agency, has been on the rise for the past two decades. In several large states, kinship placements constitute almost half of the out-of-home placements (Berrick, Barth, and Needell 1994). In addition, many children are part of informal kinship arrangements where they reside with a relative but are not wards of the state.

Among African Americans, the development of kinship care can be traced back to the "village" or collective community concept of West Africans where extended families held responsibility for children (Martin and Martin 1983). Several authors have noted the extension of this concept during slavery and throughout the history of Blacks in this country (Billingsley and Giovannoni, 1972; Martin and Martin 1985). During the 1970s and 1980s, formal kinship care among African American extended families increased due to a decline in the availability of nonrelative foster families simultaneous to a rise in urban problems, particularly substance abuse. In writing about African American kinship care, Danzy and Jackson (1997, 37) note that "the terms family preservation and kinship care are interchangeable ... both are ways of sustaining and maintaining the family system." Kinship care, among other aims, reinforces the social status that comes from belonging to a family of one's own and the sense of identity and self-esteem that is inherent in knowing one's family history and culture (Heger 1993, 370). However, the stigma that surrounds AIDS can act to silence families and create an environment of shame rather than pride within extended family systems. Thus, children may not receive the positive messages about deceased parents that is needed to instill and sustain a positive sense of parental attachment.

Historically, much attention has been given to the availability of grandparents and extended family members for children of color, particularly African American children. However, recent concerns have been raised about the state's increased use of kinship care without giving increased attention to meeting the needs of overburdened extended kinship caretakers. Children can be placed at further risk if child welfare and other agencies overlook the stress and strain experienced by relatives who take the responsibility of caring for ill or surviving well children. Caretakers, who are primarily grandmothers and aunts, are likely to have their physical and emotional capacities severely taxed. Brown and Bailey-Etta (1997) warn against child welfare agencies pursuing kinship care arrangements as a cost-effective way to avoid providing supportive services to children and families in need. The reality is that in most cases families providing kinship care are poor, suffer from the same lack of resources as the child's biological parent (Brown and Bailey-Etta 1997), and receive fewer services than do nonrelative foster care arrangements (Dubowitz 1994). Elderly grandmothers may also be in ill health (Nicholas and Abrams 1992). In some cases, AIDS may strike members of both the immediate and extended family. In essence, kinship caregivers and extended family members are vulnerable themselves as they struggle with grief complicated by poverty and role strain. The result may be more family breakdown and increased vulnerability for some children in kinship care.

THE INTERACTION OF AIDS, PARENTAL CHRONIC ILLNESS, AND RACIAL INEQUALITY

Chronic illness of a parent is a very stressful event for a family, and it can negatively impact a child's mental health (Armistead, Klein, and Forehand 1995; Beardslee and Wheelock 1994; Christ, Siegel, and Sperber 1994; Coyne and Downey 1991; Dohrenwend and Dohrenwend 1981; Mireault and Bond 1992;

Rutter 1966; Siegal et al. 1992; Stuifberger 1990). Armistead, Klein, and Forehand (1995) outline dimensions of illness that may be important in the relationship between parental illness and family functioning: disruption of parenting, parental depression, conflict between family members, and, perhaps, ultimately family breakdown. Parental chronic illness has been associated with somaticizing behaviors among children, particularly if the parent models maladaptive responses to pain and illness (Bass and Murphy 1995; Morgan, Sanford, and Johnson 1992; Stein and Newcomb, 1994) and absent or inadequate parenting (Mallouh, Abbey, and Gielies 1995). In addition, children with a chronically ill sibling are more likely than their peers to experience difficulty, decreased self-esteem, and somatic complaints (McKeever 1983).

When the parent's chronic illness is due to AIDS, children have the added stress of AIDS stigma and sometimes chaotic family life related to drug use and/or poverty (Garnier and Weisner 1994; Rotheram-Borus, Draimin, Murphy, and Reid 1997; Zayas and Romano 1994). In a longitudinal study of HIV-infected parents and their adolescent children, the parents' poor physical health was found to be significantly associated with the adolescent's internalizing mental health symptoms; adolescents with more symptomatic parents reported significantly more somatic complaints of psychosocial origin (Rotheram-Borus and 1999). Lewis (1995) notes that "a child's or adolescent's fear of the outcome for the ill family member—as well as anxiety on his or her own behalf—may lead to counterphobic risk taking that includes, in adolescents, high-risk sexual encounters and drug abuse" (52). Parents' risk behaviors and their ways of coping with AIDS as a chronic illness have serious implications for their children's mental health and behavior. Parents' substance use has been shown to be significantly associated with adolescents' externalizing behavior problems. Adolescents whose parents had high rates of substance use were significantly more likely to engage in marijuana use, risky sexual behavior, and conduct problems, each of which is an externalizing symptom of mental health problems (Rotheram-Borus and Stein 1999).

Familial reactions to HIV-infection can result in the realignment of roles between parents and children (Fair, Spencer, Wiener, and Riekert 1995; Faithful 1997). For example, children may become subject to parentification or the acting out of parental roles within the family (Stein, Reidel, and Rotheram-Borus 1999), which may cause them to feel unfairly burdened or punished (Andiman 1995). Some adolescents may immerse themselves in adultlike activities to keep busy and avoid painful feelings, get attention or approval of parents, or convey a sense of readiness to take on life's tasks in the absence of the parent (Zayas and Romano 1994). On the other hand, Anderson (1999) writes about parentification within an African American family context and makes the point that values such as collectivism and shared responsibility may explain part of what is labeled "parentified" among children of color.

Because the majority of HIV-affected children and adolescents are poor, African American, and disenfranchised, this raises great concern about the mental health and social outcomes for this population as they attempt to cope with a parent's HIV-related illnesses, especially given their already precarious status in our society (Glbert 2000). Forehand et al. (1998) examined the association between maternal HIV status and psychosocial adjustment in healthy, HIV-affected children in inner-city African American families as compared with children from non-HIV-affected families. Findings from this study indicate that maternal HIV-infection is associated with child psychological adjustment difficulties in multiple domains; internalizing problems, externalizing problems, prosocial competence, and cognitive competence. Of interest is the fact that among Forehand's total sample of inner-city African American children, scores of mental health and cognitive functioning for both groups were in the clinical (or educational) range or below average scores for many of the measures. Thus, one critical point is that the preexisting conditions of poverty and racial inequality exacerbate children's psychosocial adjustment, whether or not the parent is HIV-infected. The triple burden of loss and illness associated with a parent's HIV-infection creates the situation of a severely overburdened childhood (Draimin 1993; Hudis 1995; Rotheram-Borus, Draimin, Murphy, and Reid 1997; Zayas and Romano 1994). This may result in self-destructive coping behaviors, conduct problems at home and school, problems related to custodial placements, externalizing behavior problems (substance use, sexual risks, and conduct problems), and somatic symptoms related to their parents' physical health (Rotheram-Borus and Stein 1999).

However, with effective coping skills, HIV-affected children and adolescents can be extremely resilient (Draimin, Hudis, Segura, and Shire, 1999; Rotheram-Borus and Stein, 1999). For example, among the longitudinal sample of HIV-affected, primarily African American and Hispanic youths studied by Rotheram-Borus and colleagues, severe emotional distress and behavioral problems were lower than expected; however, the adolescents reported high levels of grief, which, *if unresolved*, will have a significant impact on their accomplishment of developmental milestones (Rotheram-Borus and Stein 1999). The emphasis must be on assisting these youth and families in resolving grief and coping with HIV-related stress and losses whether they are a part of the child welfare system, living with extended family and guardians, or living with a chronically ill parent.

RESILIENCY

The intersecting losses brought on by AIDS stigma, parental and/or sibling loss, and inequality can appear insurmountable. Yet children have been known to adapt in the most unfavorable of conditions. Valentine and Feinauer (1993) define resiliency as "the power or ability to overcome adversity, survive stress, and rise above disadvantage" (222). The ability of HIV-affected African American children and adolescents to move through their losses and effectively cope with the challenges they face is dependent on both individual traits and environmental changes. Personal characteristics leading to resilience might include ego strengths, secure attachments, a sense of competence, positive coping strategies, traits of adaptability, and a sense of empowerment (Begun 1993). Consistent with their readiness to learn, children may ask biologically specific or scientific questions about the parent's death as a way of adapting to the parental loss. Children also experience adaptive ways of mourning differently from adults. Bowlby (1980) describes three stages of childhood mourning: (1) protest or denial of death; (2) pain, despair and disorganization, and regression; and finally (3) hope prevails as children reorganize their lives for the future.

Resilience among parents and children is often related to the fact that children can provide the motivation for women to recover and abstain from drugs, as well as obtain needed resources to keep the family intact (Gilbert 1999; Gillman and Newman 1996; Hackl, Somlai, Kally, and Kalichman 1997). Thus, priority should be given to helping parents maintain a sense of integrity in their parental role (Gilbert 1999). Because most HIV-infected parents may look to close relatives and extended family to provide guardianship and other parenting assistance, it is important to heal family and kinship bonds in cases where HIV-infected parents may be estranged from extended families due to previous drug use or other issues. Thus, strengthening family bonds with extended family may also be important to helping HIV-affected children.

Reducing the parent's health and psychological distress will obviously positively impact the entire family system (Compas 1987; Compas, Phares, and Lordoux 1989; Glyshaw, Cohen, and Towbes 1989; Patterson and McCubbin 1983), and for most African American families, this involves both individual and community-based support, evident in the theme of many HIV-positive African Americans needing to be recognized and accepted, and not ostracized, by their community. Thus, the availability of supportive individuals and a responsive community can act as protective factors to decrease psychosocial risks for children and families. Clearly, children who are able to establish a sense of unconditional attachment to one or more special persons are likely to be less vulnerable to poor functioning. The community also plays a large role in the adjustment of HIV-affected youth. Children will need help within a family-based intervention approach that includes community-based services. This includes providing assistance to HIV-infected parents to increase their quality of life, which is significantly associated with a prolonging life for HIV-infected persons (Stanton et al., 1994). Holistic service delivery approaches such as substance abuse treatment, individual and family counseling, and child placement services that are truly in the best interest of the child and family are recommended. In addition, interventions which include stigma reduction approaches are crucial to helping HIV-affected families cope effectively and manage the stress related to HIV/AIDS.

SUMMARY AND IMPLICATIONS

HIV-affected African American children and adolescents face unique challenges due to the intersecting losses associated with AIDS stigma, death and chronic illness, and institutionalized racism. Any programs or initiatives aimed at this population must consider addressing these issues in tandem; however, the fact that programs do not always address multifaceted problems helps explain why African American HIV-affected children and families are also underrepresented in AIDS service utilization. This is due not only to the cultural and societal stigma of AIDS, but also because of a lack of accessibility to counseling services, slowness of social service agencies to provide culturally sensitive services, and, in many cases, a family's general mistrust of public agencies. Thus, enough cannot be said about the continued need for culturally grounded, family-based intervention programs designed specifically for HIV-affected African American families.

REFERENCES

Adams-Greenley, M., and Moynihan, M.S. (1983). Helping children of fatally ill parents. *American Journal of Orthopsychiatry*, 53 (2), 219–229.

Anderson, Louis P. (1999). Parentification in the context of the African American family. In Nancy D. Chase (Ed). *Burdened children: Theory, research, and treatment of parentification* (pp. 154–170). Thousand Oaks, CA: Sage Publications.

Andiman, W. (1995). Medical aspects of AIDS: What do children witness? In S. Geballe, J. Gruendel, and W. Andiman (Eds.), *Forgotten children of the AIDS epidemic* (pp. 32–49). New Haven, CT: Yale University Press.

Armistead. L., Klein, K., and Forehand, R. (1995). Parental physical illness and child functioning. *Child Psychology Review*, 15 409–422.

Balk, D.E. (1983). Effects of sibling death on teenagers. *Journal of School Health*, 53 14–18.

Barth, R.P., Courtney, M.E., Berrick, J.D., and Albert, V. (1994). *From child abuse to permanency planning: Child welfare services, pathways and placements*. New York: Aldine de Gruyter.

Bass C., and Murphy M. (1995). Somatoform and personality disorders: Syndromal co-morbidity and overlapping developmental pathways. *Journal of Psychosomatic Research*, 39 403–427.

Beardslee, W.R., and Wheelock, I. (1994). Children of parents with affective disorders: Empirical findings and clinical implications. In W.R. Reynolds and H.F. Johnston (Eds.), *Handbook of depression in children and adolescents*. New York: Plenum Publishers.

Begun, A. (1993). Human behavior and the social environment: The vulnerability, risk, and resilience model. *Journal of Social Work Education*, 29 (1), 26–36.

Berlinsky, E.B., and Biller, H.B. (1982). *Parental death and psychological development*. Lexington, MA: D.C. Heath.

Berrick, J.D., Barth, R.P., and Needell, B. (1994). A comparison of kinship foster homes and foster family homes: Implications for kinship foster care as family preservation. *Children and Youth Services Review*, 16 33–63.

Bifulco, A., Brown, G., and Harris, T. (1987) Childhood loss of parent, lack of adequate parental care and adult depression. *Journal of Affective Discordance*, 12 (2), 15–128.

Billingsley, A., and Giovannoni, J.M. (1972). *Children in the storm: Black children and American child welfare*. New York: Harcourt Brace Jovanovich.

Bowlby, J. (1980). *Attachment and loss,* Volume III. New York: Basic Books.

——. (1988). *A secure base: Parent-child attachment and healthy human development.* New York: Basic Books.

Brazdziunas, D.M., Roizen, N.J., Kohrman, A.F., and Smith, D.K. (1994). Children of HIV-positive parents: Implications for intervention. *Psychosocial Rehabilitation Journal,* 17 (94), 145–149.

Brown, A.W., and Bailey-Etta, B. (1997). An out-of-home care system in crisis: Implications for African American children in the child welfare system. *Child Welfare,* 76 65–83.

Centers for Disease Control and Prevention, Division of HIV/AIDS Prevention. (2002). HIV/AIDS among African Americans [fact sheet].

Chiefetz, P., Stavrakakis, G., and Lester, E. (1989). Studies of the affective state in bereaved children. *Canadian Journal of Psychiatry,* 34 688–692.

Christ, G.H., Siegel, K., and Sperber, D. (1994). Impact of parental terminal cancer on adolescents. *American Journal of Orthopsychiatry,* 64 (4), 604–613.

Cohen, F.L., and Nehring, W.M. (1994). Foster care of HIV-positive children in the United States. *Public Health Reports,* 109 (1), 60–67.

Compas, B.E. (1987). Coping with stress during childhood and adolescence. *Psychological Bulletin,* 101 393–401.

Compas, B.E., Phares, V., and Lordoux, N. (1989). Stress and coping preventive interventions for children and adolescents. In L. Bond and B.E. Compas (Eds.), *Primary prevention and promotion in the schools.* Newbury Park, CA: Sage.

Coyne, J.C., and Downey, G. (1991). Social factors and psychopathology: Stress, social support, and coping processes. *Annual Review of Psychology,* 42 401–425.

Dane, B. (1994). Death and bereavement. In B. Dane and C. Levine (Eds.), *AIDS and the new orphans* (pp. 13–31). Westport, CT: Auburn House.

Danzy, J., and Jackson, S.M. (1997). Family preservation and support services: A missed opportunity for kinship care. *Child Welfare,* 76 31–44.

Dohrenwend, B.P., and Dohrenwend, B.S. (1981). Socioenvironmental factors, stress, and psychopathology. *American Journal of Community Psychology,* 9 (2), 128–164.

Draimin, B. (1993). Adolescents in families with AIDS: Growing up with loss. In C. Levine (Ed.), *A death in the family: Orphans of the HIV/AIDS epidemic* (pp. 13–23). New York: United Hospital Fund.

Draimin, B.H., Hudis, J., Segura, J., and Shire, A. (1999). A troubled present, an uncertain future: Well adolescents in families with AIDS. *Journal of HIV/AIDS Prevention and Education for Adolescents and Children,* 3 (2/3), 37–50.

Dubowitz, H. (1994). Kinship care: Suggestions for future research. *Child Welfare.* Vol. 73 (5), 553–564.

Fair, C.C., Spencer, E.D., Wiener, L., and Riekert, K. (1995). Healthy children in families affected by AIDS: Epidemiology and psychosocial considerations. *Child and Adolescent Social Work Journal,* 12 (3), 165–181.

Faithfull, J. (1997). HIV-positive and AIDS-infected women: Challenges and difficulties of mothering. *American Journal of Orthopsychiatry,* 67 (1), 144–151.

Fein, E. (1991). Issues in foster family care: Where do we stand? *American Journal of Orthopsychiatry,* 61 578–583.

Festinger, T. (1983). *No one ever asked us: A postscript to foster care.* New York: Columbia University Press.

Forehand, R., Steele, R., Armistead, L., Simon, P., et al. (1998). The family health project: Psychosocial adjustment of children whose mothers are HIV infected. *Journal of Consulting and Clinical Psychology,* 66 (3), 513–520.

Garnier, H., and Weisner, T.S. (February 1994). A longitudinal study on the effects of family life style, values, and drug use on adolescents' achievement. Paper presented at the Society for Research on Adolescence, San Diego, CA.

Gil, E., and Bogart, K. (1982). An exploratory study of self-esteem and quality of care of 1000 children in foster care. *Children and Youth Services Review*, 4 351–363.

Gilbert, D.J. (1999). In the best interest of the child: Maintaining family integrity among HIV-positive mothers, children, and adolescents. *Journal of HIV/AIDS Prevention and Education for Adolescents and Children*, 3 (2/3), 99–117.

———. (2000). Cultural competence: Assessing child welfare, school, and community services to HIV-affected families. Paper presented at the 14th Annual National Black Family Summit Proceedings, University of South Carolina College of Social Work, Columbia, SC.

Gillman, R.R., and Newman, B.S. (1996). Psychosocial concerns and strengths of women with HIV infection: An empirical study. *Families in Society: The Journal of Contemporary Human Services*, 77 (3), 131–141.

Glyshaw, K., Cohen, L.H., and Towbes, L.C. (1989). Coping strategies and psychological distress: Prospective analysis of early and middle adolescents. *American Journal of Community Psychology*, 17 607–623.

Gould, K.H. (1991). Limiting damage is not enough: A minority perspective on child welfare. In J.E. Everett, S.S. Chipungu, and B.R. Leashore (Eds.). *Child welfare: An Africentric perspective* (pp. 58–78). New Brunswick, NJ: Rutgers University Press.

Hackl, K.L., Somlai, A.M., Kelly, J.A., and Kalichman, S.C. (1997). Women living with HIV/AIDS: The dual challenge of being a patient and caregiver. *Health & Social Work*, 22 53–62.

Hegar, R. (1993). Assessing attachment, permanence, and kinship in choosing permanent homes. *Child Welfare*, 72 (4), 367–378.

Hegar, R., and Scannapieco, M. (1995). From family duty to family policy: The evolution of kinship care. *Child Welfare*, 74 200–216.

Hogan, P.T., and Siu, S.F. (1988). Minority children and the child welfare system: A historical perspective. *Social Work*, 45 493–497.

Hudis, J. (1995). Adolescents living in families with AIDS. In S. Geballe, J. Gruendel, and W. Andiman (Eds.), *Forgotten children of the AIDS epidemic* (pp. 83–94). New Haven, CT: Yale University.

Kessler, D.T., and Klein, M.A. (1995). Drug use patterns and risk factors of adolescents with physical disabilities. *The International Journal of Addictions*, 30 (10), 1243–1270.

Land, H. (1994). AIDS and women of color. *Families in Society*, 75 355–361.

Lewis, M. (1995). The special case of the uninfected child in the HIV-affected family: Normal development tasks and the child's concerns about illness and death. In S. Geballe, J. Gruendel, and W. Andiman (Eds.), *Forgotten children of the AIDS epidemic* (pp. 50–63). New Haven, CT: Yale University Press.

Lyman, S.B., and Bird, G.W. (1996). A closer look at self-image in male foster care adolescents. *Social Work*, 41 (1), 85–96.

Maddison, D., and Raphael, B. (1972). The family of the dying patient. In B. Schoenberg, A.C. Carr, D. Peretz, and A.H. Dutscher (Eds.), *Psychosocial aspects of terminal care*. New York: Columbia University Press.

Mallouh, S.K., Abbey, S.E., and Gillies, L.A. (1995). The role of loss in treatment outcomes of persistent somatization. *General Hospital Psychiatry*, 17 (3), 187–191.

Martin, J.M., and Martin, E.P. (1985). *The helping tradition in the Black family and community*. Silver Spring, MD: National Association of Social Workers.

McIntyre, A., and Keesler, T.Y. (1986). Psychological disorders among foster children. *Journal of Clinical Child Psychology*, 15 (4), 297–303.

McKeever, P. (1983). Siblings of chronically ill children: A literature review with implications for research and practice. *American Journal of Orthopsychiatry*, 53 (2), 209–218.

Michaels, D., and Levine, C. (1992). Estimates of the number of motherless youth orphaned by AIDS in the United States. *Journal of the American Medical Association*, 268 3456–3461.

Mireault, G.C., and L.S. Bond. (1992). Parental death in childhood: Perceived vulnerability and adult depression and anxiety. *American Journal of Orthopsychiatry*, 62 (4), 517–524.

Moore, D., and Polsgrove, L. (1991). Disabilities, developmental handicaps, and substance misuse: A review. *International Journal of the Addictions*, 26 (1), 65–90.

Morgan, J., Sanford, M., and Johnson, C. (1992). The impact of a physically ill parent on adolescents: Cross-sectional findings from a clinic population. *Can J Psychiatry* 37 423–427.

Nicholas, S.W., and Abrams, E.J. (1992). The 'silent' legacy of AIDS: Children who survive their parents. *Journal of the American Medical Association*, 23 3478–3479.

Ormond, E., and Charbonneau, H. (1995). Grief responses and group treatment interventions for five- to eight-year-old children. In D.W. Adams and E.J. Deveau (Eds.), *Beyond the innocence of childhood*, volume 3. *Helping children and adolescents cope with death and bereavement* (pp. 188–201). Amityville, NY: Baywood Publishing.

Osterweis, M., Solomon, F., and Green, M. (1984). *Bereavement: Reactions, consequences, and care*. Washington, DC: National Academy Press.

Palmer, S.E. (1990). Group treatment of foster children to reduce separation conflicts associated with placement breakdown. *Child Welfare*, 69 227–238.

Patterson, J.M., and McCubbin, H.I. (1983). Chronic illness: Family stress and coping. In C.R. Figley and H.I. McCubbin (Eds.), *Stress and the family II: Coping with catastrophe*. NY: Bruner Mazel.

Perry, B.D., Pollard, R.A., Blakley, T.L., Baker, W.L., et al. (1995). Childhood trauma, the neurobiology of adaptation and use-dependent development of the brain: How states become traits. *Infant Mental Health Journal*, 16 (4).

Petit, M.R., and Curtis, P.A. (1997). *Child abuse and neglect: A look at the States, 1997 CWLA stat book*. Washington, DC: CWLA Press.

Rando, T. (1993). *Treatment of complicated mourning*. Champaign, IL: Research Press.

Raphael, B. (1983) *The anatomy of bereavement*. New York: Basic Books.

Raphael, B., Field, J., and Kvelde, H. (1980). Childhood bereavement: A prospective study as a possible prelude to future preventive intervention. In E.J. Anthony and C. Cluvard (Eds.), *Preventative child psychiatry in an age of transitions*, (pp. 507–519). New York: Wiley Interscience.

Rotheram-Borus, M.J., Draimin, B.H., Murphy, D.A., and Reid, H.M. (1997). The impact of illness disclosure and custody plans on adolescents whose parents live with AIDS. *AIDS*, 11 1159–1164.

Rotheram-Borus M.J., and Stein J.A. (1999). Problem behaviors among adolescents whose parents are living with AIDS. *American Journal of Orthopsychiatry*, 69 228–229.

Rutter, M. (1966). *Children of sick parents: An environmental and psychiatric study.* London: Oxford University Press.

Salahu-Din, S.N., and Bollman, S.R. (1994). Identity development and self-esteem of young adolescents in foster care. *Child and Adolescent Social Work Journal,* 11 (2), 123–135.

Saler, L., and Skolnick, N. (1992). Childhood parental death and depression in adulthood: Roles of surviving parent and family environment. *American Journal of Orthopsychiatry,* 62 (4), 504–524.

Sandler, I.N., West, S.G., Baca, L., Pillow, D.R., et al. (1992). Linking empirically based theory and evaluation: The family bereavement program. *American Journal of Community Psychology,* 20 (4), 491–521.

Siegel, K., and Freund, B. (1994). Parental loss and latency-age children. In B.O. Dane and C. Levine (Eds.), *AIDS and the new orphans: Coping and death* (pp. 43–58). Westport, CT: Auburn House.

Siegel, K., Mesagno, F., Karus, D., Christ, G., et al. (1992). Psychological adjustment of children with a terminally ill parent. *Journal of the American Academy of Child and Adolescent Psychiatry,* 31 327–333.

Stack, C.B. (1974). *All our kin: strategies for survival in a Black community.* New York: Harper & Row.

Stein J.A., and Newcomb, M.D. (1994). Children's internalizing and externalizing behaviors and maternal health problems. *Journal of Pediatric Psychology* 19 571–594.

Stein, J.A., Riedel, M., and Rotheram-Borus, M.J. (1999). Parentification and its impact among adolescent children of parents with AIDS. *Family Process,* 38 193–208.

Stuifbergen, A.K. (1990). Patterns of functioning in families with a chronically ill parent: An exploratory study. *Research in Nursing and Health,* 13 (1), 35–44.

Taylor, R.J., Chatters, L.M., Tucker, M.B., and Lewis, E. (1990). Developments in research on Black families: A decade review. *Journal of Marriage and the Family,* 52 993–1014.

Toth, J. (1997). *Orphans of the living: Stories of America's children in foster care.* New York: Simon & Schuster.

Valentine, L., and Feinauer, L.L. (1993). Resilience factors associated with females survivors of childhood sexual abuse. *The American Journal of Family Therapy,* 21 (3), 216–224.

Zayas, L.H., and Romano, K. (1994). Adolescents and parental death from AIDS. In B.O. Dane and C. Levine (Eds.), *AIDS and the New Orphans* (pp. 59–76). Westport, CT: Auburn House.

6

Focus on Solutions: Harlem Dowling–West Side Center for Children and Family Services: A Comprehensive Response to Working with HIV-Affected Children and Families

Melba Butler and Chedgzsey Smith-McKeever

The vast majority of HIV-affected children and adolescents are African American children, most of who experience AIDS within the context of poverty, multiple losses, and societal stigma (Fair, Spencer, Wiener, and Riekert 1995; Lewis 1995; Rotheram-Borus and Stein 1999). These children and their families are also lacking appropriate counseling and support services (Draimin, Hudis, Segura, and Shire 1999; Gilbert 2001). Programs that are able to build on the strengths of the African American family are best equipped to provide family-based mental health and supportive services in order to promote resilience in this population. The purpose of this chapter is to describe one such program, the Harlem Dowling–West Side Center for Children and Family Services, a historically Black human services agency that provides a continuum of family based, culturally grounded services to empower HIV-infected parents, their children, and family members. We first provide historical background information and a current description of the agency. Next, a case study is presented to illuminate how a continuum of services based on the strengths perspective can be highly effective in meeting the holistic needs of African American families affected by HIV/AIDS.

AGENCY BACKGROUND AND DESCRIPTION

Harlem Dowling–West Side Center (HDWC) has had a historical presence in the Harlem Community of New York City. The earliest predecessor of HDWC was the Colored Orphan's Asylum, founded in 1836 by two Quaker women in response to the absence of any caring mechanism for orphaned black children. During the 1800s, orphaned or half-orphaned Black children were not allowed admission into the Protestant and Catholic-run orphanages of the day. Rather, they lived as street urchins or were housed in the public almshouses along with poor and mentally disturbed adults. The founders of the Colored Orphan's Asylum relied heavily upon financial support from wealthy White philanthropists to sustain the organization. Yet from the beginning the Black community supported the organization through both monetary and in-kind contributions. Model programs developed by the asylum throughout the years recruited Black employees from Black churches and civic organizations. These staff members were proficient in areas such as child care, education, and trade instruction, and assisted the program with its focus on basic education, linkages with historically Black colleges, cultural and religious enrichment, on-site health care, and family-based care for children. Harlem Dowling Children's Services merged with the West Side Center in 1989 to form the oldest and one of the largest organizations in New York serving at-risk children and families of color. Currently the organization serves approximately 2,500 children and their families annually through programs and services such as family preservation, foster care, adoption, HIV/AIDS services, therapeutic foster boarding homes, summer and after-school programs, independent living, and medical and mental health programs. The organization's diverse board and staff are reflective of the population served. Both draw heavily from people who are indigenous or who share a social and historical commitment to the communities served. The board of directors is composed mostly of prominent African Americans from the local community.

The HDWC for Children and Family Services provides a range of services to children and families affected or infected by HIV/AIDS. Services range from street education and outreach to at-risk populations, to case management, early permanency planning, and foster and adoptive home placement of children who are infected and/or orphaned as a result of AIDS.

HDWC's approach to the provision of services to its clientele is based on the six principles of the strengths perspective (Saleebey 1992, 6–7):

1. All services are based on respect for client strengths.
2. Client strengths are physical, cognitive, interpersonal, social, and spiritual in nature.
3. Client motivation is based on promoting client strengths.
4. The agency/practitioner is a collaborator with the client.
5. The approach to service provision must avoid "blaming the victim."
6. Any environment is full of resources that have been untapped and unsolicited.

The provision of services is not only based on the strengths perspective, but it is also based on the understanding that the problems clients face in living with HIV/AIDS are not *one*-dimensional. They are biological, psychological, social, cultural, environmental, and spiritual in nature.

Case Study

CeCe is a thirty-seven-year-old African American mother who is living with AIDS. She has been receiving services from the Early Permanency Planning (EPP) component of the Specialized Services Department at HDWC. CeCe has a history of mild mental illness and abuse of crack cocaine and other substances and is currently in recovery. When CeCe came to HDWC to apply for EPP services, she presented several pressing issues related to her substance use recovery, mental health, HIV/AIDS related medical needs, as well as the need for permanency planning for her five-year-old son, TJ. Two years ago CeCe voluntarily placed TJ in kinship foster care with her parents.

Because the agency's approach to intervention considers the multidimensional nature of problems, the agency has service provision relationships with medical clinics; substance abuse treatment professionals; individual and family therapists of African American descent; clergy from local African American Catholic, Protestant, and Muslim congregations; and child welfare professionals. In addition, the agency has mentoring programs and support groups for children, adolescents, and adults living with HIV/AIDS. After completion of a year's participation in the support group, adults and adolescents can participate in a mentor-training program, which upon completion qualifies participants to work in paid positions within the program. The range of services offered in connection to the HIV/AIDS cases demonstrates the agency's understanding that although HIV/AIDS is, at its root, a biological problem, it also has psychological, social, cultural, and spiritual implications. Most of these services, including medical care management and child welfare services, are provided on site at HDWC. Thus, once the needed services were identified and agreed upon by CeCe and her HDWC counselor, she was able to access the services she needed quite easily.

MEDICAL AND SUBSTANCE ABUSE TREATMENT

CeCe was referred to a hospital with an established relationship with HDWC with a specific physician who works regularly with HDWC clientele. After her initial meeting, during which CeCe was diagnosed with manic depressive disorder, she opted to receive services from a mental health clinic near her home which also offered treatment for her substance abuse and recovery issues. The strengths perspective principle that the agency/practitioner is a collaborator with the client is demonstrated by the agency's practice of giving clients treatment options and giving the client the choice in the method of service delivery. Throughout her treatment CeCe's parents were very much involved in her treatment and made sure that she was diligent in keeping her appointments and following prescribed treatments. Involving her parents as active participants in CeCe's treatment also supports the strengths perspective and builds on the positive interpersonal relationship between CeCe and her parents as one of CeCe's strengths.

INDIVIDUAL AND FAMILY COUNSELING

CeCe's family received extensive individual and family counseling at HDWC to address the issues of grief, loss, and changing family dynamics, which are common issues among all HIV-affected families. During the time of the family's participation in counseling, CeCe's health worsened, and she became homebound and bedridden. The provision of counseling services then took place at the family home. Counseling to help facilitate the parent/child interactions of CeCe, her parents, and TJ was provided and thus supported CeCe in her wish to spend quality time with her family. CeCe's declining health could have been viewed as a reason that quality time among the family would be lost. Instead, using the strengths perspective, the chosen intervention avoided any "blaming the victim" and instead moved services to the home, giving CeCe a sense of empowerment in her situation.

PERMANENCY PLANNING

CeCe's family and HDWC began to address plans for TJ's future. Using a strengths perspective, the agency/practitioner is a collaborator with the client. After a great deal of counselor facilitated family discussion, CeCe and her parents decided to make adoption the permanency planning choice for TJ. CeCe signed documents surrendering her parental rights under the condition that her parents were to be the designated adoptive parents, and the process of the adoption is now under way.

One of CeCe's main concerns was that she wanted to have a very direct influence on her son's future as it relates to his culture, spirituality and religion, familial relationships, traditions, and overall well-being. The EPP process helped CeCe to collect family photographs and videos which document oral history, family outings, and events that she wished to pass on to TJ. The practice of helping clients create such resources for their children demonstrated HDWC's approach to clients as bio-psycho-social-cultural-environmental and spiritual by nature.

CHILD ADJUSTMENT

TJ has adjusted well to life with his maternal grandparents and his mother. He is appropriately bonded to all three adult caregivers. At present, grief and loss counseling services are being provided to the family, and TJ is an active participant in the counseling process. The therapist describes the family's deep spiritual beliefs as a strength. Their spiritual beliefs have helped the family to deal more effectively with both the grieving and healing process. TJ and his grandparents have joined a support group for HIV/AIDS affected families, and TJ will continue to receive ongoing individual counseling to continue to support his positive adjustment to the changing dynamics in his family.

REDUCING STIGMA

Situated in the middle of one of the most well-known African American communities and serving a primarily African American clientele, HDWC is also committed to reducing the stigma of HIV/AIDS in Harlem and its surrounding communities. This challenge is an important one to address as, according to their approach, a client is seen as a part of a social environment that has an impact on his or her overall functioning.

HDWC has an extensive community outreach and education program that focuses on reducing the level and intensity of AIDS stigma within the Harlem community. The HDWC outreach program includes monthly, communitywide educational and informational meetings which are held at local Catholic, Protestant, and Muslim churches and mosques on a rotating basis. Some meetings are focused on specific topics, such as new developments in treatment and medication, or HIV/AIDS and the Americans with Disabilities Act. Other meetings focus on general HIV/AIDS topics such as methods of transmission and prevention of acquiring HIV.

Another program that HDWC offers to reduce the stigma of HIV/AIDS is focused on the school-age child. Through outreach to and consultation with local school officials, HDWC has a mentoring and training program for adolescents living with HIV/AIDS. Once an adolescent has completed the training program, he or she can go into schools and give age appropriate presentations that focus on educating children about HIV/AIDS and prevention. It is HDWC's policy to try to make sure presentations are made to all elementary, middle, and high schools in the community on a yearly basis.

CONCLUSION

This chapter described how a community-based agency using the strengths perspective can be effective in providing a continuum of services and how important it is to approach services with the understanding that problems can be multidimensional. With its holistic approach to service provision to clients and its goal of reducing AIDS stigma within the community, Harlem Dowling–West Side Center is a model agency in providing resiliency- and strength-based social services to HIV-affected African American families.

REFERENCES

Draimin, B.H., Hudis, J., Segura, J., and Shire, A. (1999). A troubled present, an uncertain future: Well adolescents in families with AIDS. In S. Taylor-Brown and A. Garcia (Eds.), *HIV-affected and vulnerable youth: Prevention issues and approaches* (pp. 37–50). New York: Haworth Press.

Fair, C.C., Spencer, E.D., Wiener, L., and Riekert, K. (1995). Healthy children in families affected by AIDS: Epidemiology and psychosocial considerations. *Child and Adolescent Social Work Journal*, 12 (3), 165–181.

Gilbert, D.J. (2001). HIV-affected children and adolescents: What school social workers should know. *Journal of Children in Schools*, 33 (3), 135–142.

Lewis, M. (1995). The special case of the uninfected child in the HIV-affected family: Normal development tasks and the child's concerns about illness and death. In S. Geballe, J. Gruendel, and W. Andiman (Eds.), *Forgotten children of the AIDS epidemic* (pp. 50–63). New Haven, CT: Yale University Press.

Rotheram-Borus, M.J., and Stein, J.A. (1999). Problem behavior of adolescents whose parents are living with AIDS. *American Journal of Orthopsychiatry*, 69 (2), 228–239.

Saleebey, D. (1992). *The Strengths perspective in social work practice*. New York: Longman.

7

Life Transformations of HIV-Positive African American Women: Theories and Evidence of Change

Mildred Williamson

A theoretical model for understanding individual response to a life-altering, traumatic event such as major illness is the concept of stress and coping as explained by Lazarus and Folkman (1984). These authors noted that major stress, such as a crisis, causes some people to draw upon adaptive resources they never thought they had and that such people can gain strength and grow from stress.

A qualitative study of eighteen African American HIV-positive women was conducted to learn if perhaps some people do something more than "adapt" to life when faced with a major stressor such as HIV/AIDS. The study explored whether an alternative paradigm may exist: to examine if women showed evidence of "transformation," a concept that transcends adaptation. The basis for conducting the study came from the clinical experience and observations of many women served by the Women & Children HIV Program (WCHP) at Cook County Hospital/CORE Center in Chicago whose adjustment to life with HIV was characterized by reclaiming relationships with children or family of origin, reducing-high risk behaviors, and finding or reclaiming spirituality. This chapter presents an overview of the theoretical basis for the construct of transformation; describes how African American HIV-positive women in WCHP came to perceive and define life with HIV, even while living with multiple stressors; and concludes with implications for social service and public health intervention strategies with disenfranchised women of color.

DEFINING TRANSFORMATION

The term *transformation* for the purpose of the study means "to change characteristics or actions of daily living in a dramatic or profound way." Contextualized information about the women's transformative experiences were obtained from statements by WCHP participants and corroborated by the medical and social service records. Examples include:

1. If previously a substance user, to have moved from chemical dependency to prolonged recovery/sobriety (which can be measured in months/years)
2. If previously estranged from family of origin, to have achieved family reunification; examples may include:

  (a) mother regains custody of children, (if previously lost)

  (b) woman regains acceptance/trust among family of origin

  (c) woman forms "new" family, partnerships, or constructs support networks that are qualitatively different from previous ones.

3. If previously in an abusive relationship, to have moved out of the abusive situation
4. If previously engaged in illegal acts (such as paid sex work or drug sales), to have discontinued
5. If previously nonspiritual, nonreligious, to have become spiritual; examples may include joining a church or another organized religious group or personal acknowledgment of being a spiritual person, but not necessarily joining a specific religious group
6. If previously incarcerated, or serving probation/parole, to have no new arrests
7. If previously a high school dropout, to have started work toward or obtained a GED diploma; if a high school graduate, to have enrolled in college or other advanced training
8. If previously unemployed, to becoming employed or actively seeking work
9. If previously on a track of individual personal health or sobriety maintenance, to have embraced health advocacy with groups as in support group participation, HIV peer education and, peer drug prevention advocacy
10. If previously socially unmotivated, to have moved into volunteer activities, consumer activism, or health/social policy advocacy with others in groups.

The transformation definition and examples helped inform the literature review and data analysis of the participants' experiences. Several theories of change form the basis for the construct of transformation, including theories of behavioral health change, behavioral response to illness, stress and coping, and resiliency/empowerment.

Health and Behavioral Change

A uniting feature of many behavioral change theories is heavy emphasis on the individual, starting with the Health Belief Model of the 1950s, developed to understand human response to symptoms and compliance with treatment regimens (Rosenstock 1990); to the Transtheoretical Model (Prochaska, Norcross, and DiClemente 1994), which acknowledges that there are different stages of behavioral change and that strategies can be used to accommodate a person's change process. Bandura (1977, 1989) provides concepts of dynamism and reciprocity in human behavior through social learning theory, which rejects the idea that personal and environmental factors function independently. Instead, interaction between individual thought, behavior, and the environment in which the behavior is performed is the theory's cornerstone. This interaction is defined as reciprocal determinism, and when a change occurs in one area, it has implications for other areas. The interaction informs the design and implementation of strategies to reduce risk for a health problem, especially in situations in which external control is considered a causal factor. Success can be achieved through knowledge building (information sharing and skill building), with an opportunity to have the desired skills modeled. Internal and external rewards can be provided for practicing the skill, which can lead to greater confidence in performing the behaviors (self-efficacy).

Bandura (1989) identifies the most important mechanism of personal agency as a group's belief that it is capable of exercising control over the events that affect its members' lives. To raise beliefs of self-efficacy, people must feel a sense of empowerment, which refers to a sense of personal control, mastery, and power to effect change, and to a group's or organization's ability to control community resources, engage in collective decision making, and achieve shared goals (Chavis and Wandersman 1990).

Theories of Behavioral Response to Illness

Theories of behavioral response to illness contain a logic similar to the behavioral health theories. Both theoretical paradigms place strong emphasis on individual and immediate family response to illness but focus little on the interaction of individual and environmental circumstances and changes over time. Morse and Johnson (1991) rejected the medical model of illness, described as an individual living with disease, reduced to a set of physical symptoms and a treatment plan for the symptoms, resulting in diminished individual qualities, and ignores family members as participants in the suffering and recovery. Morse and Johnson's Illness-Constellation Model views illness as an experience that affects the sick person and significant others. The goal is to treat patients as persons and not as objects. The ramifications of individual illness experience cause profound changes in the interactions and relationships of those involved in the illness experience, and result in a loss of normalcy. Individual experiences with physical and psychosocial symptoms are considered, including reactions and adjustments of loved ones.

The aforementioned theoretical frameworks all assume that the ill person has loved ones to whom they can turn, but do not account for behavioral response to illnesses that: (1) carry a strong societal stigma, (2) have no initial physical symptoms, (3) are associated with drug addiction, and (4) result in economic consequences for the person, family, and community. It is indirectly assumed that loss of normalcy may mean the same to most people. Life with HIV has shown that "normalcy" lost may be liberation for some, depending on the issues that affected their risk for acquiring the infection. That is, an HIV diagnosis can be a trigger to lose some of the old "normal" behaviors that originally placed the ill person at risk, such as having unprotected sex and sharing needles. Gaining new knowledge and methods to name and pursue a new concept of normalcy may result in a departure from what was normal in the past and a welcome to the newly named and claimed "normalcy."

Kübler-Ross (1987) applied the five stages of dying to HIV disease at a time when treatments were unavailable. They are (1) denial and isolation, (2) anger, (3) bargaining, (4) depression, and (5) acceptance. Effective treatments now exist, yet there is still no cure. A positive HIV test result still means living with a potentially terminal illness.

The five stages could be applied to a behavioral response to HIV test results in this way:

1. *Denial*—one may be at risk for HIV-infection and delay being tested. Once tested, one may deny the validity of the positive test results once informed. They may fear rejection when disclosing results to significant others, therefore live with secrets, often in isolation. They may delay seeking health care due to the belief that death is imminent, anyway.
2. *Anger* may emerge at sex or needle-sharing partners whom one believes may have knowingly or unknowingly placed them at risk. One can be angry with themselves for engaging in potentially harmful behaviors, (if understood as such). Anger can emerge from perceptions of how counseling and testing procedures occurred, and over yet another adversity to live with on top of other multiple issues.
3. *Bargaining* can happen with one's self, loved ones, and/or with one's God, where promises are made to change certain lifestyle practices, in hopes of gaining more time to live free of symptoms, or to avoid a painful death, if one is at the point of end-stage disease.
4. *Depression* can emerge if one remains isolated, secretive, outside of care, or if one has disclosed and did experience rejection from their loved one(s).
5. *Acceptance* can be directional—one can "give in" to living with the virus and peacefully wait for death, or one can take ownership of the disease and claim, "yes, I have HIV, but HIV doesn't have me," as Novella Dudley[1] and others like her, did.

Theories of Stress, Social Support, Coping, and Adaptation

Lazarus and Folkman (1984) define psychological stress as a relationship between a person and the environment that is appraised by the person as taxing or exceeding one's resources and endangering one's well-being. Stressors fall into different categories such as major life events (birth/death in the family), daily hassles (work/child rearing), chronic strains (poverty/racism/unemployment), sudden disasters, and environmental pollution.

Social support is a resource that a person must cultivate and use as a component of coping with stress. House (1981) identifies three types of social support: *emotional* (empathy, love, trust, and caring); *instrumental* (tangible aid and services that assists a person in need); and *appraisal*. Appraisal support is the provision of useful information, feedback, affirmation, and social comparison for self-evaluation purposes. Coping confidence is a set of social skills people learn and draw upon in stressful encounters with the environment.

Adaptational outcomes from the variety and frequency of stress include social functioning in work and social living, morale or life satisfaction, and somatic health. Over a lifetime, social functioning is seen as an extension of coping effectiveness. Positive morale depends on consistency in appraising encounters as challenges, harms and threats as manageable, and coping effectiveness across different encounters. Somatic health quality is an adaptational outcome affected by coping effectiveness as it relates to pursuit of wellness versus risk taking regarding morbidity and mortality and, acceptance versus denial of certain behaviors as health risks (Lazarus and Folkman 1984).

African American women are burdened with a disproportionate share of all these stressors, especially varied and persistent chronic strains, which lead to poor mental health (Belle 1990). Women living with drug and alcohol addiction live in disproportionately violent situations as well (Fullilove, Lown, and Fullilove 1992). Yet, access to social support among Black women does exist (Adisa 1990; Aschenbrenner 1975; Stack 1974). Quality and consistent availability of such support varies, however, and in some cases may have deteriorated, given the growth of concentrated poverty in certain inner city areas as described by Wilson (1987). Wandersman and Nation (1998) found neighborhood characteristics to be related to mental health outcomes. Fullilove, Green, and Fullilove (1999) found that even as physical rebuilding occurs in previously deteriorated communities, full restoration requires reconstruction or new construction of social support networks.

Theories of Struggle, Resilience, and Transformation

Transformation might be considered the ultimate adaptational outcome to adversity. One may assume a new attitude about life and how to live it that didn't exist before the adverse event(s) occurred. The new attitude and behavior would significantly differ from one's outlook *before* the adversity took place. This is where the term transformation differs from resilience, which the dictionary defines as bouncing or springing back into (an original) shape or position after being stretched, bent, or compressed.[2] Wright (1998) describes resilience as the capacity for successful adaptation, positive functioning, and competence despite high-risk status, chronic adversity, and exposure to severe stressors. The term resilience assumes a return to the shape or position one previously had despite going through the adverse event(s), and then maintaining it over time.

Transformation of thought and action implies the emergence of a new attitude and behavior that qualitatively differs from the "stressed" position of the most recent adverse event *and* from positions held in the past. A transformed person may structure their lives and surroundings, so that exposure to severe stressors would be reduced, if not eliminated. Becker (1997) suggests that acceptance is a central theme of transformative metaphors. The process is not one of uncritical acceptance of certain conditions and adapting behavior to fit them. It is more complex, especially for disenfranchised populations. Uncritical acceptance is an apolitical concept that may be socially dangerous for the disempowered. If the women in this study were merely resilient, "bouncing back" to previous thoughts or behaviors before learning their HIV status could be detrimental if the original behaviors were shaped by abuse, neglect, or other mistreatment, as it was for most.

Transformation is a state of mind that says "I have a right to determine, at least some conditions; I have a right to reject or protest unfair conditions; I have a right to all information that can guide my decision-making process, and the power to act." These are sentiments usually present with *empowered* transforming behavior. Transformation can also occur from an *unempowered* standpoint. The presence of personal and/or group empowerment can be the determinant of directional outcome. Channeled, constructive health-affirming behaviors and group actions become possible. Collins (1990) explains:

The existence of Afrocentric feminist thought suggests that there is always choice, and power to act, no matter how bleak the situation may appear to be. Viewing the world as one in the making raises the issue of individual responsibility for bringing about change. It also shows that while individual empowerment is key, only collective action can effectively generate lasting social transformation of political and economic institutions (237).

Transformation is not necessarily finite, it is subject to change and has features that can elevate or deflate human progress in ways that can produce temporary or lasting effects. The presence or absence of individual social consciousness, human agency, and will helps sustain positive change over time and resist negative change attempts, despite pressures endured. It forms the content behind the old civil rights slogan that rejects complacency: "freedom is a constant struggle." Complacency helps those who are opposed to social progress gain momentum in their efforts to destroy it just as silence by those who witness injustice to others helps it continue.

Hooks (1993) suggests that in the traditional world of Black folk experience, there was a profound belief in the spiritual power of Black people to transform their world and live with integrity and "oneness" despite oppressive social realities. That folk experience and its spiritual power represent some of the ways of knowing that must be shared to assist in the emergence of empowered Black women and communities.

A transformative vision of African American thought was described by Marable and Mullings (1994) initially as a concept driven by the objective of abolishing racism, defined as an unequal relationship between social aggregates, based on power and violence. Over time, it was realized that wider power relationships such as class exploitation and oppression rooted in gender and sexual orientation must also be transformed to achieve full human equality.

How does one move from being and feeling powerless to being and feeling powerful? If living with HIV, how does gaining personal power contribute to healthier living? How does one move from a position of personal growth to involvement in collective action, including individual and community health affirming actions? These questions helped inform the choice of methodology, cohort selection, and analysis.

METHODOLOGY

Thirty in-depth, semistructured interviews were conducted with eighteen HIV-positive African American women during 1997–1998. Women were asked to identify and define factors that influenced their current social and health behaviors and what, if anything, changed for them since becoming HIV-positive. All participants were asked about the quality of their lives before and since learning their HIV status. All were asked questions to learn what impact, if any, did the improved medical treatments make upon their personal quality-of-life assessments. Using methods described by Lincoln and Guba (1985), the analysis looked for one or more common themes from the collective life accounts of the participants. Determinants of transformation as earlier defined were investigated for those that considered themselves as having changed as such, and for those who did not.

African American HIV-positive women were of specific interest because they represent the majority, 60 percent of the documented AIDS cases among women in this country (CDC data 2000). However, views of Black HIV-positive women at the time were rare in the HIV prevention and behavioral change literature. Their voices were not regularly sought or heard among the AIDS activists or mainstream policy makers around health care and research demands (Cohen 1999; Battle 1997).

Interviews were audiotaped and transcribed; postinterview notes were taken. Twelve were interviewed twice; six were interviewed once. Reasons for single interviews include one participant died before the second interview could occur; one developed AIDS dementia, prohibiting a second interview; four others explained their experiences in great detail in one interview. Most interviews (twenty-two) took place in participants' homes. Five were conducted on the campus of Cook County Hospital. Two occurred in residential addiction treatment facilities. One occurred in a homeless shelter. One occurred in the apartment of a participant's friend.

Demographic information was collected, followed by semistructured, open-ended questions. Medical records were reviewed to corroborate oral responses where possible, to verify HIV status, medical regimen, disease progression, and to note possible comorbidities.

Study Participants: Demographics

Five participants were born outside Chicago. Three were born in Mississippi, one in Ohio, and one in South Carolina. All five spent a portion of their childhoods and most of their adult lives in Chicago. Thirteen participants were born and raised in Chicago.

When interviewed, sixteen participants resided in Chicago homes or apartments. Two lived in suburban towns. One of the two exceptions lived in a homeless shelter; one lived in a subsidized apartment. Of the Chicago residents, two lived in a supportive living facility, four in subsidized apartments, nine in rented homes or apartments, and one resided in a residential chemical dependency facility for women. Some moved between the first and second interviews. One participant who resided in a friend's home during the first interview was living in her own apartment by the time of the second. One moved from a homeless shelter, married, and became a homeowner shortly after the study was completed.

The youngest participant interviewed was age 20; the oldest two women were both age 52. Eight participants were age 35 or younger; 10 were between 36 and 52 years of age. Fifteen of the participants were parents to a total of 51 children, including 3 mothers who had 5 HIV-positive children among them. One woman had 7 children, the most of the cohort; one woman had only one child, the least. One participant was married; 10 were single/never married; and 7 were divorced or separated. Four were grandmothers.

All participants were poor when interviewed. Four were Supplemental Security Income (SSI) disability recipients, and received Temporary Assistance for Needy Families (TANF) for their children. Seven were SSI recipients only. Two were TANF recipients. Four worked full- or part-time jobs; one was unemployed with no income at the first interview, but was a full-time factory worker by the second interview—her first job in ten years.

One participant was a dependent, living with her mother who was employed. Two participants had incomes of $1,200 per month, the most reported in the cohort. The majority had incomes of $484 per month (from SSI). One participant reported receiving child support from the father of her children. The range of educational attainment for the women spanned from completion of eighth grade through completion of two years of college. Three completed between one and two years of college; three graduated from high school; one completed a General Equivalency (high school) Diploma (GED) program. Eleven completed between the eighth and eleventh grades of high school. One of the eleventh-grade completers was in a GED program when interviewed, but died before she could finish. The most reported reason for leaving high school among those who dropped out was pregnancy.

Eleven participants reported a transmission risk of sharing needles for intravenous drug use; five reported unprotected sex with someone HIV-infected; two reported that their risk could have been from sharing needles and/or unprotected sex with someone HIV-infected. The length of time participants knew their HIV status ranged from one to twelve years. All participants tested positive for HIV between the years 1985 and 1996. Three had an AIDS diagnosis at interview; fifteen did not. Fifteen women were taking the highly active antiretroviral therapy (HAART) regimen at interview; three were not. All three who were not taking HAART were recommended to start by their doctors, but were reluctant to do so. Reasons for fear fell in two categories: fear of adverse side effects and general fear of taking any medications for any reason. Three women on HAART complained of painful side effects from the medication when first interviewed; two of them stopped the regimen by the time of the second interview. No participant credited the availability of HAART or taking the regimen with either positive or negative influence on their quality-of-life views. Ten of the women were participants in one or more National Institutes of Health (NIH)–sponsored clinical trials or studies; three of them were members of the community advisory boards (CAB) associated with specific protocols.

Thirteen women had a history of chemical dependency; of this total, eleven were in recovery for one year or more, and two were in recovery for at least six months when interviewed. Two admitted to relapse during their most recent recovery period. The lowest number of years reported for substance use was eleven. Four had lived with drug/alcohol addiction for 15–19 years; 6 had 20–24 years; 2 reported 25-plus years of addiction to drugs. The two most common drugs abused were heroin (injected and snorted) and cocaine (snorted; or mixed with heroin and injected). Most reported that substance use began with marijuana, alcohol, and other drugs when they were 11–15 years old, except for 2 who were introduced to drugs at ages 16 and 18. Five women had no history of chemical dependency. Ten had a history of mental illness, with 6 having had depression (3 of whom had suicide attempts in their past) and 2 with anxiety disorders. Two were hospitalized for mental illness with suicidal ideations or attempts earlier in their lives. Both were sexually abused as children. One reported being sexually assaulted in the mental health facility. One reported repeated physical abuse. Other illnesses women had were epilepsy, dementia, asthma, hypertension, and herpes.

Nine participants were sexual assault survivors, six of them survived multiple rapes. Four women who survived rape as adults were also survivors of childhood sexual abuse. Ten women were survivors of physical abuse. All except one of them were survivors of domestic violence; one recalled being beaten badly on her head by five white youths as she deboarded a bus, which resulted in hospitalization.

Eight participants were incarcerated at some earlier point in their lives. Seven had drug-related offenses ranging from stealing/shoplifting, prostitution to drug possession and sales. One was arrested and convicted of trespassing on Chicago Housing Authority (CHA) property, in that she and others often used an abandoned CHA apartment to use drugs.

All but a few participants had an earlier fear of disclosure to families and loved ones about their status. Some have become open with everyone about their status, with a few being open from the beginning. For former substance-using women, fear of disclosure was compounded by guilt and shame for the impact their substance use had on themselves and their families over time. HIV was yet another "burden" to place on their loved ones and another possible reason to be rejected. Participant #2 first told her family she had cancer and then later told them the truth:

I lied to my mom. I told my mom and my sister that I had cancer. My mom said, that's ok baby, we gonna still love you. If you do have cancer, that's alright. But then I heard my sister go over there and tell her, she got cancer alright—she got that stuff! And I said, what stuff you talking about? The doctor told me I had cancer. 'Cause when I went back to the doctor's office, he said I was positive and that was all. And I was so angry and upset with him for disclosing my status on the phone,[3] I just walked up out the office and left. And she said, I know this for a fact, our other sister is HIV-positive, also, and I was like whoa! I said, what? So, come to find out that I was positive and my sister is positive, also. So, now I'm worried about my mom.

Most of those with unprotected sex as their risk did not want to be identified as "bad," or be mistaken for someone who used substances, or engaged in sex for drugs or money. Surviving rape, childhood sexual or physical abuse, poor educational attainment, or little or no work experience were common features with most participants interviewed, with few exceptions, regardless of risk factor for infection. Several women survived more than one of these events multiple times. Former substance users had the majority of their adult lives consumed with addiction-driven demands, which may have been triggered by abuse endured over time. Those with and without addiction histories had been emotionally, physically, or sexually abused or assaulted by men and/or were poorly educated or labeled cognitively impaired in some way. All were vulnerable and at risk for HIV-infection.

In sum, the collective backgrounds of the participants show lifetime burdens of abuses and stressors, to which the diagnosis of HIV disease was later added. These demographic trends are consistent with earlier research with WCHP patients (Boxer and Coon 1994; Cook et al. 1990; Driscoll et al. 1994; Ruble-Soro et al. 1994; Taylor et al. 1990).

RESULTS: ANALYSIS OF WOMEN'S EXPERIENCES

All participants were asked if they felt that the quality of their lives had changed in any way since learning their HIV status. Among the eighteen participants, fifteen considered their lives and outlook transformed in some way. Three did not view their lives as being transformed in any way, though there was evidence that transformation "criteria," as explained earlier, was met. The analysis is arranged to reflect the differences between the two groups: nontransformed and transformed.

Nontransformers

Several observations were made among the three participants whose lives were not "transformed." All three had the same risk factor for acquiring HIV: unprotected sex with someone HIV-infected. None had a history of drug or alcohol addiction. All three were labeled "slow learners," or cognitively challenged in some way, with apparently little or no developmentally appropriate interventions at the time. For example, participant #3 reported:

The school I was going to was an occupational high school; they find you jobs. It was for EMH [Educable, Mentally Handicapped], 'cause I was in you know, a slow classroom. This was the school I went to. They get you a job, and you go to school part time, and work part time. Or whatever they want you to do, or however the scores is. If they feel, you know, you're not ready, you got to stay in school for the whole full time, and they don't get you no job. So I was ready. So, they took me out of that school, and that's when I went to Westinghouse (another high school). But I didn't like it there. So I went back. I wanted to go back to my home school, 'cause I just knew so many people, I got along. So, I just stayed there until I graduated.

All three endured difficult relationships with men; one had been in a long-term relationship characterized by physical, emotional, and financial abuse (#10). She explained:

That man did me so bad 'til my family hated him. My brother told me one day ... something happened, I think I lost my job and lost my apartment. Oh, I had to move out. That's a lot of things, too, when I was with him because he was real loud and violent and tearing up stuff, she [the landlady], said "but that man got to go. I live upstairs and I can hear him down here jumping on you and I just can't take that." She told me that. I said, this is my house and I pay rent here. She said, "but you all are young, you got a gorgeous son and you don't have to take that." I was getting mad with her, just 'cause I was in love with him. I didn't want to hear that. My momma, daddy, my sisters, my brother—my brother wanted to kill him a whole bunch of times. I can't go back there.

Participant #10 also expressed despair and fear:

I don't know, I just have this weak thing with men. If they say "Boo," I jump. I always have ... I don't have too much [self] esteem. I have this thing about ... I don't want to talk about it 'cause I'll start crying. I just don't feel love anymore for myself. Every since I been infected with this virus, I am very particular. Sometimes, I feel like I'm out of place. I scared, I am really, deep down, scared of having a relationship, period.

Coincidentally, two of the three reported deception by a man who knew he was HIV-positive at the time he had unprotected sex with them. Each of the two women who were deceived by the same man independently recounted events. Each thought she was involved in a monogamous relationship with the man. They each reported similar feelings upon learning that they were mistreated and infected by the same man; their initial mistrust of one another was followed by subsequent friendship.

One of the two women was sexually assaulted by two other men at another time. Life with HIV was a stressor added to surviving sexual assault for participant #12 who explained:

What made it so bad is, one of the dudes that raped me is the one I used to go with. Two years ago, when I went into this lounge, I seen the dude who raped me and he had the nerve to come to my face and ask me when he raped me, did I get pregnant. That's why I don't talk, I don't say nothing. I was standing on the corner, catching the bus to come to the clinic and I seen him and he got on the bus, he was just looking at me. And I looked at him. And when I got off the bus, he got off the bus, he said something to me. I said, if you come to me, I'll cut you down. Don't say anything else to me. He kept trying to tell me, he didn't do it, he didn't do it. It ain't his fault, he was sorry. What made it so bad, I had went to court and they threw it [the case] out.

The hometowns of these two women are in the South, not more than ten miles apart. Their stories reflect what is becoming the sad epidemiology of HIV-infection in the southern United States. HIV in the rural south is disproportionately a disease of economically poor and poorly educated African Americans, as compared with other groups, with unprotected sex slightly leading injection drug use as the main risk factor for infection for women. AIDS cases among women in the South are four times higher than in the Midwest and West (CDC 1999).

All three "nontransformed" women had children; all felt that parenting motivated them to "keep going," despite their general pessimistic outlooks. One had an HIV-positive child. All expressed a desire to be present to watch their children grow up. All were hurt, angry, and perplexed to have been mistreated, taken advantage of, ironically infected in the name of love. Participant #3 had a view shared to some extent by other nontransformers:

I got a lot from [the support group], but everybody there was in recovery [from drug addiction]. I was the only person there who wasn't. At first I felt this is not for me. I didn't want to talk about that. I wanted to talk about, why God didn't even watch over me, and I didn't do nothing wrong. All I was doing was taking care of my kids, never dealt with drugs. I guess he punished me, because I wasn't going to church. That's what I thought.

In summary nontransformers felt that multiple injustices were done to them; that they were badly mistreated not only by the virus, but by the men in their past lives. Nontransformers were also disturbed over their previous lack of knowledge about why unprotected sex is risky for more than just pregnancy. Once again, participant #3 explained:

When I met him, we started using condoms, and I wanted a girl, so after I went out, you know, I was using condoms, because we were together for a year and a half. I decided I wanted to have a baby by him, 'cause I knew, this was the one! That was when I, we stopped using condoms, and I wish I would have never did that.

Finally, these three women all stated that their lives had not changed in any way for the better, despite making several accomplishments. Participant #3 completed the WCHP HIV Peer Education training and became knowledgeable about HIV and sexually transmitted diseases (STD). She obtained employment by the time of the second interview, after formerly being an unemployed TANF recipient. Participant #10 left an abusive relationship after twelve years' endurance. Participant #12 obtained an apartment by the time of the second interview, making it possible for her children to live with her instead of her mother. She took a GED test, failed by a slim margin, and vowed to try again. Yet all three women still did not consider their quality of life as improved, thus they were characterized as nontransformers.

Transformers

Two participants went through a process of transformation and had a risk factor of unprotected sex and no drug/alcohol addiction history. However, they felt their quality of life had improved since learning their HIV status. What was different about them? Participant #8 reported that she never heard of HIV before the announcement of Magic Johnson's seropositive status in 1991. While surviving and getting out of a previous abusive relationship, she later met and married someone who knew that she was HIV-positive, accepted her and her children as his family. In her case, it was another chance at happiness in a relationship, which she embraced. She explained why she feels better about herself today than before:

Well, for one thing I got saved and I rededicated my life to the Lord. I look at life different, I don't take things for granted anymore. I treat other people around me better. By being saved I try to love everybody. I used to have an attitude that I was better than other people. Certain people, like if I see somebody bummy or not dressed right, when they were down on their luck, I would look down on them. Now, I don't have that attitude. Now I have a spirit that wants to let out my hand to that person and help them. It's like my eyes have been opened up.

The other woman who said her life had changed positively was the youngest participant (#13). She was twenty years old when interviewed, and testing HIV-positive to her was like a wake-up call to change her lifestyle, which, by her account, was played out more in the streets of the various cities she lived in over time than in the schools she attended during her teen years. She also found out that she enjoyed public speaking about HIV prevention. She said, "I used to like to fight. Now, I don't like to fight. I'm an outgoing person. I like speaking to folks about HIV prevention and I've been doing it with some young people. I feel good about that. I'm set to go back to school soon, to an alternative high school, too." She became spiritually active and found a church she likes to attend with a new partner who she said shared her spiritual interests. These events motivated her to return to school.

Thirteen women had long histories of drug addiction, mostly heroin and cocaine. Some tried and failed treatment programs before they learned their HIV status, with a few trying and failing multiple times. Some were in a treatment program when they learned their HIV status, and it served as a prompter to be more successful with sobriety than in past attempts. Some had a long period of sobriety, relapsed, and quickly got back into some form of treatment. In evaluating those cases, the emphasis is not on the relapse itself, which is common; the emphasis is on the quality of how the person handled the relapse events.

For example, participant #7 has lived with HIV since 1985. She had twenty-five-plus years of addiction, survived three sexual assaults, many incarcerations, and violent encounters. She began recovery in 1987, and reported three relapses before regaining sobriety for three years prior to the interview. She was most proud to have been living sober without methadone for about a year, which was accomplished with the help of a WCHP psychiatrist. She explained:

I've been in the hospital for depression and I've been on methadone, but now I've been put on Prozac and I feel great. I don't take the methadone anymore. I'm taking the new medicines [HAART] and I haven't had side effects. It's only in these last three years that I really stopped being ashamed of my past. Now I've been in some theology classes with my pastor and I want to be an evangelist. Before, I thought because of my past, I couldn't talk to other people about believing in God. Now I realize my own experiences could help other people in similar situations find their way to God, too.

Participant #9 survived childhood sexual abuse, domestic violence, and eighteen years of drug addiction. She was a mother and grandmother, and obtained a GED diploma while an adult. After three years of sobriety, she relapsed in the time between the first and second interviews. She called the WCHP psychologist the day after relapse event, which resulted in a hospitalization. She returned to the program support group after being discharged and began the HAART regimen before the second interview, after expressing skepticism about taking HAART in the first interview. When asked if life had changed for her, she said:

Every time I be honest I used to get into trouble, like the first time I told my mother I was molested, she whooped me, 'cause she didn't believe me. But now people respect me being honest. I used to be afraid of people in authority. Now I speak up for myself and I speak up for others. I have a checking account now, that's an accomplishment. I'm just dating now—no sex, just want to have a nice time. I'm practicing celibacy. Spiritually, I'm experiencing God now. I was thinking that God must really love me. I have no scars, except mental scars, but it's over with. But it's something that happened, but I'm glad He allowed it to happen, so if somebody else did go through it, I could be there for them. Pain ... I guess when you get tired of feeling the pain, it motivates you to change your life. I even have a better relationship with my kids, but I am just really learning how to love 'em.

In these cases, both women were already motivated by what they had accomplished while living sober, free from abuse, and reengaged with their families. They were proud to have lived many years with HIV, most without symptoms. Both endured years of physical, emotional, and sexual abuse, rape, and incarceration, and survived. Each had a role-model-like stature among many WCHP patients, a phenomenon that can be a source of pressure to relapse. Peers get to know you, learn of your behavioral changes, become inspired, and try to emulate you. Pressure is raised on role models to be flawless in their own recovery. Such pressure is unrealistic and unintentional, but it does happen, and it can lead to relapse.

Participant #9 once worked part time for WCHP, and advocated for patients regularly. Participant #7 was one of the first to graduate from the peer HIV education training program, and was admired by her peers for living so long with

HIV—mostly free of symptoms. Her longevity gave hope to women just beginning to learn to live with HIV.

Each of the former substance-using women experienced their longest period of sobriety ever since learning of their HIV status. Prior to that, most had little or no experience with sobriety during their adult years. Perhaps for the first time, long-term experience with sobriety was a good state to be in as reported by participants in recovery. They were beginning to like their lives without drugs, and, for most, this also meant life without enduring physical or emotional abuse. Typical statements in the interviews were:

I just want to be an example for anybody that's addicted. Just be an example to let them know that you can change your life. You can live without the use of drugs. I didn't know I could function without drugs. I didn't think I ever could. I thought I was gonna die a dope fiend. I am responsible now, I can do things on my own. [I feel better about my life today] ... because I'm being a mother to my children and an example in the community. This is the best my life has ever been.—#11

I now enjoy the relationships I have with my kids, especially my daughter, the oldest one. We like buddies, almost. My son, he's leery because he always known me to be irresponsible, but now he sees that I'm responsible. He brings his buddies around me now. For a long time he wouldn't bring a friend, but now he brings his friends around. I've got an apartment in my name. I'm a paying consumer. I do speak out for those afflicted and affected by this virus. I get a lot out of it. I get more than I give.—#17

Finally, this participant expressed a new outlook that is in place:

Today, I look at my life as a productive member of society. Today I'm a responsible parent. I'm a responsible person today. My mother trusts me now to go to the store and get her groceries, and bring her groceries and change back. I came a long way to get where I am today, and I refuse to let the devil destroy me and take away my joy, because when I broke up my relationship with my [abusive] fiance, he said you won't be there long. And I said like, no, he won't take me back to the bottle. ... What I really thought about doing if God answer my blessings is open up a recovery house for women and children, for women that are HIV-positive or have AIDS. It took me a long time to accept I'm HIV-positive, about two years. And I finally made up my mind, get some acceptance with it. Life goes on, and you know about it, and you know there is treatment for it.—#2

Transformers, with and without substance use backgrounds, arrived at a certain "peace" or acknowledgment of the unprotected sex and needle-sharing actions that placed them at risk for HIV-infection, even though they may not have understood it at the time they were engaged in those behaviors. Some even came to understand how enduring repeated abuses in childhood and beyond damaged self-esteem and set them up for prolonged engagement in what they now know as risky behaviors. They came to this viewpoint either without the added baggage of self-imposed judgment, or at some point they later dropped the judgment baggage from their thinking. As a result, dropping that baggage may have effectively made it more difficult for others to impose judgmental attitudes upon them.

There are different examples of dropped baggage. Participant #5 concluded that she couldn't be a parent and achieve and maintain sobriety at the same time, and consented to place her youngest child for adoption. Upon acceptance of the circumstances, she achieved her longest period of sobriety ever in life (ten months) and obtained a full-time job, her first in ten years. She described how she made her decision:

I've had baby after baby. And they have been with those people since they were babies. I don't want to fool myself, those people are giving my kids love and support they need that I don't have. I need to get myself together, and not being together and trying to have a baby is not going to work. It's rough trying to get me together. I'm going through so many changes, physically, emotionally, mentally, all of that.

In contrast, participants #4 and #14 concluded that they wanted to be parents strongly enough to fight successfully to regain custody of their children. Participant #14 described in detail how she regained custody of all six of her children:

They told me that 30 days of treatment and six weeks of parenting and you can have your children back. My ass was whipped so bad, I went into treatment 20 months and 8 months of parenting. That still wasn't enough. Once I completed the programs, I did outpatient [addiction treatment] for one year. Then they found out that I was HIV-positive, that's a separate issue. They didn't know what stage I was in the disease. They felt if I had my children returned home to me, I might get sick and die next month. This was a real issue. I fought it, I really fought it in court. I told my worker; my worker was the same one who took my children. This social worker had been with me for so many years. I couldn't stand her because she be so right all the time. She was really right. She was telling me what I needed to do and I didn't want to hear that shit because I always wanted to do what I wanted to do as opposed to what I needed to do. Doing what you need to do is no fucking fun. I got a doctor's statement that I was fine and healthy enough to take care of my children. We went into the courtroom and my health issue came up, the day I told my lawyer about it. The judge was like, "we're going to take a break and then I need to see all the attorneys in my chamber." I was real nervous and scared, they stayed away for 40 minutes. Then they called us back in. The judge said, "Ms ———, I see no reason why your child cannot go home with you." It was a party in the courtroom! We had a ball! Me and my son walked out of that courtroom together. My other five children were all gradually returned within that same year.—#14

Freedom from judgmental burden allowed new personal visions to develop, for healthier, safer decision making and for transformation to have a chance to emerge.

Transformation and Spirituality

Most participants reported movement toward leading more spiritual lives. For some, the journey began before learning their HIV status, later strengthened from living with HIV. Some formally joined a place of worship. Others embraced spirituality less formally, but no less meaningfully, as an anchor for making healthy decisions. Large Bibles and other faith articles on tables, gospel music on the stereo, and biblical names and symbols on jewelry were visible in the homes or on the person(s) of many participants. Participant #1 shared her beliefs:

Since I've been sober, my eyes are more open now. God's gonna be with me, you know. If it's meant, it's gonna happen. I can't change that. You know the only thing I can do is thank Him for letting me be here, and being able to walk, being able to talk, laugh, breathe and smile, look at the birds, you know. Since I've been sober, I really see life. It's a whole lot that I didn't see before. Life is beautiful, just like the flowers and stuff they plant out there. You see, even I've got a little plant.

"Trouble in My Way" is an old gospel song that participant #4 referred to, and occasionally sang, almost as if it were her theme song. She obtained all five of her children from Illinois Department of Children and Family Services (DCFS) custody after completing addiction treatment. Treatment worked on her third attempt, she thinks, because of the inspiration she got from her father who successfully completed a treatment program, and she liked what she saw in him as a result. She explained:

Haymarket [the treatment program] broke my ass down. They really helped me. I started liking myself. My friends today are all different—I don't have no "using" friends. I go to church four times a week with all my kids, the same church as my daddy, and I was never religious, before. I'm just taking care of myself and my kids, and all my kids are in school. I love being a peer [HIV] educator on the OB [CCH obstetric] wards and I tell all those women about myself, too.

Participant #11 became a Suni Muslim several years before learning her status, and it remained as source of strength for her over time. She explained:

I met a man who was a Muslim in 1980 and he liked me. So during that time, I started finding out more and more. It was something about the way he lived that was totally different from living a Christian lifestyle. People would say, "Your husband made you convert." But that was not it at all, even though he played a big part in introducing me to it. It touched my heart, and that's what made me convert.

Participant #8 had a special experience that she described:

It all started when I was in the hospital. I was so scared, I was just talking to the Lord, talking to Him and praying to Him, and talking to Him out loud like I'm talking to you. And I really believe He heard me because then that woman came to see me, like a day later, she came. She sat down and told me about how I could be saved and I need to repent for my sins. From that moment on, I've established a steady relationship with the Lord. Then, that following December, I got baptized, speaking in tongues and everything. It was nice. I was saying all kinds of stuff I didn't even know what I was saying. I had never had that type of experience before. God is why my life is better than before.

Participant #9, although not a member of a specific faith congregation, explained the role that spirituality was beginning to play in her life:

I am trying to become dependent of God, and it's like I am experiencing Him, now, believing what He says. That's what I really want to do—people say you can't be perfect, but I am going to try to be perfect. But I don't want to say that I'm Christian and still doing things I'm not so supposed to. I'm either a Christian or I'm not. Like the Bible say do this and do that, and don't curse and all like that. Like today, I did say a couple of [curse] words, but it's a difference in saying a couple of words, from every word coming out of your mouth. My kids say I sound funny when I curse. I do have a relationship with my children. But I am learning to love them. But people say they love their kids automatically, I know that's my responsibility. I have them and they belong to me. So I know I'm supposed to take care of them—but that don't mean I have to love them, so that's an accomplishment.

In summary, the quest to make sense of life and all the experiences included spiritual examination by most participants, with twelve of them naming a personal spiritual belief from which they found strength from an additional membership and participation in some faith-based institution. Eleven transformers began to include spirituality in their lives, as did one of the nontransformers. As they personally defined it, spirituality seemed to be an important anchor upon which transformative thinking and action could have its chance to emerge.

Race/Class/Gender, Advocacy, and Transformation

There remains a social context under which people live, and it has an impact on the transformation process, whether realized fully by the person or not. Race, class, and gender concepts and practices in U.S. society provide a significant part of the social context of everyday living. Some participants gave such examples; most did not. Participants #1 and #2 endured race-based mistreatment by other Blacks, including family members. Participant #1 responded to a question about childhood relationships: "Well, my childhood friends, I always kinda got in trouble with them. And, they used to tease me. They used to call me 'big lips' and I didn't get along too well with them. The ones I did get along with were the ones I used to sit around with and we would have drinks and do little things we didn't have no business doing."

Perhaps friends who did not use substances were a turnoff because of the teasing they did. Nonteasing friends represented other negative influences. The teasing logic is that big lips are considered ugly; they did not fit the imposed standard of what was considered beautiful at the time (thin lips). It is an example of internalized oppression when a person behaves in such a way that accepts or internalizes racist stereotype images or myths as fact.[4] Such images can be generationally passed on, thereby assuring continuation of the stereotyping process. The images get "played out" as teasing daggers among children. A different observation on this theme is made by participant #2:

My grandfather used to always tell me, "you light skinned." "You don't belong in this family. All the rest of my grandchildren is dark skinned, you is not my son's daughter." And, I held a resentment against him for a long time. And, I said, well I don't belong in this family. I don't need to be here, no way. When I get older, I'm getting away from them. As soon as I could figure out a way to get away, I'm gonna get away.

It is not known if the grandfather resented how he perceived "light skinned" Blacks were treated compared with Black people of a darker complexion at the time, and if that was held against his granddaughter, or if he actually thought she wasn't biologically related. What's important is that the statement made her feel unwanted and excluded from her family.

The workplace is one place where different nationalities regularly interact. Only four women in the sample were working when interviewed, and only two worked full time. Participant #11 (a full-time worker) shared her feelings about it:

The department I work in is mostly female. All three supervisors are White women. It's subtle. They make you feel welcome, but in the same breath, they want their demands done. It's not just them, it's the group in particular. Like the college kids that work there are young, White kids. They go out to work and they [the supervisors] take them out to lunch. They don't do that with me. Sometimes, I don't feel good enough. Like I was working one of my temporary assignments and I was paired with this White girl. She was really petty to me. At that point, I felt low.

Participant #11 may have actually felt low because of a perception about skill differential between herself and the coworker as her next statements in the interview were about plans to enroll in college classes. Yet she expressed her feelings based on physical comparisons. The imposition of western beauty standards continues to be a source of excess judgmental baggage to be dropped for those who do not fit the mold.

The concept of gender is complicated. The partners and/or attackers of these women were mostly Black men. Black men as a group do not have the same economic or political power in society as White men, yet they are influenced by male supremacy. The practice of abuse transcends race and class. When abuse begins in childhood, especially when prolonged, one's idea of trust, self-appreciation, respect, and dignity becomes a difficult, if not impossible, concept to grasp as one's deserved everyday human right. Some participants grew up under prolonged abusive conditions that were basically repeated in their adult relationships. Along with enduring abuse, addiction to substances often follows (Cohen et al. 2000; Cassese 1993).

Participants experienced abusive treatment that ranged from verbal/emotional to physical and sexual. Unlike the racial issues, they had more examples to share. Interpretations of their experiences varied. Some felt their mistreatment was a consequence of living an addiction lifestyle, and the social dangers associated with it, as described by participant #11:

Fast life, period. Fast money, fast life, that's what put me in danger. I was smoking crack cocaine while I'm in a methadone program. I called myself detoxing from one drug and got addicted to two. The last time I got high, I woke up, laying next to a man that I didn't know, who looked like a lizard. That's when I knew I needed to get out of there and into treatment.

Some considered survival of childhood sexual abuse as a contributor to their endurance of abuse in adulthood and/or to their addiction to substances. As participant #14 explains:

I didn't have a childhood. It was nothing like I wanted it to be. So much happened to me. So much adults had done to me that I had no control over it, and it went on for years to me. I didn't have any self-esteem because of the abuse—for years, it wasn't like a one time thing. Once, my sister and her friends were going up to this building to smoke marijuana together, and I went. I tried it, and I loved it. It got to the point where I needed to have something to drink with it. First it was beer, then wine, and the other drugs came later. I was a gangbanger. I got pregnant, the father of my first four children was physically abusive. We was together seven years. He was drinking. I was doing drugs, selling drugs. He was doing all that stuff. He was gangbanging. By me being young, I thought it was cute. I was this tough girl. It was just so crazy.

Although gender-based mistreatment was a more accessible subject for them, linking their own experiences to gender inequality in society was difficult for all but a few participants.

There is a big problem with racism in society, you know, with the police, employment, welfare, the community, the environment and living conditions. A white man in my building called me an—, just recently. I was really mistreated as a woman, especially when I was a prostitute. Even when you say no to [sex with] men, you get this "bitch this, bitch that," response. Rape is forced sex . . . I was raped three times. There was one other time when I woke up in a strange place, naked and sore.—#7

Despite enduring these violations, participant #7 was optimistic when she said: "I feel great. I go to support groups, I have a good counselor and I can talk with her almost anytime I want to. I even have good fellowship with my housekeeper [personal assistant] I don't think my life changes have been profound, but I do feel my life has changed, and I'm still changing."

Class was a more clear-cut concept. It was clear in that the women knew they were poor. However, some were not as poor as they had become when interviewed. Some had more income in their previous lifestyles, though illegally obtained for some. They were adjusting to living on a fixed SSI income, as participant #6 explained: "I always made money. I did a little of everything. I boosted [meaning shoplifted] clothes; I sold drugs. Now, I can only do so much. I don't have no money to really get around, I don't have no car. It's a lot of things I be wanting that I have to do without, 'cause I don't have nothing to get nothing with. It's just one of them things."

Some women were just beginning to assume parenting responsibilities for the first time, and had to adjust to budgeting for six or eight, rather than one or two. Some had been raised in working to lower middle-class households and were just beginning to live on their own, without parental or partner assistance, and through legal means. Participant #15 explained:

If it don't happen, it don't happen. If I don't have it, I don't have it. If I can't get it, I can't get it. It feels better to earn it. 'Cause I can connive anybody out of some shit, but it don't sit right, anymore. That came from learning about myself. I learned that it's not always the street way. And that was instilled in me coming out and why I saw my mother struggle. That was the way to do it, not the street way. All you have to do is earn it and you can have it. I took for granted that [my mother and father] had it, but I didn't take it for granted that they saved to have it. My mother and them said when I get sixty years old, all the money I took from people during my addiction, some young man, seventeen years old gonna take all my checks.

Several participants talked about the unfairness of welfare "reform." Some commented that it wasn't enough money to live on, and they would rather work it they could find it; others complained about how hard it was to find work and child care. As #2 described: "I'm struggling to keep the place that I have. I've been going on job interviews. I'm gonna go back to school and get my GED, and then go on and get my certificate in substance abuse. 'Cause I don't really want to be on Social Security or public aid, because they give you the run around." Participant #3 shared similar sentiments as well:

I still want to be a nurse, but I can't go to school right now, because I need a job. I'm looking for work. I gotta do one or the other, because the baby-sitter ... it's hard, it's hard. I don't think I can get a baby-sitter and go to school, and I ain't got nothing to pay her with. So, I just have to get me a job, so I can afford a good baby-sitter. You *have* to look for work on public aid. You only gonna be on it for five years. If I just go to school, and then I'm still on [public] aid, and then they cut me off, and then what?

Participant #9 looked at the struggle for a decent income in another way:

I said God got a plan for me ... you know those same women be coming here [to WCHP], the majority. It's like they're satisfied with their lives being the way they are. And I don't want to be like that. It's like they in a rut. It's like they jumped to SSI. And I refuse to go on SSI. It's like they accepting this. And I don't want to be like that, so I try to get ahead. I don't think I'm better than they are. I don't want people thinking HIV people are all like that. I want them to think good of us. I do understand that some people have to get over to SSI, but I feel that all of us don't have to be there, though. And that's what make me strive for better.

Examples of some qualitative life change that was socially positive, despite their illness, were given even from nontransformers. However, race, class, and gender inequality was *objectively* important, but not necessarily *subjectively* interpreted as such by the participants, including risk factors for acquiring HIV. Most had not begun to place their experiences in the context of what it means to be an African American woman in U.S. society, which indicates that their transformation was largely on the personal growth level. Political transformation had not emerged for most, despite triumphs over multiple adversities. Their life stories revealed how their societal status and limited, disempowered choices led them to harmful situations, including the increased risk of HIV-infection. Most of them, however, found a way to move from disempowered to empowered personal decision making—with most doing so after learning their HIV status. What prompted that movement?

Perhaps the impact of new knowledge and the opportunities to use it forms a bridge from individually centered transformation to a different form that exposes people to new possibilities, particularly in helping others. Several participants completed a course in HIV peer education.[5] These included transforming and nontransforming participants. One participant completed a similar course elsewhere. When interviewed, eight of those who completed the course lead some form of peer HIV education at least on an occasional basis, ranging from weekly to a few times per year. One conducts regular peer HIV education with postpartum women on the Cook County Hospital obstetric-gynecological wards and refers women for HIV counseling and testing with health professionals. One cofacilitates a support group for HIV-positive women seeking recovery from addiction; one is a peer HIV educator with new patients in one WCHP clinic session; two others volunteer on a weekly basis in the clinic. Being a peer HIV educator was important to many participants interviewed, and emerged as an unsolicited empowering phenomenon identified by several of them. For example, participant #1 said, "I like being a peer educator. I like talking to the patients ... I love that job, talking to new patients coming in, and letting them know you can live with this virus."

New knowledge emerged from other sources besides the WCHP peer education training program. Some participants also expressed new perspectives based on what they learned from drug treatment or participation in other programs. New knowledge had a profound effect that participant #14 described:

There's a lot of things that's been going on with me, my life history. I didn't talk about ... none of this stuff was ever dealt with. It builds up and builds up and as a result, drug abuse is the last result of the problem. Drug abuse is not even my problem, that's the end result of the problem. By so much stuff happening to me, when I started using drugs, it was too late already. If things could have been dealt with as they happened, I probably never would have resorted to drugs. But I would encourage a person to talk about what's going on with them, because if they weren't taught that talking about problems helps to heal you, they're not gonna talk. I deal with people now. Whenever people call me, I go [to speak about drug/HIV prevention]. I don't give a shit if it's all the way in Kankakee. I will talk and try to help because I've been there ... I walked in those shoes.

New knowledge and practice opportunities through educating others can lead to advocacy on behalf of and with others as well. WCHP's first peer educator, Novella Dudley, demonstrated it; participant #7 acknowledged that Novella's friendship and remembrance of her work inspired her to advocate on behalf of people living with HIV, as well as to educate about HIV prevention. Participant #17 described a different variation on the advocacy theme:

My life is like a revolution—from the person I was to the person I am now. I'm more like the person I was, way back in the beginning, when I was kind. I'm getting back to that. I'm getting back to the person I was when I was younger, which wasn't a bad person. When my life revolved around drugs, I was a lost soul. I was in a lot of pain and misery, but I didn't know it. The only time I recognized it was when I got busted and went to jail. I'm aware of mortality, now. At one time, I thought I had from now on. But now, I know that ain't the case. What's different now is that I face problems. I used to walk away. I got relationships. I pay bills, I pay rent. Brought me back to humanity, so that I could think. ... Last year, I went to Springfield to the legislature. I would love to do more of that—be a voice for minority Black women. I spoke at a couple of schools on the south side. I enjoyed it, and they needed it bad. Some of them so hardheaded, they want to be the class clown. I said, you might be standing up here next, if you don't pay attention.

"Dropped baggage" of negative self-judgment and at least some of those life-time multiple stressors seemed essential for transformation to grow and develop. In each case of those who transformed, one or more major stressors were elim-inated, which then allowed for life with HIV to emerge as a perhaps liberating and enlightening phenomenon, even as the potential of fatality coexists.

DISCUSSION

This project was an attempt to learn more about multiple stress, serious ill-ness, and life changes among the participants, and to see if the stress and coping concepts of Lazarus and Folkman (1984) was a sufficient explanation for the dra-matic life changes that occurred among most participants. For these authors, coping includes all efforts to manage stress; it separated in two categories: emo-tion-focused and problem-focused. Emotion-focused efforts occur when an ap-praisal concludes that nothing can be done to modify harmful or threatening environmental conditions. The problem-focused approach is derived from an ap-praisal that deems conditions amenable to change and is directed at managing the problem causing distress.

The experiences of these participants were in sharp contrast with Lazarus and Folkman's (1984) example. They did not have resources, they did not have two seemingly episodic crises to arise simultaneously that suddenly produced mul-tiple stressful conditions. Most were very poor, living with multiple, persistent stressors before and during the time they learned about their HIV status. Sev-eral experienced multiple traumatic events in their lives, such as imprisonment, sexual abuse, and physical beatings. Several reported that they lost siblings or other loved ones to murder or drug overdose; others lost custody of their chil-dren. Their accounts of childhood and adult life experiences were more similar with those described as "overwhelmed" by Hopps, Pinderhughes, and Shankar (1995). Overwhelmed clients were defined as economically poor persons who were "prey to physical, emotional and psychological problems; spotty (if any) employment; family violence, substance abuse and child abuse; truancy, teenage pregnancy, and financially irresponsible fatherhood" (2).

The cohort comprised mostly African American families that failed, succeeded, and partially succeeded in improving family functioning with help from social service agencies. Some families succeeded and relapsed back to what was char-acterized as family dysfunction. Success was described as movement toward social functioning that manifests improved self-esteem, social and psychological competence, educational competence, and the capacity to develop skills that lead to self-sufficiency and dignity (93).

Overwhelmed fairly characterizes most participants interviewed, at least for a time. At previous points in their lives, several participants who considered themselves transformed or in process when interviewed, appraised their situation and concluded that nothing could be done to alter it. They made emotional adjustments where they could to improve their ability to cope with the circumstances. Sometimes their adjustment was to suppress all emotion toward themselves and others. Some participants stayed in physically and emotionally abusive relationships, continued to doubt their ability to recover from addiction, tried and failed or never entered addiction treatment, continued illegal acts, and other harmful behaviors.

At some point, a reappraisal took place among these women. For some, this act occurred before the HIV status was learned, as in the case of participants #4, #11, #14, and #15. These women entered addiction treatment and later learned their HIV status. They credited their treatment experience and recovery process as sources of strength to remain sober, deal positively with their HIV status, and face parenting and custody issues with their children, among other things. Others had their reappraisal experience to occur later, in some cases a year or more after the HIV status was learned, as in the case of participants #1, #2, and #7. All three of these women had addiction problems and tried to get as high as possible upon learning of their HIV status or shortly thereafter. In somewhat different scenarios, when it was discovered that their drug binges did not kill them, they chose to live, instead.

Making the choice to live seems to include making the choice to live life differently than before. In several cases, study participants literally removed themselves from certain stressful situations, such as an abusive relationship, or they chose not to return to certain stressful environments such as prison, friendships with active drug users, or even the neighborhood in which they previously lived. Examples of such movement were reported by transformers and nontransformers. Most women interviewed changed their circumstances and entered new ones with a different outlook and a different sense of personal self-confidence. They set goals they planned to achieve. They began to think and do things in a profoundly different way—seeds of transformation, perhaps.

Lazarus and Folkman's (1984) coping definition included the words "constantly changing cognitive and behavioral efforts." On the one hand, this concept fits the experiences of the women interviewed. They did try different things to alleviate stressful demands or forget past or recent abuses. For several, drugs were things used for stress relief, to diminish pain or as emotional escape devices. In recovery programs, in prison, or through other counseling, the women learned and accepted the fact that they did not work. As new knowledge was learned and accepted, new strategies were tried by them to reduce the stressful demands.

However, on the other hand, for several women the reappraisal process of their situations allowed them to consider for the first time or redefine specifically what situations were taxing and exceeding their personal resources. For instance, participant #5 never experienced an intimate relationship that was not narrowly defined by sex and or physical dominance of her partner(s). She reported that ten of her childhood years were marked by sexual abuse from several adult men. Prior to gaining a different understanding, she did not have a reference that a relationship should or could be anything different. Her years of enduring the abuse distorted her ability to appropriately define a loving or caring relationship. She suffered emotionally and physically through drug use, poor health, and the birth of seven children, having custody of none. However conceptually, her adolescent and adult intimate experiences were cognitively not too taxing for her until she learned and understood better—a process that was still continuing when interviewed. She explained:

My mom told me if somebody liked me and wanted to have sex with me, make sure I got some money from it. So that's how I started. My first boyfriend was six years older than me. He was twenty-one and I was fifteen, and all we really had going was sex, and I used that to get anything I wanted. And I did it with men and they were unprotected. At the time, there wasn't things going on like they are now [meaning HIV]. If he looked good, I was hooked on good looks. And if he looked good, he could have some. With this last baby, I told my mom I couldn't do it no more—the drugs, even the cigarettes. I didn't want those enticing clothes. I told my mom to go through my closet and get all those nasty things out of my life. For a minute, I stopped wearing makeup, because even makeup for me was a trigger because I liked to look pretty. It made me big headed when I would go in and out of treatment and I would look so good. It went to my head, I got so many compliments from men and my shape was real nice, and I had this nasty little walk that I don't walk anymore today. Praise God, thank you Jesus. I don't have to put on no mask to be somebody that I am not. To me, that was devastating because I almost died. I almost died. Hitting that bottom was enough there for me.

Reappraisal for participant #5 was also perhaps an investigation and discovery of herself, as well as a reassessment of past practices as too demanding for her current frame of mind. Lazarus and Folkman (1984) point out that these cognitive processes often persist in the postimpact period (of crises or stressful events), and that a host of new considerations and tasks emerge. They then ask: "Can one return to the *status quo ante*, or have things changed appreciably?" (148). That question assumes that the situation was manageable and acceptable before the stressful event(s). For many of these women, their most "manageable" period is the present, and several expressed interest in building upon whatever progress they had recently achieved, such as raising their children themselves, continuing sobriety, exploring their spiritual side, working at their jobs, and/or enrolling in school. Even nontransformers spoke of being busy pursuing such endeavors. It is possible that one can revert back to past practices, including unsuccessful coping strategies; but if things have changed appreciably, especially with time, then it may indicate something more than coping variation—perhaps seeds of personal transformation. If it is a transformation, how long can it last?

Perhaps reappraisal is the point where dropping the baggage of guilt, shame, poor self-esteem, and imposed stigma occurs among the previously overwhelmed women. Perhaps elimination of some of the other multiple stressors allowed the women to then "cope" with the stress associated with an HIV-positive diagnosis. Coping with HIV for most grew to include coping with being a full-time custodial parent for the first time; full- and part-time employment for the first time (or in a long while); return to school or other training; and living sober. Each of these new activities has inherent in them other potentially stressful features that were viewed by the participants as challenges to be met with confidence—not as demands exceeding their personal resources. Most participants also pointed out human, spiritual, and service resources in their lives that they could consider for support, if needed, which represented a change from their past when they could not name a reliable, positive source of support. Resources mentioned included family of origin from which they had previously been estranged, addiction and mental health counselors, medical providers, and formal and informal peer support (other HIV-positive individuals and support group members).

Lazarus and Folkman (1984) acknowledged spiritual belief as a source of effective coping, as did several of the participants. Two actually referred to pastoral support (#7 and #10). This is significant, because it indicates that these women were members of congregations that allowed them to feel comfortable enough to disclose their HIV status to their clergy leaders and actually reported being supported after doing so. Spiritual support for persons living with HIV in the United States has been mixed, ranging from advocacy and compassion to indifference and judgmental rejection among the various religious orders in many communities, including the African American one (Cohen 1999; Dalton 1989).

Multiple kinds of support helped participants succeed in their decisions to achieve several goals identified by them while they also managed life with HIV. For example, avoiding re-arrest, for those who were formally incarcerated, required substantial, sustained behavioral change, as did maintaining sobriety, returning to school, seeking/obtaining employment, and becoming or reestablishing oneself as a responsible parent. Several participants rose to the occasion when challenged, and resisted pressures to return to previous decision-making tactics.

Participant #11 began to use an emotion-focused form of coping with her son's undesirable behaviors while continuing to use problem-focused (problem-solving) skills in dealing with her own multiple goals of maintaining sobriety, providing full custodial parenting to her children, holding on to her job (a first in many years), and managing life with HIV. It is doubtful that she could maintain sobriety and provide sensible, even if not fully accepted, counseling to her son without having discarded past stressors of drug abuse and prostitution.

Dropping the baggage of imposed stigma, shame, and guilt seemed to make it possible for coping skills to improve from minimalist emotional suppression to a combination of emotion-focused skills designed to maintain hope and optimism. A transformative vision had a chance to emerge where one begins to consider what is possible, instead of what cannot possibly be achieved. It is a vision that "reappraises" concepts or goals that seemed unthinkable or impractical in the past to concepts and goals that are thinkable and obtainable in the present or near future. The new concept that propels such thinking into the equation is personal power.

The perception of power (personal control) or lack thereof, is the conceptual ingredient in an appraisal decision that something or nothing can be done to alter or change the stressful event or condition. The perception that power is unobtainable leads some women to give up trying to cope, due to belief that it is hopeless to do so: a symptom of depression. Learned helplessness is a theory based on an experiment with animals that learned through prior conditioning that they were helpless in the face of "uncontrollable" shock, and so gave up trying to cope behaviorally and instead passively cowered in the cage (Seligman 1975). These results were offered as one explanation of human depression. Contrast that with Goodrich (1991) who defined power as the capacity to gain whatever resources necessary to remove oneself from a condition of oppression, to guarantee one's ability to perform, and to affect not only one's own circumstances, but also more general circumstances outside one's intimate surroundings. Hopps, Pinderhughes, and Shankar (1995) conclude that power involves the capacity to influence for one's own benefit the forces that affect one's life space; powerlessness is the inability to exert such influence.

Many participants began to exercise personal power for themselves and their families, and they spoke about it when interviewed. Most, with some exceptions, had not yet moved to consider political or collective power beyond their personal boundaries. A few began to consider themselves as advocates. Such a movement is an important first step to participation in the world of HIV policy making, a world with very few women like those interviewed at the decision-making table.

IMPLICATIONS FOR SOCIAL SERVICE AND PUBLIC POLICY

The accounts of the women interviewed suggest that health care and human service providers may need to establish new or to strengthen existing empowerment practices. Such practices should have an atmosphere for transformation to emerge, to promote a partnership between workers and clients, and to include clients as leaders, planners, and evaluators of policies, agencies, programs, and services. Empowerment practice compliments Mann and Taratola's (1996) concept of reducing personal and programmatic vulnerability for HIV-affected populations. The more one is able to make such decisions, the more empowered they are. Conversely, the least capable they are of making such decisions, the more vulnerable they are. Programmatic vulnerability refers to the role of HIV/AIDS programs in reducing or increasing personal vulnerability through three intervention elements: information and education, health and social services, and nondiscrimination toward people living with HIV/AIDS. The societal vulnerability concept recognizes that broader, contextual issues such as government structure, gender relationships, and attitudes toward sexuality, religious beliefs, and poverty influence the capacity to reduce personal vulnerability to HIV, both directly and as mediated through programs.

There are empowerment practices in the United States that have effectively served people living with HIV/AIDS (PWAs), including African American HIV-positive women. Most are comprehensive medical and psychosocial programs supported by the federal Ryan White CARE Act.[6] The component of the CARE Act that is the most woman, adolescent, and family specific is Title IV. This title is the legislative mandate to provide HIV comprehensive care services, primary and secondary prevention services, and access to research and clinical trials for women, children, and youth affected by HIV/AIDS. These and many other CARE Act–supported programs have demonstrated commitment to empowering their clients to participate in their own healthy decision making and program design, as well as in broad HIV policy making in their local areas.

Local participation must lead to input in national and, increasingly, international HIV program development, advocacy, and policy making. The movement is growing to assure that women, men, youth, and caregivers of color are better represented in this arena. The AIDS Alliance for Children, Youth & Families is a national organization of AIDS activists of all backgrounds. Title IV service providers, and consumer partners, which include adult and young PWAs, affected loved ones, and caregivers. It was founded in 1994 as the AIDS Policy Center for Children, Youth & Families on the premise that consumers and service providers can work together to achieve maximum effectiveness in identifying service needs and policies for these populations. Its mission has since expanded to include education and training for consumers and providers, which resulted in the name change. In 2000, AIDS Alliance launched a national training institute for consumers, who, in turn, provide self-empowerment training to their peers. These consumer-led training help young people, women, and families to navigate the HIV/AIDS care system successfully, build partnerships with providers, and get involved in program planning, implementation, and evaluation (AIDS Alliance Annual Report 2000). At this writing, it was learned that the AIDS Alliance has a complementary youth corp leadership project to begin in 2001, which marks the twentieth year of the AIDS pandemic as we know it.

Findings from this study suggest that programmatic training and advocacy efforts as just described are examples of empowerment practice. These interventions help create an atmosphere for transformation to emerge for some, move the transformation process forward for others, which is perhaps a way to help sustain powerful attitudes and actions over time, if given a chance. Much has been learned about the biological, epidemiological, social, and behavioral aspects of this virus and the millions of people it affects. Among our greatest lessons learned is that inequality driven by race, class, gender, sexual orientation, disability, and educational/professional differences is a causal agent of vulnerability. Reduction and elimination of vulnerability where possible may be the key ingredient to reducing new HIV infections and improving optimal care and services for all who live with HIV/AIDS.

NOTES

1. Novella Dudley (1951–1996) was an African American woman patient and the first to be trained and graduate as a peer educator by the Women & Children HIV Program in 1989. She led her first peer HIV-education session at her storefront church in Chicago's Englewood neighborhood, and went on to lead HIV-risk-reduction sessions all over the country. She soon became a nationally recognized leader in influencing public policy for women living with HIV disease. She served on several local and national policy-making councils and founded the organization Women Resourcing Women to assure HIV-positive women would have a vehicle of their own in which to advocate for their health care and political rights.

2. M.T. Fullilove was instrumental in pointing out the distinction between the two terms.

3. Participant #2 explained earlier in the interview that her test results were actually given to her sister by mistake, over the telephone by a health care worker, who assumed that they were speaking to the patient at the time.

4. Yamato (1998) defined internalized oppression as the emotional, physical, and spiritual battering of the target group to the point that they actually believe that their oppression is deserved and their mistreatment is justified. Like a virus, the author said, it's hard to beat racism, because by the time you come up with a cure, it's mutated to a "new cure-resistant" form.

5. The Women and Children HIV Program began a course for patients in 1989 that educates them about HIV-prevention and risk reduction and prepares them to educate others (peers) about HIV. The content is adapted from a Red Cross HIV Prevention training curriculum. It is an eight-session course; each session is two hours. Each course concludes with a graduation. Each graduate can, if she chooses, lead formal and informal HIV prevention presentations with audiences of any type and get paid a stipend for doing so.

6. The Ryan White Comprehensive AIDS Emergency (CARE) Act is the name of the $1.7 billion federal program that, second to Medicaid, funds the bulk of HIV medical, dental, and psychosocial services in the United States, including financial subsidy of the cost of HAART medications for the medically uninsured or underinsured (Stein 1998). It began in 1990 and is named after Ryan White, an AIDS-diagnosed hemophiliac who suffered stigma and abuse, including exclusion from school before he died at age eighteen. Client participation in program decision making is one of the cornerstones of the CARE Act. Collective action by PWAs and allies made the original legislation possible. Continued advocacy has sustained it over time.

REFERENCES

Adisa, O.P. (1990). Rocking in the sun light: Stress and Black women. In E.C. White (Ed.), *The Black women's health book: Speaking for ourselves*. Seattle: Seal Press.

AIDS Alliance for Children, Youth & Families. 2000 Annual Report: *AIDS: We're in this together*. Washington, DC.

Aschenbrenner, J. (1975). *Lifelines: Black families in Chicago*. New York: Waveland Press, Inc.

Bandura, A. (1977). *Social Learning Theory*, Englewood Cliffs, NJ: Prentice-Hall.

———. (1989). Human agency in social cognitive theory. *American Psychologist*, 44 (9), 1175–1184.

Battle, S. (1997). The bond is called Blackness: Black women and AIDS. In N. Goldstein and J.L. Manlowe (Eds.). *The gender politics of HIV/AIDS in women: Perspectives on the pandemic in the United States* (pp. 282–291). New York: New York University Press.

Becker, G. (1997). *Disrupted lives: How people create meaning in a chaotic world*. Berkeley: University of California Press.

Belle, D. (1990). Poverty and women's mental health. *American Psychologist*, 45 (3), 385–389.

Boxer, A. and Coon, L. (1994). *Issues facing HIV+ women with a history of Illinois Department of Children & Family Services (DCFS) involvement*. Report prepared for DCFS, Chicago.

Cassese, J. (1993). The invisible bridge: Child sexual abuse and the risk of HIV infection in Adulthood. *SIECUS Report*, 21 (4) April/May. Sex Information and Education Council of the United States, New York.

Centers for Disease Control and Prevention. (1999). *HIV/AIDS Surveillance Report*, Midyear Edition, 11 (1).

Centers for Disease Control and Prevention (2002). Women and AIDS Factsheet, L264 update 3/4/2002. Slide series slide #2.

Chavis, D.M. and Wandersman, A. (1990). Sense of community in the urban environment. *American Journal of Community Psychology*, 18 55–81.

Cohen, C.J. (1999). *The boundaries of Blackness: AIDS and the breakdown of Black politics*. Chicago: University of Chicago Press.

Cohen, M., Deamant, C., Barkan, S., Richardson, J., et al. (2000). Domestic violence and childhood sexual abuse in HIV-infected women and women at risk for HIV. *American Journal of Public Health*, (90) 4, 560–572.

Collins, P.H. (1990). *Black feminist thought: Knowledge, consciousness and the politics of empowerment*. New York: Routledge.

Cook, J., Boxer, A., Camarigg, V., Cohen, M., et al. (1990). The impact of AIDS on inner-city minority women: The role of emotion management in risk factor reports by women attending a public hospital HIV clinic. Presented at the 85th Annual Meeting of the American Sociological Society, Washington, DC.

Dalton, H.L. (1989). AIDS in Blackface. *Daedalus: Journal of the American Academy of Arts and Sciences*, 118 (3), 205–227.

Driscoll, M., Cohen, M., Kelly, P., Taylor, D. et al. (1994) Women and HIV. In A. Dan (Ed.), *Reframing Women's Health*. Thousand Oaks, CA: Sage.

Fullilove, M.T., Green, L., and Fullilove, R.E. (1999). Building momentum: An ethnographic study of inner-city redevelopment. *American Journal of Public Health*, 89 (6), 840–844.

Fullilove, M.T., Lown, A., and Fullilove, R.E. (1992). Crack 'hos and skeezers: Traumatic experiences of women crack users. *Journal of Sex Research*, 29 (2) 275–287.

Goodrich, T.J., Ed. (1991). *Women and power: perspectives for family therapy*, p. 10. New York: W. W. Norton.

hooks, b. (1993). *Sisters of the Yam: Black women and self recovery*. Boston: South End Press.

Hopps, J.G. Pinderhughes, E., and Shankar, R. (1995). *The Power to care: Clinical practice effectiveness with overwhelmed clients*. New York: The Free Press.

House, J. (1981). *Work, stress and social support*. Reading, MA: Addison-Wesley.

Kübler-Ross, E. (1987). *AIDS: The ultimate challenge*. New York: Macmillan Publishing.

Lazarus, R.S., and Folkman, S. (1984). *Stress appraisal and coping*. New York: Springer Publishing.

Lincoln, Y.S., and Guba, E.G. (1985). *Naturalistic Inquiry*. Thousand Oaks, CA: Sage Publications.

Mann, J. and Taratola, D., Eds. (1986). *AIDS in the World II*, pp. 441–462. New York: Oxford University Press.

Marable, M., and Mullings, L. (1994). The divided mind of Black America: Race, ideology & politics in the post–Civil Rights Era. *Race & Class*, (36) 1, 61–72.

Morse, J.M., and Johnson, J.L., Eds. (1991). *The Illness Experience: Dimensions of Suffering*. Thousand Oaks, CA: Sage Publications.

Prochaska, J.O., Norcross, J.C., and DiClemente, C.C. (1994). *Changing for good: The revolutionary program that explains the six stages of change and teaches you how to free yourself from bad habits*. New York: William Morrow & Company.

Rosenstock, I.M. (1990). The health belief model: Explaining health behavior through Expectancies. In K. Glanz, F.M. Lewis, and B.K. Rimer (Eds.). *Health behavior and health education: Theory, research and practice*. San Francisco: Jossey-Bass.

Ruble-Soro, N., Harris, K., Demain, L., Cohen, M., et al. (1994). Milieu treatment in a multidisciplinary women and children's HIV program. Poster session, American Psychological Association Conference on Psychosocial and Behavioral Factors in Women's Health, May 12–14, Washington, DC.

Seligman, M.E.P. (1975). *Helplessness*. San Francisco: W.H. Freeman.

Stack, C.B. (1974). *All our kin: Strategies for survival in a Black community*. New York: Harper & Row.

Stein, T.J. (1998). *The social welfare of women and children with HIV and AIDS: Legal protections, policy and programs*. New York: Oxford University Press.

Taylor, D., Irvin, Y., Rodriguez, A., Cohen, M., et al. (1990). The Evolution of Dignity. Poster Session, Sixth International Conference on AIDS, June 20–24, San Francisco, CA.

Wandersman, A., and Nation, M. (1998). Urban neighborhoods and mental health: Psychological contributions to understanding toxicity, resilience and interventions. *American Psychologist*, 53 (6), 647–656.

Wilson, W.J. (1987). *The truly disadvantaged: The inner city, the underclass and public policy*. Chicago: University of Chicago Press.

Wright, M.O. (1998). Resilience. In E.A. Blechman and K.D. Brownell, (Eds.), *Behavioral medicine and women: A comprehensive handbook*, pp. 156–161 New York: Guilford Press.

Yamato, G. (1998). Something about the subject makes it hard to name. In M.L. Andersen and P.H. Collins (Eds.), *Race, class and gender: An anthology*, Third Edition, pp. 89–93. Belmont, CA: Wadsworth Publishing.

8

Making a Way Out of No Way: Spiritual Coping for HIV-Positive African American Women

Ednita M. Wright

> It has been a struggle, and such that I never attempted suicide but it was al-
> ways an option, in the back of my mind. The minute I got diagnosed suicide
> went right out the window.

We know, now, that all types of diseases are associated with an increased stress level. "One of the more recent findings has been that there is evidenced linking stress and the body's ability to fight disease" (Humphrey and Thomas 1992, 31). And even though a definition of the nature and degree of stress remains problematic, it is postulated that stress causes changes to the immune system that lead to infectious, neoplastic, or autoimmune disease (King 1993). The subject of stress and its effects on the immune system is beyond the scope of this work. However, a factor is important to note, particularly, given the stress-producing situations African American women must contend with "normally." Added to the diagnosis of HIV-infection or AIDS, racism, gender inequities, poor economic conditions, inadequate health care, and negative stereotypes may further increase stress.

Despite the stressful conditions that African American women encounter, they continue to be individuals who persist. Aptheker (1982) noted that African American women do not see themselves exclusively or primarily as victims, but display resistance and strategies for survival in the face of oppression. In their work regarding stress, Lazarus and Folkman (1984) found emotion-focused coping is avoidance of the future implications of a problem, in order to maintain hope and optimism. It seems that the individual's appraisal of a situation and coping strategies best predict health outcomes (Rose and Alexander-Clark 1996). Additionally, existential beliefs, such as faith in God, fate, or some natural order in the universe are general beliefs that enable people to create meaning out of life, even out of damaging experiences, and to maintain hope (Lazurus and Folkman 1984).

Hope was one of the ingredients that the women in the study relied on to move them from seeing themselves as dying victims to living individuals. In the lives of these women, it was how they appraised and coped with the stress of HIV/AIDS that predicted their quality of life, which seemed more important than health outcome.

In this chapter, I revisit the lives of the women introduced in Chapter 2 (May, Glow, Wind, Angel, Dell, Rose, Shell, and Dar) in order to illustrate the theme of spirituality, variously defined by the women, as a way that most of the women coped with their HIV-infection. In their multiethnic study of fifty-three women with HIV/AIDS, Kaplan, Marks, and Mertens (1997, 88) found that "prayer and rediscovery of self were their most frequent coping responses." However, African American women tended to "try to keep their feelings to themselves" more than Latina and White women in the study. Both these findings are relevant for the women in this study. Most of the women came to accept that AIDS was not the true tragedy in their lives: not living is the tragedy, and if one is going to live, then sometimes that means transforming and redefining ourselves.

Each of the women in my study, like most people when they are told they have a terminal illness, are locked, at first, into the shock of the diagnosis; they see themselves as dying. May described when asked, her fears after being diagnosed.

Me—me dead and wondering what was going to be next whether I am going right away or how long I am going to be here. And after the doctor, cause I had two doctors and the social worker, up there, after they got me in the room and I am just boo hooing they say you don't have to die because you HIV. I said well HIV is AIDS—pure AIDS. He said no, it is not. He said you just got the virus.

The description that May provides regarding her fear is consistent with my initial assumption, as I began my study, which was that the women would view AIDS as a horrible nightmare. I was less prepared for the experience expressed by the women in the study. They moved past the initial shock, and through a process of searching for the reasons why for their situation, they had concluded that AIDS was providing them an opportunity to see life and live it differently. As Glow so eloquently states as she reflects on her perspective on life before her diagnosis: "I was watching the *Birdman of Alcatraz*, which I hadn't seen in twenty-five years, the movie had nothing to do with reality. Burt Lancaster said the first task of life is to live. When you are born your job is to live and I don't know if I could have said that two years ago."

There were times when living day to day with AIDS was scary and difficult. As the women transformed their identities from one who was dying to one who was living, they expressed belief that the disease was necessary to inform their new capacities. It was not that they were in a state of denial about the debilitating and fatal aspects of this disease, but rather that their focus moved to life instead of death. They had transformed the meaning of this disease in such a way as to make the disease work for them. The disease had become a revelation about some segment of their life.

Dar and Glow best describe this feeling. Dar believed that being HIV-positive gave her the opportunity to live her life for the first time the way she wanted to and that she had things to share with others.

I don't know [why I have AIDS], maybe my kids, maybe just living and being happy for once in my life. Because I never been happy all my life and I never did anything that I just wanted to do. I mean when I did drugs, I didn't want to do them. It was something that had to be there to medicate. Then I had to do things that I didn't want to do to get the drugs. The only thing that I wanted to do that I managed to do was stay with [my lover] and to keep my kids. I think now is the time for me to grab a hold of the shit, because it has been holding me down long enough.

HIV is an opportunity that will take me places that I have never been before. Like maybe even sharing my feelings with people that are ignorant to [AIDS], or being able to just be there for a poor young Black woman that has just been told that she is HIV-positive. To let her know that it is not the end of the world and that she shouldn't do anything that is health wise dumb to kill herself.

Glow was raised as an "army brat"; therefore, maintaining relationships or even admitting that there was a need for close emotional relationships was hard for her.

I have absolutely no one up here wherever we are. My relatives are downstate, Massachusetts, my brother is in South Jersey and then I have relatives down South. However, there is no one at all except me here in Upstate. There is no other blood relative or even friend, that is long term, I am up here by myself. But I am a military brat and so you get use to stupid stuff like that—

Glow finally had met her match in AIDS. She could not run from AIDS, so she had to deal with it.

I wasn't able to stand on my own two feet, but I have discovered that I am stronger than I think. I can carry more burdens than I think. Because being a military brat I have always been able to walk away from things. But you can't walk away from AIDS, so this is the first real barrier I have had in my life.

They say that HIV and AIDS is a warning. It's not a warning in terms of health, it is a warning in terms of life—to wake up and smell the coffee. It is not just health related and I needed to wake up and smell the coffee.

In *Man's Search for Meaning*, Viktor Frankl (1959) asserts that human beings have the capacity to transcend tragic aspects of the human condition. Although Frankl's text concerns those that survived the Holocaust, I believe that the women in my study experienced a similar process, as both groups come face to face with their own deaths.

It is difficult to describe a process that is fluid, concerned with sustenance, that is not physical, and cannot be easily discerned. It is complicated, further, by the fact that language does not adequately reflect the complexity of what is involved. Being diagnosed HIV-positive or having AIDS assaults our plans for the future, the principles by which we make decisions, and who we think we are (Bartlett 1993, 14); it changes our relationship with living. Even in the face of living with dying, however, Dell speaks about the "joy" that has been brought into her life because of AIDS. "It has brought more joy in my life since I had the virus. You know I had so much bitterness, pain, and hurt, being able to express it and let it out has brought me joy. It is really something." When asked how she defined "joy," Dell makes clear that there just are not any words. "How would I define joy? It is this warm feeling in my heart. I really can't explain joy. But I know I feel really good. I just feel good and I feel that I don't even have the virus. I don't know if that is joy or anything but I really can't express it, but I know I really feel good."

Each of the women in the study defined the meaning being diagnosed with AIDS would have in their lives. The diagnosis was used as a vehicle to set some things straight, to become more connected with self and others, and to change their relationship with life. It is not my intent to present the women in my study as "superwomen." I seek only to reveal the process they related to me, as they made a way out of no way. Their process of moving from seeing themselves as dying to recognizing how they could, in fact, live with AIDS progresses through four subthemes, which are presented through the women's words in the remainder of this chapter.

SEPARATING ONESELF FROM THE VICTIM ROLE

> I mean I was so sick that I wanted to die because the suffering was getting to me.

Although death, for most of us, is the ultimate loss, there are other losses that affect us significantly, that occur with any change. One is the loss of self, as we perceive the suffering it entails. It isn't that these women had a quixotic notion of death but that the reality of death was seemingly less cruel than the meaning of the dying process. As May explains, dying is hard, but the changes that will occur to her physical appearance are of primary concern to her.

Dying—the hardest thing is dying. I don't think really dying is the problem anymore. I think it is the way I am going to look. You know some people get really little. I mean they just fade away and their eyes and stuff go back in their heads and I don't want to look like that, I want to look like this—the way I am now. That is the scary part—how I am going to look. Cause I already done said and I told my daughter, that I don't want nobody looking at me if I look that bad.

Dar's mother took care of a friend of the family's that was dying of AIDS. Dar's concerns are similar to those of May.

I hope I don't look like my friend [P]. She is the only one I have ever seen that come from HIV and get full-blown AIDS and I watched her literally die. My mother was taking care of her and when I went up to see her a couple of times. She is a real cool lady; you know what I am saying, real cool. Her youngest child is younger than mine. And each time I went to see her and would look at her, I would leave and go and get stone drunk because of the reality.

My mother came home one night, she said Dar will you please take care of yourself, please. Please take care of yourself because I can't see burying you like that and I said, I don't want to die like that. I am so scared of dying like that—I am scared to die. Never really thought about it before since this last month. Never thought about dying but it is a scary thing to know, if you don't take care of yourself.

There are also circumstances that add to the identity we create for ourselves. For some of the women in the study, chemical addiction had become a way of life, although they knew that it was a self-inflicted death sentence. Shell clearly articulates until her diagnosis that her role as an alcoholic was hard for her to release.

Well I am hardheaded. I am one of those people that had to learn the hard way, but if I hadn't, I probably would have been dead now any ways cause I was drinking so much. Because I mean I think I will live longer being HIV-positive than I would have lived being out there on the streets still drinking and stuff. It was only an existence. My days consisted of—well I lived right across the street from a liquor store. It was so convenient and I had a bootlegger that lived next door to me. I was set. It didn't matter what it was, I drank it.

Even though physical death is not a transition that is usually met with open arms, it is one that "we cannot buy or yell or deny our way out of" (Levine 1982, 239) for long, because we have no control over it. Either one has to start gearing up to leave the world or start preparing to live. Glow alludes to the fact that her trump card in life was that if the going got too rough, she had the option of suicide.

I never had to do that, I was always planning into the future. Now I have no choice but to take one day at a time. I was always in a hurry to go nowhere and still am but a little less than I use to. I never comfortably adapted on an emotional, interpersonal level with other people—never. It has been a struggle and such that I never attempted suicide but it was always an option, in the back of my mind. The minute I got diagnosed—suicide went right out the window.

Each of the women in her own way came to accept that she had a disease that would kill her. In doing so, they also had to decide what their relationship to living was going to be, until death came. Wind explains, "You know I was being like a victim because there was nothing else over me that could help me. I, by myself, couldn't follow all of the stuff and I had lost that feeling of spirituality, that feeling of connection with a higher power."

Wind had her first opportunistic disease before feeling the full impact of having AIDS. She exposes her transition from focusing on dying to living with AIDS, as she relinquishes the role of victim.

My acceptance of the disease didn't really come until winter when I was sick in the hospital. That's when it really hit me that I really had this disease and I am going to die from it. I said I really have AIDS and I freaked out. I was really depressed, at first, and my thing was [just] let me die, now.

I mean I was so sick that I wanted to die because the suffering was getting to me. The being incapacitated was and is what I can't handle. I lost control of my bowels and my eyes turned all red and my leg, there was no definition between my leg and my thigh. But what I had begun to do was be a victim. And as soon as I got out of the hospital I decided I am not having this. I am not a victim and my people are not victims and we can do something.

I didn't understand it, I just knew something had happened and I felt I could breathe and I felt life and I felt hope. Maybe I really could live what I call above ground because I had lived most of my life below ground. Maybe I could try.

It was important to the women in the study not to see themselves as victims. They lived with AIDS. They are women living with AIDS, not "an AIDS victim or an AIDS sufferer and mercifully only from time to time an AIDS patient" (Bartlett and Finkbeiner 1991). As Wind clearly states, her acceptance did not come until she separated herself from the victim role. Her transition was directly tied to her feeling of connection to a power outside herself. She named the power, hope.

A NEW REASON TO LIVE

Maybe I really could live what I call above ground because I had lived most of my life below ground. Maybe I could try.

Wind had never felt any real sense of self-esteem before her diagnosis. She had been a drug addict for over twenty years and had behaved in ways that made her deeply ashamed. Wind tells us being diagnosed with AIDS changed her entire perception of herself and gave her a reason to want to live "above ground."

And I thought I had something to live for and I knew it had to do with AIDS, but I didn't know about AIDS. I was just working on me, and how was I going to deal with [AIDS] and that all came from a sense of hope that I just hadn't felt [before].

And here I was thirty-seven and I felt this hope and that is what I kept coming back to and even when I felt bad, I would come back to that hope. I kept pulling on that and drawing on it for strength and that is all I really did the first year was drawing on that and saying I am not going to die.

It was this "hope" that each of the women spoke about that gave them the strength and permission to reevaluate both the disease and themselves and to develop new ideas to reflect their changed circumstances (Weitz 1991). Speaking about the Holocaust survivors, Frankl (1959) states that the prisoners did not survive with just the will to live, but had to find their own personal meaning in the suffering. If they did not, they perished more quickly. "Whenever there was an opportunity for it, one had to give them a why—an aim—for their lives, in order to strengthen them to bear the terrible how of their existence.

Woe to him who saw no more sense in his life, no aim, no purpose, and therefore no point in carrying on. He was soon lost" (Frankl 1959, 76).

Robert Firestone, in his article "Individual Defenses against Death Anxiety," cites Frankl's definition of "tragic optimism": "an optimism in the face of tragedy and in view of the human potential which at its best always allows for: 1) turning suffering into a human achievement and accomplishment; 2) deriving from guilt the opportunity to change oneself for the better; and, 3) deriving from life's transitoriness an incentive to take responsible action" (1993, 500). The women in my study and the Holocaust survivors had been stripped of their usual roles and were forced to find something else that was worth living for.

As Wind moved away from the role of victim, her faith in the power of "hope" increased and, subsequently, so did her desire to live.

See, all of this is making sense now—even though at first I wasn't dealing with the AIDS issue, not really, I was just dealing with this newfound sense of, I like me and I don't have to take this and it was more of feeling this power that I never felt before. I was empowered because I had AIDS and I wanted to live for the first time in my adult life I wanted to live.

When I say spiritual awakening that is what that was because it was this weight and this hope. It wasn't like I saw Christ or I heard him. I just had a hope. For me that was a spiritual awakening because for me because I could do something, that I was worthy to have a better life and I could go for it. And I just built on that and mostly I built on it.

In not dealing with her illness, it could be said that Wind was in a state of denial. Denial seemed to be a useful defense mechanism against the reality of her illness. It is not that the knowledge that one has a fatal illness is very far from the surface, but that there were times where the weight of what it means, every day, to live with AIDS is suspended for a while. Each woman adapted her life to include the reality of AIDS without yielding to it.

By moving from feeling like a victim to feeling empowered, Wind began to "turn her suffering into accomplishment." Advocating for persons with AIDS became her "divine mission."

It is a divine mission and I have to do this. All these brothers that are out here perpetrating, saying they are serious about helping people who are infected and helping people to prevent it, well, I know that they are not doing that. They talk about outreach and at the same time, they are over fucking some broad. I am ratting on all of y'all. I am telling them I got it, you know.

See I can do those kind of things, but I couldn't do that feeling like a victim and having real doubt there was a higher power. And so, I couldn't die and AIDS couldn't kill me, I had too much to do. I had too much to live for and I started putting the energy, I had put into being a victim and dying, into advocating for myself, at first. And then I realized the stuff I was doing other people was having the same problem. It was never like I set out to do a lot of this stuff, it was just that nobody had done it and I was on this mission.

Shell's achievement was sobriety.

People say things happen for a reason and if I hadn't stopped drinking I'd have died. Something had to happen—the purpose of being raped was so I would get this disease and—and this is going to really sound sick but this was meant to happen. This happen to me to save my ass. There was nothing else that could possibly stop me from drinking. Now I can do something positive with my life and not just stand on a corner and drink. I can do positive things.

Angel was not sure what her purpose was, but felt that God was not ready for her to die because there was still something out there that she needed to accomplish.

I was nuts and when I woke up, I just felt oh God why—you know—cause then I had to deal with the shame of what I was doing and it didn't work. There is nothing worse to me than someone that wants to commit suicide and doesn't do it—it just didn't work. I was ready to go and I would just not die. I was shooting air into my veins for weeks before I finally ended up in the hospital.

I think there is a purpose for everything. There is something that I am supposed to do or accomplish and that is the only reason that I am still here and God means for me to do it or accomplish this thing—what it is, I don't know. I am trying to find out, but I don't know.

For Dell, the disease meant an opportunity to enhance her own self-esteem and to repair a significant relationship in her life. Dell felt that without the onset of the disease she might never have reached out for the help that she needed to increase her ability to show love toward her children.

I think, I guess it happened, for me to get myself together because—to find out what are my feelings, and what I can do. You know, I thought I couldn't do anything, especially without a man. [It also helped me] to get in touch with my kids, because I've showed no love toward them. I know that I love them but I couldn't show it to them, and that's what I am working on now. Showing my love toward them. I think that's why it happened for me to get here, where I am now. And I am grateful, but it's awful harsh, though.

I am coming around. I am a worthwhile person and I need to tell myself that even more because I have been—I didn't care about myself. I didn't think I was worth it and I thought that way for a lot of years so that is why I need to keep telling myself that. 'Cause I can also go back to feeling that way—it is so easy to go back to feeling that way.

In Dell's account, focusing on the opportunities the disease has revealed does not mean that living day to day with AIDS is not scary or difficult. However, she emphasizes that one must be continually vigilant in maintaining the changes made to improve self-esteem.

Glow felt that without her illness she would not have felt as if she had become an adult.

It is very recent that I have determined who I am as an individual, but I still really didn't know. I have also wondered so what—so what is the purpose to life. That has never been clear to me. It is becoming clear because of HIV. I am growing up for the first time in twenty years. I have been a child for twenty years and this [having AIDS] has forced me to grow up quick, fast, and in a hurry. And it wouldn't have happen if I hadn't gotten ill.

Weitz, in *Life with AIDS* (1991), provides other examples of how individuals create opportunities for self-enhancement. She summarizes by saying that "[p]erhaps more surprisingly, they can develop new cognitive frameworks that enable them to use their illness not just to maintain but actually to improve their self-esteem. As individuals discover within themselves the emotional resources needed to confront illness, stigma, and dying with dignity, their self-esteem can increase" (137).

A majority of the women in the study felt that living with AIDS brought with it the possibility of learning to love themselves, in ways they had not before. Wind eloquently expresses this feeling in the following quote: "[Even though] I have the disease and I can visibly see people cringe, and that is hard, I wasn't dealing with the AIDS thing. My self-esteem was so profound, I was feeling so good about me that they couldn't touch me. Nobody could touch me because for the first time in my life, I liked myself."

As this "hope" fed their sense of purpose and strengthened their self-esteem, it also strengthened their conviction that they knew what they needed in order to live with HIV/AIDS. Because of this, each in her own way became more assertive in areas of their lives where they had not been before. Concerning medical care, May felt she, rather than her doctor, knew how far to push her body.

I am not going to let nothing get me down and I am going to push until every strength is out of my body and I said I think I can do it. Now like I can't walk up that hill sometime [to the doctor]. I will make myself do it and then I come back home and I lay down and take a cat nap. That is all it is, and my doctor said if I got to take them naps—take it—don't push it away because that will just make more problems.

Wind explains her response when her doctor attempts to give her something to quiet her down, instead of respecting her knowledge of her physical condition. "When I am telling you I have a cold sore on my tongue, there is something happening here. I didn't ask you for valium or codeine and I started hollering, and all that came because I had this sense of hope."

HIV/AIDS provided Dell the strength to deal with her addiction and to change what she would allow others to do to her.

I'm glad I'm in recovery. Sometimes, I can say, I'm glad I have this virus, too. Because I don't have to let nobody walk over me any more. This program has taught me that I don't have to let anyone walk over me anymore and I have the right to be angry and express my feelings. Sometimes it is still hard for me to do that and that I can love me. It's okay to love me.

For Michelle, having HIV/AIDS has kept her sober.

It [has] kept me sober. I probably wouldn't be here if I hadn't come down with this disease. I really think so. Because I wasn't ready for recovery. You know I just wanted to go
into a rehab and get my P.A. and cut back on drinking and then go back out there and do
what I was doing before. And not that I am—I am scared of dying—but [having AIDS]
is working, it is keeping me sober.

All the women spoke about how HIV/AIDS had forced them to look at their
relationship with life.

It is in the tradition of Black folks that death is respected, but not feared (hooks
1993). Being immersed in that tradition does not mean that the women in the
study were not afraid of death. It just means that each had been told, at some
point during their lives, that "life was not promised" (hooks 1993, 100) and that
death was as much a part of life as breathing whether this source of strength
was the "hope" that began to well up inside, or a deepening or return to traditional Christian beliefs, or drawing on the relationships with the ancestors. Each
woman relied on her source of strength to keep her going when things became
overwhelming.

GAINING THE STRENGTH TO GO ON

> I stand on those promises. When I feel myself getting worried or feeling sick
> I say Lord you promised me. You promised me that I was going to be here
> to see the grandbaby. I talk to the Lord like that—we old-timers can talk to
> the Lord that way.

When Rose made this statement to me, there was no hint of doubt in her voice
that the Lord would uphold the promises he made to her. Her certainty reminded
me of historical Black women who believed that the Lord would deliver them
from hardships. Rose didn't see herself as any different from any one else, except that she had "promises" from the Lord to stand on. "I am no different than
no body else but I know I have some promises. I stand on them promises. You
know you can have some promises and still be worried about things, but I stand
on those promises."

Throughout the history of this country, Black women have relied on spirituality to sustain us, to renew our hope, to strengthen our faith. This spirituality
has often had a narrow dimension, and we have internalized without question
dogmatic views of religious life reinforced by intense participation in patriarchal religious institutions (hooks 1993, 184). Although the views of some of the
women in the study were from the perspective of an institution, these women
also had a more personal relationship with their God, as Dar describes here.

Having the Lord in your life or having a power greater than yourself—I will put it that
way because you know people believe in different things. You know when you just believe and trust in yourself which—you know if I believed and trusted in myself I ain't
never done anything right in my life. When I don't pray about it I make big time mis-
takes. So, I believe in something higher than myself because when you trust in the

doctor or a friend to help you or just yourself it is not going to get it or this medicine that you take.

In Dar's case, she felt that her God would continue to give her strength as she adjusted to living with dying. She remarks that this faith was not reliant on a miracle.

You know I don't even know how to pray. I just get on my knees and talk and thank God for helping me get through this day and watch over my babies. I be talking to Him like He is right there and sometimes I feel so foolish. I really haven't asked Him to take this HIV away from me I really haven't asked Him to do that. Because I think it is there for good and I am not asking for a miracle. Help me to be able to accept it in everyday life without pulling all my hair out and crying and stomping and carrying on. Just if He would give me the strength to deal with it but not take it away.

Dell's diagnosis with HIV/AIDS was just another tragedy in her life. Moreover, although she did not always understand the reason for it, she continued to rely on her source of power, not only to comfort her but also to put people in her life to help her.

I guess, sometimes I still don't understand. I don't understand why all of this happened, but I know that God is in it helping me out. I know that I have not made it this far without Him. I also had two other kids. I have five kids all together. One was a still born. My second child was a still born, but my first child, he, hum, he hung himself. He hung himself at the age of eight. Through all of this I know that there is a God. Because I know that I should be in a nut house somewhere.
   God put people in my life for me to get around and do the things I need to do to keep myself going that is why I say God plays a big part in this.

May's parents were not living, but they were not absent. May drew her comfort from the presence she felt was their spirits.

I am more scared at night, and I lay there and I talk to dad and I talk to mom. I say dad I need you and I say I'm scared daddy, but I love you. You know I am always scared of the dead, so I don't want to see your face right now. I just want you near me and all of a sudden I could feel someone in the room with me. And I guess that why I don't be afraid because I know. I guess if I didn't know him, I would be really frighten. You think I am wrong?

May considered it might be seen as improper for her to commune with the spirits of her parents. However, deriving comfort from our ancestors is a tradition that goes all the way back to Africa. In Patricia Jones-Jackson's *When Roots Die*, she recounts an excerpt from an interview with a very religious man from the Sea Islands, who validates May's belief in the presence of her parents. "Listen to me good now: When you die in this world, you see the . . . soul of a man go home to the Kingdom of God, but your spirit's still here on earth" (1987, 25). Jackson further elaborates: "This concept of a tripartite body, soul, and spirit, with the body and spirit remaining on earth after death and able to influence the living, is widespread in West Africa today. The spirit of one's ancestors is considered the closest link to the other world. Thus, on the Sea Islands as well as in Africa, spirits are asked to intervene on behalf of a living relative" (25).

This communion with the ancestors is one of the secrets of healing for traditional Black people. It continues within healing practices in some Black communities and is similar in some ways to psychological counseling. Its purpose is to understand complex mysteries in daily life and to create ways to intervene and enhance health and well-being (hooks 1993, 103). For the nine women in the study, the use of this customary practice fortified them as they lived with dying. Wind describes:

But never lose your faith. Don't lose your spirituality cause that is always going to get you through. It's just that don't worry about the church doctrine, don't feel that you have to be a part of an organized church. You keep dwelling on what you have come through without being in religion. That there was some other hand guiding you.

SPIRITUALITY—INDIVIDUALIZED DEFINITIONS

It is what makes me love my sisters, because they got work to do and they will do it.

Spirituality is problematic because it has no agreed-upon definition. The women spoke of the power as "hope" or "joy" as what they stood on. I have heard my aunt define the power as grace. My aunt says that grace builds on nature, meaning that it enhances our own abilities. Grace is the power by which we are being invited to go beyond our capacities. Living by grace does not earn credit in a heavenly book. Grace is the act of being alive, living life to its fullest, and doing for others. By the act of telling their stories, the women in the study have given testimony, so that others living with AIDS would see themselves and possibly experience the power of grace.

The women's talk about this power really describes a shift in their relationship with living. Therefore, spirituality could be defined as a relationship, to self, to others, and to a power. Spirituality could be considered a process in which we experience standing outside ourselves to consider the meaning of our actions, the complexity of our motives, and the impact we have on the world around us. As the women in the study describe, this process for them was anchored in the belief that life has meaning and purpose, and found expression in a sense of gratitude and acceptance.

As the women show, inherent in this process was the way that the gratitude and acceptance weaved in and out of the anxiety associated with living with dying. As Glow tells us, she can appreciate the opportunity that HIV/AIDS has given her now, but that might not be the case once she becomes more ill. "There are things I needed to learn about life and about me that might have eluded me without AIDS, and I can appreciate it because I am not prostrate in a hospital bed. Now when that time comes it will be a different story."

Nevertheless, the fear would eventually subside and each of the women would return to the hope. Wind tells us: "It was because I kept feeling like I have to live because I have this hope and because of that, life is good."

As this power that they felt became stronger, it fortified them. As May describes, it fortified her enough to then pass on what she was experiencing with her community:

I don't want anyone seeing me but the group. The reason why I want the group to see me is as they can know how they may look or feel other than that I don't want no one else to see me. But at some funeral homes they make you look like there was nothing wrong with you. Like a picture of health and I notice that.

Rose, like May, was concerned about how she looked. But Rose felt the Lord was keeping her looking good, so that others she came in contact with would know that living with dying did not have to be tragic.

I say the Lord is keeping me looking good cause I am a—I have to testify. I can't be sick and down and out because you know, a lot of people look at that and say, my goodness, how much can the Lord be doing if you looking like that, down and out and stuff. The Lord keeps me looking good because I am a testimony.

The central characteristic in the lives of the women in the study was their ability to transform this time of trial and adversity to one of opportunity. This transformative process included, in some sense, a spiritual awakening or deepening and informed other aspects of their lives. Wind explains:

I had tried everything else in the world and nothing ever made me feel good about me, nothing had made my life bearable. Being diagnosed with HIV/AIDS was the first sense of hope I had ever had. I had never felt hope in twenty-two years. I never had hope of getting out of addiction. That's why rehab never worked for me, because I didn't believe that I could do it. Any of the rehab programs will tell you that someone with long-term use, they don't generally want to take the chance on you. They figure by the time you are thirty that you are pretty much lost. This hope is what I drew on to not just live with AIDS, but also stop my addiction.

Although we live in an age when there seems to be a psychological explanation for everything, something much deeper than psychological cause and effect is reflected in these attitudes (Anderson 1991, 44). The women in the study had made a way out of no way. In so doing, in the tradition of Black women, they felt compelled to share their experience, thus, forming community.

We all need someone to lean on and to talk to and that is why groups are important. Our own network works very well where we call each other and know that we can rely on each other. We don't die, at least some of us, until we have taken care of business. Like one of the women we knew was hanging on until she knew her daughter was going to be taken care of and when the papers came in, for this woman she wanted to take her child, the next day she died. And this is the thing, as sad as [living with dying] is, hearing us talk is what makes me love my sisters, because they got work to do and they will do it.

Throughout this chapter the women have revealed that they saw having HIV/AIDS as a "blessing" and that feeling or belief was integral to their perception as women living as opposed to dying with HIV/AIDS. The "blessing" came in different forms—an opportunity to set some things straight in their lives, to become more connected with themselves or other significant people in their lives, or to change their relationship with life itself. These women did not see themselves as extraordinary women but they felt that to give up hope and faith would be more of a tragedy than dying with HIV/AIDS.

REFERENCES

Aptheker, B. (1982). Race and class: Patriarchal politics and women's experience. *Women's Studies Quarterly*, 10 (4), 10–15.

Bartlett, J.G., and Finkbeiner, A.K. (1991). *The guide to living with HIV infection*. Baltimore, MD: Johns Hopkins University Press.

Frankl, V.E. (1959). *Man's search for meaning: An introduction to logotherapy*. Boston: Beacon Press.

Firestone, R.W. (1993). Individual defenses against death anxiety. *Death Studies*, (17) 497–515.

hooks, b. (1993). *Sisters of the Yam: Black women and self-recovery*. Boston: South End Press.

Humphrey, J.H., and Thomas, C.C. (1992). *Stress among women in modern society*. Springfield, IL: Charles C. Thomas.

Jones-Jackson, P. (1987). *When roots die: Endangered traditions on the Sea Islands*. Athens, GA: University of Georgia Press.

Kaplan, M.S., Marks, G., and Mertens, S.B. (1997). Distress and coping among women with HIV infection: Preliminary findings from a multiethnic sample. *American Journal of Orthopsychiatry*, 67(1), 80–91.

King, M.B. (1993). *AIDS, HIV and mental health*. Cambridge: Cambridge University Press.

Lazarus, R.S., and Folkman, S. (1984). *Stress, appraisal, and coping*. New York: Springer.

Levine, S. (1982). *Who dies? An investigation of conscious living and conscious dying*. New York: Anchor Books.

Rose, M.A., and Alexander-Clark, B. (1996). Coping behaviors of mothers with HIV/AIDS. *AIDS Patient Care*, (10) 44–47.

Weitz, R. (1991). *Life with AIDS*. New Brunswick, NJ: Rutgers University Press.

9

Focus on Solutions:
Black Churches Respond to AIDS: Interview with Pernessa C. Seele, Founder and CEO of The Balm In Gilead

Dorie J. Gilbert

The Balm In Gilead is a national, nonprofit organization located in New York City and the only organization in the United States dedicated to empowering churches in the struggle against the devastation of AIDS in the Black community. The organization's mission is to work through Black churches to stop the spread of HIV and AIDS in the African American community and to support those infected with and affected by HIV. Since 1989, the organization has diligently advanced its goals to motivate and equip Black churches with the tools to take an active role in HIV prevention. The goals of the organization are multifaceted:

1. To build the capacity of Black church congregations to provide compassionate leadership in the prevention of HIV, disseminate treatment information, and deliver supportive services to those infected and affected in their respective communities
2. To build the capacity of community-based organizations (CBOs) and state and local agencies to collaborate effectively with Black churches to address the AIDS pandemic in the African American community
3. To raise awareness in the community at large of the Black church's unique strengths in facilitating the eradication of AIDS in the African American community and the need to support the church's development in this area

Among its many successful programs, the Black Church Week of Prayer for the Healing of AIDS had its roots in Harlem and was the result of one woman's zeal and determination. The story of how this now national, and increasingly international, organization advanced from a prayer gathering in Harlem in 1989 to an astoundingly progressive and nationally successful response to AIDS from Black churches unfolds in this interview.

Gilbert: Pernessa, the Rev. Canon Frederick B. Williams, chair of the National Clergy Advisory Task Force, has said that in 1989, "God sent a messenger, in the person of Pernessa Seele, to the religious communities of color, with a 'wake up call' about our failure to confront the devastation that HIV/AIDS epidemic was wreaking among our people." What was it like to have been that "messenger"?

Seele: Well, I had no intentions of having a national organization or an international focus. Whatever I did to start this, I never had in mind that I would get here, to this point as a national or international organization. My background is in immunology. I moved to New York to work as an immunologist in malaria research at Rockefeller University. I quickly ended up instead at Sloan Ketterling Memorial Hospital working in the area of cancer. Well, I was in my twenties, and I soon decided to quit by job there and to just work little jobs. And I was doing these little jobs and was very happy. Then AIDS happened. Suddenly my master's degree in immunology came into play. I had the opportunity to conduct the first AIDS education in New York City. As such, I developed one of the first AIDS education programs in a methadone center. From there, I went to work at Harlem Hospital as an administrator in the AIDS Initiative Program. In that role, my function took me on the wards, and I had to actually go and see people in beds dying of AIDS. I was really struck by the lack of spiritual support—not one pastor, clergy at the bedsides of these dying individuals.

So, I became something like the spiritual counselor. I *did not* feel called to do that, and I certainly wasn't trained to do so. I was naïve at the time about AIDS and about why even though there were 352 churches surrounding Harlem Hospital in the center of the community, the churches were so distant. I was very naïve; I really didn't understand stigma, homophobia, or exactly what the lack of response was all about.

One morning on my third day on the job, I was already burned out and didn't want to go to work. I was having a hard time getting motivated, and I didn't want to go back to the job. So, I had a talk with myself and God, and I asked, "Why me, God? Where is the church?" I thought, we have to really pray on this one.

You have to understand that I was born with the gift of ideas. And suddenly I had the idea to mobilize the religious community of Harlem, not just the Christian churches but the entire religious community. A week of healing of prayer for AIDS—yes, in the African American community, we believe in prayer.

I didn't know a soul in Harlem; I had just moved there. So, I went to my supervisor and told her I wanted to try to bring the religious community together around AIDS. She told me that several people had already tried it, but none of them were successful. But I was determined and so I just started with picking up the church directory. I went to church on Sunday and I just started to tell people, "We're having a Harlem Week of Prayer." Of course, at that time the "we" really meant me and thee that was having this week of prayer because I was doing all of this by myself at first. But it all came together. We had a coming together of the total religious community to pray and to incorporate AIDS education into that week. We had Christians, the Muslim community, the Ethiopian Hebrews, the Yoruba, and the Islamic community—all coming together on the third week in March back in 1989. There were also Native Americans in Harlem that were involved.

It was modeled after an old-time revival. Of course, this model was based on my general understanding of life. As a child growing up in Lincolnville, South Carolina, twenty miles from Charleston, an all Black town in South Carolina, the idea of a revival and motivating people to come together around prayer was a natural part of my upbringing.

I just could not understand why the churches weren't involved. If I knew then what I knew now, I would have never done it, but it happened. It happened, and it was the first time anyone had mobilized all the religious sectors, all African American, and all praying to one God. In 1989, everybody had already been touched by HIV, but they didn't know how to talk about it, sexuality, homosexuality, and all that stuff. So, when I came up with this the "week of prayer" idea, it worked. Everyone thought, yea—we can do this! But I'm not a prophet. Call me a crazy woman, but not a prophet [laughing].

It was amazing to me that they were listening to me—all the major leaders in Harlem were listening to me. And of course we had to do the drama thing, you know cultural dramatics, with everyone walking around Harlem Hospital in their religious garb—Christians, Africans, Muslims, carrying pyramids and religious and universal symbols and such. All these Black people with such different religious affiliations coming together and adding the AIDS educational programs. It was exciting!

Gilbert: How did things progress from there?

Seele: From there, I was determined *not* to do this again [laughing], but it was spiritually on me to do it again. People were excited about it. So, the next year I did it again. After the second year, people began to hear about it all over the country. Harlem became the central voice. People wanted to know about the Harlem Week of Prayer [HWOP]. I was invited to speak at what was then called the National Minority AIDS Conference on faith-based issues in California. This was my first introduction to the national scene, and I was amazed at how many people had heard about the HWOP. People talked about needing this in their community and how they wanted to do their own week of prayer. On the plane coming back to New York, I had another idea: "Why don't we just do it nationally. Let's try that." We did it, and it worked.

It's always been the case that what Black people do best is word-of-mouth mobilization. We started with several cities doing what we could with absolutely nothing or few resources. Soon after that, with the help of funding from the Centers for Disease Control, we formally replicated the Week of Prayer program in six cities—across the United States.

Then people started to look at me as a national organization. That was very far from the truth. Then, some big-time lawyers came to my assistance to help me obtain the 501C status. They asked, "What are you going to call this thing?" I didn't know. Then one morning I was riding my bike, that is my stationary exercise bike, and it came to me. I was riding my bike and I saw this book on the bookshelf—*The Balm in Gilead* by Sarah Lightfoot. My spirit was saying, "Name the organization The Balm in Gilead." And I thought, no way! That name doesn't say AIDS, doesn't include anything about the church. But my spirit kept saying, "Name the organization The Balm in Gilead." OK—FINE! There goes the name. But the miraculous surprise was that, with that name, when they heard that name, they knew that I was coming to talk about HIV. It immediately took hold in the bosoms of Black people. We keep that front and center because Black folks organize around prayer.

Gilbert: To what do you credit the initial success of the organization?

Seele: It's truly been hard work—but more than my hard work. Ten thousand churches later and seventy community organizations implemented with a growing number of churches from Africa and the Carribean, we have come along way. And I must thank the Harlem community—it really embraced me, Pernessa, as the spear-header of the movement. The ministers and a cadre of renowned leaders were there for me—Wyatt T. Walker, Canon Fredreck Williams, Calvin Butts, Bishop Norman Quick, James Forbes, and numerous others!

If you take any denomination, every one has a famous church and famous minister in Harlem. And these religious leaders did embrace me, just embraced me as the leader—and they took the message to the country. Nobody knew me. The Rev. Dr. Preston R. Washington was the first minister I spoke to. He could have killed it, but he opened the door. He allowed me to come in and talk to the clergy, one on one with them, and they just embraced me. Whenever I'm talking to anyone, I must say that it was the full support of the Harlem community that supported and launched the national and international collective response. I am just your average Ms. Mary.

Gilbert: Can you describe all of the initiatives currently implemented by the Balm In Gilead?

Seele: Well, now we're looking at a twelve-year spectrum. Now we see churches coming on board with the Week of Prayer as the entry point. From there they branch out to training, having workshops in their communities, assisting people in getting HIV testing, and then some churches are developing housing and testing sites in their church basements.

The Black Church Week of Prayer for the Healing of AIDS, begins on the first Sunday in March of each year. During this week, across the nation Black churches engage their congregations in a dialogue about issues of HIV. This week of prayer generally serves as a catalyst for the development of ongoing efforts within the church to get more involved in addressing AIDS in their respective communities.

From this initial dialogue, churches can then receive national training and technical assistance on HIV prevention through the Black Church HIV/AIDS National Technical Assistance Center which is funded by the Centers for Disease Control and Prevention. The center provides assistance to church members, pastors, public health departments, AIDS Service Organizations [ASO], CBOs, students, and the media on issues related to effectively mobilizing the Black churches to become community centers for HIV/AIDS education and compassion. The center provides expert guidance in developing and implementing faith-based HIV/AIDS programs for Black communities on resource materials, sermon development, program suggestions, speaker identification, publicity and promotion, and evaluation. Churches can call us and get assistance in developing programs, or gaining referrals and information from their local ASOs. We also offer assistance in helping to build the capacity of local health departments, ASOs, and CBOs in partnering with and mobilizing their local Black churches. From there, the church participates in workshops and trainings that are based in their perspective communities.

We also have an annual national conference at Tuskegee University where we educate pastors, Sunday School teachers, and others about how to put AIDS education into the structural body of the church. Tuskegee is a meaningful place because of the Tuskegee Syphillis Study, which is still part of the reason why Black folks don't get into clinical trials and other medical regimens.

The Black Church Lights the Way is a national HIV Testing Campaign organized by the Balm In Gilead. The campaign takes place during the month of June and is designed to assist Black churches in educating and encouraging African Americans to get tested for HIV and to get more Black churches involved in addressing HIV. The initiative is seen as a "call from the pulpits" to get tested and as a way to say that the church is prepared to assist persons in receiving the best treatment and services. The first television commercial sponsored by the Black church was aired in New York, Chicago, San Francisco, Atlanta, and Washington, D.C., with Oprah Winfrey and Ozzie Davis in a thirty-second announcement advertising the Black Church Lights the Way national HIV Testing Campaign.

Gilbert: What church-based success stories can you share in terms of a community that has been effectively impacted by the work of the Balm In Gilead?

Seele: So many churches are making a huge difference in their community. One way that churches make a difference is through their prison ministries, such as the New Jersey Prison Initiative. This program has effected the mind-set in prisons and advocates for AIDS education and medical care in prisons. As a result of the Black Church Lights the Way HIV Testing Campaign, some churches have turned their basements into testing sites. In Harlem, one of the ministers, Preston Washington, has obtained city funding to build housing units for persons living with HIV. The work in Harlem has been developed primarily through the Harlem Congregation for Community Improvement through which churches have impacted the community through housing and outreach programs and street-based resource and condom distribution centers.

In Nashville, Tennesee, Rev. Edwin E.W. Sanders, president of the Black Clergy Association of Nashville, has developed an extraordinary comprehensive program on HIV outreach out of his church, the Metropolitan Interdenominational Church. Rev. Sanders helped to initiate the African American Clergy Summit on AIDS at the White House in 1994. This was the first summit of its kind, and as a result of this meeting, participating clergy signed the African American Clergy's Declaration of War on HIV/AIDS. After this summit, Rev. Sanders pledged to make HIV a part of his weekly sermons for one year. Since then, his church has developed a women's ministry, a needle-exchange program, a men's program for HIV-positive men, and a program for substance abusers and homeless individuals. Recently, Dr. Sanders also purchased land in Durban, South Africa, that would be used by women in that community to raise AIDS orphans in Africa. His is truly a Balm In Gilead success story. Although many other churches have become partners with the Balm In Gilead, there is still so much more work needed to eradicate this disease that is destroying our people. Churches, the most important institutions owned and operated by and for Black people, can and must lead the struggle to stop the spread of HIV/AIDS. The message that I would like to end with is that we need to continue to break the chains of silence and rise up to overcome this devastating disease.

NOTE

The Balm In Gilead is located at 130 West 42nd Street, Suite 450, New York, NY. For more information visit their Web site at www.balmingilead.org or call toll-free (888) 225-6243.

III

African American Adolescent Females: Invisible and at Risk

African American adolescents are leading the statistics when it comes to new HIV-infection rates among adolescents in this country. The number of AIDS cases is growing at a faster rate for African American adolescents than for any other major ethnic group according to statistics from the CDC. Critical responses to alleviating the prevalence of AIDS in African American communities must include special attention to our young people, both our young men and young women. Gibbs (1988) described young black males as an "endangered species" over a decade ago, and today this still appears to be a relevant term within the context of rising HIV-infection rates. The chapters focus on African American females, which is not meant to deny the existence of the males with whom they interact. Neither is it meant to discount the sexual diversity among young African American teens. The fastest growing population of HIV-infection is among eighteen- to twenty-five-year-old African American young men who have sex with men. However, the aforementioned relatively high prevalence (estimated as much as 36 percent) of gay males of color who also engage in heterosexual sex cannot be left out of the equation of what puts young, heterosexual African American girls at risk.

The three chapters in this section focus on young African American women. From poor, urban environments to a historically Black college campus, our young women are faced with many barriers to HIV-prevention, some of which we are still attempting to understand. Kelly, in Chapter 10, highlights the lack of inclusion of African American females in most studies of female sexuality. It appears African American females do not have sufficient information and support to construct a positive sexuality and to avoid unintended pregnancy and sexually transmitted diseases. Instead, these youths tend to be heavily influenced by outwardly imposed images, much of which cast them in negatively stereotyped roles. These internalized negative attitudes about oneself based on stereotypes and denigrated status by mainstream society can have devastating consequences on an individual's psyche. McGee and Johnson (1985, 3) conceptualized four areas of identity problems associated with being African American that interact with propensities for substance abuse and other behavioral problems among Black youth. These include:

1. Perceived negative physical attraction due to dominant Euro-American standards of beauty
2. Internalized negative stereotypes which result in low self-esteem
3. Racially based role expectations that grow out of stereotypes and media portrayals of African Americans and cause youth to limit their role experimentation and self-concepts to narrowly, externally defined choices
4. Low self-expectations based on others' opinions, negative stereotypes, and labels such as "at risk" and "minority" which cause children to question their own worth and competence

Although there is still much more to learn about African American female sexuality, it is becoming increasingly clear that mothers hold the crucial key to promoting positive self-image and gender identity among their daughters. Discussing her school-based group intervention with American adolescent females, Burson (1998) notes two case studies that offer poignant examples of how mother's involvement perception can make a remarkable difference in the way daughters define their sexuality. Mothers who validate the daughter's feelings, help her formulate goals, and helping to build her self-confidence and positive self-esteem can help their daughters achieve a positive sense of sexuality. Dancy, in Chapter 11, provides details of an HIV-prevention approach that targets mother-daughter dyads within a community context.

Although African-American college students have a good understanding about AIDS and HIV transmission, this knowledge does not readily translate into behavioral change that reduces risk (Johnson 1993). Even when attending college, African American youth may still be influenced by a narrowly defined group identity, strongly influenced by the media, limited life choices, and problems with formulating a positive ethnic identity. In Chapter 12, Katz points out that by focusing exclusively on the poor African American adolescent population's high HIV risks, college women may not see themselves as vulnerable to HIV. Katz discusses how a computer-based, culturally sensitive HIV prevention program can be used to reach African American college women. Qualitative findings of the young women's reactions to the program are informative and can be used to further similar HIV prevention programming.

REFERENCES

Burson, J.A. (1998). AIDS, sexuality and African American adolescent females. *Child and Adolescent Social Work Journal*, 15 (5), 357–365.

Gibbs, J.T., Ed. (1988). *Young, black, and male in America: An endangered species*. Dover, MA: Auburn House.

Johnson, E.H. (1993). *Risky sexual behavior among African-Americans*. Westport, CT: Praeger Publications.

McGee, G., and Johnson, L. (1985). *Black, beautiful and recovering*. Center City, MN: Hazelden Foundation.

10

African American Adolescent Girls: Neglected and Disrespected

Ella Mizzell Kelly

Although African American adolescent girls represent about 8 percent of American adolescents (U.S. Census 2000), they account for 58 percent of new AIDS cases reported among youth between the ages of thirteen and nineteen (CDC 2000).[1] This frightening statistic depicts the intersecting demographics of the HIV/AIDS epidemic in the United States where race, gender, class, and youth converge. Estimates of the numbers of U.S. youth infected with HIV vary from a low of 110,000 to a high of 250,000 (Rotheram-Borus, O'Keefe, Kracker, and Foo 2000). Ninety-two percent of identified HIV-infected youth acquire the illness through sexual transmission, and 8 percent acquire it through injection drug use (CDC 1998). Within the African American community, two subgroups are disproportionately at risk: young women who become infected primarily through heterosexual contact, and young men who engage in unprotected sex with other men.

Although both African American male and female youth are at high risk for HIV-infection, this chapter addresses the unique condition of African American adolescent females. The increasing number of African American adolescent girls infected with HIV raises the troubling question of whether the African American community can cope with an additional drain on overburdened institutions. The disproportionate number of African American adolescent girls with HIV also raises questions about our society's commitment to provide high-quality preventive services and care for these young women.

Shaping high-quality preventive services for African American adolescent girls requires a knowledge of their sexual behaviors and beliefs, as well as an understanding of the intersecting cultural, social, and ecological factors that make it more difficult for them to make wise decisions. This chapter describes current sexual behaviors and HIV/AIDS knowledge among African American adolescent girls compared with all adolescents and explores cultural, social, and ecological issues in their lives. We conclude with recommendations for HIV-prevention services for this population.

CURRENT SEXUAL BEHAVIOR AND HIV/AIDS KNOWLEDGE

Individual Sexual Behavior

Increase in adolescent sexual activity: Heterosexual activity among all U.S. adolescents has increased dramatically since the 1970s (Rotheram-Borus, O'Keefe, Kracker, and Foo 2000). Current studies have found the age of sexual initiation for most adolescents is between sixteen and nineteen years (UNAIDS/WHO 1998) and is about the same across genders by age sixteen. However, for U.S. urban youth, irrespective of race/ethnicity, heterosexual intercourse is occurring at an earlier age, with a median age of twelve to thirteen according to some studies (Levy et al. 1993). Once engaged in sexual intercourse, however, sexual activity varies, with about 34.8 percent of sexually active high school students reporting intercourse in the last three months; older students in grades eleven and twelve are more likely to be sexually active (e.g., 68.2 percent by college age [CDC 1997]). Clearly efforts should be made to retard the age of coitus initiation, as it is the precursor to sexual activity.

There are modest disparities in sexual activity among never-married female adolescents. African American adolescents typically begin having sex earlier than Anglo American adolescents (i.e., 16.4 years for Anglo American versus 15.5 years for African American girls [Tolman 1996; Vera, Reese, Paikoff, and Jarrett 1996]). African American adolescent girls tend to reach menarche earlier than Anglo American adolescent girls (Wyatt 1990), which puts them on an earlier physiological developmental timetable. In addition, African American adolescent girls often have sexual partners who are older than they are, and in those cases, the chance of initiation of sexual intercourse is increased by 44 percent (Marin et al. 2000).

Contraceptive use: African American adolescents tend not to use contraception until after the initiation of sexual intercourse, which accounts for why one-fifth of their pregnancies occur within one month after initiation of intercourse. Murry (1996) found more than 45 percent of Hispanic and African American adolescent girls did not use contraception at first intercourse, and 60 percent stated that they used no methods at last intercourse. When methods were selected, the African American girls used medically prescribed methods and Hispanic girls used over-the-counter methods, resulting in a greater amount of the African American girls (40 percent) becoming pregnant. With low-income African American communities more likely to be epicenters of HIV-infection than majority group communities, the likelihood of infants being born with HIV also increases. In fact, 75 percent of all babies born to infected mothers are African American (Dryfoos 1990). Unfortunately, the pregnancy rate among African American adolescent girls has led to a focus on policies to prevent unwanted pregnancies, to the exclusion of policies that would help prevent sexually transmitted diseases (STDs) (Rotheram-Borus, O'Keefe, Kracker, and Foo 2000; Whaley 1999).

The high rate of STDs among U.S. adolescents is a clear reflection of the prevalence of unprotected sex. Adolescents between the ages of fifteen and nineteen years have the highest rates of gonorrhea, syphilis, chlamydial cervicitis, and hospitalization for pelvic inflammatory disease (PID) (Kipke, Futterman, and Hein 1990). The implications of the impact of sexuality-related problems on the overall health of African American adolescent girls cannot be ignored, as these conditions are often precursors to HIV infection.

Alcohol and drug use: The use of alcohol and other noninjection drugs also exacerbates the risk of HIV by increasing the likelihood of unsafe sex (Keller et al. 1991; Kipke, Futterman, and Hein 1990; Rotheram-Borus, O'Keefe, Kracker, and Foo 2000). Drug use among African American and non–Anglo American youth is higher than or equal to rates of Anglo American youth in every major drug category except for inhalants and hallucinogens (NIDA 1979). In the younger adolescent age group (ages twelve to seventeen), 31 percent of African American teens, male and female, reported they had used marijuana, and 29 percent said that they had used alcohol (NIDA 1979). By 1982, however, there had been a decrease in the prevalence of marijuana use for young African American adolescents to 23 percent; however, the rate was 61 percent for youth aged eighteen to twenty-five. These figures may not show the true prevalence of African American drug use, as African American youth are less likely to report their drug use than their Anglo American counterparts (Myers 1989).

A recent analysis (Grant, Gilbert-Martinez, and White 1998) of the impact of alcohol and other substances on the development of African American youth has suggested that a new paradigm, addressing both direct and indirect factors across childhood and adolescent phases of human development, should be applied. Researchers noted that the physical, maturation, peer group membership, and identity development tasks of early development leave African American adolescents particularly vulnerable. The pressures of peers and the overwhelming adolescent need to achieve group membership are fundamental to African American adolescents' sense of identity, safety, and belonging.

Further, African American youth may also be at risk because of the rapid physical change they undergo during adolescence, when many perceive that they are at a physical disadvantage compared with their Anglo American and Hispanic counterparts due to weight, body image, or unattractiveness. Concurrent research has found that adolescents who are dissatisfied with their weight and who considered themselves unattractive use illicit substances, drank alcohol, and got drunk more often that those who were satisfied with their physical selves (Page, Scanlan, and Allen 1995).

HIV/AIDS Knowledge

[*Knowledge about sexual risk*: Even though knowledge about prevention of HIV infection is necessary to reduce exposure to the virus, misinformation persists among most teenagers (Kaiser Family Foundation 2000; Rotheram-Borus, O'Keefe, Kracker, and Foo 2000; Sells and Blum 1996). Even when youth have some knowledge of HIV transmission and risk, studies have found little association between knowledge of STDs and condom use (DiClemente, Brown, Beausoleil, and Lodico 1993; Jemmott et al. 1992; Shrier, Goodman, and Emans 1999).

In the Kaiser Foundation survey of Teens on HIV/AIDS (2000), most teens reported that they were personally concerned about becoming infected, and African American and Latino teens reported even higher levels of concern. One in six teens reported that they knew someone who had AIDS, had died of AIDS, or had tested positive for HIV; for African American and Latino teens, the ratio was one in four. Further, the survey found that fewer than one-third of teens that say they are sexually active have been tested, although 16 percent say they have considered getting tested (Kaiser Family Foundation 2000). Most teens reported that they get their information about HIV/AIDS from varied sources, with school being their primary source, followed by parents. The media also play a role in providing information about HIV/AIDS, with half of the teens reporting getting at least some information from TV or movies, and at least some information from magazines. This was true for girls in general, and African American and Latinas in particular (Kaiser Family Foundation 2000).]

[*Negotiating condom use*: Studies that focused on condom use among adolescent girls with their partners found that these young women lack self-efficacy in negotiating condom use with a partner, lack sufficient knowledge of HIV/AIDS, and believe that condom use reduces sexual pleasure (MacDonald et al. 1990; Rotheram-Borus, Kelly, Kracker, and Foo 2000). Adolescent female participants also reported their concern about how they would be perceived if they insisted that their male sexual partner use condoms (e.g., that sex was planned), whereas not using them showed love and trust in their partner (Sugarman, Hergenroder, Chacko, and Parcel 1991)] They also shared their discomfort with the use of condoms and their inability to negotiate the purchase of condoms (Berlin, Hingson, Strunin, and Heeron 1990; Hudson, Freeman, Krepcho, and Petty 1990), and there was reduced motivation among females who use oral contraceptives to get males to participate in HIV prevention (Brookman 1990). Some researchers (Amaro 1995; Rosenthal, Gifford, and Moore 1998) have noted that the female socialization process may render most young women unable to successfully negotiate the twin demands of their sexual health needs and their desires for long-term heterosexual relationships, and have suggested that future HIV/AIDS research focus more fully on the gender-based underpinnings of the epidemic.

Complicating our understanding of the sexual health of African American adolescent girls is the reality that these young women are seldom the sample upon which theories of sexual health are developed. When studies of HIV/AIDS knowledge, attitudes, and beliefs do include them, present findings are generally confounded by problems of study design (Forrest and Singh 1990; Wyatt 1990; Zabin and Hayward 1993). Conceptualizing two-parent families as the norm, despite the fact that alternative family constellations are increasingly prevalent among the larger population (U.S. Bureau of Census 1992, 2000; Wyatt 1990, 1991) can render the health of African American adolescent girls and women as invisible to sexual health researchers. In addition, there is the ongoing concern for the continued confounding of race and class (Forrest and Singh 1990; Zabin and Hayward 1993), and the use of race consistently as the correlate of sexual activity (Foshee and Bauman 1992; Muram, Rosenthal, Tolley, and Peeler 1991). Perpetuation of this methodological flaw limits our understanding of the sexual health of African American adolescent females from a variety of perspectives (e.g., class, geography, religious influence, etc.).

HIV/AIDS RISK IN CONTEXT

Race and Increased Risk

Geographical risk: Race, income status, and gender combine to place African American adolescent girls at high risk for HIV-infection. Rates of HIV-infection tend to be highest in low-income, inner-city urban areas with total populations over one million (CDC 2000). These epicenters—areas with HIV-infection rates of 7.5 percent or higher per 100,000—have been relatively stable since 1984, when the majority of adolescent HIV-infection cases were found in New York, Florida, Texas, Puerto Rico, and New Jersey. By 1999, however, the epicenters of adolescent HIV/AIDS had shifted to the major metropolitan areas of the northeastern and southeastern United States: District of Columbia, New York, U.S. Virgin Islands, Florida, Puerto Rico, Maryland, New Jersey, North Carolina, Massachusetts, Delaware, Georgia, Connecticut, Louisiana, Pennsylvania, and Mississippi (Bowler, Sheon, D'Angelo, and Vermund 1992).

Income status and increased risk: Historically, African American women are the only group in the United States who were enslaved and brought to the United States to work, to produce, and to reproduce (Almquist 1995). Although the legacy of racism and sexism has been well documented (Giddings 1984; Reid 1988), less has been written about the burden of class. The incomes of African American women in the United States lags far behind the incomes of Anglo American men, African American men, and Anglo American women, even when differences in levels of education are controlled (Horton and Smith 1993).

Single parenthood family status: Single parenthood and the impact of the socioeconomic disadvantage that comes from reduced economic resources is a reality for many African American children. In 1991, 54 percent of all African American children lived in mother-only families. Sixty-five percent of these children were poor, compared with 19 percent of African American children who lived in two-parent families (U.S. Bureau of Census 1992). The risk of poverty in mother-only families is high, resulting from factors such as low wages for women, unfavorable economic conditions, the low educational attainment of many single mothers, the large number of single mothers who are adolescents, and the large number of fathers who provide no financial support for their children (Ellwood 1988; Houston, McLloyd, and Carcia 1994).

The erosion in the economic well-being of working-class African American men in particular has been accompanied in the African American community, and the larger U.S. society, by a decline in marriage rates, an increase in divorce rates, an increase in the number of mother-only families, and an increase in childhood poverty. Marriage rates for African American females fifteen years of age and older dropped from 54 percent in 1970 to 38 percent in 1991 (McLloyd and Hernandez-Jozefowicz 1996). During the same period, divorce rates for this group increased from 4.4 percent to 11 percent, and the proportion of mother-only families to all African American families increased from 28 percent to 46 percent (U.S. Bureau of Census 1992). Between 1971 and 1990, the poverty rate for African American children under eighteen years increased from 40.7 percent to 44.2 percent, with the sharpest increase occurring during the 1980s. It has been argued that the major cause of these trends is the deteriorating economic status of African American men (Wilson 1987).

Limited housing options: One outcome of reduced economic resources is that African American women and their children have limited options about where they will live; geography, then, becomes a correlate for risk of HIV-infection. Low-income inner-city communities typically have high neighborhood seroprevalence rates, resulting from high rates of drug use and drug dealing. Within this context there is the probability of heterosexual transmission that has been associated with more frequent intercourse (Gerrard and Warner 1994), less consistent use of condoms (Norris and Ford 1998), and, multiple sex partners within relatively short time periods (Ford and Moscicki 1995; Seidman and Rieder 1994). These are also communities where other stresses are present. Myers (1989) has written extensively of the multiple stressors that assault the mental health of urban African American youth, leading to their overrepresentation in all major mental health categories: psychiatric disorders, juvenile delinquency and violence, suicide and related self-destructive behaviors, as well as substance use and abuse (Myers 1989). However, Myers (1989) also calls attention to the social and economic context of these stressors, such as substandard housing, chronic unemployment and underemployment, the higher risk for a variety of physical illnesses and disabilities, injuries, socioemotional maladjustments, and higher levels of death than for most other American youth.

Low-income, young African American girls must learn to navigate the hazards of low-income neighborhoods as a form of self-protection and survival. Research on the developmental context of African American girls found that upper elementary-school girls in low-income communities consistently reported the hassle of unwanted sexual advances from older men (Anderson 1999; Spencer, Dupree, Swanson, and Cunningham 1998) and feelings of vulnerability and fear of victimization in their immediate surroundings (Vera, Reese, Paikoff, and Jarrett 1996). In addition, these studies reported the difficulties these young girls had in finding peer groups who valued noninvolvement in early sexual activity, their concerns about the absence of adults and "safe spaces" to provide the social and psychological support they desired (Pastor, McCormick, and Fine 1996).

Oppressive schooling environment: For the mothers of these young girls, the search for support as they attempt to protect their daughters from physical and sexual harm can be daunting. The logical institution for this support is the public school; however, African American youth consistently report that urban schools, in their efforts to reduce violence, have been transformed into virtual prisons (Pastor, McCormick, and Fine 1996), where surveillance of behavior has taken priority over the provision of personal and group guidance. African American adolescent girls report that their desire to discuss personal issues with school guidance counselors diminishes when they perceive that their personal stories will be used against them (Fine and Zane 1989). This perception of disrespect for their privacy as individuals can be devastating to the young women. Once they perceive that school authority figures do not respect them, they no longer share their most pressing personal concerns with these authority figures. The resulting lack of communication between the young female students and the school authority figures denies these young women access to adults from whom they desire to engage in open and honest discussion about many of the problems they incur as they mature (Kelly, in submission; Pastor, McCormick, and Fine 1996).

The failure of urban schools to help accommodate the developmental needs of African American adolescent females discourages young women's pursuit of academically rigorous work, as learning about social oppression can be problematic for low-income young women of color, especially if they perceive that their conditions cannot be overcome. In research conducted with an inner-city junior high school population in New York City, students were asked to project themselves forward and list possible occupations for themselves (Pastor 1993). Responses were correlated with measures of perceptions of racism and limited economic opportunities. The findings were that greater awareness of racism and limited economic opportunities were significantly correlated with lower-prestige-level occupational aspirations. Thus, it appears that students of color with sophisticated social consciousness of race and class relations may also have the most depressed sense of what is possible for themselves (Pastor, McCormick, and Fine 1996).

The diversion from high school completion and higher education aspirations for African American adolescent girls can be fatal. Young women who persevere in their education are able to construct a world of possibilities that does not succumb to hopelessness, cynicism, or alienation (Pastor, McCormick, and Fine 1996). What is more important, the participation in high-risk sexual activity that can lead to HIV-infection correlates highly with HIV-infection, the infection of other STDs, and unintended pregnancy for African American adolescent girls. School achievement and completion, therefore, is a critical buffer for African American adolescent girls to sexual health risks of all kinds.

Low parental support for career aspirations: Not only is support for school achievement and higher education aspirations of African American girls important to the avoidance of sexual health risks, but also support by significant others in the lives of these young women is requisite. Research (McLloyd and Hernandez-Jozefowicz 1996) on the perceptions and expectations of African American mothers for their adolescent daughters' economic futures found two areas of mother-daughter agreement concerning the daughter's economic future, both related to the daughter's academic ability and the importance of good grades. Adolescents' perceptions of their academic abilities are based largely on the perceptions of significant others, such as parents (Eccles-Parsons, Adler, and Kaczala 1982) and teachers (Eccles-Parsons, Kaczala, and Meece 1982). Mothers' perceptions of their daughters' abilities still have an effect on daughters' expectancies of economic hardship. This latter finding suggests that mothers who perceive their daughters as lacking academic skills can dampen their daughter's expectations of economic success, regardless of the daughter's self-perception of abilities (McLloyd & Hernandez-Jozefowicz 1996). Care should be given by low-income mothers, especially of their achieving daughters, in projecting their concerns about economic hardship and uncertainty on their children.

Gender and Increased Risk

Dual developmental scripts: Adolescence provides the developmental link between childhood and adulthood. A major developmental task of adolescence is to consolidate one's sense of identity, which, according to Erickson (1968) is based in part on one's ethnicity and gender. A major task for African American youth is learning to live among Anglo American people in America while becoming an African American (DuBois 1938; Greene 1990). For African American adolescent girls, this requires that they learn to negotiate the intersection of race and gender in a society that devalues both. To accomplish this task, African American adolescent girls must confront two differing worldviews: one of the majority culture in the United States, and, the other of their own African American ethnic minority (Boykin 1986; Greene 1990). The majority culture focuses on the importance of the individual, usually accomplished through individualism and competition. In the African American ethnic culture, the focus is generally on group survival that requires cooperation. In general, African American ethnic culture places a premium on behaviors that emphasizes spirituality and affect; whereas, to a greater degree, the majority culture emphasizes behavior focused on materialism and reason.

Some researchers (Lightfoot 1976; Myers 1989) have noted that African American adolescent girls are equally as likely to be victims of neglect and invisibility as they are to be denigrated. This may be due to a number of factors. For example, compared with their male counterparts, African American adolescent females have a tendency to exhibit fewer behavioral difficulties (Myers 1989). Moreover, because Anglo American women have been the forerunners in the women's movement, they have tended to research themselves and Anglo American female adolescents, leaving the assumption that many of the educational and socialization problems facing Anglo American girls also apply to African American girls (Kelly 2001). Although the socialization processes are similar for both groups, there are important cultural and historical differences between them. The result has been, however, that little attention has been given to either how an African American adolescent girl perceives herself as a female or how others perceive her (Smith 1982).

The presence of these dual scripts can be a source of opportunity and challenge. On the one hand, there is the opportunity for African American young women to become competent in both, or bicultural, moving between both cultures (Rotheram-Borus, Dopkins, Sabata, and Lightfoot 1996); on the other hand, this "dual consciousness" can be a source of tension, unease, and even shame when an aspect of the self is negated and/or stigmatized (DuBois 1938; McCombs 1986).

Mother-daughter relationships: The individual best able to facilitate the integration of racial and sexual identity for African American adolescent girls is the mother and/or mother surrogates within the community. The special bond between mothers and daughters in the African American community has long been recognized, and when African American young women are asked to identify the most influential relationship in their lives, they routinely describe the relationship with their mothers as the most rewarding (Armsden and Greenberg 1987; hooks 1990). At the same time, African American girls describe adolescence as the period of greatest conflict with their mothers (Montemayor 1986). The issues most likely to be the source of conflict are those of autonomy and control, when the establishment of rules regarding increasing independent behavior and family-related obligations and responsibilities are in flux (Cauce et al. 1996).

Although there is little research in the literature regarding the relationship between African American mothers and daughters, of the few studies that do exist (Cauce et al. 1996; McCombs 1986), they report that the mothers are overwhelmingly concerned about the safety of their daughters, who must navigate on a daily basis the dangerous and hostile environment in which they live. Lost in the breach between mother and daughter is the opportunity for the older generation to share family history and stories of group pride that are essential to the identity formation of adolescent youth. Without a knowledge of who she is and the role that family history and pride can play in identity formation, young African American adolescent girls may not develop a strong sense of self which can serve as a buffer to negative stereotypes of Black femininity.

Developing a healthy sexuality: Despite mothers' concerns for their daughters' physical safety, there still remains the silence around issues related to adolescent female sexuality (Burson 1998). Much of this silence is embedded in the usual fears about unintended pregnancy; for African American mothers, however, it may also be an unintended consequence of their own oppression within the African American community where human sexuality is often discussed within the context of deviance (Quinn 1993; Townes 1991). Some scholars have suggested that the resistance on the part of the Black church to place the integration of the sexual self with the spiritual and physical aspects of personhood may also militate against efforts of some mothers to discuss issues of adolescent sexuality in an open manner (Burson 1998; Townes 1991).

In a major study of adolescent sexuality, African American adolescent females reported that their parents only warn them to stay away from boys or to avoid physical contact (Banks and Wilson 1989). The young women were left to develop a definition of sexuality based on unreliable information from their peers or from broadcast and visual media. Research by Kaplan (1997), however, has suggested that there may be an intergenerational pattern of not discussing issues of female sexuality and sexual desire, especially for those women who may have been teen-parents themselves. Kaplan suggests that much of the inability of the mothers to discuss issues of maturation and sexuality with their daughters may be a function of the mother's own lack of information. She notes that in interviews with the some of the mothers of the adolescent girls in her study many related that their mothers had not discussed the changes their bodies were undergoing during adolescence, nor were their any conversations about addressing feelings of sexual desire. Accordingly, although many of the women wanted to help their daughters, the conversations with their daughters often reduced to "do as I say and not as I did" (Kaplan 1997).

African American adolescent girls and their mothers share the connection of race, gender, and a common history of sexual exploitation. From that history emerged the sexual coding of Anglo American women as "good," embodying asexual virtue and purity and African American women as "bad," embodying deviant female sexuality (Caraway 1991; Painter 1992). By understanding their history and engaging in open and honest communication about their bodies, their sexual desires, and their aspirations, mothers and daughters can craft an image of their sexual selves that affirms them as African American women (Flannery, Rowe, and Gulley 1993; Townes 1991).

Reducing the impact of media on sexual identity: African American adolescent females do receive information about human sexuality from the visual media, where they are routinely exposed to sexual images. Ninety-eight percent of all American households have at least one television set, making television the dominant source of information and entertainment in the United States. It matters for African American adolescent girls, when television program content renders them invisible or portrays them in marginal, negative, or unrealistic roles (Berry 2000). Media researchers (Berry 2000; Kaufman et al. 1993) have noted that although the number of African Americans has increased over the years, the characters are more likely to be presented in highly a stereotyped manner than European American characters in terms of occupational level, social role, and behavioral characteristics.

Complicating the media portrait of African American girls are popular rap music artists (many of whom are young adult African American males) who routinely scorn adolescent females for not having a male sexual partner. Their music reinforces the message that teen female popularity is dependent on attracting a male partner. "Having a man" has come to exemplify the prescribed gender role for African American adolescent females who are urged to make themselves subservient to their male partner in order to preserve the relationship. Many African American adolescent females (especially those who are unsure of their identity, ill-informed about their bodies, and bereft of appropriate adult role models) embrace these lyrics and use them as the framework for their own sexual development. The tension between parental and religious admonitions to avoid sexual activity and media messages to engage in sexual behavior can be overwhelming (Berry 2000; Brown 2000; Zillman 2000).

Confronting the dilemma of male-female relationships: Another important developmental task for African American adolescent girls is learning how to live with African American males. Ideally, this takes place in the context of a loving family where adult males nurture, support, and protect her as she develops into womanhood. For many African American adolescent girls, this learning process is often filled with the pain of absence and/or trauma. From an early age, many young girls encounter physical, sexual, and emotional violence and abuse from African American men as varied as fathers, stepfathers, brothers, male cousins, and mothers' boyfriends (Greene 1990; Wyatt 1990). Feminist researchers (Gilligan 1993; Miller 1987) have offered "female relationships" as an alternative paradigm for understanding the identity construction of women and girls to the commonly accepted paradigm of Erickson (1968). They aver that the key relationship for young women is that of their mother's. But Kaplan (1997) noted in her research with low-income African American adolescent girls their preference for male love (121) as a central construct of their identity formation. She describes young women who are emotionally needy, creating fantasy fathers, while their mothers make the love of their brother central to their (the mother's) lives, diminishing the quality of their relationship with their daughters. This is often referred to as "loving their sons and raising their daughters" (Greene 1990). The results are often that the young women are left as emotional prey to young African American males whose social scripting for displaying their masculinity requires that this emotional vulnerability be exploited (Anderson 1999; Kaplan 1997).

During adolescence, as dating begins, young African Americans must negotiate their sexual safety with their partners. In a study (Vera, Reese, Paikoff, and Jarrett 1996) of the contextual factors for sexual risk-taking for young, inner-city girls (African American and Latina), parents reported their daughters having unsafe sex with gang members in order to "buy safety" from violence in their community and coercion to have sex on the part of their daughters' boyfriends as a means of proving love and affection. Current research (Elders and Albert 1998) has documented that child and adolescent sexual abuse is a risk for teen pregnancy. Sexual abuse is generally an antecedent to pregnancy (66 percent of teen girls report histories of sexual abuse; Boyer and Fine 1992). A history of sexual abuse is linked to high-risk behaviors that may account for increased risk of early unplanned pregnancy, including young age at initiation of sexual intercourse (Boyer and Fine 1992; Nagy, DiClemente, and Adcock 1995; Widom and Kuhns 1996), failure to use contraception (Boyer and Fine 1992; Widom and Kuhns 1996), prostitution (Boyer and Fine 1992; James and Meyerding 1977; Widom and Kuhns 1996), physically assaultive relations (Nagy, Diclemente, and Adcock 1995), and abuse of alcohol and drugs (Boyer and Fine 1992; Widom and Kuhns 1996). In addition, the presence of abuse can lead to feelings of helplessness, hopelessness, and severe depression, which combined reduce the likelihood of successful mental health intervention and health promotion (Sanders-Phillips, 1994).

Recommendations for Reducing HIV Risk

The intersection of race, low-income, and gender need not be overwhelming for African American adolescent girls. If we are to have any success in reducing HIV risk among low-income, African American adolescent girls, we need a new approach that addresses the relationship of adolescent behavior, that is, risky sexual activity and drug use, and the context of their behaviors. Most prevention approaches currently aim to reduce adolescents' vulnerability to HIV by focusing on important intrapersonal and interpersonal mediators of behavior such as HIV knowledge, attitudes, and beliefs; developing peer norms to support HIV-prevention practices; promoting the mastery of risk-reduction skills; and motivating the adolescent to adopt prevention practices. Some individual level interventions produced evidence of effectiveness in reducing adolescents HIV-associated risk behaviors, but some researchers (DiClemente and Wingood 2000) have suggested that these interventions may not be sufficient to sustain any newly acquired behaviors over time. Thus, prevention efforts must target adolescents, as well as attend to the ecological factors that impact and affect their behavior: attention to family constellations, community-level interventions (especially to influential institutions such as school and religious organizations), and public health and community welfare services (such as housing, child care, media, etc.). In addition, policy level interventions are necessary to address the structural context of the HIV-risk generation: community violence reduction, providing culturally specific and culturally competent public health services, improving and expanding the quality of housing for low-income and working-class families, increasing social services such as child care and afterschool care, increasing employment opportunities for older youth and adult residents of low-income communities, providing low-income transportation in low-income communities, and expanding opportunities for the arts and more public places for exercise and recreation.

In attending to the unique needs of African American adolescent girls, however, prevention efforts must attempt to reduce the insidious overlapping or race, class, and gender; these efforts should include:

1. *Developing enhanced communication between mothers and daughters*: Mothers are their daughters' first teachers. Young girls learn from their mothers who they are, how they are perceived and valued in the family, and where the family fits in the larger society. Strength has become the primary coping mechanism for African American women, and it is this coping mechanism that African American mothers try to instill in their daughters (Shorter-Gooden and Washington 1996). If we want young, low-income African American girls to grow strong, healthy, and proud, we must educate their mothers in the competencies and skills necessary to teach their daughters about their bodies and their emotions during adolescence so they will feel good about their physical and emotional selves and be able to develop integrity and a sense of wholeness.

2. *Support the educational advancement of young girls*: Success in school is the best predictor of school completion and continued school performance. Expecting and supporting school success beginning in the elementary grades is the best predictor of continued school performance. Continued school performance is the best predictor of risk behaviors such as delayed sexual activity; use of alcohol, tobacco, and other drugs; and the likelihood of unintended pregnancy. High school completion is the critical milestone for entry into the world of work and the prospect of economic independence. For low-income African American girls, getting an education is the best deterrent to HIV risk.

3. *Introduce information about career options early in the education of girls*: The pervasive reality for too many low-income African American adolescent girls is that they end up as female heads of households. If the economic deprivation that most often attends this status is to be changed, young girls must be exposed to the possibility of more favorable economic options as soon as possible in their development. Female-headed household status need not be synonymous with economic deprivation. Motivating young girls to aspire to nontraditional careers where the economic rewards can be favorable should be at the center of any prevention effort.

4. *Support the rights of girls and women*: Sexism is the "dirty secret" in the African American community. Although African American women have always played a prominent role in the Black civil rights movement, the movement has often been silent on the issue of gender-based violence. Boys, young males, and adult males all engage in abuse of their female counterparts, and the traditional Black civil rights organizations should begin to elevate the issue of violence against African American women by African American men to the top of their domestic agenda. Part of this agenda should address the critical need for places in low-income, inner-city communities where young girls can feel safe from sexual coercion. Chronic ecological violence has a depressive effect on inner-city populations and can lead to feelings of helplessness, hopelessness, and dependency. It is important that the issue of safety be addressed for the children and youth of inner-city communities, male and female.

5. *Develop parallel programs that address the sexual health of young African American males*: Most girls and women desire to have a life that is shared with a male partner who loves and respects them. Indeed, it is fair to say that a primary ingredient in the health of African American women and girls is their relationship with their male partner. Just as special intervention programs are needed to help young African American adolescent girls develop as strong, healthy, and proud women, similar programs that address the unique issues of young, minority male development are needed to support

and sustain them. This means addressing their need for developing a positive masculine identity that does not exploit women, addressing racial injustice that does not lead to loss of life and incarceration, striving for intellectual growth and stimulation, and pursuing a healthy lifestyle that addresses nutrition, sports, and exercise, as well as reduced or no use of alcohol, tobacco, and other illicit drug substances.

6. *Provide low-cost, accessible health care for all adolescents to ensure the health of sexually active young females and males*: African American adolescent males and females desire to have high-quality information about their bodies, access to information about contraception for the prevention of STDs, HIV/AIDS, and pregnancy, and access to HIV/AIDS testing. African American adolescents represent increasing percentages of the more than 110,000 documented HIV-infected youth in the United States (Rotheram-Borus, O'Keefe, Kracker, and Foo 2000). Although about 44 percent of adults who are infected get tested, only about 4 percent of adolescents have been tested (Kaiser Family Foundation 2000). With such low rates, African American adolescent youth are seldom aware of their sero-status (Rotheram-Borus et al. in submission). When HIV-related services are accessed, the youth are typically symptomatic (mostly gay and bisexual youth) or are being evaluated for pregnancy (CDC 1992). If we are to maintain the health of African American adolescent girls and boys, we must develop the appropriate health programs that are responsive to their needs and are equipped to outreach and service the diversity they present.

NOTE

1. Numbers and percentages for reporting adolescent data vary by source, and are reflected in this chapter. For purposes of this chapter, "adolescent," unless otherwise noted, refers to youth between the ages of thirteen and nineteen; "preadolescent" refers to youth between the ages of nine and twelve.

REFERENCES

Almquist, E.M. (1995). The experiences of minority women in the U.S.: Intersections of race, gender, and class. In J. Freeman (Ed.), *Women: A feminist perspective* (pp. 573–606). Mountain View, CA: Mayfield Publishing.

Amaro, H. (1995). Love, sex and power. *American Psychologist, 50* (6), 437–447.

Anderson, E. (1999). *Code of the Street: Decency, violence and the moral life of the inner city*. New York: W.W. Norton.

Armsden, G.C., and Greenberg, M.T. (1987). The inventory of parent and peer attachment: Individual differences and their relationship to psychological well-being in adolescence. *Journal of Youth and Adolescence*, 16 427–453.

Banks, I.W., and Wilson, P.I. (1989). Appropriate sex education for Black teens. *Adolescence*, 24 233–245.

Berlin, B., Hingson, R., Strunin, L., and Heeron, R. (1990). Changes in adolescent condom use, knowledge, and beliefs about AIDS in Massachusetts, 1986–1989. *International AIDS Conference*, 6 (233) (Abstract No. S.C. 576).

Berry, G.L. (2000). Multicultural media portrayals and the changing demographic landscape: The psychosocial impact of television representations on the adolescent of color. *Journal of Adolescent Health*, 27 (2), 57–60.

Bowler, S., Sheon, A.R., D'Angelo, L.J., and Vermund, S.H. (1992). HIV and AIDS among adolescents in the United States: Increasing risk in the 1990s. *Journal of Adolescence* 15 349–371.

Boyer, D., and Fine, D. (1992). Sexual abuse as a factor in adolescent pregnancy and child maltreatment. *Family Planning Perspectives*, 24 14–11.

Boykin, A.W. (1986). The triple quandary and the schooling of Afro-American children. In E. Neisser (Ed.), *Achievement and achievement motives*. Hillsdale, NJ: Erlbaum.

Brookman, R.R. (1990). Adolescent sexual behavior. In K.K. Holmes (Ed.), *Sexually transmitted diseases*. New York: McGraw-Hill.

Brown, J.D. (2000). Adolescents' sexual media diets. *Journal of Adolescent Health*, 27 (2), 35–40.

Burson, J.A. (1998). AIDS, sexuality and African-American adolescent females. *Child and Adolescent Social Work Journal*, 15 357–365.

Caraway, N. (1991). *Segregated sisterhood*. Knoxville: University of Tennessee Press.

Cauce, A.M., Hiuraga, Y., Groves, D., Gonzales, N., et al. (1996). African-American mothers and their adolescent daughters: Closeness, conflict and control. In B.J.R. Leadbeater and N. Way (Eds.), *Urban girls: Resisting stereotypes, creating identities* (pp. 100–116). New York: New York University Press.

Centers for Disease Control (1992). Publicly funded HIV counseling and testing—United States, 1990. *Patient Education and Counseling*, 19 219–228.

Centers for Disease Control and Prevention (1997). Youth risk surveillance. National college health risk behavior survey—United States, 1995. *Mortality and morbidity weekly report*, 46 (SS-6), 1–58.

Centers for Disease Control and Prevention (1998). *Young people at risk—Epidemic shifts toward young women and minorities*. Atlanta, GA: Centers for Disease Control and Prevention.

Centers for Disease Control and Prevention (2000). *HIV/AIDS surveillance: December 1999 Year-end edition*, 11 (2). Atlanta, GA.

DiClemente, R.J., Brown, L., Beausoleil, N., and Lodico, M. (1993). Comparison of AIDS knowledge and HIV-related sexual risk behaviors among adolescents in low and high AIDS prevalence communities. *Journal of Adolescent Health*, 14 231–236.

DiClemente, R.J., and Wingood, G.M. (2000). Expanding the scope of HIV prevention for adolescents: Beyond individual-level interventions. *Journal of Adolescent Health*, 26 377–378.

Dryfoos, J.G. (1990). *Adolescents at risk: Prevalence and prevention*. New York: Oxford University Press.

DuBois, W.E.B. (1938). *The souls of black folk*. Chicago: A.C. McClurg & Co.

Eccles-Parsons, J.S., Adler, T.F., and Kaczala, C. (1982). Socialization of achievement attitudes and beliefs: Parental influences. *Child Development*, 53 310–321.

Eccles-Parsons, J.S., Kaczala, C., and Meece, J. (1982). Socialization of achievement attitudes and beliefs: Teacher influences. *Child Development*, 53 322–339.

Elders, M.J., and Albert, A.E. (1998). Adolescent pregnancy and sexual abuse. *Journal of the American Medical Association*, 280 (7), 648–649.

Ellwood, D.T. (1988). *Poor support: Poverty in the American family*. New York: Basic Books.

Erickson, E. (1968). *Identity: Youth and crisis*. New York: W.W. Norton.

Fine, M., and Zane, N. (1989). Bein' wrapped too tight: When low-income women drop out of high school. In L. Weis, E. Farrar, and H.G. Petrie (Eds.), *Dropouts from school: Issues, dilemmas, and solutions.* Albany: State University of New York Press.

Flannery, D., Rowe, D., and Gulley, B. (1993). Impact of pubertal status, timing and age on adolescent sexual experience and delinquency. *Journal of Adolescent Research,* 8 (1), 21–40.

Ford, C., and Moscicki, A.B. (1995). Control of sexually transmitted diseases in adolescents: The clinician's role. *Advances in Pediatric Infectious Diseases,* 10 263–305.

Forrest, J., and Singh, S. (1990). The sexual and reproductive behavior of American women, 1982–1988. *Family Planning Perspectives,* 22 206–214.

Foshee, V., and Bauman, K. (1992). Gender stereotyping and adolescent sexual behavior: A test of temporal order. *Journal of Applied Social Psychology,* 22 (20), 1561–1579.

Gerrard, M., and Warner, T.D. (1994). Comparisons of Marine and college women's HIV/AIDS-relevant sexual behaviors. *Journal of Applied Social Psychology,* 24 (11), 959–980.

Giddings, P. (1984). *When and where I enter: The impact of Black women on race and sex in America.* New York: Bantam Books.

Gilligan, C. (1993). *In a different voice.* Cambridge, MA: Harvard University Press.

Grant, D., Gilbert-Martinez, D.J., and White, B.W. (1998). Substance abuse among African American children: A developmental framework for identifying intervention strategies. *Journal of Human Behavior in the Social Environment,* 1 137–163.

Greene, B.A. (1990). What has gone before: The legacy of racism and sexism in the lives of Black mothers and daughters. *Women in Therapy,* 9 28–29.

hooks, b. (1990). *Yearning: Race, gender, and cultural politics.* New York: Basic Books.

Horton, C.P., and Smith, J.C. (1993). *Statistical record of Black America,* 2nd ed. Detroit, MI: Gale Research.

Houston, A., McLloyd, V.C., and Carcia, C. (1994). Children and poverty: Issues in contemporary research. *Child Development,* 65 275–282.

Hudson, R., Freeman, A., Krepcho, M., and Petty, A. (1990). Adolescent school-based AIDS knowledge and behaviors among teenagers, Massachusetts statewide surveys, 1986 to 1988. *Pediatrics,* 85 24–29.

James, J., and Meyerding, J.J. (1977). Early sexual experience and prostitution. *American Journal of Psychiatry,* 134 163–169.

Kaiser Family Foundation (2000). *National survey of teens on HIV/AIDS.* Menlo Park, CA: Henry J. Kaiser Family Foundation.

Kaplan, E.B. (1997). *Not our kind of girl.* Berkeley: University of California Press.

Kaufman, K.L., Brown, R.T., Graves, K., Henderson, P., et al. (1993). What, me worry? A survey of adolescents' concerns. *Clinical Pediatrics,* 32 (1) 8–14.

Keller, S.E., Barlett, J.A., Schleifer, S.J., Johnson, R.L., et al. (1991). HIV-relevant sexual behavior among a healthy inner-city heterosexual adolescent population in an endemic area of HIV. *Journal of Adolescent Health,* 12 44–48.

Kelly, E.M. (2001). Female, young, African-American and low income: What's feminism got to do with her? *Feminism and Psychology,* 11 (2), 152–155.

———. (In submission). *Beyond illness: Reconstruction of identity through relationships for HIV-positive women.*

Kipke, M., Futterman, D., and Hein, K. (1990). HIV infection and AIDS during adolescence. *Medical Centers of North America,* 74 1149–1166.

Lightfoot, S.L. (1976). Socialization and education of young black girls in school. *Teachers College Record*, 78 239–262.

MacDonald, N.E., Wells, G.A., Fisher, W.A., Warren, W.K., et al. (1990). High-risk STD/HIV behavior among college students. *Journal of the American Medical Association*, 263 3155–3159.

Marin, B.V., Coyle, K.K., Gomez, C.A., Carvajal, S.C., et al. (2000). Older boyfriends and girlfriends increase risk of sexual initiation in young adolescents. *Journal of Adolescent Health*, 27 409–418.

McCombs, H.G. (1986). The application of an individual/collective model to the psychology of black women. *Women in Therapy*, 5 67–80.

McLloyd, V.C., and Hernandez-Jozefowicz, D.M. (1996). Sizing up the future: Predictors of African-American adolescent females' expectancies about their economic fortunes and family life courses. In B.J.R. Leadbeater and N. Way (Eds.), *Urban girls: Resisting stereotypes, creating identities* (pp. 355–379). New York: New York University Press.

Miller, J.B. (1987). *Toward a new psychology of women*, 2nd ed. Boston: Beacon Press.

Montemayor, R. (1986). Family variation in parent-adolescent storm and stress. *Journal of Adolescent Research*, 1 5–31.

Muram, D., Rosenthal, T., Tolley, E., and Peeler, M. (1991). Race and personality traits affect high school senior girls' sexual reports. *Journal of Sex Education and Therapy*, 17 (4), 231–243.

Murry, V.M. (1996). Inner-city girls of color: unmarried, sexually active nonmothers. In B.J.R. Leadbeater and N. Way (Eds.), *Urban girls: Resisting stereotypes, creating identities* (pp. 272–290). New York: New York University Press.

Myers, H.F. (1989). Urban stress and mental health in black youth: An epidemiologic and conceptual update. In R. Jones (Ed.), *Black adolescents* (pp. 123–154). Berkeley, CA: Cobb and Henry Publishers.

Nagy, S., DiClemente, R.J., and Adcock, A.G. (1995). Adverse factors associated with forced sex among Southern adolescent girls. *Pediatrics*, 96 944–946.

National Institute on Drug Abuse (NIDA). (1979). *National survey on drug abuse*. Washington, D.C.: U.S. Government Printing Office.

Norris, A.E., and Ford, K. (1998). Moderating influence of peer norms on gender differences in condom use. *Applied Developmental Science*, 2 (4), 174–181.

Page, R.M., Scanlan, A., and Allen, O. (1995). Adolescent perceptions of body weight and attractiveness: Important issues in alcohol and illicit drug use? *Journal of Child and Adolescent Substance Abuse*, 4 (4), 43–55.

Painter, N. (1992). Hill, Thomas, and the use of racial stereotypes. In T. Morrison (Ed.), *Racing justice, engendering power*. New York: Pantheon Press.

Pastor, J. (1993). *Possible selves and academic achievement among inner-city students of color*. Master's thesis. City University of New York, NY.

Pastor, J., McCormick, J., and Fine, M. (1996). Makin' homes: An urban girl thing. In B.J.R. Leadbeater and N. Way (Eds.), *Urban girls: Resisting stereotypes, creating identities* (pp. 15–34). New York: New York University Press.

Quinn, S.C. (1993). AIDS and the African-American woman: The triple burden of race, class, and gender. *Health Education Quarterly*, 20 (3), 305–320.

Reid, P.T. (1988). Racism and sexism: Comparisons and conflicts. In P.A. Katz and D. Taylor (Eds.), *Eliminating racism: Profiles in controversy* (pp. 203–221). New York, NY: Plenum Press.

Rosenthal, D., Gifford, S., and Moore, S. (1998). Safe sex or safe love: Competing discourses? *AIDS Care*, 10 (1), 35–47.

Rotheram-Borus, M.J., Dopkins, S., Sabata, N., and Lightfoot, M. (1996). Personal and ethnic identity, values and self-esteem among black and Latino adolescent girls. In B.J.R. Leadbeater and N. Way (Eds.), *Urban girls: Resisting stereotypes, creating identities* (pp. 35–52). New York: New York University Press.

Rotheram-Borus, M.J., Kelly, E.M., Gillis, R., Kennedy, M., et al. (In submission). Alternative format for HIV testing among adolescents.

Rotheram-Borus, M.J., O'Keefe, Z., Kracker, R., and Foo, H.H. (2000). Prevention of HIV among adolescents. *Prevention Science*, 1 (1), 15–30.

Sanders-Phillips, K. (1994). Correlates of health promotion behaviors in low-income, black and Latino women. *American Journal of Preventive Medicine*, 21 71–83.

Seidman, S.N., and Rieder, R.O. (1994). A review of sexual behavior in the U.S. *American Journal of Psychiatry*, 151 330–341.

Sells, C.W., and Blum, B.W. (1996). Morbidity and mortality among U.S. adolescents: An overview of data and trends. *American Journal of Public Health*, 86 513–519.

Shorter-Gooden, K., and Washington, N.C. (1996). Young, Black and female: The challenge of weaving an identity. *Journal of Adolescence*, 19 465–475.

Shrier, L.A., Goodman, E., and Emans, S.J. (1999). Partner condom use and adolescent girls with sexually transmitted diseases. *Journal of Adolescent Health*, 24 357–361.

Smith, E.J. (1982). The Black female adolescent: A review of the educational, career and psychological literature. *Psychology of Women Quarterly*, 6 261–288.

Spencer, M.B., Dupree, D., Swanson, D.P., and Cunningham, M. (1998). The influence of physical maturation and hassles on African-American adolescents' learning behaviors. *Journal of Comparative Family Studies*, 29 189–200.

Sugarman, S.T., Hergenroder, A.C., Chacko, M.R., and Parcel, G.S. (1991). Acquired immunodeficiency syndrome and adolescents. *American Journal of Diseases in Children*, 145 431–436.

Tolman, D.L. (1996). Adolescent girls' sexuality: Debunking the myth of the urban girl. In B.J.R. Leadbeater and N. Way (Eds.), *Urban girls: Resisting stereotypes, creating identities* (pp. 255–271). New York: New York University Press.

Townes, E.M. (1991). The price of the ticket: Racism, sexism, heterosexism, and the church in the light of the AIDS crisis. In S.E. Davies and S.H. Haney (Eds.), *Redefining sexual ethics* (pp. 67–73). Cleveland, OH: Pilgrim Press.

UNAIDS/WHO (1998). Report on the global HIV/AIDS epidemic, June. Washington, D.C.: UNAIDS, World Health Organization.

U.S. Bureau of Census (1992). The black population in the United States: March. *Current population reports*. Series P20, no. 464. Washington, D.C.: U.S. Government Printing Office.

U.S. Bureau of Census (2000). *Population estimates of the United States by age and sex: April 1, 1990, to July 1, 1999, with short-term projection to November 1, 2000*. http://www.census.gov/population/estimates/nation/intfile2-1txt.

Vera, E.M., Reese, L.E., Paikoff, R.L., and Jarrett, R.L. (1996). Contextual factors of sexual risk-taking in urban African-American preadolescent children. In B.J.R. Leadbeater and N. Way (Eds.), *Urban girls: Resisting stereotypes, creating identities* (pp. 291–308). New York: New York University Press.

Whaley, A.L. (1999). Preventing the high-risk sexual behavior of adolescents: Focus on HIV/AIDS transmission, unintended pregnancy, or both? *Journal of Adolescent Health*, 24 376–383.

Widom, C.S., and Kuhns, J.B. (1996). Childhood victimization and subsequent risk for promiscuity, prostitution, and teenage pregnancy: A prospective study. *American Journal of Public Health*, 86 1607–1612.

Wingwood, G.M. and DiClemente, R.J. (2000). Expounding the scope of HIV prevention for adolescents: Beyond individual level interventions. *Journal of Adolescent Health*, 26(6) 377–378.

Wyatt, G.E. (1991). Examining ethnicity versus race in AIDS related sex research. *Social Science and Medicine*, 33 (1), 37–45.

———. (1990). Changing influences on adolescent sexuality over the past forty years. In J. Bancroft, J.M. Reinisch, and J. Machover (Eds.), *Adolescence and puberty* (pp. 182–206). New York: Oxford University Press.

Zabin, L., and Hayward, S. (1993). *Adolescent sexual behavior and childbearing*. Newbury Park, CA: Sage.

Zillman, D. (2000). Influence of unrestrained access to erotica on adolescents' and young adults' dispositions toward sexuality. *Journal of Adolescent Health*, 27 41–44.

11

Focus on Solutions: A Community-Based Mother/Daughter HIV Risk-Reduction Intervention[1]

Barbara L. Dancy

African American mothers represent an important link to reducing the risk of HIV-infection among adolescent girls. If African American mothers have comprehensive and correct HIV sexual risk-reduction information and skills, they can become protective factors for their daughters in deterring HIV sexual high-risk behaviors (Romer et al. 1999). When African American mothers, prior to their adolescents' first sexual encounter, actively engage their adolescents in conversation about condoms and sexual risks, their adolescents are more likely to use condoms during their first sexual relationship and in subsequent sexual relationships and to postpone early initiation of sexual activities (Lock and Vincent 1995; Miller, Levin, Whitaker, and Xu 1998; Romer et al. 1999).

However, far too often African American mothers do not have the comprehensive and correct HIV sexual risk-reduction information needed to promote risk-reduction behaviors (Hamburg 1997; Hockenberry-Eaton et al. 1996; Wyatt 1997). Consequently, mothers' guidance may be lacking at a time when their daughters need it most. This lack of guidance is especially apparent for African American mother/daughter dyads because, compared with other ethnic groups, African American adolescents are less likely to have talked to their mothers about sex or HIV/AIDS (Player and Frank 1994; Wyatt, 1997).

African American mothers' abilities to assist their adolescents could be greatly enhanced if the quality of their HIV-related information were improved. With enhanced knowledge and skill, mothers might be more inclined to assume their unique position as viable role models. Health care providers can enhance mothers' ability to be effective role models by teaching them HIV knowledge and risk-reduction skills so that they can then teach to and model for their daughters.

To date few studies have tested the effects of training mothers to directly teach HIV risk-reduction behaviors to their adolescent daughters. Therefore, the purpose of this pilot study was to develop and test the feasibility of the Mother/Daughter Risk Reduction (MDRR) intervention for inner-city, low-income African American adolescents who range in age from ten to sixteen. The development of the MDRR was based on theory, as well as on information from a series of focus groups conducted with low-income, inner-city African American mothers and their adolescent daughters. The MDRR was further refined based on critiques of mothers and daughters who actually attended the intervention when it was implemented in the community.

THEORETICAL BACKGROUND

The theoretical basis of the MDRR intervention takes into account the intersections of behavioral intention, beliefs, and self-efficacy. In this case, *behavioral intention* is the adolescent's plan not to engage in sexual activity, or to use condoms if she does become sexually active. Her behavioral intentions are contingent upon her *beliefs* or thoughts about the behavior. *Self-efficacy* is the adolescent's confidence in her ability to master refusal skills and consistent condom use. As such, behavioral intention, beliefs, and self-efficacy interact to influence the adolescent's acquisition of healthy behaviors.

The development of the MDRR was guided by an integration of Bandura's (1982) behavioral skills and self-efficacy acquired through modeling and performance accomplishment, integrated with Ajzen and Fishbein's (1980) beliefs and behavioral intentions. Bandura advocates the use of modeling, a structured action-oriented approach, as the primary mode of acquiring new behavioral skills. Through the process of modeling, the adolescent learns new behavior by extensive practice and corrective feedback that enhance self-efficacy to accomplish the behavior (Bandura 1994). Suggestions from focus groups and critiques of the intervention were incorporated in the development of the MDRR to ensure that the behaviors and the situations depicted in the intervention were realistic and credible (Rosenthal and Bandura 1978).

THE PILOT STUDY

Since the goal of the pilot study was to develop a culture-, gender-, and age-specific mother/daughter HIV risk-reduction intervention based on the specific needs of mothers and daughters in a community setting, the pilot study required two phases. In Phase 1, mothers and daughters provided information about their perceptions of HIV risks. In Phase 2, this information was used to develop a 2-segment intervention in which mothers first learned crucial HIV-prevention techniques and then taught these techniques to the daughters.

Phase 1

In Phase 1, a convenience sample of mother/daughter pairs were recruited from two geographically distinct but demographically similar study settings.

The mothers and daughters participated in focus groups designed to elicit their perceptions of adolescent girls' HIV risk behaviors and situations, as well as their perceptions of an effective HIV risk-reduction program for adolescents.

Mother/daughter pairs were assigned to one of three categories based on the daughters' ages: 10 to 11 years old, 12 to 14 years old, and 15 to 16 years old. Separate focus groups were conducted for mothers and for daughters within each category. As such, a mother of a 10- to 11-year-old daughter would be in a focus group with other mothers of 10- to 11-year-old daughters. Likewise, a 10- to 11-year-old daughter would be in a focus group with other 10- to 11-year-old daughters. Focus groups lasted approximately one hour and tended to be small, ranging in size from three to ten participants.

A total sample of 116 mother/daughter pairs participated in the focus groups: 38 pairs in the age 10 to 11 category, 56 in the age 12 to 14 category, and 22 pairs in the age 15 to 16 category. The demographic characteristics of mothers and daughters were similar across the two study settings. Mothers ranged in age from 27 to 67 years with an average age of 36.58 years, and 42 percent had less than a twelfth-grade education. The majority (66 percent) of the mothers had never married. Due to their low educational achievement, 60 percent were receiving public aid, and 72 percent had a monthly income of $899 or less. Nearly half (47 percent) were unemployed. The daughters ranged in age from 10 to 16 with an average age of 12.45 years, and 99 percent were currently enrolled in school. Their grade level ranged from third to eleventh grades. Forty-one percent reported that they were B students; however, 20 percent reported that they had failed a grade. A large percentage (61 percent) reported that they were in afterschool programs.

Results of Phase 1

Focus group data were analyzed using content analysis. The analysis revealed that not using condoms was the most frequently reported HIV risk behavior for daughters across all three age groups, whereas sharing drug paraphernalia was reported by daughters age 12 and over. Compared with the 15- to 16-year-old daughters, the 10- to 11-year-old daughters were more likely to report behaviors that were not HIV risk: "drinking off someone," "smoking off someone," and "eating out of someone's mouth." For mothers across all three age groups, the most frequently reported HIV risk behaviors for girls were failure to use condoms and sharing drug paraphernalia. For all mothers and daughters, girls not using condoms was reported as the most risky HIV behavior.

In terms of what HIV risk behavior would be hardest for an adolescent to change, the general consensus was the discontinuation of sharing drug paraphernalia and the incorporation of condom use. Daughters reported that the most likely place where unprotected sex occurred was in the girl's home when her parents were not present. *With the exception of the 10- to 11-year-old girls, all daughters reported cars and friends' homes as places where unprotected sex occurred.* Only the fifteen- to sixteen-year-old girls reported hotels and the boys' homes as places where unprotected sex occurred.

The boy's home was the most difficult place for 15- to 16-year-old girls to either resist sex or to demand condom use, whereas the 12- to 14-year-old girls reported the friend's home and the 10- to 11-year-old girls reported being home alone. Additionally, girls 12 and older reported that sharing drug paraphernalia took place in the girl's home when her parents were not present, followed by a friend's home and drug houses. Girls 12 and older reported that parties and in a friend's home were situations in which they found it most difficult to refuse drugs, including sharing paraphernalia. The 15- to 16-year-old girls also reported drug houses. *Consistent with the reports of daughters 12 and older,* mothers generally reported that girls their daughters' age would not be able to resist substance use at a party or at a drug house.

Mothers reported that an effective HIV risk-reduction program would expose adolescents to the different types of protective barriers, namely, male and female condoms and dental dams, and would stress the positive benefits of condom use. They thought that adolescents should be given opportunities to practice condom application and receive pamphlets to reinforce learning. They also suggested that someone living with AIDS should talk to the girls to discourage risky behavior. Lastly, they thought that the intervention should have visual aids and should allow the adolescents to participate in HIV-related games to stimulate interest and learning. The girls agreed, adding that they needed information on HIV transmission and on how to say no to sex.

Phase 2

In Phase 2, the MDRR intervention was developed based on the results of the content analysis of the focus group data. The MDRR intervention was conducted with a convenience sample of mother/daughter pairs from the same study settings as in Phase 1. The first segment of the intervention was to provide extensive training for mothers; *the second segment was for mothers to provide the training to the daughters.* As in Phase 1, mother/daughter pairs were assigned to training groups based on the daughters' ages.

Each intervention consisted of two-hour classes that were presented weekly for four weeks. In the first and third weeks, the research staff presented information to the mothers. In the second and fourth weeks, the mothers demonstrated what they had learned and practiced imparting that information to others in class. They received constructive feedback aimed to enhance their understanding and presentation skills. After each class, mothers provided feedback that was used to revise the intervention.

Upon completing their training, the mothers entered into the second segment of the intervention, the delivery of the intervention to their daughters. Three mothers from each training group volunteered to deliver the intervention to their group of daughters, but all mothers were required to attend their daughters' classes. The mothers' presence modeled their acceptance of the content and communicated that they viewed the content to be important. After each class, daughters provided feedback, and revisions were made based on this feedback.

In Phase 2, sixty-four mother/daughter pairs participated in the MDRR intervention. Fifty-four pairs of the sixty-four pairs had participated in Phase 1. The Phase 2 retention rate at fourteen weeks for the MDRR was 86 percent for the MDRR.

Mothers ranged in age from 26 to 56 years with an average age of 37.28 years, and 64 percent reported that they had never married. As in Phase 1, a large percentage had less than a twelfth-grade education (41 percent), were receiving public assistance (55 percent), and reported being unemployed (47 percent). In addition, 77 percent had a monthly income less than $1,100. Daughters ranged in age from 10 to 16 years with an average age of 12.65 years, and their grade level ranged from third to eleventh grades. The majority of these girls (86 percent) were currently enrolled in school, with 52 percent reporting that they participated in afterschool programs. Thirty-seven percent reported that they usually made Bs.

Results of Phase 2

Content analysis of the mothers' and daughters' feedback on the MDRR revealed that daughters thought that there was too much content in each session and that more time should be allocated for games, the group discussion, and the role-plays. The daughters particularly liked the role-plays because they represented real-life situations and gave them an opportunity to model HIV risk-reduction behavior. The suggestions made by the mothers and daughters led to the development of credible role-plays, thus enhancing the effects of modeling as proposed by Bandura (1982, 1994). Mothers of 10- to 11-year-old girls rejected the abbreviated version of condom application that was developed for 10- to 11-year-old daughters, so all daughters received the same condom information and practice. *The feedback from mothers and daughters participating in Phase 1 and Phase 2 of the pilot study was used to refine the intervention for future use with other mother-daughter pairs in similar communities.*

Description of the Final Revised Intervention

The participants' feedback yielded a group skill-building intervention that is culture-, gender-, and age-specific. The intervention has two components. Component 1 is a twelve-week group for mother training in which health experts teach mothers HIV risk-reduction knowledge and skills. Component 2 is a six-week daughter-training group in which mothers teach the daughters what they have learned in Component 1.

Component 2 has six sessions. Session one covers sexual development. Using three-dimensional models of the reproductive system, female and male sexual body parts and their functions are discussed. Each adolescent demonstrates on the models that she knows the body parts. At the end of the session, the girls participate in the "Who Knows the Body Game" as a means of summarizing the content of the session. Sessions two and three focus on knowledge of sexually transmitted diseases, including HIV. Guided discussion, games, and a colorful poster using animal figures to demonstrate the physiology of HIV enhance understanding. Daughters play other games, such as the "Risk Behavior Game," where they rate the degree of HIV risks for several thoughts and behaviors. The girls learn the rates of HIV and AIDS among African American adolescents and are to come prepared the following week to discuss the reasons for these high rates.

Session four begins with a group discussion of the reasons for the high rates of HIV and AIDS among African American adolescents. The group discusses rules governing male-female relationships and condom use that put African American adolescent girls at risk. Afterward in this session and subsequent sessions, HIV risk-reduction strategies are presented. Assertive behavior skills and decision-making skills are discussed in detail, followed by behavioral rehearsal with corrective feedback. In addition to engaging in prepared scenarios for behavioral rehearsal, the adolescents are encouraged to create a scenario where a really cute boy is pressuring them to have sex. Their homework assignment is to practice refusal skills at home with their mothers.

In session five, after hearing a story about a young woman who contracted HIV when she was an adolescent, the girls are encouraged to discuss their reactions. They play the "Abstinence Game," a board game designed to provide further practice in the use of refusal skills. After the game, the adolescents are given information about Pap tests, cervical cancer, male and female condoms, and dental dams. Female and male condom application is demonstrated, and adolescents are given an opportunity to practice condom application with corrective feedback. They role-play several scenarios and are to continue to practice refusal skills with their mothers and to add condom application to their practice. During the last session, adolescents demonstrate that they know condom application for both the male and female condom. Afterward, working in groups of threes, the adolescents complete a crossword puzzle that covers the content of all the sessions. In teams, the adolescents develop a fifteen-minute presentation to inform girls their age about sex. Each team gives its presentation to the large group and receives feedback.

CONCLUSION

The pilot study suggests that it is feasible for health experts to model HIV risk-reduction knowledge and skills to mothers, who then model the knowledge and skills to their daughters. The pilot study should be extended to a large-scale study to test the effectiveness of the MDRR. If this approach proves to be successful in reducing HIV risk behavior among African American adolescent girls, then similar programs could be implemented on a larger scale.

NOTE

1. This project was funded by the National Institute of Mental Health as a Supplement Grant, RO1-MH055937.

REFERENCES

Ajzen, I., and Fishbein, M. (1980). *Understanding attitudes and predicting social behavior*. Upper Saddle River, NJ: Prentice-Hall.

Bandura, A. (1982). Self-efficacy mechanism in human agency. *American Psychologist*, 37 (2), 122–147.

———. (1994). Social cognitive theory and exercise of control over HIV infection. In R.J. DiClemente and J.L. Peterson (Eds.), *AIDS theories and methods of behavioral interventions* (pp. 25–59). New York: Plenum Press.

Hamburg, D.A. (1997). Toward a strategy for healthy adolescent development. *American Journal of Psychiatry*, 154 7–12.

Hockenberry-Eaton, M., Richman, M.J., DiIorio, C., Rivero, T., et al. (1996). Mother and adolescent knowledge of sexual development: The effects of gender, age, and sexual experience. *Adolescence*, 31 35–47.

Lock, S.E., and Vincent, M.L. (1995). Sexual decision-making among rural adolescent females. *Health Values* 19 47–58.

Miller, K.S., Levin, M.L., Whitaker, D.J., and Xu, X. (1998). Patterns of condom use among adolescents: The impact of mother-adolescent communication. *American Journal of Public Health*, 88 1542–1544.

Player, M.L., and Frank, D.I. (1994). Families as a source of AIDS information for school age children. *Clinical Nurse Specialist*, 8 321–327.

Romer, D., Stanton, B., Galbraith, J., Feigelman, S., et al. (1999). Parental influence on adolescent sexual behavior in high-poverty settings. *Archives of Pediatrics & Adolescent Medicine*, 153 1055–1062.

Rosenthal, T.L., and Bandura, A. (1978). Psychological modeling: Theory and practice. In S.L. Garfield and A.E. Bergin (Eds.), *Handbook of psychotherapy and behavior change: An empirical analysis* (pp. 621–658). New York: John Wiley & Sons.

Wyatt, G.E. (1997). *Stolen women: Reclaiming our sexuality, taking back our lives*. New York: John Wiley & Sons.

12

Focus on Solutions: A Culturally Sensitive, Computer-Based AIDS Prevention Program Targeting African American Women on College Campuses

Heather A. Katz

African American women are eight times more likely to contract HIV than White women and three times more likely than Hispanic women are (Fears 1998).

"In 1999, more African Americans were reported with AIDS than any other racial/ethnic group. Almost two-thirds (63%) of all women reported with AIDS were African American" (CDC 2001). Thus, females in the early and late adolescence developmental stage are at very high risk, and many of these women are college students, for whom few prevention programs are targeted. Prevention efforts targeting young African American women on college campuses need to be gender and cultural specific and also take into account the environment that places the target audience at risk for HIV-infection. Furthermore, the program should take into account the unique learner characteristics that are not only shaped by racial/ethnic characteristics but also are influenced by one's present learning environment and past learning experiences. This chapter describes a user-friendly, computerized HIV/AIDS prevention program specifically developed for African American women on college campuses. The program considers age, race/ethnicity, and individualized learner characteristics, and the college milieu in providing HIV/AIDS prevention education and interactive skills-building information for this population.

HIV-PREVENTION BARRIERS FOR AFRICAN AMERICAN WOMEN ON COLLEGE CAMPUSES

Numerous barriers prevent African American college-age women from accessing culturally appropriate and representative HIV/AIDS prevention

education. First, the majority of HIV/AIDS prevention programs do not address the diversity within group characteristics and unique HIV prevention
needs among African American women, and existing programs typically are
not designed for the African American females within the university or college
campus milieu. Many HIV/AIDS prevention programs target either the "know-
it-all" teenager (Stevenson, McKee Gay, and Josar 1995), low-income Black
women (Flaskerud and Nyamathi 1990), African American women having low
levels of education and high unemployment (Weeks et al. 1995), or African
American early adolescents who live in urban low-income neighborhoods
(Stanton et al. 1995). The investigation of HIV/AIDS prevention programs involving African American women from variant age and educational groups (see
Dancy 1996) is minimal. In addition, the stigma associated with HIV and AIDS,
coupled with an inability to tolerate open and honest discussions about sexuality, maintains a sense of shame and secrecy for most young adults in our society, and particularly within various African American populations, thus
maintaining the high rates infection and death rates from AIDS among African
Americans (Stolberg 1998).

As a result of these barriers, many young African American women feel un-
comfortable seeking information about HIV/AIDS or become resistant to or reject HIV/AIDS prevention programs that are not representative of their race,
culture, and socioeconomic status (Stevenson, McKee Gay, and Josar 1995; Weeks
et al. 1995). For example, Renee, a twenty-two-year-old African American
woman, expresses her concern about seeking HIV testing at a local hospital, "Everything there was labeled, and I didn't want anyone seeing me" (Stolberg 1998,
A1). When AIDS prevention information is not culturally grounded, the material can be interpreted as "It doesn't pertain to me" or "It's not my problem."
The attitude of "it's them, not me" exists within the group among African American women and can be a special problem for young African American women
on college campuses who may view themselves as disassociated with the "poor,
inner-city, African American women" who are often highlighted as being at high
risk for HIV-infection. Thus, the existence of the aforementioned barriers re-
veals both the lack of and the need to develop HIV/AIDS prevention programs
that are representative of the college-campus, African American female population. Yet, it is also important to take into consideration the variant learner characteristics and unique learning needs of this population.

WHY AN INTERACTIVE AND COMPUTERIZED PROGRAM?

HIV/AIDS prevention education that is disseminated via a popular interactive medium, which has both culturally relevant and credible content, and represents the same race, cultural, and socioeconomic status background of the
target audience, is purported to have not only a higher rate of viewer engagement and acceptance but also improves the accurate perception of one's health
risk (Pittman, Wilson, Adams-Taylor, and Randolph 1992; Stevenson and Davis

1994, 1995; Stuber 1991; Wingood and DiClemente 1992). However, this presents a challenge for HIV/AIDS prevention education programs to meet the various needs of the diverse subgroups that exist within a specific population; for example, the African American female audience that resides within our nation's higher education system—from the local community college to the private and state universities. In fact, Stephens, Braithwaite, and Taylor (1998) state: "One cannot over-emphasize the effectiveness of using mediums that are developed within the cultural and environmental influences of the target audience" (135). Weeks et al. (1995) conclude that the "need for African American women … to protect themselves from HIV-infection … demands development of AIDS-prevention designs that address gender, class, and ethnic specific issues at work in the environment which increases these women's risk" (261). Nationally, the Centers for Disease Control calls for the design of culturally appropriate HIV prevention efforts for sub-populations within the African American community at large (CDC 2001). There is a collective call to action for new and innovative ways to disseminate culturally appropriate HIV/AIDS intervention programs that are specific to the unique needs—age, education level, socioeconomic status, and environment—of diverse subgroups that exist within the African American community.

Research shows that various media—video (Stevenson and Davis 1994), talking-computers (Stanton, Li, Galbraith, Feigelman, and Kaljee 1996), and hip-hop music therapy (Stephens, Braithwaite, and Taylor 1998)—can be effective in delivering innovative HIV/AIDS prevention education. The following section describes the instructional hypermedia HIV/AIDS prevention education program that was specifically developed for African American women on college campuses. The program considers age, race/ethnicity, and individualized learner characteristics, and the college milieu in providing HIV/AIDS prevention education and interactive skills-building information for this population.

PROGRAM DESCRIPTION

The instructional hypermedia program entitled *HIV & AIDS Prevention Education for African American Women* was designed as part of a larger study by Katz (2001) and seeks to educate women of color about HIV and AIDS, how to communicate about HIV and AIDS, and the protection options that are available to protect oneself against contracting HIV, the virus that causes AIDS. The program is designed specifically to meet the culturally unique needs of African American women on college campuses and responds to the call to the stated need for AIDS prevention programs that "build on the use of ethnic cultural concepts, racial and other social relations, and acknowledge issues specific to minority women in order to prevent their infection with HIV" (Weeks et al. 1995, 251). It incorporates hip-hop and rap music, ethnically appropriate graphics, and videos depicting young African American women in college settings. The program's CD-ROM format requires minimal computer skills and is self-paced. These characteristics allow viewers to use the program in private settings on individual computers at their own learning speed. Subject matter experts[1] in the areas of social and cultural implications regarding HIV/AIDS, and HIV/AIDS content accuracy provided formative evaluation of the program. The program's instructional content references HIV/AIDS public domain information disseminated by the Centers for Disease Control, and is composed of three core modules having information specific to young African American college women:

1. *Facts*—includes two separate submodules: *HIV Facts* and *AIDS Facts*. The *HIV Facts* and *AIDS Facts* submodules include an interactive activities that requires the user to determine if statements about HIV and AIDS are fact or fiction.
2. *Protection*—includes two separate submodules: *Abstinence* and *Safer Sex*. The *Abstinence* submodule includes videos of women explaining why they choose abstinence as their protection option, as well as a series of questions to help the user determine if abstinence is right for her. The *Safer Sex* submodule includes various interactive media that discuss safer sex and women's protection options, while providing instruction on the use of both male and female condoms and how to make a dental dam from both a latex glove and a latex condom.
3. *Communication*—includes two separate submodules: *What to Say* and *How to Respond*. The *What to Say* submodule includes videos that display women negotiating safer sex and interactive activities which allow women to practice communication skills that they can use when talking to their partner about the facts surrounding HIV and AIDS and the need to practice safer sex. The *How to Respond* submodule includes audio and video vignettes of potential excuses that men might use to avoid both safer sex and talking about HIV/AIDS. Interactive activities allow women to respond to such excuses by typing in their own responses after hearing the excuses presented via audio files.

The program supports the different learning needs of variant learners by providing cognitive tools that are available anytime during the program. The purpose of the cognitive tools is to assist the users with their information processing while they learn about HIV and AIDS. They allow one to "Bookmark" screens for instant repeated viewing, search for words/phrases using the "Find," view HIV/AIDS terms in the "Glossary," ask for "Help" with using the program, navigate and get a bird's-eye view of the program with the "Map," and use the "Notebook" to answer questions and process one's thoughts and feelings—in a journaling format—about how their life is affected by HIV/AIDS. This program acknowledges that people have different learning styles and use different learning strategies to acquire information; hence, the cognitive tools are supplied to meet users' individual learning needs as they navigate their own path through the program, viewing modules in the order that they choose.

FINDINGS

Fifty undergraduate women volunteers from a small rural southern state HBCU (historically Black college and university) responded to a questionnaire about their experience with using the instructional hypermedia HIV/AIDS program. Participants' ages ranged from eighteen to thirty-one years old. This population represented the "nontraditional student" in that most were older students—either married with children or single mothers, employed full- and/or part-time, and received financial aid. Many of the students came from neighboring towns in which they were born and raised. A professor from this HBCU described the academic competencies of the majority of the students as having "comparable levels to that of community college students who were in need of or had taken remedial courses prior to enrolling in their freshman undergraduate courses." Moreover, as a result of the HBCU having limited computer technology, students did not have access to multimedia instructional programs. The majority of participants had minimal computer skills and multimedia learning experience: $MEAN = 2.6$ on a Likert scale of 1–4.

Participants' interviews were analyzed using grounded theory guided by a feminist approach. This analysis allowed relevant themes to emerge that reflected the participants' experience while maintaining their perspectives as young African American women. The following nine themes surfaced: customized instruction, supported information processing, navigation assistance, classroom connections, attention getting, fostered problem-solving, real-life connections, educational/informative, and change in knowledge, attitude, beliefs, and behavior.

Customized Instruction

It is evident that these women want control over what and how they learn about HIV and AIDS. The hypermedia element of this program allows the users to customize their instruction as they set their own pace and choose the order in which they view the instruction. This allowed for a positive and personally relevant learning experience that met their unique learning needs: "I just used the ones [modules/sections] that I picked. Basically because it seemed more interesting, things that I really didn't know about just so I could learn more about them. So, I picked most of the things that I really didn't know ... hadn't heard a lot of information about." The different lengths of time that the users spent in the program indicates that these women learn differently from one another. On average, participants spent 1 hour 20 minutes viewing the program, and had a range in viewing times from 21 minutes to 2 hours 49 minutes.

Supported Information Processing

This population benefited greatly from having the notebook tool. Not only did it assist participants to organize their thoughts regarding the facts about HIV/AIDS, it acted as a journaling tool in which each could write about her real-life experiences and process how the program information related to her life: "I thought it was useful to have the notebook in the program, because as I went ahead I could take notes. I thought it helped me out a lot. I take information in when I write it down … it helps me out better when I can go back … and look at the notes that I took." Furthermore, in a society where talking about sex and HIV/AIDS isn't always easy for a young woman due to gender stereotypes regarding a woman's sexuality and the stigma associated with HIV/AIDS, the notebook provided a safe and confidential place to reflect/journal about how HIV/AIDS affects their lives: "Yes, I do regret having unprotected sex but I am glad everything is fine. However, I wish I would have waited just to have sex until I got married. You should make sure that you don't put yourself in any type of position that you do not want to be in so you want have to make any serious or hard choices."

Additionally, having the notebook to record answers proved thought provoking: "it made me think about, you know, the certain things [about HIV/AIDS] I hadn't thought about [before]."

Navigation Assistance

The map satisfied the participants' desire for HIV/AIDS information on demand. This population knew what they wanted to learn, and the map assisted the learners with not only navigating through the various modules in the order that they chose but in keeping track of which modules they completed: "the map was like the most helpful part for me, [it showed me] where I go next, [what] had I completed already and what do I need to complete."

Classroom Connections

The users transferred learning strategies from their classroom and study experiences to the HIV/AIDS hypermedia program. Many users expressed that they learn best from repeated reading and taking notes. The program allowed the users to repeatedly view various media and text, and take notes in the notebook: "the videos, it made me … like in class when the teacher said something, if you didn't write it down you still had it kind of in your memory. I had to look at the videos so when they asked the question … it pulls, if you weren't sure it made me think back to what those people in the video were saying [about HIV/AIDS]."

Attention-Getting

In order to be effective, HIV/AIDS intervention programs need to keep the participant's attention—*the video helped … it got my full attention*—while providing comprehensive HIV/AIDS information: "It was a nice program because it had a lot of information ya know like the videos and a lot of information that tells you about the different ways you can contract AIDS, the prevention methods you can use. It was an interesting program."

Fostered Problem-Solving

Young African American women need numerous opportunities to practice problem-solving skills so that they can feel empowered to protect themselves against contracting HIV. Participants expressed that the notebook gave them the opportunity to safely practice communication and negotiation skills regarding HIV/AIDS prevention. They used the notebook to reflect about past sexual experiences and how they would handle future situations. In this manner the notebook was used as a tool to facilitate role-playing: "when it asked me a question about what I thought and how I would handle the situation [negotiating safer sex], I went back and typed in what I would do and what I wouldn't do ... you got a chance to put your opinion in, and [how] you would handle a certain situation if you were encountered with it."

Real-Life Connections

Young African American college women respond to gender and culturally appropriate HIV/AIDS education programs that are sensitive to their needs and grounded in "their" reality. Users of this program related to the African American characters depicted in the program while drawing relevance to their own lives: "When I was watching [the video] I think there was an individual on there, a girl and we had a lot of stuff in common and I am looking at her like this is me here and it can happen to her ... I need to slow myself [down, sexually] you know I'm thinking, so it's helping me out like somebody like my mother or father is talking to me." The videos and interactive activities mirrored real-life scenarios and allowed the users to practice their communication skills, for example, negotiating safer sex with a reluctant partner: "It made me think about things I hadn't thought about like when I encounter something like that. What would I really do? It made me really feel like I was in the situation when it was asking me the questions [about negotiating safer sex]."

Educational/Informational

Participants enjoyed the opportunity to access sexual health information that was not only related to HIV and AIDS but also went beyond the basics. They found themselves broadening their knowledge by learning information that they previously were unaware of: "it had a lot of information, I went under herpes and it showed pictures and different stuff I hadn't really seen about different diseases. I thought that was very interesting too. It helped me learn a lot more about AIDS that I really didn't know."

Change in Knowledge, Attitude, Beliefs, and Behavior

Higher education is found to influence one's AIDS knowledge and prevention, yet research has found that the cognitive awareness of HIV/AIDS prevention has little effect on African American women's sexual behavior and ability to negotiate HIV protection with their partner (Braithwaite et al. 1998; Dancy 1996). However, women who viewed this program reported that they were strongly impacted by the instruction and put forth serious efforts to modify their sexual activity: "Yes! It really would [change my behavior] 'cause I learned a lot of stuff that I really didn't know about AIDS and different other stuff, so yes it did increase my knowledge. My behavior [laugh] most definitely cause I slowed down in a lot of different areas [sexual behavior] since I went through the program." Moreover, participants reported that viewing the program increased their awareness regarding the importance of practicing safer sex and of African American men who insist upon safer sex:

For instance being protected all the time cause with AIDS how a person looks you really can't tell, and so certain things like that and like using a condom all the time and talking about [safer sex]. Ya know some boys on there [in the videos] really made me think about it—they were saying they just wouldn't have unprotected sex. So that made me think, 'cause most boys you find they don't act like that. You have to be protected all the time if you gonna have it [sex].

One participant felt the program reinforced her belief to "*wait to you get married*" to have sex. Conversely, it changed the view of another participant who took it upon herself to educate her relatives—"I changed my views on thinking abstinence is the best way and I really have been talking to my little teenage sister and cousins about it, trying to keep them away from it [sex] until they're ready."

CONCLUSION

This instructional hypermedia program used gender and culturally relevant material to reflect the college milieu of African American women. Doing so not only addressed this population's unique HIV/AIDS prevention needs but also provided a safe, private, and customizable learning and journaling environment to practice and reflect on HIV/AIDS communication and prevention skills, respectively. The participants reported that they could relate to the program's characters of like race, socioeconomic status, and college lifestyle, and described themselves as being more informed of their HIV risk status and empowered about their protection options. Notably, this program impacted participants to elicit serious efforts to change their sexual behavior and to practice safer sex as a form of protection against contracting HIV.

The program required only minimal computer skills, which allowed the participants to take advantage of the cognitive tools to personalize their learning experience. Descriptively, the map tool was used by the participants an average of 10 times for 1.79 minutes, while the notebook tool was used on an average of 12.89 times for 18.72 minutes. The map allowed this population to self-prescribe a personally relevant sequence of instruction that met both their individual learning and HIV/AIDS prevention education needs. The notebook provided these women confidential journaling opportunities to express how their lives are affected by HIV/AIDS. The interactive activities allowed them to practice communication skills, which are essential when communicating to their partners about HIV/AIDS and negotiating safer sex.

The overall heuristic implications for the use of culturally relevant hypermedia programs in HIV/AIDS intervention programs are boundless. First, culturally relevant programs can address the unique HIV/AIDS prevention needs of other group populations—age, education level, sexual orientation, gender, and race/ethnicity. Second, intervention programs that are grounded in hypermedia and educational research can meet learners' variant learning needs. Moreover, this medium can be used to provide culturally and gender relevant health intervention programs to other populations with other content such as violence reduction and substance abuse prevention.

NOTE

1. Experts were from a southwestern state university and included a social work professor, who has conducted extensive research in the area of HIV and AIDS and women of color, and two sexual health educators.

REFERENCES

Braithwaite, R., Stephens, T., Sumpter-Gaddist, B.W., Murdaugh, H., et al. (July 1998). Sex-related HIV/AIDS prevention among African American college students: Issues for preventive counseling. *Journal of Multicultural Counseling and Development*, 26 177–193.

Centers for Disease Control and Prevention—National Center for HIV, STD, and TB Prevention, Divisions of HIV/AIDS Prevention. (2001). HIV/AIDS among U.S. women: Minority and young women at continuing risk. *FactSheet*. Atlanta: Department of Health and Human Services.

Fears, D. (1998). AIDS among black women seen as a growing problem. *Los Angeles Times—Washington Edition*, July 24, p. A1.

Flaskerud, J., and Nyamathi, A. (1990). Effects of an AIDS education program on the knowledge, attitudes, and practices of low income Black and Latina women. *Journal of Community Health* 15 (6), 343–355.

Katz, H.A. (2001). The relationship between learners' goal orientation and their cognitive tool use and achievement in an interactive hypermedia environment. Unpublished doctoral dissertation. University of Texas at Austin.

Pittman, K., Wilson, P.M., Adams-Taylor, S., and Randolph, S. (1992). Making sexuality education and prevention programs relevant for African American youth. *Journal of School Health*, 62 339–344.

Stanton, B., Black, M., Freigelman, S., Ricardo, I., et al. (1995). Development of a culturally, theoretically and developmentally based survey instrument for assessing risk behaviors among African-American early adolescents living in urban low-income neighborhoods. *AIDS Education and Prevention*, 7 (2), 160–177.

Stanton, B.F., Li, X., Galbraith, J., Feigelman, S., et al. (1996). Sexually transmitted diseases, human immunodeficiency virus and pregnancy prevention. *Archives of Pediatric and Adolescent Medicine*, 150, 17–24.

Stephens, T., Braithwaite, R.L., and Taylor, S.E. (1998). Model for using hip-hop music for small group HIV/AIDS prevention counseling with African American adolescents and young adults. *Patient Education and Counseling*, 35 127–137.

Stevenson, H.C., and Davis, G. (1994). Impact of culturally sensitive AIDS video education on the AIDS risk knowledge of African American adolescents. *AIDS Education Prevention*, 6 40–52.

Stevenson, H.C., McKee Gay, K., and Josar, L. (1995). Culturally sensitive AIDS education and perceived AIDS risk knowledge: Reaching the "know-it-all" teenager. *AIDS Prevention and Education*, 7 (2), 134–144.

Stolberg, S.G. (1998). Eyes shut, Black America is being ravaged by AIDS. *New York Times*, June 29, p. A1.

Stuber, M.L. (1991). Children, adolescents and AIDS. *Psychiatric Medicine*, 9 441–454.

Weeks, M.R., Schensul, J.J., Williams, S.S., Singer, M., et al. (1995). AIDS prevention for African-American and Latina women: Building culturally and gender-appropriate intervention. *AIDS Education and Prevention*, 7 (3), 251–263.

Wingood, G., and DiClemente, R.J. (1992). Cultural, gender and psycho-social influences on HIV-related behavior of African American female adolescents: Implications for the development of tailored prevention programs. *Ethnicity and Disease*, 2 381–388.

IV

Community and Policy Action: A Call to Action

Clearly, it is time for critical responses to the alarming loss that is ravaging African American communities. Throughout the two-decade history of HIV and AIDS in this country, preexisting concepts, paradigms, and societal constructions of those groups primarily affected by HIV and AIDS have shaped the public policy response over the changing course of the epidemic. The fact that AIDS was initially linked to gay males and now is having a devastating effect on populations who have been historically disempowered sets the background for examining AIDS activism and social policy legislation related to the epidemic.

Schneider and Ingram (1993) proposed that the "social construction of target populations" in society is based on the target population's social construction and level of political power, and these constructions influence the distribution of policy benefits or policy burdens (negative consequences of policy action or inaction) among different groups. Social constructions of target populations are "stereotypes about particular groups of people that have been created by politics, culture, socialization, history, the media, literature, religion, and the like" (335). The authors theorize that politically powerful, positively constructed target populations receive more policy benefits over policy burdens as compared with politically weak, negatively constructed groups, based on the following four categories:

Advantaged target populations are positively constructed and politically powerful, and therefore this group is most likely to receive policy benefits

Contenders target populations are politically powerful yet negatively constructed. This group receives benefits when largesse is concealed but public opinion may drive policy makers to inflict policy burdens when public interest is high and unfavorable toward the group.

Dependent target populations enjoy a positive social construction yet lack political power, and like contenders, push policy makers in two opposing directions. Despite lawmakers' sympathetic stance few direct resources are directed toward this group.

Deviant target populations are both politically weak and negatively constructed, making this group the least likely to reap policy benefits. This group may receive policy burdens as a result of policy ineffectiveness.

Schroedel and Jordan (1998) reported that this model successfully predicted trends in Senate voting patterns between 1987–1992 based on the following categorization of HIV-infected target populations: (1) advantaged (war veterans, health care workers); (2) contenders (gay and bisexual men, and general population with AIDS); (3) dependents (spouses, patients, the public); and (4) deviants (intravenous drug users, criminals, prisoners, and foreigners).

However, Schroedel and Jordan's (1998) analysis did not consider the role of race and ethnicity. Given the highly disproportionate number of African American populations comprising the growing HIV-infection and AIDS cases, combined with their historical disenfranchisement, one would arguably place African Americans, particularly poor African Americans associated directly or indirectly with drug use, within a target population of those both politically weak and negatively constructed or stereotyped by mainstream society. In addition, African Americans are disproportionately represented among both the intravenous drug-using, as well as the prison population. This model would explain what Perry, in Chapter 15, refers to as a legacy of nonprogressive, nonresponsive HIV/AIDS-related policy development and social activism, which has existed not only nationally toward African Americans, but also is visible in the slow responsiveness from leaders within the African American community to support HIV-infected African Americans. Indeed, as has been discussed elsewhere in this book, African American drug users, criminals, and homosexuals—deemed deviant—all suffer additional stigma from within the African American community on top of the racial stigma and oppression they experience from mainstream society. Thus, the call for action is twofold. First, national HIV/AIDS and related policy development must continue to take steps toward reconceptualizing how best to curb this epidemic among African Americans. Second, African Americans must reconceptualize this epidemic for themselves, engage in honest self-evaluations, and act in collective ways to address the AIDS crisis within our communities.

Thus, a call to action is also a call to African Americans—not to look exclusively to White America for solutions. In his noteworthy essay, "AIDS in Blackface," Dalton (1989) stated over a decade ago "as the drama unfolds, we cannot simply ask white actors to put on blackface and favor us with their best rendition of 'life in de ghetto.' Instead, we need to turn to black actors and black leaders" (224). Dalton speaks about our paralysis regarding AIDS, as well as our conflicting emotions of guilt, anger, shame, horror, fear, sympathy, aversion, affinity, and uncertainty of how much we can expect mainstream White America to commit to sociopolitical action toward eradicating AIDS, now that it is overwhelmingly a disease of the most politically weak and negatively socially constructed target population.

In Chapter 13, Stewart discusses that the first step toward critical action is the need for healing, for healing among African American women through counseling and culturally appropriate mental health services that take into account the underlying causes and conditions of the presenting problems. Stewart's account is a personal reflection of many years of working with disenfranchised African American women and their families. Her account includes a discussion of the vicarious trauma—the anger, rage, and sadness that Dalton (1989) also speaks of—when, as an African American helping professional, she sees client after client visibly confirming the grim statistic that African American women are sixteen times more likely to be HIV-infected than their White counterparts.

The changing face of AIDS has presented challenges to AIDS services organizations, and there is a need for all agencies to be trained in culturally appropriate service delivery strategies. In an interview with Phil Wilson, executive director of the African American AIDS Policy and Training Institute at the University of Southern California, he made the following comment on how the demographic shift of AIDS has impacted AIDS service delivery and AIDS Services Organizations (ASOs):

Some of the folks who got involved in AIDS work did so because the disease appeared to be an issue of gay White men. If the disease had manifested itself in another community, they might not have gotten involved. Now some of those individuals and organizations are undergoing honest self-examination to assess whether they are still passionate about the work. (Villarosa 2000, 1)

This is clearly an aspect of the future of HIV and AIDS services that will have to be worked out. Traditional ASOs, which were formed on a model to serve predominantly gay, White, male clientele, will either need to make drastic changes to their approach in order to serve the populations most affected or make room for others to do it, specifically those who can offer culturally congruent services. It is clear that services, including prevention messages, need to be community-specific. This speaks to the importance of organizations that are black-initiated, and specifically equipped to offer culturally congruent services to various African American communities. In Chapter 14, Dana Williams discusses the programming of Blacks Assisting Blacks against AIDS in St. Louis, Missouri. This *Focus on Solutions* chapter aims to promote the programming and organizational structure and service delivery strategies that can be effective in HIV/AIDS prevention and intervention work with African Americans. More such organizations are needed, particularly in the southern United States. Funding, however, is a crucial issue. It is very important for Black-implemented programs to maintain coalitions and secure funding to remain a strong force in the community and to advocate for federal policies that support culturally tailored services.

In the book's final chapter, Perry reviews HIV/AIDS-related policies and initiatives over the last two decades and how policy development has moved from apathy to action. The chapter addresses the need for African American leaders and policy makers to define and articulate policies based in an Afrocentric perspective, a paradigm that builds on the collective needs of the African American community and is grounded in a history of African American survival. The Congressional Black Caucus has responded strongly in the last few years, as well as other African American organizations; however, the magnitude of the problem is far from diminished. Moreover, Perry makes the point that the solution rests beyond HIV/AIDS-related policies. Policies that alleviate poverty, poor housing, unemployment, and health disparities for African American women and African Americans, in general, must also be tackled.

REFERENCES

Dalton, H.L. (1989). AIDS in blackface. *Daedalus*, 118 (3), 205–227.

Schneider, A., and Ingram, H. (1993). Social construction of target populations: Implications for politics and policy. *American Political Science Review*, 87 (2), 334–347.

Schroedel, J.R., and Jordan, D.R. (1998). Senate voting and social construction of target populations: A study of AIDS policymaking, 1987–1992. *Journal of Health Politics, Policy and Law* 23 (1), 107–131.

Villarosa, Linda. (2000). "Speaking out to make AIDS an issue of color. A conversation with Phil Wilson." *New York Times*, p. 7, column 1.

13

Culturally Grounded Responses: HIV/AIDS Practice and Counseling Issues for African American Women

Patricia Stewart

There are many ways to approach the subject of counseling relative to African American women living with HIV. To speak of the contemporary concerns of the HIV-positive African American woman, one needs to be mindful of her in the context of her rich and capable role in the family, in the community, in society, and, of course, in history. This chapter broadly addresses the following: (1) salient issues that surface in practice, (2) the importance of addressing causes and conditions for those issues, and (3) key practice strategies—suggestions for insightful, respectful, culturally competent practice, which include counseling. The stress of living with HIV/AIDS is compounded by the stress inherent in being a woman and in being African American and, for many, in being poor. Sandra Crouse Quinn (1993) refers to this phenomenon as the "triple burden." This chapter discusses counseling issues in practice with African American women living with HIV who also live in poverty, because they are the most visible to the service delivery system and are more likely to need assistance accessing quality mental health care that is affordable. I use interchangeably "African American" and "Black"; the same is true for the words "counseling" and "therapy." Also, as a social worker, I speak from that disciplinary perspective and refer to other designations, such as "practitioner," to be inclusive and respectful of other human services helping professionals.

BACKGROUND

For years, as I have been working in the field of HIV, I have been concerned about the vulnerability of women, especially those in long-term and/or "committed" relationships or marriages. This epidemic initially struck gay men and then injection drug users with such fury that prevention and intervention efforts were focused on them and appropriately so. When I began clinical work in HIV in the early 1990s, there was much concern about the increase in infections among women, but much of that concern was coupled with the exposure to children. At that time, I worked in a hospital-based, family-focused HIV program in which we received two to four new referrals of newly diagnosed women with children per week. Largely because of the way women and men were thinking (or not thinking) about their risk for infection as observed in my clinical work, I developed grave concern about the potential for a sharp rise in the number of infections among women in heterosexual relationships. How does a woman who has been having unprotected sex for years, decades, negotiate for condom use to protect herself if she believes her mate is sexually involved outside of the relationship? How does she move herself out of the deeply entrenched denial about her partner's extra-relationship activities? Is she in a violent relationship, at risk for grave harm if she asserts herself to protect her health? If she is HIV-positive, what does she do if she has had lifelong desire to have children or how does she respond to her partner's pressure or interest in children?

To whom was she to turn for guidance? Who was there to educate and support her in her decisions? Many of the AIDS service organizations were built on a model to serve people with different issues and life experiences. The fact that the silence and the shame about AIDS extended to institutions in the Black community that traditionally address social problems compounded the perception that Black people need not be concerned about contracting HIV. And if one was known to be HIV-positive, the message was, at the very least, "Don't talk about it."

One way of putting the issues and needs of women in context is to acknowledge the "deafening silence" in the African American community about AIDS. Not only was there the deeply rooted belief that AIDS is a gay disease or for those who "use needles," but also that "the government created it to keep us from having children." The Black community, on the whole, stood still from community to Congress.

Now it is reality that there are dramatically rising numbers of infections among women, who are disproportionately African American and poor, with nearly virtually all cases attributable to injection drug use or heterosexual contact, of which the majority of cases are due to heterosexual contact with an intravenous drug user. More than ever, this has implications for what is happening in the relationships and in the bedrooms of African American men and women. Along with that, though, are also many opportunities for growth and healing in those relationships.

SALIENT PRACTICE CONSIDERATIONS

The HIV practitioner knows all too well that women can attempt to balance a number of issues that tend to burden and potentially overwhelm. From the time that the epidemic began affecting "traditional" families, it was apparent that women tended to be the primary caregiver for those around them who were living with the virus, that is, their children, their spouses or partners, and friends. It was also apparent that sometimes this care was given at the expense of the woman, who devoted relatively little time and energy to attend to her own health and well-being. To some extent, this remains the case. The goal of treatment, in this regard, is that the woman, who is often naturally inclined to be the "mother/nurturer," put herself high on the list of those for whom she gives high quality care.

Counseling African American women, in general, is an experience with much richness and depth. It takes a great deal of courage and fortitude for anyone to get to the point of asking for and accepting support. I believe that it is even more poignant for a woman of African descent for a number of reasons, not the least of which is her great capacity for self-sufficiency and survival. It is usually a crisis that will help someone to get to the point of opting for therapy. Many in the general population suffer, often in silence, for a very long time, as though there were no recourse. Being diagnosed with and then getting on with the business of living with HIV can push the envelope—some women are unable to handle the diagnosis and may attempt to evade the pain, by relapsing into an addiction for example. Some take time to adjust to the diagnosis on their own; others become ready for support of outsiders.

Mindful that we are outsiders, it is important to remember that, though we may have much to offer, we must also earn the privilege of access to the woman's private life and issues. Assessing the needs of African American women is best done from a strength perspective. A client will initiate discussion with her pain—problems for which she is seeking help and/or support. In my experience, it is safe to say that each factor, identified as a problem, can point to positive correlates in character and in functioning. My wish is that we seek always to learn of that positive, and having identified the positive strengths, we can share these as a gift with the woman when the pain has subsided enough for her to be able to hear it.

Commonly addressed in therapy are issues of trust and fidelity and power dynamics in relationships, which have for generations been a source of pain and confusion. Women who feel that they must have a man at all costs are at great risk—the same is true when this phenomenon is apparent among lesbian women with whom I have worked. A faulty concept of self-worth is often at the core of dependent, enmeshed relationships in which decision making is impaired.

Women tend to present for testing and, thus, treatment later in the progression of their disease, and they die more quickly. This can mean that, in addition to adjusting to a major diagnosis, there is the stress of facing their own mortality before having the opportunity to experience, over time, the range of feelings about being infected.

If the woman has children, there is the anguishing process of facing her own mortality by making a plan for their care after her death. And how does she discuss her disease with her children, or anyone else in her life for that matter? Disclosure—when to tell, whom, for what reason, and with what supports—is a complex issue that women bring to the helping relationship.

Other concerns may be having enough income/resources to meet the basic needs of food, clothing, and shelter; level of maturity, problem-solving skills;

and coping ability. Of course, issues will be highlighted relevant to age. Having worked with women at ages spanning the life cycle, and regardless of life circumstances, there is one issue that is consistently high on the list of concerns. That is the shame of having a sexually transmitted disease for which there is no cure. If acquired sexually, societal and familial shame-based messages come to the fore, in part accounting for sexual shutdown. Imagine that!—women, in the prime of life who have stopped enjoying the sexual aspect of their being! They respond well to messages that counter the shame. If drugs are a factor for the woman or her partner, that tends to add to the shame extra layers of emotion, such as guilt and anger, often directed inward. As a practitioner, it is important to develop the ability to distinguish depressed mood from the more serious but treatable clinical depression. This can be learned by regular access to a good, culturally competent clinical consultant, such as a clinical social worker, psychologist, or psychiatrist. And of course there is no substitute for good clinical supervision. Furthermore, it is helpful to be familiar with how to research symptoms in the DSM IV, not necessarily to diagnose, but for assistance in understanding and identifying the issues.

Some women that we encounter will have psychiatric illness underlying or predating the diagnosis that is exacerbated by the stress of coping with the HIV. For them, as for other troublesome symptoms of concern, a referral for evaluation is indicated. And here presents another potential for refusal due to a cultural construct—that of taking medication to relieve symptoms of an emotional nature. The resistance to accepting medication for HIV or issues of compliance to a medication regimen seem easy to address compared with those for psychiatric meds, such is the stigma in the community. Professional perseverance and respectful seeking to understand the breadth of the woman's reasoning for not wanting to take the meds are ways to address these concerns. As with anything, we need to stand ready to let go of our agenda, recognizing the client's right to self-determination. I have outlined a number of issues that make it readily apparent that African American women with HIV/AIDS may benefit from counseling support. However, there are, again, contextual issues to consider in determining what kind of support is desired and deemed to be helpful to her. The key to understanding the type of support needed is a good understanding of causes and conditions underlying the counseling needs of African American women living with or at increased risk for HIV.

UNDERLYING CAUSES AND CONDITIONS

A number of contextual issues should be considered when counseling African American women around issues of HIV/AIDS, including the role of sexuality and sexual partners, the historical context of the African American experience, quality of social support, burdens, addictions, and prevalence of traumatic experiences.

The Role of the Invisible Partner

It goes without saying, then, that it is past time to change the practice of denying the existence, importance, and worth of the African American man in the lives of the women and children that present for care. To negate the man is an ingrained notion in the human services community that is simply wrong—the social worker has the power and the responsibility to address and change it on many levels from the way she shapes her microinterventions to advocacy in the agency and community. We must get creative in including the partners in treatment, even when funders only see the "women and children." I often say that to work only with the woman and exclude or make no mention of her male partner is a setup for intervention failure or at least diminished effectiveness. If we are wondering why, after all our best efforts, our interventions with women fail, we can look first to our program design in relation to her partner. If we exclude Black men, or if we have a heterosexist approach to work with women, we are possibly competing with messages countering ours in the vulnerable, proverbial "midnight hour" by someone whose message is much sweeter, and who makes her feel a whole lot better than we do in our program or agency. We cannot afford to overlook the importance of the partner of a woman—whether lesbian or straight—in her life and in her decision making. If we do, not only is our work shortsighted and incomplete, but sexism and racism have closed us off from the possibility of counseling, testing, treatment, in short, an opportunity to serve the partner. I discuss the issues, particularly related to Black men, at length in other works (Stewart 1998; Stewart 2000).

The Role of Stigma and Mistrust

I have spoken earlier about the "deadly silence" about emotional need that I have witnessed among African American clients. We just don't talk about a lot of what ails us. There is considerable stigma in seeking professional health care for emotional or psychological issues. Along with that, historically, Black people have learned from experience to be skeptical of and to not trust the system, especially when it comes to talking about "our [personal] business." There can be fear that information will be used later to harm them. Anyone who is poor and had to interact with agencies for assistance may have had humiliating experiences in which they were not helped and were disrespected in the process (Stewart 2000). Coming for treatment is often misconstrued as an admission that one is "crazy." Also, there is the phenomenon of willingness and/or ability to carry great burden, mentioned earlier. And of course, the stigma, the shame of having HIV is difficult to talk about, especially with a stranger.

With these factors in mind, it is important to take great care in referring the African American woman living with HIV for therapy. I am of the opinion that such a referral should not be made early in the casework relationship, unless there is clear and present danger. Rather, it is important for the social worker or other practitioner to take time to develop their own relationship with the woman, which in itself can be *therapeutic*. Trust can be built more easily when one sees that the practitioner is genuine, consistent, and nonjudgmental. Moreover, African American people tend to want to see tangible evidence of that caring and assess whether *we*, the practitioner or counselor, are competent and worthy of *their* trust by the manner in which we follow through on the provision of concrete services and goods. Issues, such as the severity and chronicity of problems, feelings of safety in current circumstances, and stigma about counseling, may prevent the woman from attending therapy for a long time, if ever. Hence, the therapeutic relationship of the social worker/case manager becomes of primary importance. Simply being "heard" about that issue and not being subjected to us pushing our agenda with people gives them space within which to grow. Except in extreme circumstances of psychosis or severe mood disorder, a counseling referral is best done when the woman is ready. Until then we can plant the seed, share our opinion or rationale for the recommendation, but leave the driving to her. "Counseling" is a dreaded issue in some segments of the African American community. If a woman is responding in reasonable measure to your care, that may be all she can or will do for now. If you feel as though her needs are beyond your skill level, seek resources to develop and sharpen your skills and consult supervisory experts, but keep doing what you are doing. A good rule of thumb is this—your effectiveness is measured in terms of her response to you. Sometimes we recommend referrals when what we are doing is enough!

The Role of "Bearing the Cross"

It is important to know in as much detail as possible what kind and how much support the woman has. This issue is universal; however, I have found that among African American women, there can tend to be an understating of the nature of support, that is to say, of truly safe space. All too often, I have worked with women who have someone—mother, sister, for example, someone to whom there is deep loyalty rather than intimacy, closeness, and genuine support. In fact, what may be the case is that the woman who is in *need of support* may in essence *be the support* for those whom she has identified as supportive to her, while her own needs go unmet. What I make of this is that there is such a tendency to bear such great amounts of stress—burdens, if you will—that it can seem the norm to add HIV to a long list of life's stressors which to the observer may seem insurmountable. In my experience, this phenomenon of "problem bearing" transcends age difference and is likely passed on from one generation to another, like a badge of honor. Sometimes Christian principles can be misconstrued, fostering this notion of expectation of trials and tribulations—of having a "cross" to bear.

For example, for years I have worked with African American children and adolescent girls in the child welfare system. From the point of initial assessment, I am repeatedly struck by the nonchalant way in which they share their histories with me. As they recount "tales of horror," often doing so devoid of emotional affect, they are seemingly oblivious to the magnitude of what they have experienced and the impact of the past on their current self-concept and ability to be happy or to function optimally.

Similarly in my work with adults, from the young to middle age to older adults, I consistently encounter African American women with significant history about which they have not grieved or even acknowledged as significant to their lives today. Moreover, there is a tendency to minimize or to dismiss as relevant their experience of trauma and its impact. Later, I discuss trauma theory and its relevance to this work.

This minimizing and other aspects of the coping style mentioned earlier are often referred to as "denial," an overused and often poorly understood concept that practitioners use to explain client behavior. But this is more than denial. First of all, we sometimes forget that denial is a defense mechanism, initially called upon by the human psyche to protect it. Denial can help us survive—emotionally, mentally, and physically. And then, through growth and maturation, we are hopefully able to replace the denial with awareness of issues/circumstances about which we have genuine feelings, as we process the grim realities from which we initially sought to protect ourselves. People can only make these changes when ready. The consistent, positive support of the social worker or other practitioner creates the safe space conducive to that readiness. We cannot change others, simple as that seems. I think most practitioners know that, but out of frustration or in response to demands or expectations to "fix it" can arise the tendency to then blame the client for not changing.

The Role of Racism

According to bell hooks (1993), the social correlate to the myth of white supremacy is the myth of Black inferiority and the expectation of suffering. I believe that this suffering, which is often unacknowledged or, if known, is done in silence, is learned behavior passed along and dating back to the devaluing and dehumanizing institution of slavery. It has implications for how the African American woman sees herself and her needs and for how she relates to herself and others. It has implications for our counseling strategies.

Second, when I compare the ways in which I have observed that African American women and White women see themselves in relation to their problems and issues, there are distinct differences. For the Black woman, I see a sort of resignation to and expectation that she be a "problem bearer," that she "grin and bear it" or "suck it up." As I think about it, it is as though years of lack of emotional nurturance in the personal environment, compounded by oppressive, hostile treatment from "helping professionals," have taught them *not to expect* to be treated well. Bear in mind that I am not speaking of all African American women, but rather of the hundreds I have seen who live in poverty and who are visible to the system. They do not have the often righteous indignation about receiving harsh, inadequate treatment that I have repeatedly seen in their White counterparts. Instead, the anger expressed is often more situational and directed inward or at each other, seemingly without the indignation about being worth more than to be treated poorly.

I also believe that this negative self-valuation has major impact on the approach to parenting, and this manifests in the early losses in the lives of many women. I have never met an African American woman who did not love her child, but I have met many who clearly do not know how to communicate that love in a nurturing way because they may not have had that experience themselves. You cannot give what you do not know or have or what has been denied to you as a group through historical oppression. The role of the counselor then, is to be alerted to assess for that need and to know that the counselor's role may need to be broadened to include not only supporter and guide, but also *nurturer*. In that regard, we can model for the woman the behavior we would like to see her learn, always mindful of the fact that it is the woman that decides whether and when she wants to learn new behavior.

The Role of Addictions

At experiencing unresolved mental health issues, women may be self-medicating the pain via various addictions to substances such as alcohol, tobacco, and prescription and other "legal" drugs, as well as the more commonly thought-of abuse of or addiction to so-called street drugs such as marijuana, heroin, and crack cocaine. This also creates fertile ground for the process addictions, such as to sex and love, codependency and gambling, to name a few. No matter the way it is manifest, addiction is painful, progressive, and debilitating and leads to spiritual death.

Consider the effects of addiction to substances. In some cases, the drugs and the drunkenness actually mask clinical depression which, when untreated, sends ripples of pain through families and communities. When one is addicted to a drug, including alcohol, it is not possible to have meaningful relationships with partner, spouse, children, mother, or father, and thus, drugs destroy our sense of community in countless ways (hooks 1993).

The successful mental health practitioner will not only support the recovery efforts of the identified client and proceed with treatment, but will also work with the client to strengthen and maintain healthy relationships and, with her permission, to offer to include in treatment such significant others as family and extended family members. The longer I do this work, the more I realize that to increase the chance for success, that is, symptom relief and behavioral change, it is important to consider the communal aspect of the heritage of African Americans and to include family. And it is necessary to define broadly the concept of family to extend to others in the community that significantly impact the client's well-being. What this means is that there is a need for the practitioner to develop skills in couples and family assessment and treatment specific to African Americans living in poverty and to develop a database of capable practitioners with those skills to which the family can be referred for more intense work.

The process addictions are equally as devastating, but much less frequently recognized and addressed. Of those mentioned earlier, the addiction to others, as in sex and love addiction and codependency, are some of the most painful elements in the lives of women, and men living with HIV. Frequently in my experience counseling HIV-positive women, including, but not limited to, those recovering from addiction to substances, I have found that they are faced with process addictions that were not immediately apparent. As in the substance addictions, addiction to others and the denial of self that accompanies it, such as is seen in adult children of alcoholics and people who suffer sex and love addiction, are acutely and chronically painful. Often, it is not readily recognized as an addiction disorder, which means that there is difficulty for both the client and the practitioner to have a context within which repetitive, self-defeating, behavior can be understood and treated.

The Role of Childhood Sexual Abuse in the Lives of African American Women

Studies have shown a relationship between childhood sexual abuse and HIV-infection. In a study by Trisdale (2000), more than 50 percent of HIV-positive women reported physical or sexual abuse in the past. In childhood, 21 percent were physically abused, and 25 percent were sexually abused. As adults, 33 percent were physically abused, and 29 percent were sexually abused. "Childhood sexual abuse victims reported much higher numbers of lifetime sexual partners (46 versus 11 for non-abuse victims), probably because early sexual abuses can lead to a woman feeling like she has no control over her body . . . 20% of women with HIV reported that they had been physically harmed since finding out they were infected" (Trisdale 2000, 4). Although we do not know exactly what percentage of HIV-positive African American women have histories of childhood sexual abuse, other literature as well as my clinical experience do substantiate that large numbers of African American women living with HIV suffer post traumatic stress disorder (PTSD) at alarming rates. We can add to the above list of traumas "that many women living with HIV have . . . had children or romantic partners die from HIV, many have been through the traumatic experience of prison and many live in areas where poverty or crime can result in severely traumatic experiences" (Trisdale, 2000, 4) I will go as far as to say that the experience of being African American in and of itself is traumatic, because of the daily issues of overt and covert discrimination that one faces, regardless of socioeconomic status (Stewart 1998). The literature is replete with information about the aftereffects of all forms of abuse. Fortunately, much has also been written in the popular "self-help" books that have been instrumental in disseminating this information widely among lay people. E. Sue Blume (1990), in her book *Secret Survivors*, has a checklist of behavioral symptoms characteristic of incest survivors. This checklist can be used to help women identify their behavioral patterns associated with past trauma. Women need permission to honestly explore their past, uncover memories, acknowledge the current-day ramifications of abuse, and begin the process of healing.

RELEVANT THEORETICAL CONCEPTS: TRAUMA THEORY AND BEHAVIOR CHANGE THEORY

This brings me to the discussion of two theoretical concepts helpful in practice with people, and, in my experience, particularly helpful in understanding behavior and the decision-making processes of women who live in poverty, who are African American and HIV-positive. They are trauma theory and behavior change theory.

Sandra Bloom, M.D., is a psychiatrist and activist who has made a unique contribution to the field through clinical work and extensive research about the physical, cognitive, emotional, social, and behavioral responses to danger. Quoting Perry and Pate, she states that the number of children traumatized in the United States in one year equals the number of combat veterans who served in Vietnam for a decade. "We are all part of a society that is organized around unresolved traumatic experience." (Bloom 1997, 195). The work of Patrick Carnes, a pioneer in the field of sexual addiction, which is often an outgrowth of sexual trauma, is also particularly relevant. In his *Betrayal Bonds* (1997), he uses trauma theory to help the reader understand and break free of exploitive relationships. Carnes notes that the alarm state induced by trauma becomes the gateway for addictive behavior (e.g., gambling, high-risk sex, stimulant drugs, etc.). Carnes outlines five areas of trauma responses:

1. *Trauma Blocking*

    Trauma survivor avoids fear, numbs the pain

    Addictions are compulsive, repetitive efforts to calm the mind

    Neuropathway—satiation

    Behaviors, substances that induce calming, relaxing, numbing—Create neurochemical reactions in the brain (analgesic fixes)

    Neurochemical bottom line is anxiety reduction

2. *Trauma Splitting*

    Takes many forms—

    Amnesia

    Feel detached from body—jokes about "the lights are on but no one is home"

    Multiple personality disorder, dissociative identity disorder

    Addiction is an important partner to the dissociative process in that it creates altered reality

3. *Trauma Abstinence*

    Driven by terror and fear, there is core belief of self-unworthiness

    Compulsive deprivation or abstinence (deny self good things, especially memories of success). There is high stress, shame, anxiety

    Compulsive debtors or "returners"—binge-purge cycle of buying and returning

4.*Trauma Shame*

Shame-based. Feel unlovable/unworthy. Impostor syndrome. All experiences processed as extremes

Results in excessive self-hatred

Results in self-destructive behavior

Living in emotional shell shock; propensity for re-creating trauma.

5.*Trauma Repetition*

Effort to bring resolution to the traumatic

Repeating behaviors, seeking situations or persons that re-create the trauma experience

Examples are repeated abusive relationships & self destructive relationships

It is clear to see the effects of trauma on functioning, including decision making, personal style, capacity for intimacy in relationships, and so on. This knowledge can prepare the practitioner so that certain client behaviors alert us to explore causes and conditions. Women who continually turn to self-defeating behavior without benefit of this framework question their own sanity and even their worth. Sharing with them this knowledge about trauma can help to make sense out of lifelong behaviors, and it increases the likelihood that the woman has deeper insight into her own behavior which is a catalyst for change!

What about this phenomenon of change? That is the goal of all treatment, yet the process of change can be long and arduous. James Prochaska and colleagues (1994) have submitted to the literature a very useful model for understanding the process by which people make change. In their Transtheoretical Model of Behavior Change (TTM), they have found that successful behavior change is most likely when the following conditions prevail:

• A personal readiness to change one's behavior (stages of change)

• A personal belief that one can carry out the proposed change in various settings or situations (situational confidence)

• The belief that the pros outweigh the cons of the proposed behavior change (decisional balance)

One of the model's major contributions is the recognition that behavior change unfolds through a series of stages. That is, individuals progress through a series of stages in recognizing the need to change, contemplating a change, making a change, and finally sustaining the new behavior. Typically, most people are in the early stages of a change and are not prepared to take action. The TTM helps us to understand how shifts in behavior occur. The model suggests it is critical to understand and identify the stage an individual is in before a successful change intervention can be designed and applied. The stages are:

- Precontemplation
- Contemplation
- Preparation
- Action
- Maintenance

In this model, the authors chose a six-month period of time that it takes for each stage, because that seemed to be about as far into the future as people plan, at least for changing behaviors. Furthermore, progression through the stages is usually not linear. People can progress repeatedly from contemplation to action and back to contemplation. This kind of nonlinear progression may feel like "going in circles," but Prochaska et al. (1994) suggest that these circles are spiraling upward. In this spiral of change, people revisit stages when the work of that stage is not complete. As each stage is revisited, issues are dealt with in greater depth. The changer is actually making progress toward change, even if she seems to be "backsliding" in her behavior. Prochaska refers to this as "recycling," not slipping (O'Keefe 2000). Prochaska's model has applicability to virtually every issue that about which there is a desire for human change. O'Keefe (2000), a long-time HIV/AIDS social worker in the Philadelphia area, has applied this theory with victims/survivors of family violence, an area highly associated with women's vulnerability to HIV-infection.

What this model can teach helping professionals to see is that there is significant value in supporting the client by finding ways to accept her at whatever point she presents by working with her at her own pace. It seems it can be particularly effective in working long term with women who are balancing all the ramifications of an HIV diagnosis in addition to attending to the myriad issues that predate and sometimes supersede the attention to HIV. It can also help to sustain the helper emotionally in this difficult work.

Understanding and embracing these trauma and behavior change theories can help to reduce the frustration that helpers can feel about the repetitive, self-destructive behaviors of clients and what can seem like their unwillingness or incapability to change. These important concepts help us to be more patient. They provide a new lens for viewing these actions that is nonjudgmental and blameless. Also helpful is understanding our own process—working with traumatized people has a potentially dangerous effect on the helper. This is known as secondary or vicarious traumatization and is also known as compassion fatigue. Paying attention to that reality can help us to put the frustrations into perspective as we realize that we must enlist our own supports and strategies for healing the wounds of working with the wounded, who also invariably touch in us something from our own life experiences.

PERSONAL REFLECTIONS OF AN AFRICAN AMERICAN PROFESSIONAL: KEY PRACTICE STRATEGIES

About halfway through this work, I was acutely aware that this has been a difficult chapter to write. Then it finally hit me! As an African American woman—first-generation professional, old enough to have known my grandparents whose parents were enslaved—writing about the counseling needs of African American women has been more than an intellectual endeavor. It calls forth much sentiment and many issues—some of which are deep-seated and very personal. These are issues that have to do with both my own personal history and my contextual experience of being a woman of African descent in a deeply divided racist and sexist society.

Every time I see the statistics—telling of rising numbers among African people in Africa and in the Diaspora, every time I see that juxtaposed with the declining numbers in communities "not of color," every time I am faced with the fact that not only do African people bear a grossly disproportionate share of the incidences of HIV but also, in the United States, Black women are the fastest growing group of the newly infected, every time I see it and hear it and sit with women who are it, I feel it deeply. I feel the sadness about her living with a disease that has stricken her in the prime of life and that will likely consume her before her time. I feel the anger about it affecting her at sixteen times the rate of White women and about the veil of poverty that disproportionately predisposes and exposes her to more than her share of medical and social ills. I feel the fear and the loneliness of the children who watch their parents and perhaps their siblings struggle to live with the disease and eventually die, leaving them to live with a legacy of pain in the homes of strangers or the estranged or extended families, overwhelmed themselves and dealing with loss.

But it does not stop there. I feel the fear and the rage and the absolute terror as I watch a disease that provides profit and employment and status and power for so many while it ravages and devours the world's population of African people. And I sit and I wonder, "Why?" It is often said that HIV is a disease about what you do, not who you are. And I fundamentally agree with that. Yet the shrewd variable of racism, that teaches all its subjects to devalue a people, seems to belie that fact. After all, when we see people sharing similar characteristics, particularly ethnic identity, rolling through the doors of the hospitals and clinics with very familiar life stories and circumstances, HIV can very much *look like* it is about who you are. This poses a challenge for even the most liberal, most conscious, most sensitive practitioner to provide individualized care and attention of high quality that is more than professional practice—it is "soul work." it requires us to be intimately in touch with our humanity—with humility that reminds us that we are one with our so-called client. We must look beyond the presenting behavior, issue, problem into the heart and soul of that human being who is in so much pain as to present with whatever behavior it is that we would, in a lesser space, condemn or judge.

As a social worker of more than two decades and spanning a number of areas of practice, I have seen much and have many thoughts about it. What I attempt to communicate around the counseling needs of African American women living with AIDS must be viewed through the lens of my experiences with them in the capacity of social worker, confidante, soul mate, "SisterFriend." These roles are not taught in academia. In fact, what is seen as appropriate is to maintain "professional distance." And I do agree that there should be good boundaries when we interact with others, particularly our so-called clients. Clarity in the relationship with them keeps them safe to do the work they need to do and ultimately models for them the experience that healthy relationships are attainable and desirable.

However, and I want to be truly heard on this, when I say that, given the many grave variables that create the profile of women living with HIV/AIDS, we can risk *not* making connection if we subscribe rigidly to the tenet of "professional distance." What I have learned is that what makes me effective with women who are poor and African American and "down and out," whether HIV-positive or not, is that I am genuine, present, and consistent with them. And there is one more essential ingredient—love.

Now there is a radical thought in relation to those with whom we work. Love is all of those things mentioned earlier, communicated in the context of unconditional positive regard. People, especially people who have withstood generations of shame and lies and pain and who have known all too well how it feels to be devalued, benefit greatly to know that, without strings attached, they truly matter to someone. Moreover, it is important to know that there is a safe space within which they can be heard from their depths; the ability to be who they are is life giving. When the practitioner is adequately evolved on her/his own journey and can be there in that way with the "client," it is a rare and special gift that transcends and surpasses the confines of traditional counseling. I might add that my colleagues, regardless of race, who are able to be with "clients" in similar ways are also effective and highly appreciated by the women (and men and children) with whom they work. That gives me gratification and much hope.

I began by saying there are many different ways to treat the issue of counseling African American women living with HIV. I chose to do so broadly to hopefully provide practitioners in a range of roles with helpful, culturally meaningful strategies and tools, which only begins the discussion. In the tradition of Ghana, I bid you "Safe Journey" for yourself and for the African American women living with HIV for whom you are supporter, advocate, nurturer, and guide.

REFERENCES

Bloom, S. (1997). *Creating sanctuary: Toward an evolution of sane societies*. New York: Routledge.

Blume, E.S. (1990). *Secret survivors: Uncovering incest and its aftereffects in women.* New York: John Wiley & Sons.

Carnes, P. (1997). *Betrayal bonds: Breaking free of exploitive relationships.* Deerfield Beach, FL: Health Communications, Inc.

hooks, b. (1993). *Sisters of the yam: Black women and self-recovery.* Boston: South End Press.

O'Keefe, P. (2000). The transtheoretical model of change and its relevance to family violence. Workshop for Providers, Philadelphia Physicians for Social Responsibility, transcribed by Sandra Dempsey, MSS.

Prochaska, J., Redding, C., Harlow, L., Rossi, J., et al. (1994). The transtheoretical model of change and HIV prevention: A review. *Health Education Quarterly*, 21 (94), 471–486.

Quinn, S.C. (1993). Perspective: AIDS and the African American woman: The triple burden of race, class and gender. *Health Education Quarterly*, 20 (3), 305–320.

Stewart, P. (1998) Social work practice with African Americans with HIV/AIDS: Challenges to mind, body and spirit. In L. Gant, P. Stewart, and V. Lynch (Eds.), *Social workers speak out on the AIDS crisis: Voices from and to African American communities.* Westport, CT: Praeger.

———. (2000). HIV/AIDS issues among African Americans: Oppressed, gifted and black. In V. Lynch (Ed.), *HIV/AIDS at the year 2000: A sourcebook for social workers.* Boston: Allyn & Bacon.

Trisdale, S. (September 2000). HIV/AIDS and posttraumatic stress disorder. *WORLD.* Oakland, CA.

14

Focus on Solutions: Blacks Assisting Blacks Against AIDS: Taking Care of Our Own

Dana Williams

As an African American woman directly involved in the struggle against AIDS for the last fifteen years, it is clear that the need for HIV/AIDS services organizations and agencies, which are initiated and implemented by Blacks, is imperative for the survival of our community. Unfortunately, for years we as a community have embraced the stigma, denial, and discrimination attached to the word AIDS. Now in the twenty-first century, we have witnessed the devastation of this disease across the country and the world. As AIDS ravishes our community, taking away thousands of women who are the keepers of life, we are forced to face our fears. AIDS has now become a pandemic. African Americans and other minorities are now taking the brunt of this deadly disease. With a vaccine potentially years away, treatments becoming more expensive with unknown long-term effects, and more children becoming orphaned as a result of parents dying from AIDS, we have no other recourse except to take drastic measures. Education by way of persons who come from our own communities who look like us, speak like us, and can relate to the cultural barriers that keep us from accepting our responsibility to take care of our own will be key to reducing the rates of HIV/AIDS infection. Now is the time to step up and meet the demands and challenges our communities face in dealing with this epidemic.

A number of Black-implemented programs specifically targeting African Americans are currently in operation across the country. Many are making remarkable changes in communities of color. In this focus on solutions discussion, I simply discuss the organization and programming of one such agency, Blacks Assisting Blacks against AIDS (BABAA), located in St. Louis, Missouri. The existence of such services are more concentrated in the northeastern and West Coast areas and nearest to AIDS epicenters. It is important for existing programs to reach out and share programming information, disseminate findings about the effectiveness of programming, and act in ways to support more such organizations throughout the country.

THE MISSION OF BABAA

Our mission is to advocate, educate, and act as a resource for the St. Louis Metropolitan African American community, with particular regard to support services and resource development for individuals who are HIV-challenged—a term which is less stigmatizing than HIV-infected and encompasses those that face serious challenges to remain HIV-negative. The staff of BABAA consists of African American professionals who are dedicated to providing the most efficient and confidential service available.

NEW TRANSITIONS

This innovative program provides a holistic approach to enhance HIV/AIDS health care and support services for African American women recently released from prison. This program is a collaborative effort with BABAA and the St. Louis Judicial Court system, more specifically Drug Court. Drug Court is a specific court that deals with women who are arrested for drug use, drug possession, and/or prostitution. All the women in this project are at high risk or infected with HIV/AIDS.

This holistic and comprehensive program is designed with four key components:

1. Transitional Case Management, which provides HIV/AIDS-positive women who are incarcerated access to Care Case Management services and discharge planning.
2. Prevention Case Management, which helps women who are HIV/AIDS-positive as well as women who are at high risk for HIV/AIDS to adopt and maintain strategies for how they can reduce their risk for HIV-infection. It also helps women access various resources (i.e., housing, substance treatment, mental health, and concrete services) to meet their basic living needs.
3. Care Case Management, which provides HIV/AIDS-positive women access to all Ryan White care services needed to maintain a healthy lifestyle and basic standard of living.
4. Mental Health/Therapeutic Services, which is geared toward HIV/AIDS-positive women or high-risk women and their families and partners, provides emotional and moral support. In addition, the agency maintains strict rules of confidentiality, an element of service that we find is essential to working with African American populations. This component allows clients to look at the underlying issues related to their incarceration.

STEPS TO LIVING

The Steps to Living Program provides education, information, and support services to African Americans living with HIV/AIDS, and/or those who are providing care for HIV-challenged persons. The program is administered by African American facilitators with HIV/AIDS training, and consists of five eight-week workshops over a one-year period. Weekly meetings are held in two-hour sessions. The first hour is designed for HIV-relevant education on topics such as nutrition, safer sex behavior modification, reinfection prevention skills, disclosure, universal precautions, medical issue, legal issues, and resource identification. Education presentations are made by professionals in the community who have experience working with clients who are HIV-challenged and their families.

The second hour provides support group therapy, with the goals of facilitating communication, supporting and reinforcing behavior modification, encouraging information and experience sharing, and alleviating anxiety while fostering a sense of mutual aid. Participants are encouraged to attend the entire eight-week workshop in order to maximize the benefits of ongoing support. Support group facilitators are volunteers trained in HIV/AIDS knowledge and group dynamics.

In addition to education and support, Steps to Living also provides participants with a hot home-style cooked meal and on-site child care by a volunteer certified through the American Red Cross Baby-sitting course. Additionally, transportation to and from meetings is routinely provided, as this can be a major barrier for many participants.

Although Steps to Living is geared toward meeting the needs of the African American community, we continue to serve clients who identify as Caucasian, Native American, Caribbean, African, and biracial. Additionally, clients are able to participate regardless of sexual orientation or gender. Steps to Living has been in existence since 1992 and continues to receive recognition as an excellent model for providing support services to the African American community, through federal, state, and local entities.

COALITION EMPOWERING FAMILIES AFFECTED BY AIDS (CEFAA)

CEFAA exists to empower women, children, youth and families affected by or at risk for HIV-infection. The coalition works in collaboration with AIDS service organizations and community-based organizations to identify and address barriers to services. CEFAA works to identify and address barriers and to eliminate them, in order to maximize services and to advocate for a comprehensive service delivery system. CEFAA came to fruition in 1998 as a direct result of the need to educate and support women with HIV infection and AIDS and to identify gaps and barriers to providing services to women. CEFAA is made up of four critical subcommittees. They are as follows.

Advocacy and Maximizing Services

The primary purpose of this committee is to work toward a comprehensive continuum of care for HIV-affected families through the mobilization of and networking with existing child welfare, AIDS service, and community-based organizations through other systemic and legislative change. The advocacy committee seeks to provide community leadership in the recognition of key issues/needs that impact the lives of HIV-affected families and to work toward effective solutions to address these needs. This committee is responsible for the annual toy drive for over 600 children and an annual school supply drive for over 400 children. They also submit quarterly legislative updates to be included in the newsletter and developing a quarterly roundtable discussion on current topics.

Education and Prevention

This committee works toward educating community-based organizations that serve women, children, youth, and their families infected and affected by HIV/AIDS, as well as those individuals who are infected and affected by HIV/AIDS.

This committee is responsible for monthly educational sessions to CEFAA members and CEFAA's annual summer conference and fall forum, as well as any other project as it relates to education regarding women, children, youth, and their families pertaining to HIV/AIDS.

Membership Outreach

This committee's purpose is to reach out to the community through active membership recruitment activities, the media, and legislative involvement. This committee is responsible for the production of the quarterly newsletters, legislative updates, and media attention and membership recruitment activities throughout the year.

Administration

The officers consist of a president, vice president, secretary, and treasurer. The officers sit as part of the board of directors, as well as being the chair and cochairs of each subcommittee. Additionally, there is an executive director that is responsible for the overall functions of the coalition. Currently there are over twenty-five agencies that are a part of the coalition. The body of the coalition is made up of federal and state agencies, as well as community-based and AIDS service organizations. The coalition is also made up of individuals who are infected and affected with HIV/AIDS.

15

HIV/AIDS Policy and African American Women

Tonya E. Perry

"Invisible," "triple burdened," and "falling through the cracks" are among the ways in which the position of African American women within the context of the HIV/AIDS epidemic have been represented in the literature (Caravano 1991; Corea 1992; Hammonds 1990; Quinn 1993; U.S. House of Representatives 1991). As these characterizations suggest, the ways in which our society has responded to the HIV/AIDS crisis among African American women and other stigmatized groups is a reflection of the complex interaction of cultural, social, and moral factors. These factors shape AIDS social policy (Brandt 1988), and, in effect, result in policies that do not equally benefit all. In fact, though HIV/AIDS-related policies and programming have led to a significant decline in the total number of reported AIDS cases among White Americans, the total number of AIDS cases reported among African Americans, and African American women, specifically, has increased dramatically (CDC 1999; Kaiser Family Foundation 1998). Despite the degree to which African American women are affected by HIV/AIDS, policy-initiated programming aimed at reducing HIV/AIDS incidence among African American women and responding to the special needs of those women who are HIV-positive or AIDS-diagnosed is lacking. This chapter examines key HIV/AIDS-related social policies affecting African American women. In addition, the chapter explores the extent to which HIV/AIDS-related policies have been responsive to the needs of African American women and major advancements in HIV/AIDS-related policy development that may assist African American women. Finally, the chapter ends with recommendations for future policy development.

AFRICAN AMERICAN WOMEN AND FEDERAL AIDS POLICIES

> ...a failure by scientists and policy makers to appreciate the interaction between social, economic and cultural conditions and the propagation of HIV/AIDS disease has often led to public misunderstanding and policy mistakes about the epidemic. (National Research Council 1993, 9)

The history of AIDS-related policy development is plagued by a pattern of delayed, reactive, and noncontextualized responses. Although the first reported U.S. cases of AIDS-related illnesses such as *pneumocystis carinii* pneumonia (PCP) were reported in 1981, nearly ten years passed before a comprehensive federal policy response was implemented (Stein 1998). By the time the Ryan White Comprehensive AIDS Resources Emergency Act was passed by Congress in August 1990, an estimated one million people were HIV-positive, and approximately 140,000 persons had already been diagnosed with AIDS (CDC 1999).

The passage of the Ryan White Comprehensive AIDS Resources Emergency Act and early AIDS-related initiatives were significant milestones toward the provision of essential AIDS-related programming. However, the policies failed to encompass the full range of the AIDS experience by failing to acknowledge and address women's experiences—most particularly the experiences of African American women and other population groups who are disproportionately affected by HIV/AIDS. For example, though it was clear that African American and Latina women were disproportionately affected by HIV and AIDS as early as 1982, it was not until 1983 that the CDC actually augmented its classification system to include heterosexual partners of AIDS patients as an identified risk group (African American AIDS Policy & Training Institute 1999).

In addition to exclusionary policies impacting AIDS diagnosis, clinical drug trials have often excluded women—particularly African American women and members of other minority groups (Quinn 1993). Following hearings held by the House of Representatives in 1992, the government acknowledged that not enough had been done to examine the ways in which women are differentially affected by HIV and AIDS. Subsequently, two major governmental offices were formed: the Office of Research on Women's Health and the Office of AIDS Research. Among the objectives of the offices was a charge to enhance the level of representation of women in all facets of AIDS research, including clinical drug trials.

The efficacy of policies aimed at increasing women-focused research and the participation of women in clinical trials has yet to be established. Research conducted by Williams and colleagues (1997) and by the National Center for HIV, STD & TB Prevention (1998) suggests that women from minority groups continue to be less likely to participate in clinical drug trials and more likely to enter treatment further along the illness trajectory. Existing AIDS policies reflect a generic approach to HIV/AIDS prevention, treatment, and research that has obviously failed miserably in preventing HIV and in providing equitable HIV-related treatment and services to African Americans.

BENEFIT AND STATUS-CONFERRING POLICIES

Given the history of HIV/AIDS policy development, it should not be surprising that HIV/AIDS-related policies that are designed specifically to meet the needs of African American women are lacking. Consequently, any discussion of HIV/AIDS-related policy development directed toward this group must necessarily revolve around a critique of existing social policies designed to meet the needs of the AIDS-affected population at large.

There are six major policies through which HIV/AIDS-related benefits are administered. These policies are Social Security Disability Insurance (SSDI), Supplemental Security Income Program (SSI), Medicaid, Ryan White Comprehensive AIDS Resources Emergency Care Act (Care Act), Housing Opportunities for People with AIDS Act (HOPWA), and the Alcohol, Drug Abuse and Mental Health Administration Reorganization Act (ADAMHA).

These benefit-conferring policies are supported by other key policies, known as status-conferring policies, which were not specifically designed to address the needs of HIV-positive and AIDS-diagnosed persons but which function to provide antidiscrimination protection and legal redress for such persons (Feldman and Fulwood 1999; Stein 1998). These status-conferring policies include the Vocational Rehabilitation Act (VRA) of 1973, the Americans with Disabilities Act (ADA) of 1990, and the Fair Housing Act (FHA) of 1988. Even though these policies are not the focus of the current discussion, it is important to note their significance in guaranteeing protection to African American women and others affected by HIV/AIDS against discrimination in employment, education, housing, transportation, public accommodations, and social services (Feldman and Fulwood 1999; Stein, 1998).

Social Security Disability Insurance and Supplemental Security Income

People with HIV/AIDS who meet categorical and financial eligibility criteria may receive cash benefits under various titles of the Social Security Act. Title II, Social Security Disability Insurance (SSDI), is employment-linked and available to insured workers and/or their families who meet eligibility requirements. Title XVI, the Supplemental Security Income program (SSI), is based solely upon disability and financial need. Claimants for both SSDI and SSI must be classified as disabled, be categorically eligible, and pass through a multistep evaluation process. SSI applicants must also pass a means test (Social Security Administration 2000; Stein 1998).

To meet eligibility criteria set forth by the Social Security Administration, an HIV-positive person must demonstrate the existence of a qualifying condition. Qualifying conditions include opportunistic infections such as PCP, as well as cervical cancer, a T-cell count of less than 200, and pulmonary tuberculosis (Stein 1998). The paucity of knowledge regarding the natural history of HIV among women creates an inherent bias in the AIDS case definition classification system. This bias poses great difficulty to women in meeting specified disability criteria. This means that HIV-positive women may have extended post-HIV-qualification periods, making them much sicker and much poorer before they qualify to receive cash assistance.

Consistent with other federal assistance programs, persons applying for SSI cash assistance must pass a means test—an assessment of income and assets in order to determine that the individual applying for assistance does not already have the resources to maintain a minimal level of subsistence (Zastrow 2000). The SSI means test imposes additional qualification obstacles, particularly for the working poor. The monthly income cap from all sources is less than $700, and the total assets cap is $2,000 for single persons and $3,000 for married persons (Social Security Administration 2000). The presumption is that persons who are well enough to earn incomes at or above the monthly income cap may not be disabled. Although symptomatic, HIV-positive women not receiving SSI or Temporary Assistance to Needy Families (TANF) who are among the working poor may be required to work to support themselves and their families, making them categorically ineligible to receive SSI benefits. Inversely, women who receive SSI assistance may be placed in the precarious position of needing or wanting to earn a greater income but not being able to afford to lose SSI benefits from which they would be disqualified to receive for having earnings that exceed the established income cap.

Medicaid

Within the context of the HIV/AIDS epidemic, one may observe a link between poverty and ethnicity and a lack of accessibility to medical care. Specifically, African Americans and Latinos who are disproportionately affected by poverty and HIV/AIDS are most likely to be uninsured (Ethier, Ickovics, and Rodin 1996; Leigh 1995; McBarnette 1996). As a consequence, they rely heavily upon public programs such as Medicaid to provide for their medical care. Even if African American women with HIV/AIDS are able to afford private health insurance, they may not be able to access it because many insurance companies impose policies that restrict the coverage of HIV and AIDS as preexisting illnesses (Stein 1998). Thus, African American women and others who may be financially able to access private health insurance are also forced to turn to the public sector to gain access to care. Many African American women with HIV are heads of households with incomes that place them below the poverty line. Impoverished and in need of medical services, many turn to Medicaid for assistance.

Medicaid, which is administered under Title XIX of the Social Security Act, is the principal payer of health care for people with HIV and AIDS. Stein (1998) reports that Medicaid serves an estimated 40 percent to 50 percent of persons with HIV and approximately 62 percent of persons in the later stages of AIDS. Although many people with private insurance have turned to Medicaid because of insurance restrictions, Medicaid is the primary means of accessing health for a disproportionate number of African American women who have limi options (McBarnette 1996). Medicaid eligibility is needs-based and linked to age, disability, or membership in a needy family with dependent children (Stein 1998). Medicaid is jointly administered by the federal and local governments, and though income limits extend from SSI policy guidelines, states have the latitude to offer coverage to persons not meeting income limit criteria. This includes extending coverage to persons who cannot afford to pay for medical services but who earn too much money to qualify for cash benefits through SSI and SSDI (Stein 1998).

Ryan White Comprehensive AIDS Resources Emergency Care Act

The Ryan White Care Act is the most significant piece of legislation affecting the provision of services to persons with HIV/AIDS. The intent of this law is to strengthen the accessibility and efficacy of care for individuals and families affected by HIV/AIDS (United States 1990). Initially passed in 1990, the Ryan White Care Act was reauthorized in 1996, The Ryan White Reauthorization Bill. H.R. 4807, was passed by the U.S. House of Representatives on July 25, 2000, following the unanimous passing of a companion bill in the U.S. Senate on June 6, 2000. The passage of H.R. 4807 reauthorized the Ryan White Care Act for another five years (U.S. House of Representatives, 2000). The Ryan White Care Act represents a partnering of federal, state, and local governmental organs, community-based providers, and consumers of services working to meet the needs of HIV/AIDS-affected persons in local communities.

Consisting of five titles, the Ryan White Care Act provides funding for primary health care, AIDS medications, adherence support, case management, and other supportive services for the thousands of persons living with HIV and AIDS (AIDS Action 2000; United States 1990). Each title of the act awards competitive grants to different entities, including metropolitan areas demonstrating increased prevalence of AIDS-diagnosed persons; states, territories, and the District of Columbia; community-based clinics and public health entities serving traditionally underserved populations (50 percent of whom must be homeless); primary health care providers; and "projects of national significance."

These projects of national significance include replicable projects serving HIV/AIDS-affected populations which (1) increase the number of health care facilities that serve low-income individuals and families; (2) provide drug abuse and health care services; (3) support respite care services in minority communities to facilitate participation in family-based care networks; and (4) provide health care and support services to underserved populations such as minorities, including Native Americans, people in rural areas, the homeless, and prisoners (Stein 1998, 57). Additionally, funds are allocated to support AIDS Education and Training Centers (AETCs) that are intended to promote competence and compassion among service providers by equipping them with the most current HIV/AIDS information and methodologies (AIDS Action 1999).

Housing Opportunities for People with AIDS Act (HOPWA)

Persons with HIV/AIDS may receive special assistance through the Housing Opportunities for People with AIDS Act (HOPWA). This piece of legislation grants states the funds to develop long-term strategies for providing adequate housing to persons with HIV/AIDS and their families. Grants awarded through HOPWA may be used to support both coordination of housing-related programming, as well as direct provision of shelter and supportive services (Stein 1998).

Alcohol, Drug Abuse, and Mental Health Administration Reorganization Act (ADAMHA)

The Alcohol, Drug Abuse, and Mental Health Administration Act was passed in 1992 in response to a need to address the overwhelming correlation between intravenous drug use and HIV-infection, which is particularly evident among women (Stein 1998). Through this legislation, block grants are awarded to states for the provision of drug and alcohol services. Additionally, ADAMHA provides for awards to be made through the Center for Substance Abuse Treatment (CSAT). These awards are granted to service providers who will provide outreach, early intervention, and residential treatment services to pregnant women and their children (Stein 1998).

PREVENTION

In addition to federally mandated programs that address the cash assistance, health care, and social service needs of AIDS-affected populations, there are also policies that address the prevention of HIV/AIDS in populations that are at risk. These prevention funds are chiefly appropriated via the Ryan White AIDS Prevention Act, which provides funds to the U.S. Department of Health and Human Services, which in turn disperses the funds to the CDC for the administration of prevention-related programming. By far, the CDC accounts for the majority of federal spending aimed at HIV/AIDS prevention, with a fiscal year 2000 budget of $694.7 million and an approved fiscal year 2001 budget of $760.9 million (AIDS Action 2001). The CDC estimates that roughly 36 percent of prevention funding targeting racial/ethnic groups is directed toward African Americans. In 1999, the CDC pledged an additional $12.5 million to support the $156 million government initiative to address the AIDS crisis in communities of color. Most recently, the CDC has designated $27.4 million in additional funding to be directed toward fiscal year 2001 HIV/AIDS ethnic/racial initiatives (African American AIDS Policy & Training Institute 1999; AIDS Action 2001; CDC 1999; Serant 1998).

Additionally, the CDC supports a number of community-based organizations that specifically target the prevention and treatment needs of African Americans. The CDC also continues to support a faith-based collaboration initiative initiated in 1987 which received nearly $1 million in funding in 1997; nearly half of this funding went directly to the African American faith community (CDC 1999). Given the $27.4 million increase in funding specifically allocated to support initiatives targeting HIV/AIDS in racial and ethnic communities and the Bush administration's current interest in faith-based initiatives, it is anticipated that African American faith communities will receive an even greater portion of CDC prevention dollars.

Table 15.1 provides a summary of fiscal year 2001 appropriation levels for each of the key policies discussed. A budget package passed by the House of

Table 15.1
Fiscal Year (FY) 2001 Appropriations Levels for Federal AIDS Programs

PROGRAM	FY 2000 FINAL	FY 2001 President's Budget Request 2/7/00	FY 2001 HIV/AIDS Need	House Action L, HHS 5/24/00 VA, HUD 6/20/00	Senate Action L, HHS 5/11/00 VA, HUD 9/13/00	FY 2001 FINAL* L, HHS P.L. 106-554 VA, HUD P.L. 106-377
CDC: Prevention	$694.7m (+$36.9m)	$734.7m (+$40.0m)	$984.7m (+$290.0m)	$724.4m (+$29.7m)	$762.4m (+$67.7m)	$760.9m (+$66.2m)
HRSA: Ryan White CARE Act Total	$1,594.8m (+$183.7m)	$1,719.8m (+$125.0m)	$1,931.4m (+$336.6m)	$1,725.0m (+$130.2m)	$1,650.1m (+$55.3m)	$1,776.0m (+$181.2m)
Title I	$546.6m (+$41.5m)	$586.6m (+$40.0m)	$635.6m (+$89.0m)	$586.6m (+$40.0m)	$556.5m (+$9.9m)	$596.5m (+$49.9m)
Title II: Care Services	$296.1m (+$19.2m)	$310.1m (+$14.0m)	$341.1m (+$45.0m)	$310.1m (+$14.0m)	$296.1m (+$0m)	$315.0m (+$18.9m)
Title II: ADAP	$528.0m (+$67.0m)	$554.0m (+$26.0m)	$658.0m (+$130.0m)	$554.0m (+$26.0m)	$538.0m (+$10.0m)	$589.0m (+$61.0m)
Title III	$138.4m (+$44.1m)	$171.4m (+$33.0m)	$184.4m (+$46.0m)	$173.9m (+$35.5m)	$166.4m (+$28.0m)	$168.9m (+$30.5m)
Title IV	$51.0m (+$5.0m)	$60.0m (+$9.0m)	$70.0m (+$19.0m)	$60.0m (+$9.0m)	$58.4m (+$7.4m)	$65.0m (+$14.0m)
Part F: AETCs	$26.7m (+$6.7m)	$29.2m (+$2.5m)	$30.3m (+$3.6m)	$31.6m (+$4.9m)	$26.7m (+$0m)	$31.6m (+$4.9m)
Part F: Dental Reimbursement	$8.0m (+$0.2m)	$8.5m (+$0.5m)	$12.0m (+$4.0m)	$9.0m (+$1.0m)	$8.0m (+$0m)	$10.0m (+$2.0m)
NIH: AIDS Research	$2,006.0m (+$207.6m)	$2,111.0m (+$105.0m)	$2,329.0m (+$323.0m)	$1.02b NIH increase overall; OAR increase uncertain	$2.7b NIH increase overall; OAR increase uncertain	$2,267.0m (+$261.0m)
SAMHSA (Substance Abuse Prevention & Treatment Blockgrant)	$1,600.0m (+$15.0m)	$1,631.0m (+$31.0m)	$2,000.0m (+$400.0m)	$1,631.0m (+$31.0m)	$1,631.0m (+$31.0m)	$1,651.2m (+$51.2m)
HUD: HOPWA	$232.0m (+$7.0m)	$260.0m (+$28.0m)	$292.0m (+$60.0m)	$250.0m (+$18.0m)	$232.0m (+$0m)	$258.0m (+$26.0m)

*The final totals do not include the FY01 increases for the minority AIDS initiative or the global LIFE initiative, see next page for those totals.

AIDS *Action* 1906 Sunderland Place, NW • Washington, DC 20036
phone: (202) 530-8030 • fax: (202) 530-8031 • e-mail: network@aidsaction.org • www.aidsaction.org

Table 15.1 (continued)

Increases over FY00:

+$27.4M	for the Centers for Disease Control and Prevention (CDC)
+$36.1M	for the Health Resources and Services Administration (HRSA)
+$37.4M	for the Substance Abuse Prevention and Treatment Blockgrant (SAMHSA)
+$7.0M	for Mental Health Services (SAMHSA)
+$0M	for emergency spending to end ethnic and racial health disparities
-$8.7M	for the National Institutes of Health
+$0M	for the Office of Minority Health

$99.2 M   FY 2001 INCREASES

Totals for the accounts for FY01:

$88.0M	for the Centers for Disease Control and Prevention (CDC)
$110.2M	for the Health Resources and Services Administration (HRSA)
$92.1M	for the Substance Abuse and Mental Health Services Administration (SAMHSA)
$0.0M	for the National Institutes of Health

$290.3M

$50.0M	for emergency spending to end ethnic and racial health disparities
$ 9.7M	for the Office of Minority Health

$350.0 M   FY 2001 TOTAL

All updates regarding these funds will be posted on the Office of Minority Health Resources Center's website at www.omhrc.gov (1-800-444-6472) We know there is an interest in the status of these funds and appreciate your patience.

FY2001 GLOBAL HIV/AIDS INITIATVE

LIFE (Leadership and Investment in Fighting an Epidemic)

For FY2001, **$464.5 million (more than $200M over FY00)** will be invested in the LIFE initiative to enhance the federal response to the global HIV/AIDS epidemic that includes assistance in the areas of prevention, care, orphan care, and infrastructure development.

FY00	**$225 million**
FY01	**$464.5 million (+$239.5M)**

AIDS *Action* 1906 Sunderland Place, NW • Washington, DC 20036
phone: (202) 530-8030 • fax: (202) 530-8031 • e-mail: network@aidsaction.org • www.aidsaction.org

Representatives and the Senate on in October 2000 included increases for Ryan White, CDC funding, and HOPWA. Fiscal year 2001 appropriations also include $350 million in funds designated specifically for the Minority AIDS Initiative—which is an increase of $100 million over the fiscal year 2000 appropriation. Also noteworthy is the $464.5 million appropriation for the Global HIV/AIDS Initiative (AIDS Action 2001).

This policy review suggests that though current HIV/AIDS-related policies were not developed to benefit African American women, there are mechanisms through which their HIV/AIDS-related prevention, treatment, services, and research needs may be addressed. The discussion now turns to a critique of the effectiveness of these policies in responding to the needs of African American women along the dimensions of HIV prevention, access to care, and coordinated services/quality of care.

HOW AIDS PUBLIC POLICY HAS FAILED AFRICAN-AMERICAN WOMEN: FAILURES, GAPS, AND OVERSIGHTS

The burden is great, and public health policy greatly inadequate. Little attention has been given to AIDS education, outreach and treatment for women of color. (Bair & Cayleff, 1993, p. 284)

Eight years later, and two decades into the epidemic, Bair and Cayleff's (1993) words are still true. Maldano (1999) and others (Office of Minority Health, 1999; Waters, 1999) assert that the national investment in HIV/AIDS-related prevention, treatment, care and research has been effective in realizing significant improvements in the health and welfare of persons affected by HIV/AIDS. Unfortunately, these improvements have not extended to African Americans and other members of racial/ethnic minority groups. The failure of HIV/AIDS policies framing the national prevention response to HIV/AIDS is most pronounced among African American women whose rates of HIV infection have increased at an alarming rate. Epidemiological data, which has been outlined in great detail in previous chapters of the book, offer the greatest evidence that existing HIV/AIDS policies have failed to be effective in significantly lessening the rate of HIV/AIDS among African-American women—with African American women accounting for roughly 13% of the United States population and more than 60% of all reported AIDS case among women, there is no doubt that HIV/AIDS policies have not been effective in reducing the incidence of HIV infection among African American women. Further, research suggests that these policies have also failed to realize accessible and equitable treatment for African-American women who are HIV-positive or AIDS-diagnosed.

There is no question that African Americans bear the greatest burden of the epidemic, yet are the group that is benefiting the least from our national investment in HIV/AIDS-programs. (Maldano, 1999, p. 1)

HIV PREVENTION

Unquestionably, the national prevention response to HIV/AIDS has failed miserably in slowing the spread of HIV/AIDS in African-American communities. Prevention efforts have been plagued by a preoccupation with applying generic intervention models to reduce HIV/AIDS risk among African Americans. Funding bodies which support HIV/AIDS prevention research have failed African-American women and other most affected groups by neglecting to require interventions based on theories related to the sociocultural nature of behavior change. Such models would incorporate cultural norms, beliefs, and practices and recognize the contributions of socio-environmental factors on HIV/AIDS risk behaviors among African Americans. Such models would also need to be responsive to the tremendous diversity that is the African American cultural experience—an experience which incorporates diverse languages, beliefs and values reflecting a shared African experience across the broad boundaries of the Diaspora—including the varied speaking nations of the Caribbean and the Americas (McBarnette, 1996).

Research strategies which would allow us to gain meaningful insight into the health-related beliefs and behaviors of African-American women are sorely needed (McBarnette, 1996). Such strategies would incorporate both positivistic and qualitative methodologies in identifying and contextualizing core variables associated with African-American women's risk for HIV. More importantly, such research may provide important insight into HIV-related protective behaviors employed by African American women and variables that promote such behaviors. Given the magnitude of the epidemic among African American women, HIV/AIDS prevention action models, which elicit the active participation of women in HIV/AIDS education while facilitating the collection of data relevant to possible correlates of HIV-related protective behaviors, are especially needed. Additionally, the underrepresentation of African Americans as principal investigators on HIV/AIDS prevention projects targeting African Americans is troubling and may in part be a precipitant of culturally baseless, ineffectual prevention research. As the incidence of HIV/AIDS among African Americans continues to escalate, the need to redefine prevention policy takes on more urgency. A fundamental shift in HIV/AIDS priorities and approaches is needed to create effective prevention models that reflect the cultural realities of African Americans.

ACCESS TO CARE

African American women, who are disproportionately represented among the poor and uninsured, face tremendous obstacles in accessing medical care (Gollub 1999; Leigh 1995; McBarnette 1996). A lack of health insurance impedes a woman's ability to access preventive care and encourages delayed help seeking. This is a dangerous pattern—both for women who are at risk for HIV and for those who may be HIV-positive or AIDS-diagnosed. The implications are tremendous both for the women who will be delayed in getting tested for HIV, as well as for the women who will enter treatment further along the HIV/AIDS illness trajectory.

Limited access to health care translates into delayed treatment for African American women with HIV/AIDS. Data suggest that African American women are diagnosed with AIDS much later than their White counterparts. Compared with White men, African American women also have higher viral loads and lower CD4 cell counts upon initiation of treatment. Forty-two percent of African Americans are symptomatic upon commencing antiviral therapy (National HIV/AIDS Treatment Survey 1998).

In the absence of universal health care, many African American women will continue to rely upon Medicaid to access needed health care. Without universal access to health care, many African American women will continue to compromise their health. Those who are at risk for HIV will delay testing and early treatment, and those who are HIV-positive or AIDS-diagnosed will not benefit from antiviral therapy and continuity of care.

COORDINATED SERVICES AND QUALITY OF CARE

There is evidence to suggest that persons with HIV and AIDS who must rely on Medicaid to access medical services—which is the case for many African American women—may not only have difficulty accessing care but may also receive inferior care (Bennett, Horner, and Weinstein 1995; National HIV/AIDS Treatment Survey 1998). Findings from a multisite study conducted by Bennett and colleagues (1995) suggest that African American and Latino HIV-positive persons covered by Medicaid are less likely to receive prophylaxis for PCP. Additionally, they found that these patients had significantly lower survival rates than privately insured patients.

These findings are supported by results from the National HIV/AIDS Treatment Survey (1998) and research conducted by Shapiro and colleagues (1999) which indicate that women and minority group members tend to receive less aggressive care than White males. In their cross-sectional study of 501 persons living with HIV, Wingood and colleagues (1998) found that African Americans were 70 percent more likely to have never been prescribed AZT, 80 percent more likely to have not been enrolled in clinical trials for experimental treatments, and 70 percent more likely to have not been treated with experimental drugs. Results from the National HIV/AIDS Treatment Survey (1998) also indicate that African American women with HIV/AIDS are also more likely than White men to be treated by less experienced physicians.

Maldonado (1999) reports that though African Americans account for a significant number of clients served under Title I of the Ryan White Care Act, they are less represented among the client population served under Title II and the AIDS Drug Assistance Program (ADAP). These data are significant in that they suggest that African Americans with HIV/AIDS may not be receiving critical services such as home-based care and assistance in purchasing AIDS-related drugs as provided under Title II. Unfortunately, programs operating under Title I, Title II, and ADAP are not required to provide data regarding health outcomes for the African American clients they serve; therefore, few conclusions may be reached about the nature and the quality of the services they receive.

Based on available epidemiological data and information regarding services and the quality of care received by African Americans with HIV/AIDS, it is apparent that they are receiving neither equitable levels of care nor equitable quality of care. This kind of disparate treatment translates into poorer survival times for African Americans living with HIV/AIDS. In addition to implementing comprehensive treatment protocols specifically designed for African Americans, policies must be put in place that mandate that programs receiving Ryan White funds be required to report data relevant to health-related outcomes for all clients served. This would be an important step toward understanding the nature of the obstacles impeding the equitable treatment of African Americans with HIV/AIDS.

Along the domains of prevention, access to care, and coordination and quality of care, we observe that African Americans are in fact not reaping the benefits of the national investment in HIV/AIDS prevention, treatment, and research. Although the Ryan White Care Act continues to be the major source of appropriations for persons with HIV/AIDS, including services and program delivery to African American women, the context within which this important legislation was created has changed. As the "face of AIDS" has changed so too must the face of AIDS policies. The author concurs with Wright (1998, 58), who suggests that we must "consider ways to critique and challenge the paradigm that has defined the response strategy ... and defined treatment, prevention, services and research."

CLINTON ADMINISTRATION INITIATIVE TO ADDRESS HIV/AIDS AMONG RACIAL AND ETHNIC POPULATIONS: INROADS TO REDEFINING THE HIV/AIDS POLICY AGENDA

In what was heralded as an unprecedented commitment, President Clinton, along with the Department of Health and Human Services (HHS), the Congressional Black Caucus, and the Congressional Hispanic Caucus announced in October 1998 that $156 million in additional funds would be appropriated to support initiatives aimed at addressing HIV/AIDS among racial and ethnic minorities (African American AIDS Policy & Training Institute 1999; Office of Minority Health Resource Center 1999). Table 15.2 provides a summary of the initial cluster of initiatives supported by the 1999 special appropriation that launched the Initiative to Address HIV/AIDS among Racial and Ethnic Minority Populations. The Initiative includes funding directed toward cooperative arrangements between faith-based organizations, minority community-based organizations, and collaboratives. The initiatives are aimed at addressing disparities in HIV/AIDS prevention, treatment, services, and research among African Americans and other minority groups disproportionately affected by HIV/AIDS.

It should be noted that the Initiative to Address HIV/AIDS among Racial and Ethnic Minority Populations, also referred to as the Minority HIV/AIDS Initiative is one of the six major components of the broader HHS Initiative to Eliminate Racial and Ethnic Disparities in Health by 2010. The Minority HIV/AIDS Initiative, which was announced in 1998 and initiated in 1999 with a $156 million appropriation, has expanded significantly. The initial appropriation was increased to $251 million in fiscal year 2000 and to $350 million in fiscal year 2000 (Office of Minority Health 2001). The Minority HIV/AIDS Initiative is the vehicle through which the CDC prevention initiatives previously discussed are funded. Four additional agencies also receive funding via the Minority HIV/AIDS Initiative to respond to the HIV/AIDS crisis in racial and ethnic communities. These agencies include the Health Resources and Services Adminis-

Table 15.2
Clinton Administration Initiative to Address HIV/AIDS Among Racial and Ethnic Minority Populations[1]

Organization	Name of Initiative or Program Activity	Description of Initiative	Eligible Entities	Type of Funding	Amount of Funds
Centers for Disease Control and Prevention	*Directly funded Community-Based Organizations (CBO's)*	• For direct funding of grant applications of indigenous organizations with a history of working with African-American communities to target high-risk populations. Goals: (1) provide financial and technical assistance to indigenous CBOs to provide HIV prevention services to primarily African American populations for which gaps in services are demonstrated; (2) support HIV prevention programs that reflect national programs that reflect the HIV prevention priorities outlined in the jurisdiction's comprehensive HIV plan; and (3) promote the collaboration and coordination of HIV prevention efforts among CBOs and other local, State, and federally funded programs.	Minority CBO's, including faith based organizations (must have 501(c) status)	Cooperative agreements	$10 million
Centers for Disease Control and Prevention	*Investment in Minority CBO's Providing Prevention*	• Approximately $4.0 million was awarded through state and local health departments by CDC on a competitive basis to support racial and ethnic minority CBOs in 30 locations to address high priority HIV prevention need in African American and Latino populations. • These CBOs must have a governing board composed of more than 50 percent racial or ethnic minority members, a significant number of minority individuals in key program positions, and an established record of service to racial or ethnic minority communities.	State and local health departments, (some of these funds may be competitively available at the state and local level)	Cooperative agreements	$4.0 million
Centers for Disease Control and Prevention	*Faith Based Initiatives*	• For developing HIV and substance abuse prevention programs at divinity school located at Historically Black Colleges and Universities (HBCU), and for expanding the ability of other faith-centered programs in this area.	Faith-based CBO's/HBCU Divinity Schools	Cooperative agreement	$1.5 million
Centers for Disease Control and Prevention	*Community Development Grants for HIV/STD/TB/ Substance Abuse Integration and Linkages*	• The goal of this program is to improve the health status of African-American community members by increasing access to linked networks of health services, including, HIV, STD, TB, and substance abuse prevention treatment and care. • This will be accomplished by planning and developing a linked network between HIV, STD, TB, and substance abuse programs.	Local non-profit health, social service, or voluntary service organizations, or CBO's with 501(c) tax exempt status and a governing or advisory body composed of more than 50 percent of the racial or ethnic minority population to be served.	Cooperative agreements	$8.0 million

Table 15.2 (continued)

Organization	Name of Initiative or Program Activity	Description of Initiative	Eligible Entities	Type of Funding	Amount of Funds
Centers for Disease Control and Prevention	Strengthen the Requirements in CDC's HIV Prevention Community Planning	• This initiative will strengthen the requirements in CDC's HIV prevention community planning cooperative agreements so that State allocation decisions must reflect the demographics of the HIV epidemic in that State. • This activity reflects a redirection of funds within the existing HIV prevention cooperative agreements to ensure that currently available resources are spent proportionate to the epidemic in a given locale, and does not fully address substantial unmet needs.	State and local health departments	Cooperative agreements	Approximately $15 million will be redirected towards African American communities.
Centers for Disease Control and Prevention	Reducing Transmission Among People of Color	As part of CDC's initiative to reduce HIV transmission among people of color, $400,000 has been awarded to develop population-specific strategies aimed at (1) better targeting of HIV prevention resources toward those communities experiencing the greatest impact of the HIV/AIDS epidemic, and (2) improving the capacity of CBPs to deliver effective interventions.	Academy of Education Development	Task order contract	$400,000 continuation
Centers for Disease Control and Prevention	Research and Program Intervention Models for HIV+ Minority Communities	• To start research projects that evaluate innovative preventions for HIV+ African-American women and their sex partners. • This will complement existing CDC research on developing interventions for HIV+ men.	State and local health departments	Cooperative agreements	$1.0 million
Office of Minority Health, Office of Public Health and Science	Minority Community Health Coalition Demonstration Program (competitive)	• The purpose of this Program is to improve the health status, relative to HIV/AIDS, of targeted minority populations through health promotion and education activities. • This program is intended to demonstrate the effectiveness of community-based coalitions involving non-traditional partners in: (1) developing an integrated community-based response to the HIV/AIDS education and outreach demonstration projects for hardly reached populations; and (3) addressing sociocultural and linguistic barriers to HIV/AIDS treatment.	Public and private, nonprofit minority community-based organization which represent an established community coalition of at least three discrete organizations. (Applicants must be located in the 15 metropolitan statistical areas identified by the CDC in its HIV/AIDS Surveillance Report for 1996 and 1997 as having the highest number of newly reported AIDS cases in 1995, 1996, and 1997;	Competitive	$500,000
Office of Minority Health, Office of Public Health and Science	Addressing AIDS in Minority Populations	• The purpose of this Program is to provide ongoing information and programmatic support to racial/ethnic individuals and organizations addressing HIV/AIDS in disadvantaged populations.	National Minority AIDS Council	Non-competitive award	$100,000

Table 15.2 (continued)

Organization	Name of Initiative or Program Activity	Description of Initiative	Eligible Entities	Type of Funding	Amount of Funds
Health Resources and Services Administration	Ryan White Title I Supplement for Areas with Substantial Need for Services	• This is supplemental funding to Title I grantees, directed to be allocated by formula to eligible metropolitan areas that have 30% or more African American and Latino HIV/AIDS cases in an effort to improve the quality of care and health outcomes for African Americans living with HIV/AIDS.	Title I metropolitan areas with 30% or more African American/ Latino AIDS cases	Formula grants	$5 million
Health Resources and Services Administration	Ryan White Title III Planning Grants	• To be used for targeted planning grants designed to build new capacity for primary care provider organizations to link with community based organizations in highly impacted minority communities to deliver needed health care services.	CBOs, community health centers, and other medical facilities	Competitive grants	$3 million
Health Resources and Services Administration	Ryan White HIV/AIDS Care for Children, Women, Youth, and Families (Title IV Supplemental Grants)	• Grants to support care and access to care and research for children, women, youth and families affected by HIV/AIDS. • The majority of clients served by this program are from racial and ethnic minority groups.	Currently funded Ryan White CARE Act Title IV grantees, which include State and local health departments, community health centers, hospitals;	Limited competition	$12.2 million ($2 million in new funding in added FY99)
Health Resources and Services Administration	Training Programs to Help CBOs	• Replication of a demonstration program targeted at developing capacity among minority community based organizations through training and technical assistance in selected cities.	National Minority AIDS Council	Cooperative agreement	$1.1 million continuation of FY98 funding

The Department is finalizing two Additional Proposals:

Organization	Name of Initiative or Program Activity	Description of Initiative	Eligible Entities	Type of Funding	Amount of Funds
	Technical Assistance and Capacity Development	TBA	TBA	TBA	$5 million
	Community Leadership Development	TBA	TBA	TBA	$2.5 million

Source: Office of Minority Health Resource Center (1999), *Clinton Administration Initiative to Address HIV/AIDS Among Racial and Ethnic Minority Populations.*

tration (HRSA), the Substance Abuse and Mental Health Administration (SAMHSA), the National Institutes of Health (NIH) and the Office of Minority Health (OMH) (AIDS Action 2001).

The Minority HIV/AIDS Initiative is significant in that its appropriations have and will translate into programming, services, and research beneficial to African Americans living with HIV or at risk for contracting the virus. It is also particularly important because it was birthed, shaped, extended, and advocated for by African Americans on behalf of African Americans. President Clinton's announcement came upon the heels of the May 1998 Congressional Black Caucus (CBC) declaration of the AIDS crisis in the African American community as a state of emergency. Led by Representative Maxine Waters (D-CA), a collective of African American leadership, AIDS advocates, and supportive others, the fight to realize this major fete was long overdue; it represents an awakening of the leadership to acknowledge HIV/AIDS in the African American community as a crisis of epidemic proportion (Whitfield, Kaplan, and Krochmal 1999).

People such as Cornelius Baker, executive director of the National Association of People with AIDS and an African American living with AIDS, acknowledge the CBC's declaration and the pressure leveraged against the Clinton administration as the culmination of years of anger over the nation's apparent disinterest in the plight of hundreds of thousands of African American people affected by HIV/AIDS (Whitfield, Kaplan, and Krochmal 1999). Although the Initiative is indeed a most aggressive response to the disproportionate numbers of African Americans and other ethnic minorities affected by HIV/AIDS, it must be seen as an important first step toward redefining the HIV/AIDS policy agenda to better reflect the HIV/AIDS-related prevention, treatment, service delivery, and research needs relevant to African Americans and other ethnic minority communities disproportionately affected by the HIV/AIDS epidemic.

Thus far, our discussion has provided an examination and critique of key HIV/AIDS-related social policies affecting African American women. The next section of the chapter explores contextual issues surrounding the long-standing apathy regarding HIV/AIDS-related policy development and substantial changes that have taken place to better address the AIDS crisis among African American communities.

FROM APATHY TO ACTION

It is clear that HIV/AIDS is destroying us—as has been the case since the beginnings of the epidemic; however, it seems that we have only recently become impassioned enough to demonstrate and agitate for increased governmental attention to our plight. Most troubling has been the inaction of our leaders. Gant (1998) and Cohen (1999) present compelling data demonstrating the relative ambivalence of African American organizations and the national African American leadership to the AIDS epidemic among African American communities.

Gant's (1998) preliminary results of a search for HIV/AIDS-related policy statements and action guidelines produced by the Congressional Black Caucus (CBC) and the Joint Center for Political Studies, which are the premier African American policy centers, indicate that no major policy statements were issued by either entity between 1981 and 1997. Gant's (1998) survey of over 200 African American social organizations, fraternities, and sororities also failed to yield a solitary HIV/AIDS-related position statement. Cohen's (1999) survey of professional and nationalist organizations, faith communities, and traditional African American organizations such as the Southern Christian Leadership Conference and the National Association for the Advancement of Colored People sadly yielded similar results. With the exception of the faith community's Nation of Islam and the professional community's National Association of Black Social Workers, there has been a demonstrable level of apathy among these organizations.

Based on her extensive research and interviews with members and leadership of national African American organizations, Cohen (1999) asserts that, at best, the leadership has "demonstrated a conflicted response to AIDS" (288). She indicates that though a few organizations have instituted strategies to illuminate the understanding of HIV/AIDS within African American communities, most organizations have elected to frame HIV/AIDS as an issue of others, or they have resigned themselves to providing essential HIV/AIDS-related prevention, treatment, and service programming without pursuing an activist agenda. Cohen's (1999) and Gant's (1998) work indicates that African American organizations and leadership have responded to the HIV/AIDS crisis among us with ambivalence. Regardless of whether organizations that have developed programmatic responses to the epidemic have sought to organize themselves to realize larger policy-oriented goals, they should be applauded for their part in seeking to diminish the HIV/AIDS crisis.

The unfolding of a series of significant events suggests a reversal in the trend of organizational apathy toward the AIDS crisis in our communities. These events include the founding of the African American AIDS Policy and Training Institute, the surgeon general's African American community HIV/AIDS Satellite Conference, and the CBC-driven Clinton Administration Initiative to Address HIV/AIDS among Racial and Ethnic Minority Populations.

Founded in May 1999, the African American AIDS Policy and Training Institute emerged as a response to the CBC-defined "State of Emergency" regarding AIDS in African American communities. Through their policy-related activities, the Institute is committed to: (1) reducing new HIV infections in African-American communities; (2) increasing access to treatment and resources; and (3) improving the quality of life for African Americans living with HIV (African American Policy and Training Institute 1999, 44). Particularly significant are the Institute's policy development efforts, which have led to the creation of the Nia Plan, a comprehensive action agenda to direct efforts aimed at reducing the spread of HIV/AIDS within African American communities and enlisting the support of various constituencies and stakeholders in our communities such as HIV/AIDS service organizations, universities, and faith communities. The Institute holds great promise for formulating, disseminating, and lobbying for the funding of policy initiatives that are responsive to the HIV/AIDS crisis among African Americans.

In November 1999, U.S. Surgeon General Dr. David Satcher hosted a satellite conference on HIV/AIDS in African American communities. This historic event featured panel discussions highlighting the perspectives of a broad cross-section of African American physicians, service providers, researchers, clergy, and HIV-positive or AIDS-diagnosed persons. The conference, which was telecast live from the Charles Drew University of Medicine and Science, Howard University College of Medicine, Meharry Medical College, Morehouse School of Medicine, and Tuskegee University, emphasized the devastating impact of HIV/AIDS among African Americans and provided basic information regarding the epidemiology and treatment of HIV/AIDS.

Particularly heartening is the CBC-led victory of an initial $156 million appropriation toward addressing the HIV/AIDS crisis among racial and ethnic minorities (Office of Minority Health Resource Center 1999). As previously discussed, the initial $156 million fiscal year 1999 appropriation has translated into a $350 million investment in addressing the HIV/AIDS crisis among communities of color. The effort is a clear example of what may be achieved through determination, collective work, and responsibility. And yet, I must question why the effort was so late in coming. There is ample evidence that African Americans are indeed concerned about HIV/AIDS; a lack of concern is not the issue. Perhaps the apathy that seems so pervasive is not a simple absence of concern but more of an absence of impassioned concern—concern that, until recently, has not been broadly translated into action.

This is not to suggest that there have not been activists among us fighting for funding to support prevention, treatment, and service-related needs. On the contrary, since the early years of the epidemic, organizations such as the Black Coalition on AIDS, the National Black Leadership Commission on AIDS, and the activist voices of such people as Sandra Singleton-McDonald, Tracie Gardner, and Debra Fraser-Howze have been educating, advocating, and lobbying for needed changes in HIV/AIDS-related policies (African American AIDS Policy and Training Institute 1999).

With few resources and little support from national African American organizations, African Americans have been responding to the AIDS epidemic through localized, grassroots efforts across the country (Whitfield, Kaplan, and Krochmal 1999). Numerous African American owned community-based AIDS organizations such as Family and Medical Counseling Services of Washington, D.C., and Chicago's South Side Help Center have been meeting the HIV/AIDS prevention, treatment, and service needs of African Americans for years.

Although, as a collective, African American faith communities have been shamefully silent concerning the AIDS epidemic which is ravaging our community, faith-based entities such as The Balm In Gilead, Glide Memorial United Methodist Church's Glide Goldett HIV/AIDS Project of San Francisco, and Antioch Baptist Church's Cleveland-based AGAPE collaborative are responding to the crisis within our communities by offering comprehensive HIV/AIDS-related services (Krochmal 1999).

Just as we cannot deny the impact of all the "isms" on the HIV/AIDS crisis in our communities—racism, classism, and sexism—or fail to hold our national leadership responsible for not doing enough, it would be a great mistake to ignore the significance of personal responsibility and decision making in the HIV/AIDS transmission equation. Arguably, the decision to engage in HIV risk behaviors such as unprotected sex, intravenous drug use, and multiple partnering is strongly linked to complex interactions among sociocultural, socioeconomic, and sociopolitical factors. At the same time, it is clear that a major barrier to reducing HIV/AIDS incidence among African Americans is a refusal by many members of our community to both accept the gravity of the epidemic's effect on our communities, as well as to encourage us to accept personal responsibility for protecting ourselves from HIV-infection.

Until we have accepted the sheer magnitude of the epidemic within our communities, we will neither be compelled to personally protect ourselves from HIV-infection nor driven to collectively to mobilize ourselves against it.

ADOPTING AN ACTIVIST STANCE TO SAVE OUR WOMEN, OUR MEN, OUR COMMUNITIES

> Depending on others to develop and implement both treatment and prevention strategies is ultimately disempowering for African Americans and evokes slavery and ownership metaphors ... local African-American communities must relearn and implement again the social political strategies historically used by African-American communities. ... African-American communities must simply act—with intelligence, political sophistication and urgency. (Gant 1998, 93–94)

Despite the magnitude to which HIV/AIDS is affecting African Americans, a lack of what Hallett (1997, 6) terms as "activist control" over the social construction of HIV has resulted in the absence of a powerful, collective voice that would define the AIDS crisis from our perspectives and determine our change agenda. Since the inception of the AIDS epidemic, the dominant activist voice has been that of the White, homosexual, AIDS-affected population. As such, African American women and other devalued and silenced groups have been virtually excluded from the dialogue surrounding HIV/AIDS-related policy development.

It is quite clear that we must begin to define and articulate a change agenda that reflects our perspectives and understandings of the epidemic and the ways in which the epidemic may be best addressed. Such an approach requires that we operate from a worldview that is consistent with our cultural values and philosophical assumptions. An Afrocentric paradigm offers a useful foundation from which to generate policy solutions to the problem of HIV/AIDS in the African-American community (Schiele 1997). In embracing such a paradigm, we commit ourselves in part to being guided by the values of collectivity, primacy of the community over the individual, and reciprocal obligation. Application of this paradigm to address the HIV/AIDS crisis would frame the strategies and priorities driving the change agenda. Applying an Afrocentric paradigm to outlining an issues agenda and plan of action relative to policy development that is responsive to African Americans affected by HIV/AIDS suggests in part, that we:

- Recognize that we are a part of a collective that is being destroyed by HIV/AIDS. We must begin to come to terms with the degree to which our communities are being affected by HIV/AIDS. This includes recognizing that our destiny is linked to the destiny of each of our members—to include those members who fall under one or more of the known HIV/AIDS risk groups.
- Promote HIV/AIDS education by educating ourselves and our communities.
- Approach HIV/AIDS as an issue of social justice.
- Become knowledgeable regarding the political process and use that knowledge to influence HIV/AIDS-related policy development.
- Network with local, state, and national HIV/AIDS advocacy groups and organizations.
- Lobby for increased funding to support culturally specific drug treatment and prevention programs.
- Lobby for increased funding to support culturally specific HIV/AIDS prevention programming directed toward African Americans and other most affected populations. Prevention efforts targeting African Americans should be prioritized to address the most vulnerable populations among us. This would include African American women and adolescents, who are demonstrating the fastest rising HIV/AIDS incidence rates.
- Lobby to support policies which promote the civil liberties of persons affected by HIV/AIDS to include anonymous testing and voluntary partner notification.
- Lobby to support policies that support families. This includes policies that prioritize the basic sustenance of the family and policies that support extended families in caring for children whose parents are no longer able to care for them because of an AIDS-related condition.
- Support universal policies that promote the welfare of the collective. This includes policies intended to reduce inequalities along the domains of health, economics, gender, education, housing, and employment.

Persistent disparities in health between African Americans and White Americans will continue until we have adequately addressed poverty, racism, lack of access to health care, unemployment, and other critical issues that contribute to disparity. As we advocate for the development of HIV/AIDS policies that are responsive to African Americans, we must prioritize the push for an end to poverty and support the provisions of decent housing, full employment, universal health care, and equal access to education.

We must be particularly diligent in our efforts to lobby for universal health care. It is clear that access issues determine who will receive care as well as the quality of care they will receive (Bayne-Smith and McBarnette 1996; Leigh 1995). As illuminated in this chapter, differential access to care received by African Americans not only influences the treatment they receive prior to a positive HIV test but it also drives the nature of treatment they receive once they find out that they have HIV. We must continue to support policy development aimed at destroying the extraordinary gulf that separates the majority of persons who will become infected with HIV and those who will not—between those who will receive quality care and those who will not—between those who are able to access services and those who are not.

Certainly, the aforementioned action recommendations are not all-encompassing. The strategies offered are meant to serve as launching points for action regarding pressing issues of concern relevant to African Americans and others affected by HIV/AIDS. The suggestions offered reflect actions that we may take as individuals and or as members of families, communities, and organizations.

The action strategies outlined emphasize one of the central tenants of an Afrocentric social welfare philosophy, which is that "there is a mutually dependent and morally affirming concept of government and individual responsibility" (Schiele 1997, 28). Although we must agitate for increased governmental attention to reduce the impact of HIV/AIDS within our communities, history has taught us that we cannot afford to wait for the government to respond to our needs. African Americans have a history of overcoming—of making a way out of no way. A fundamental part of our survival has been the implementation of collective strategies to meet our needs (Hill 1972). African American women, in particular, have been organizing ourselves in defense of ourselves for centuries (Gray-White 1999). In mounting a response to the HIV/AIDS crisis within our communities, we need only look to the past to identify proven models of collective responses to critical needs.

The sheer magnitude of the epidemic and the urgency with which we must act demands that we adopt an activist stance in our approach to action. Within the context of the HIV/AIDS epidemic, to adopt an activist stance is to assume the role of an active, impassioned advocate on behalf of our communities which are being ravaged by HIV and AIDS. Zealand (1995) describes the advocate as one who not only speaks for and on behalf of a cause but one who also truly believes in that cause and the possibility of realizing change. As we assume an activist stance in working toward implementing an HIV/AIDS policy agenda that is responsive to African Americans, we are not only committing ourselves to taking actions which contribute to the cause of reducing the prevalence of HIV/AIDS but we are also committing ourselves to embracing the notion that we will be successful.

Unconquered and eternally united, let us commit ourselves to lending our significant creativity, talents, and problem-solving abilities to focus on educating our communities and advocating for change in order to reduce the HIV/AIDS crisis that is destroying us.

This chapter has explored HIV/AIDS policy development relevant to African American women. In so doing, the chapter provided a discussion of key

HIV/AIDS-related social policies affecting African American women, a critique of the extent to which these policies have been responsive to the needs of African American women, a review of initiatives which hold great promise for lessening the HIV/AIDS crisis among African Americans, and an outline of key issue areas that may frame a change agenda.

REFERENCES

African American AIDS Policy & Training Institute (1999). The nia plan: A comprehensive plan of action for African Americans to help reduce the spread of HIV/AIDS in our communities. Unpublished manuscript.

AIDS Action (July 26, 2000). Action Alert: House Passes Ryan White Care Act Reauthorization [Online]. Available: http://capwiz.com/aac/issues/alert [2001, April].

———. (2001, January 2). FY 2001 Appropriations levels for federal AIDS programs [Online]. Available: http://www.aidsaction.org/fy2001.html [2001, April 1].

Bair, B., and Cayleff, S.E. (1993). Community action and public health policy: Introduction. In B. Bair and S.E. Cayleff (Eds.), *Wings of gauze: Women of color and the experience of health and illness*. Detroit, MI: Wayne State University Press.

Bayne-Smith, E., and McBarnette, L. (1996). Redefining health in the 21st century. In E. Bayne-Smith (Ed.), *Race, Gender & Health* (pp. 172–194). Thousand Oaks, CA: Sage Publications.

Bennett, C., Horner, R., and Weinstein, A. (1995). Racial differences in care among hospitalized patients with pneumocystic carinii in Chicago, New York, Los Angeles, Miami and Raleigh-Durham. *Archives of Internal Medicine, 155.*

Brandt, A.M. (1988). AIDS: From social history to social policy. In E. Fee and D.M. Fox (Eds.), *AIDS: The Burdens of History* (pp. 147–171). Berkeley: University of California Press.

Caravano, K. (1991). More than mothers and whores: Redefining the AIDS prevention needs of women. *International Journal of Health Services, 21,* 131–142.

Centers for Disease Control and Prevention. (June 1999). HIV/AIDS among African Americans. National Center for HIV, STD, and TB Prevention, Divisions of HIV/AIDS prevention [On-line]. Available: http://www.cdc.gov/nchstp/hiv-aids/pubs/facts/afam.htm [1999, November 4].

Cohen, C.J. (1999). *The boundaries of blackness: AIDS and the breakdown of black politics*. Chicago: University of Chicago Press.

Corea, G. (1992). *The invisible epidemic: The story of women and AIDS*. New York: HarperCollins.

Ethier, K.A., Ickovics, J.R., and Rodin, J. (1996). For whose benefit? Women and AIDS public policy. In A. O'Leary and L.S. Jemmott (Eds.), *Women and AIDS: Coping and Care* (pp. 207–228). New York: Plenum Press.

Feldman, R.H.L., and Fulwood, R. (1999). The three leading causes of death in African Americans: Barriers to reducing excess disparity and to improving health behaviors. *Journal of Health Care for the Poor and the Underserved, 10* (1), 45–71.

Gant, L.M. (1998). When silence equals death: Advocacy and policy perspectives in AIDS and African Americans. In L.M. Gant, P.A. Stewart, V.J. Lynch, W. Green, et al. (Eds.), *Social workers speak out on the HIV/AIDS Crisis* (pp. 81–98). Westport, CT: Greenwood Publishing Group.

Gollub, E.L. (1999). Human rights is a U.S. problem, too: The case of women and HIV. *American Journal of Public Health*, 89 (10), 1479–1482.

Gray-White, D. (1999). *Too heavy a load: Black women in defense of themselves 1894–1994*. New York: W.W. Norton.

H. Res. 2391, 106th Cong., 1st Sess. Available: http://frwebgate.access.gpo.gov/cg … ry=/diskb/wais/data/106_cong_bills. [1999, October 14].

H. Res. 3804, 103d Cong., 2d Sess. Available: http://frwebgate.access.gpo.gov/cd … ry=/disk3/wais/data/103_cong_bills. [1999, October 14].

Hallett, M.A. (1997). Introduction: Activism and marginalization in the AIDS crisis. *Journal of Homosexuality*, 32 (3/4), 1–16.

Hammonds, E. (1990). Missing persons: African-American women, AIDS and the history of the disease. *Radical America*, 24 (2), 7–23.

Hill, R. (1972). The strengths of Black families. New York: Emerson Hall Publishers.

Kaiser Family Foundation. (1998). National survey of African Americans on HIV/AIDS. Prepared for The untold story: AIDS and Black Americans, a briefing on the crisis of AIDS among African Americans (pp. 1–16).

Krochmal, S.N. (1999). Black power: Advocacy and support for African-America HIVers. The body: An AIDS and HIV information resource [On-line]. Available: http://www.thebody.com/poz/survival/1_99/resources.html [1999, October 13].

Leigh, W.A. (1995). The health of African-American women. In D.L. Adams (Ed.), *Health issues for women of color: A cultural diversity perspective*. Thousand Oaks, CA: Sage Publications.

Maldonado, M. (1999). State of emergency: HIV/AIDS among African Americans. Body Positive [On-line], XII(2), 1–6. Available: http://www.thebody.com/bp/feb99/african_american.html [1999, October 13].

McBarnette, L.S. (1996). African-American women. In M. Bayne-Smith (Ed.), *Race, gender, and Health* (pp. 43–67). Thousand Oaks, CA: Sage Publications.

National HIV/AIDS Treatment Survey (1998). Results. In V. Lynch (Presenter), Symposium conducted at the Annual Program Meeting of the Council on Social Work Education, San Francisco, CA.

National Research Council (1993). The social impact of AIDS in the United States. Commission on Behavioral and Social Sciences and Education. Washington, D.C.: National Academy Press.

Office of Minority Health Resource Center. (1999). Clinton administration initiative to address HIV/AIDS among racial and ethnic minority populations. Guide to resources available through the congressional Black caucus—DHHS initiative to address HIV/AIDS in racial and ethnic minority communities [On-line]. Available: http://www.omhrc.gov/cbcdoc.htm [1999, October 13].

Office of Minority Health Resource Center (2001). Data/Statistics. Office of Management and Budgets Announcements. Available: http://www.omhrc.gov/OMH/Sidebar/datastats4.htm

Quinn, S.C. (1993). AIDS and the African American woman: The triple burden of race, class, and gender. *Health Education Quarterly*, 20 (3), 305–320.

Schiele, J. (1997). An Afrocentric perspective on social welfare philosophy and policy. *Journal of Sociology and Social Welfare*, 14 (2), 21–39.

Serant, C. (November 1998). War on AIDS gets big boost: Federal government allocates $156M. *Daily News AIDS Awareness*, p. 7.

Shapiro, M.F., Morton, S.C., McCaffrey, D.F., Senterfitt, J.W., et al. (1999). Variations in the care of HIV-infected adults in the United States: Results form the HIV cost and services utilization study. *Journal of the American Medical Association* 281 2305–2315.

Social Security Administration (October 2000). United States social security administration guide to social security and SSI disability benefits for people with HIV infection. [On-line] www.ssa.gov/pubs/10020.html.

Stein, T.J. (1998). The social welfare of women and children with HIV and AIDS: Legal protections, policy, and programs. New York: Oxford University Press.

United States. (1990). Ryan White Comprehensive AIDS Resources Emergency Act of 1990, Public Law 103–381. Washington, D.C.: U.S. Government Printing Office.

United States House of Representatives. (1991). Human Resources and Intergovernmental Relations Subcommittee of the Committee on Government Operation. Women and HIV disease: Falling through the cracks: Hearing, June 6, 1991. Washington, D.C.: U.S. Government Printing Office.

United States House of Representatives. (July 25, 2000). A bill to amend the Public Health Service Act to revise and extend programs established under the Ryan White Comprehensive AIDS Resources Emergency Act of 1990, and for other purposes; to the Committee on Commerce. Full Text [on-line], Available: wais. access. gpo.gov.

United States. Senate (June 6, 2000). S. 2311: A bill to revise and extend the Ryan White CARE Act programs under title XXVI of the Public Health Service Act, to improve access to health care and the quality of health care under such programs, and to provide for the development of increased capacity to provide health care and related support services to individuals and families with HIV disease, and for other purposes; to the Committee on Health, Education, Labor, and Pensions. Full Text [on-line], Available: wais.access.gpo.gov.

Waters, M. (1999). The black death: AIDS in the African-American community is a public health emergency. The body: An AIDS and HIV information resource [On-line]. Available: http://www.thebody.com/poz/columns/1_99/callarms2/html [1999, October 13].

Whitfield, L., and Kaplan, E., with Krochmal, S.N. (1999). The fire this time. The body: An AIDS and HIV information resource [On-line]. Available: http://www.the body.com/poz/features/1_99/leaders.html [1999, October 13].

Williams, A.B., Singh, M.P., Dos Santos, K., Winfrey, J., et al. (1997). Report from the field: Participation of HIV-positive women in clinical research. *AIDS and Public Policy Journal*, 12 (1), 46–52.

Wingood, G., Funkhouser, E., DiClemente, R., Fawal, H., et al. (1998). *Racial inequalities in the receipt of HIV/AIDS-related treatment and enrollment in clinical trials for persons living with HIV.* International Conference on AIDS, 12, 970 (Abstract no. 44166).

Wright, E. (1998). Strategies for effective intervention with African Americans. In L.M. Gant, P.A. Stewart, V.J. Lynch, W. Green, et al. (Eds.), *Social workers speak out on the HIV/AIDS crisis* (pp. 49–62). Westport, CT: Greenwood Publishing Group.

Zastrow, C. (2000). *Introduction to social work and social welfare*, 7th ed. (p. 143). Belmont, CA: Brooks/Cole-Wadsworth Publishing.

Zealand, T.P. (1995). The provider as advocate. *Bulletin of the New York Academy of Medicine*, 72, 300–308.

Index

About the Editors and Contributors

THE EDITORS

DORIE J. GILBERT, Ph.D., L.M.S.W., is Associate Professor at the University of Texas at Austin School of Social Work and a member of the School's Center for Social Work Research. Her research interest is broadly defined under the topic of stigma, more specifically investigating the cognitive, behavioral, and developmental challenges for socially stigmatized populations, with a special focus on women and persons of color living with HIV or AIDS.

She has provided community-based counseling and advocacy for women living with HIV/AIDS, and has served as a consultant on several community-based funded projects. Through the Collaborative AIDS Prevention Studies Project, funded by the National Institutes of Health, Dr. Gilbert is a Visiting Scholar at the University of California at San Francisco and is currently researching the mental health, behavioral, and social outcomes for young African American HIV-affected children. Dr. Gilbert has received funding from the National Institute on Drug Abuse to study the impact of race/ethnicity and cultural mistrust on antiretroviral medication adherence among HIV-positive individuals. She has additionally received HIV-related research grants from her university to conduct research on the life experiences of women living with HIV, AIDS service utilization among African American HIV-positive persons, and the psychosocial concerns HIV-positive parents with AIDS who have latency-age children. Her publications related to HIV/AIDS and vulnerable populations have appeared in journals and edited books. She is coeditor of the *Journal of HIV/AIDS and Social Services*. Dr. Gilbert was an active participant in the 1997 African American Social Work Leadership Summit Meeting on HIV/AIDS in Washington, D.C., sponsored by the HIV/AIDS and Social Work Training and Research Center, and continues to advocate for organized action to address the AIDS crisis among African Americans.

EDNITA M. WRIGHT, Ph.D., C.S.W., C.A.C., is President of the National Social Work AIDS Network (NSWAN), an organization comprising social workers and other professionals who provide social, educational and clinical services to people living with and affected by HIV/AIDS. For the last two decades, Dr. Wright has been an advocate for people living with HIV/AIDS, with a particular interest in African American communities. Currently, Dr. Wright is the Assistant Dean of students for diversity education and outreach at Cornell University. Her primary responsibility in this position is to create and foster community building by developing outreach services that will assist a variety of student populations on campus. Prior to October 1999, she was an Associate Professor at Syracuse University's School of Social Work. Her teaching responsibilities included a graduate practice course (Fundamentals of Social Work Practice), adolescent substance abuse course, and both undergraduate and graduate required courses in human behavior and the social environment (Persons in Social Context and Human Diversity). She completed her doctorate in 1995 through the Maxwell School of Citizenship, Interdisciplinary Social Science Program. The title of her dissertation was "Deep from Within the Well: African American Women Living with AIDS." She has consulted nationally and internationally on issues of cultural diversity, addiction, domestic violence, and infant mortality and has worked in the addiction field for more than two and a half decades. Dr. Wright has received various community awards. In 1998 she was selected for the Who's Who Among America's Teachers and from the National Association of Black Social Workers in recognition for her work in HIV/AIDS in African American communities, and in 1996 was given the Social Worker of the Year Award by NASW Central New York Region. Dr. Wright is currently interested in how educational institutions perpetuate racism and other biases, what organizational changes are needed for authentic inclusion, and how social work coupled with spirituality can move various communities through a process of social change. She continues to be committed to the understanding of addiction and HIV/AIDS in communities of color and the development of appropriate prevention and intervention strategies for both.

THE CONTRIBUTORS

MELBA BUTLER, C.S.W., began her professional career as a child care worker, and later worked as a caseworker in group home programs for adolescent girls with special needs. In 1990, she was appointed Executive Director of Harlem Dowling–West Side Center (HDWC) in the Harlem community of New York City, a comprehensive network of foster care, adoption, mental health, medical, HIV-related and family preservation programs. Ms. Butler immediately brought Harlem Dowling to the forefront of child welfare organizations and received local and national attention for successful programming and innovative projects. She continues to ensure innovative and quality service provision to over 2,500 children and their families. Ms. Butler received her master's degree in social work from Columbia University in 1979 and has been a certified social worker in New York State since 1980. She has received the following awards: the Nelson R. Mandela Citizen of the Year Award in 1992, from the New York Association of Black Psychologists, Inc.; a Special Recognition Award from the National Association of Negro Business and Professional Women; and the 1997 Business Achievement Award from the Black Retail Action Group, as well as special recognition for being *"part of the solution"* from the Board of Directors of Harlem Dowling–West Side Center. Ms. Butler is also an adjunct professor at York College in the Social Science Department. She is strongly committed to shared responsibility of diverse organizations, houses of worship, businesses, educators, community, and government in strengthening families and securing a viable future for our children.

BARBARA L. DANCY, Ph.D., researches the development and testing of innovative culturally sensitive HIV-risk reduction programs for low-income African American women and their adolescent daughters. Her initial research was the development of the "AIDS Knowledge, Feeling and Behavioral Questionnaire" to measure AIDS knowledge, feelings, and behaviors of African American women from their cultural perspective. Recognizing the importance of modeling for human learning, Dr. Dancy received federal funding to develop culturally sensitive videotapes for African American women. These tapes depicted demographic and contextual similar models who portrayed women making crucial decisions regarding HIV risk-reduction behaviors. Dr. Dancy then received funding to test the effectiveness of a culturally and gender sensitive HIV-risk reduction for low-income African American women in their reproductive years. The questionnaire and videotapes were components of this intervention. As a natural progression of her work, Dr. Dancy has developed the innovative concept of promoting mothers of adolescent daughters to the status of their daughters' HIV-risk reduction educator. She has also been instrumental in HIV-related research that deals with HIV-risk reduction among Latinos, with training professionals to enhance their HIV-risk-reduction services, and with HIV-risk reduction among adolescents in Botswana, Africa. As principal investigator, she has been funded by the National Institutes of Mental Health three times and was a recipient of the John E. Fogarty International Research Fellowship Grant Award. Dr. Dancy has published her research findings in national and international refereed journals.

CHERYL TAWEDE GRILLS, Ph.D., is a graduate of Yale University and UCLA and is currently Professor of Psychology and Coordinator of the American Cultures program at Loyola Marymount University in Los Angeles and is a licensed psychologist with a clinical practice in Los Angeles. She is also the immediate past president of the Southern California Association of Black Psychologists and the CEO of the Imoyase Group, Inc., a community-based, multiethnic research and program evaluation organization. Among her specialties is the treatment of substance abuse and dependence. She is also licensed by the Ghana National Association of Traditional Healers as a practitioner of traditional medicine in Ghana. Dr. Grills' research interests and current projects include developing and testing an African-centered model of treatment engagement with African American substance abusers, researching traditional medicine, and African concepts of consciousness in West Africa and program evaluation with community-based organizations engaged in social action, community change and prevention. She has published numerous articles and chapters on substance abuse, community-based research, and African psychology. Dr. Grills consults on a number of prevention and treatment issues, particularly regarding matters of cultural and social competence, multiculturalism, and Africentric interventions.

HEATHER A. KATZ earned a Ph.D. from the department of Curriculum and Instruction in the area of instructional technology from the University of Texas at Austin and both her M.Ed. in special education and B.S. in environmental science from Howard University. Her research interests encompass how multimedia instruction can be designed to meet the variant learning characteristics and needs of learners from diverse socioeconomic and ethnic backgrounds, and how the digital divide affects the technological literacy of disadvantaged populations. She is a contributing researcher on the Advance Placement Equity Initiative project at the Charles A. Dana Center of the University of Texas at Austin. She has presented her research both nationally and in Europe at the Association for the Advancement of Computing in Education (AACE) annual conferences Ed-Media: World Conference on Educational Multimedia and Hypermedia, in which she has also served as a peer reviewer. Dr. Katz is a member of Phi Delta Kappa, Kappa Delta Pi, and Pi Lambda Theta educational honor societies, and is listed in Who's Who Among Women in America and the International Who's Who of Information Technology.

ELLA MIZZELL KELLY, Ph.D., is a Senior Research Associate, Center for Community Health, Department of Psychiatry, UCLA Neuro-Psychiatric Institute and Hospital. Her research focuses on the intersection of chronic disease and illness on the lives of women of color. With funding support from the Office of AIDS Research, NIMH, her current research aims at understanding how the factors of identity, gender relationships and locus of control impact the ability of low-income, African American women and girls to adapt to their seropositive condition.

TONYA E. PERRY, Ph.D., is an Assistant Professor at the Howard University School of Social Work, where she teaches in the Macro and Human Behavior Sequences. Dr. Perry earned her Doctor of Philosophy degree in social work from the University of Alabama, where she also completed a minor in community health. She holds a B.A. in psychology from Edinboro University of

Pennsylvania and a master of social work degree from Tulane University. Dr. Perry is actively pursuing a research trajectory focused on HIV/AIDS and other significant health concerns of the international community of women of African ancestry. A former Johns Hopkins University International AIDS Research Fellow and NIMH/CSWE Research Fellow, Dr. Perry is actively engaged in funded research and scholarly writing related to the health issues of women of African descent throughout the diaspora. Having conducted woman-focused, health-related research in the United States, Nigeria, and Ghana, Dr. Perry recently expanded her research activities to explore the consequences of HIV/AIDs on the lives of South African women. In addition to her significant international research background and expertise, Dr. Perry has over ten years' experience in the HIV/AIDS arena. She is a dedicated scholar committed to creative teaching and mentoring. Dr. Perry regularly presents at international conferences and also serves as an HIV/AIDS program evaluator and consultant. She holds numerous memberships on local, national, and international boards and committees.

PERNESSA C. SEELE is founder and CEO of The Balm in Gilead. In 1989, while working at Harlem Hospital in New York City, **Pernessa C. Seele** was saddened by individuals suffering with AIDS with no spiritual support from the over 400-member religious community of Harlem. Realizing the missing link was the involvement of the Black church in HIV/AIDS education and spiritual care, Seele designed a plan to engage the Harlem religious community to address HIV/AIDS. With fifty Harlem churches, mosques, synagogues, and traditional African Yoruba communities, Seele launched Harlem Week of Prayer for the Healing of AIDS. On the heels of the success of this program, she founded Balm In Gilead, a national, not-for-profit organization that works exclusively to train and build the capacity of Black churches to effectively address AIDS in their respective communities. It is the only AIDS service organization in the United States that has been endorsed by over seventeen national church denominations and caucuses to provide this specific leadership. Today, Seele's Harlem Week of Prayer is the Black Church Week of Prayer for the Healing of AIDS, the flagship program of Balm In Gilead, which has engaged over 10,000 churches across the United States and a growing number of churches in the Caribbean and Africa. Many have praised Seele's work, including former President Bill Clinton, U.S. Surgeon General David Satcher, Jessye Norman, Maya Angelou, Whoopi Goldberg, and Elton John.

CHEDGZSEY SMITH-McKEEVER earned her MSW from the University of Southern California and her Ph.D. from the University of Texas at Austin. She is now an assistant professor at the University of Illinois at Chicago's Jane Addams College of Social Work and is also a Research Fellow at UIC's Institute for Research on Race and public Policy. Her research, practice and teaching interests focus on child welfare with an emphasis on African Americans. Her research areas include adoption policy and practice and the status of policy and practice with regard to the interactions and relationships between chemical dependency, criminal justice, and child welfare. Dr. Smith-McKeever is a former Council on Social Work Education Minority Research Fellow and is currently on the Board of the Society for Social Work and Research.

PATRICIA STEWART, M.S.S., A.C.S.W., L.S.W., manages an independent psychotherapy and consulting practice in the Philadelphia area and is part-time staff as a Field Instructor in Social Work Consultation Services, in Chester, Pennsylvania. Since the early 1990s, Ms. Stewart has been extensively involved in work with and on behalf of people living with HIV/AIDS. She has designed and facilitated more than fifty workshops both locally and nationally and has been involved in the planning of many conferences and institutes across the United States. She is the founder of the very successful conference "Breaking the Silence, Breaking through the Fear: HIV/AIDS African American Perspectives" held annually since 1996 in Philadelphia. She has counseled with dozens of African American women and is committed to high-quality, culturally competent care for them in her practice and training endeavors. Ms. Stewart is a contributing author to three books published about social work practice with people living with HIV/AIDS, including one for which she is coeditor. She has also written a prepublication review and commentary in a fourth book. Ms. Stewart received her master of social service degree from Bryn Mawr College, Graduate School of Social Work and Social Research, in 1981. She is licensed by the Commonwealth of Pennsylvania and is a member of the Academy of Certified Social Workers of the National Association of Social Workers.

DANA WILLIAMS is the Director of Education and Prevention for Blacks Assisting Blacks against AIDS (BABAA) in St. Louis, Missouri. She has been involved in HIV/AIDS since 1987. Ms. Williams is a national consultant for many federal and nationally recognized agencies, such as the Centers for Disease Control, HRSA, and the National Minority AIDS Council and National Prevention Intervention Network (NPIN). She is a master-level trainer and contributor to the American Red Cross African American HIV/AIDS fundamental course and currently sits on several national advisory boards, including the Office of Women's Health and the African American National Advisory Committee for the Office of Minority Health. Ms. Williams is one of the founding members of Coalition Empowering Families Affected by AIDS, a coalition of agencies addressing the gaps in services for women, children, and youth with HIV/AIDS; she has been nationally recognized for the family support program "Steps to Living." As a master trainer, she has provided technical assistance, program development, and implementation to a wide range of agencies across the country.

SHARON E. WILLIAMS, Ph.D., is an Associate Professor of Social Work and Director of the Family Violence Prevention Training Project at Florida A&M University in Tallahassee. She is an experienced family counselor and has many years of direct practice with children and their families. She has extensive training in the area of HIV/AIDS and African Americans, having studied at the University of Michigan, Institute of Social Research, Program on HIV/AIDS and African Americans. Her research interest includes African American families and mental health, particularly service delivery in rural and underserved communities, HIV/Aids and domestic violence, and HIV/AIDS and treatment compliance. She has published in the areas social work practice with African American families, culturally sensitive outcome measures, and domestic violence in rural communities.

MILDRED WILLIAMSON, Ph.D., M.S.W., is the administrator of Woodlawn Health Center, one of the ambulatory community health centers of the Cook County Bureau of Health Services, located in Chicago. She is the former administrator of the Women & Children HIV Program at Cook County Hospital and is immediate past president of the AIDS Alliance for Children, Youth & Families board of directors. She currently is a member of the HIV/AIDS Advisory Council of the Health Resources & Services Administration, Bureau of HIV/AIDS. Dr. Williamson has more than a decade of experience as a provider of HIV/AIDS care and prevention services to disenfranchised populations, and recently completed doctoral studies in social work at the University of Chicago.